GW00362151

I've asked our foreign correspondents – fellow discerning drinkers from around the globe – to update us with the latest on bars, booze and drinking habits in their various corners of the world. Friends, be warned: I'm looking for more.

OPENING SHOTS

Merlin Griffiths
Bangalore, India
Once a regular fixture on the London bar and cocktail competition scene, Merlin is now based in Bangalore, as manager of the ICE Bar and star attraction at the Taj Residency Hotel.

A city of intense traffic and noise by day, and utter peace and calm at night, beautiful Bangalore is also home to some of the world's starkest contrasts. Its intelligent, suave and hard grafting inhabitants, plus 12,000 of India's 30,000 expats, spread themselves across a huge, lively social scene that runs from dingy rock pubs to loud nightclubs and cool lounge bars, like Fuga and our very own ICE.

The main spirits of choice are either scotch or vodka: the tequila and rum revolutions have yet to hit these shores, and plenty of the premium and ultra premium spirits we know in the west are not available. But cocktail culture is certainly taking off – putting the 'Bang!' into Bangalore, as young Indian bartenders move forward with one giant leap for bartending every week. Southern India has some of the world's best spices and fruits – Kerala is famed for its black peppercorns, cinnamon and cardamom, Goa produces a cornucopia of tropical fruits – and these ingredients form the base for many exhilarating concoctions. And the expat influence is clearly visible in the growing trends for fine wines, champagnes and whiskies.

As a westerner it takes some time to get used to the licensing hours – 11.30pm is the absolute latest and most establishments call last orders at 11pm. With the exception of some 5* hotel cafés, the same applies to food.

Yet while time may be limited - some of these folk don't even finish work until 10pm - that just leads to greater enjoyment on days off. Groups start their entertainment early in the evening and on Sundays, champagne brunches are the order of the day.

Here the mood is always sunny, even when it rains in sheets. And while we're having to learn a few new tricks - making do without lemons (I always thought they were native to India?!) - my staff are exceptionally well trained. We already have the Times of India "Best Bar 2006" award and the Liquid Best Bar 2006 award, and Sandeep, Denver and I look forward to seeing you soon for a Golden Lion (Kashmiri saffron infused vodka, dry sherry, Laphroaig wash) in the land of sun, spices and smiles. Until next time -'namaste' and cheers! MG

Helmut Adam
Berlin, Germany
Helmut has worked in style bars in Vienna, Zurich, London and Berlin, but as Bartender and Executive Editor of Mixology Magazine he now mixes words more than liquor. For more on Helmut's excellent magazine see www.mixology.eu.

I've long been interested in the process of how cocktails evolve and spread. Not many of the classics are fully traceable - nobody can explain exactly where and how the Martini was developed, although there are hundreds of true stories and historical hints. Contemporary cocktails are easier. For example, we know that the London bartender Dick Bradsell created the Bramble (gin, sugar, lemon juice and a float of blackberry liqueur), which is found on many cocktail menus throughout London. We even know that Dick created the drink in the mid-eighties and that he recommends it is served and consumed quickly, to prevent excess dilution.

Here in Berlin you will find a tall drink called Watermelon Man on most cocktail menus. People keep ordering it, although its formula is not really that sophisticated: lemon and orange juice, watermelon liqueur and a dash of grenadine for colour. But the public seem to love its simple name and bright orange-red colour. Funnily enough the tale of this cocktail begins in a garage.

In the early nineties Berlin was famous for its wild underground party scene. People simply opened illegal clubs in empty buildings and moved on when they got into trouble with the city's (fairly liberal) authorities. One of these early entrepreneurs was Cookie (his nickname allegedly hints at his English ancestry), who started holding parties in a garage in the Mitte district. To distinguish himself from other clubs he served cocktails instead of the bottled beer, wine and cheap grey market vodka which still make up the illegal party diet today.

Some time around 1996 Cookie found a new cocktail name in a newspaper – Watermelon Man. He played around with the recipe, and started serving it to his growing following - mainly the bubbling core of Berlin's art, fashion and media scenes. And they loved it! They started ordering it in other places around the city and soon it made its way onto their cocktail menus. Classical bartenders pimped the drink with fresh watermelon, raising awareness even more.

And Cookie? He originally ran his club only on Tuesdays and Thursdays as he had to work three nights in another club to earn his rent. Today those days are known on the scene as 'Cookie's days', and his new club opened on the 16th January in his eleventh venue so far. Next time you're in Berlin, go see the Watermelon Man: Cookie's, Tuesday and Thursday, 9pm - 5am, Friedrichstrasse 164, 10117 Berlin. HA

Jason Scott
Edinburgh, Scotland
Australian born Jason is one of the most highly regarded bartenders north of the border and a past winner of the title 'Scotland's Mixologist of the Year'. He is a partner in Bramble, which he reviews below - I've been there and it's all true.

99 HANOVER STREET
99 Hanover Street, Edinburgh, EH2 1DJ, Scotland
Tel: + 44 (0)131 225 4680
Prematurely opened as a Fringe Festival venue last year, this all-singing, all-dancing Moulin Rouge extravaganza is now one of Edinburgh's most popular bars. Deliberately avoiding association with the sometimes pretentious 'George Street' scene, it provides sustenance to a younger, funkier, non–suited and booted clientele, with top local DJs and live acts covering a range of genres six days a week. The drinks list is short and sweet, and, depending on which bartender serves you, usually well made. A refurb and tidy up are imminent but the bar's ethos – 'Music, Fun and Liquor' – should continue.
JS

EDITOR'S LETTER

Those of you who have been following this title will have noticed a couple of changes to our cover. The 'individual' issue numbering system which confused even our distributors has gone, and instead we're naming each quarterly after the relevant season. Hence this issue, which would have been #6.1, is now Spring 07. The next will be Summer 07, then Autumn 07, then Winter 07. Next year we'll start all over again, but with 08s, of course,

I have to come clean about the other thing that's changed on our cover. Actually, it's increased – the price. I hope you don't mind too much, and I'd like to take this opportunity to thank you for forking out your hard earned wonga to purchase our humble efforts. This fact-packed tome is still only the price of a cocktail and subscribers save 10% on the cover price. Besides Dan's funky design and photography we offer loads more bang for your buck than any other booze or bar title: over 300 pages, over 500 cocktails, plus bars and restaurants from all around the world.

This issue also contains what I consider the ultimate guide to vodka (until we update it), with 110 brands from 24 countries, plus details on production and what those marketing stories actually mean (not a lot, generally, when they're talking triple distillation). So ultimate, in fact, is this capacious guide that it's squeezed our latest update on New York's fine bar scene forward into summer. Sorry! However, we have managed to squeeze in the full gen for the discerning drinker on Barcelona, Manchester, San Francisco and London's Notting Hill.

I enlisted more than a little help from my friends for this issue – you can spot them by their initials at the end of each piece. Besides the buddies who contributed our Opening Shots section – huge thanks for your excellent and individual pieces – I'd like to thank Jamie Stephenson and posse for being such great guides and drinking partners on our tour of Manchester's bars, and Sue Leckie for her note taking and sobriety on that mission, and her subsequent write up thereof. Likewise, a big thanks to Alexa Lee, Ryan Fitzgerald, Arne Hillesland, Julio Bermejo, Jacques Bezuidenhout, David Nepove, Todd Smith, Marco Dionysos, Lance Winters, Jon Santer, Joseph Ehrmann and numerous others in San Francisco for making me feel so at home. And, as ever, thanks to Mrs 'Z' the sexy sub and Dan, our talented and long-suffering designer, for the cracking photography (see particularly Barcelona and Manchester) and stunning layouts which bring my words to life.

Cheers

Simon Difford

simon@diffordsguide.com

ISBN: 978-0-9546174-4-8 **ISSN:** 1749-0855

CONTENTS

Don't blame us:

- This guide is intended for adults of legal drinking age.
- Please enjoy alcohol and cocktails in a responsible manner.
- Consumption of alcohol in excess can be harmful to your health.
- The high sugar levels in some cocktails may mask their alcohol content.
- Please do not consume cocktails and drive or operate machinery.
- Great care should be exercised when combining flames and alcohol.
- Consumption of raw and unpasteurised eggs may be harmful to health.
- Please follow the alcohol content guidelines included in this guide where a shot is equal to 25ml or 1 US fluid ounce (29.6ml) at most. A 25ml measure of spirit at 40% alc./vol. is equal to 1 unit of alcohol. Most men can drink up to three to four units of alcohol a day and most women can drink up to two to three units of alcohol a day without significant risks to their health.
- Women who are trying to conceive or who are pregnant should avoid getting drunk and are advised to consume no more than one to two units of alcohol once or twice a week.

diffordsguide are: Publisher & Editor Simon Difford, **Art Director** Dan Malpass, **Photography** Rob Lawson & Dan Malpass
Published by Sauce Guides Limited, Milngavie Business Centre, 17 Station Road, Milngavie, G62 8PG, UK **www.diffordsguide.com**

Lulu

Bramble

Lulu

AMICUS APPLE
17 Frederick Street, New Town, Edinburgh, EH2 2EY, Scotland
Tel: +44 (0)131 226 6055, www.amicusapple.com
Renowned for its clean white lines and friendly, although sometimes overly ambitious staff, this six month old venue is under new management and en route to a more approachable look and offer. The cutting edge interior and striking murals have given way to large doses of vermilion red and an oversized plasma screen. An 'apres ski' theme delivers modern gas fires and ample couching opportunities to waste away a cold, wet Scottish Sunday with a warming mug of mulled wine. There are plans for a lounge-tastic weekend VIP area at the rear of the bar and once the drinks menu has been converted to a focus on classic cocktails, twists and otherwise, this space should be put to good use. The main dining area at the front currently looks a little unfinished but these are early days. JS

BRAMBLE BAR & LOUNGE
16a Queen Street (corner of Hanover Street), Edinburgh, EH2 1JE, Scotland
Tel: +44 (0)131 226 5959
Our drinking den cum cocktail lounge is focused on product and service, with a back bar dominated by gin and a cocktail list that blends forgotten classics with original libations like the award winning 'Red Rum' (a favourite of Mr Difford's) and the 'Maya's Daiquiri' - rum, fresh avocado, fresh lime juice and agave syrup. There's a hint of bachelor pad to the space, with wall art including vintage 80s ska spectaculars resting alongside some curious alcoves, such as the 'Lovers Corner' where gilded mirrors adorn the ceiling above a mattress laden with cushions, pillows and a crimson coloured sheepskin. Named for Dick Bradsell's modern classic cocktail, Bramble is by name as Bramble is by nature: uncomplicated, inventive and downright tasty. JS

LULU
125b George Street, Edinburgh, EH2 4JN, Scotland
Tel: +44 (0)131 225 5005, www.luluedinburgh.co.uk
This nightclub is the newest addition to Montpelier Group's magnum opus, the town house at 125 George Street. The pimped out, blinged up interior works well, with beautiful red floral wall coverings, a chain mail DJ booth and an underlit dance floor clearly designed for your modern day Tony Manero.

At the bar I had one of those cocktails you'd be afraid to order again, just in case it wasn't as amazing as the first one – a Makers Mark Whiskey Sour complemented with an orange twist. After just two brief visits, when I found the bar relatively quiet and minus the 'cash flashing and finger clicking' clientele, I'm already a fan of Lulu. JS

Robert Hess
Seattle, USA

Robert is the group manager of Windows Evangelism at Microsoft but better known in these parts as a cocktail geek of some repute. He is the creator of www.drinkboy.com and its associated message board which is a daily must-read for cocktail enthusiasts around the world.

When thinking of Seattle, it's easy for liquid to be part of the discussion. Sure, rain might be the first thing to come to mind, but we are also well known for our dedication to coffee, while the Pacific Northwest has been a major player in the wine industry and the spread of craft beer. More recently, Jones Soda and Dry Soda have shown that soda pop presents some interesting craft opportunities, while Seattle also happens to have a very dedicated collection of absinthe connoisseurs (who regularly bemoan the products passed off as such by various online retailers).

Seattle has also been quietly cultivating a cocktail culture that reflects similar culinary sensibilities. Yet while coffee, wine, and beer are all products that can be exported to other ports of call, cocktails need to be experienced in situ. Without a trip to Seattle, you might never realize what is transpiring within our bars and cocktail lounges, unless you happen to be hanging around in the right circles, or reading the right materials.

A tour of some of the more notable cocktail establishments of Seattle has to start with our flagship location:

ZIG ZAG CAFÉ
1501 Western Ave (#202), Seattle, Washington, WA 98101, USA
Tel: +1 206 625 1146, www.zigzagcafe.net
The Zig Zag Café was one of the first local Seattle establishments to really embody the concept of the cocktail as craft and art form, and it still sets the bar [no pun intended] for others to aspire to. Yet it is unpretentious to a fault: an innocent tourist might easily walk in and order a Screwdriver, gin & tonic, or Long Island Iced Tea and not even realize how shockingly they are misusing their opportunity. Zig Zag regulars, however, know where they are, and how to take advantage of it. Murray Stenson is well known as Seattle's best bartender, and it is often difficult to find a seat at the bar on the evenings that he works (Tue-Fri).

Let's transition now from old to new, from casual to sleek:

VESSEL
1312 5th Ave, Seattle, Washington, WA 98101, USA
Tel: +1 206 652 5222, www.VesselSeattle.com
Vessel is the new kid on the block, having opened in Oct 2006. The owners have no previous experience of running bar, but they did have the foresight to attract the right pe in the form of Jamie Boudreau, to do so for them. The amb is glass, metal, and white, with very large picture window allow a two-way visual conversation between the outside the in. Even customers unfamiliar with the typical cocktail a trements will easily notice that things are just a notch above - from ice-cubes that are truly cubes of crystal clear ic glassware that is swooping and elegant. And the d themselves are elevated out of the ordinary, with double str juices, flamed Chartreuse and maple syrup foam deftly emp in the creation of some unique cocktails. Their exqui executed bar snack menu is a match for these creations.

From a place that is cocktails first and food second, it be useful to look at someplace that is food first cocktails second:

FU KUN WU AT THAIKU

5410 Ballard Ave NW, Seattle,
Washington, WA 98107, USA
Tel: +1 206 706 7807

Ballard Avenue is quickly turning into a restaurant row, with a wide variety of choices for the evening just steps from one another. ThaiKu is a popular Thai restaurant that has maintained a solid reputation for several years, and Fu Kun Wu is their cocktail lounge, decked out with the façade of a Chinese apothecary. But the theatre doesn't stop there. Bar manager Perryn Wright specialises in unique elixirs that fit the surroundings, from an Oolong Tea-ni, which includes black tea, to a variety of drinks that include a dash of yohimbine, supposedly an aphrodisiac and stimulant.

Before leaving Ballard, we owe it to ourselves to swing by a relatively new bar that has a popular following:

SAMBAR AT LE GOURMAND

425 NW Market Street, Seattle, Washington,
WA 98107, USA
Tel: +1 206 781 4883

Located amongst a quiet residential community, this little restaurant, a Ballard fixture, has been serving exquisite French food to a steady clientele for many years. Recently they added a little extension to one side in order to add a separate bar. It's hard to say what took them so long, but it was a welcome addition: Sambar is now a favourite hangout not only for the local neighbourhood, but for others who are interested in well made classics and finely crafted original cocktails.

From one restaurant which opened a separate bar, to another:

LICOROUS

928 12th Ave, Seattle, Washington,
WA 98122, USA
Tel: +1 206 325 6947, www.licorous.com

Lark is one of the newer restaurants in Seattle, and has gathered a lot of attention since its opening. It has a small bar counter in the back, mostly for preparing cocktails for its dining guests but with several stools for barflies. The owners clearly saw the direct association between cocktails and cuisine, and decided that they had to have a bigger space in order to give their cocktails room to play. So they opened a sister establishment next door, and Licorous was born. There are many things to like about Licorous. Not only do they make their own bitters, their cocktail menu even includes specific cocktail/food pairings, and prices them as a combo ($10.50). What better way to extend restaurant to bar? RH

ANLIS

576 Aurora Ave N, Seattle, Washington, WA 98109, USA
el: +1 206 283 3313, www.canlis.com

here is no Seattle restaurant with as long, or esteemed, a story as the Canlis. It is one of THOSE restaurants, where oung men save for months in order to take their dates, where usinessmen take out-of-town clients to really up the stakes, nd where couples make it an annual event on their anniversaries. The food is top notch, the view is spectacular, and the alets are famous for driving your car up for you almost the oment you step out the door. There was a time, however, hen their cocktails were made with lacklustre ingredients and o inspiration at all – not an uncommon occurrence in staurants, particularly not the more upscale establishments. ortunately Canlis has changed with the times and fully mbraced the culinary potential of the cocktail, guaranteeing at diners can enjoy not only an exquisite meal but an equally xquisite cocktail.

loving from fancy to fanciful, our next stop is in Ballard, a uburb just slightly north of downtown Seattle:

Martin Cate

California, USA

Our resident Tiki god, Martin fled South London to discover Tiki paradise, presently his Forbidden Island Tiki Lounge in Alameda, California. Martin is passionate about Tiki and knows more about the subject than anyone I have met.

By now, it's a well-known fact that the tiki bar is an imaginary concept. We all know that there is really no rum production to speak of in the South Pacific; the region is home to a diverse and fascinating variety of peoples whose arts & crafts are not merely interchangeable tchotchkes to be hung on the walls of a saloon; and that tiny paper umbrellas really provide very little protection from the elements. No, the tiki bar is a uniquely American invention, born from a sense of exploration and ingenuity, informed by the experience of World War II, the new statehood of Hawaii, and much, much more. Besides, it had to be an American who first looked at an innocent puffer fish and thought, "You know, if I gutted that, stuck an airhose up its behind and inflated it, covered it in lacquer and glued googly eyes on it, that might be swell. But if I stick a light bulb in it and call it a lamp, then I'll really be on to something!"

Yes, at the end of the day, it's all a lot of nonsense. But what wonderful nonsense it is.

A great tiki bar can provide a literally intoxicating sense of escape, shelter, adventure, camaraderie, mystery, danger - all at the same time. When the cocktails are right, they can be as dynamic and fascinating as anything invented by the most creative mixologists working today - even though the great recipes are often 60 or more years old. A truly great tiki bar is unquantifiable - you'll just know by the third round of drinks – yet before I talk about my favourite tiki bars, I want to mention a few of the more identifiable elements (besides the cocktails) that make a great tiki bar great.

The Darkness - A great tiki bar should be enveloped in perpetual twilight. Like being on a torch-lit lanai at dusk, the warm colours of a good tiki bar fill you with a sense of relaxation. Amber lights, accented by a colourful variety of illuminated glass floats and fish traps provide all you need. Most importantly… no windows! With escape being such a vital component of a memorable tiki experience, the last thing you want on your trip to the South Seas is to look out at the pharmacy across the street. Tiki bars came of age in America at a time when drinking in a bar was something you didn't want to advertise yourself doing - fortunately the resulting lack of windows became a design element in the tiki bar.

The Water - There is something truly enchanting about th sound of running water in a tiki bar. A stream, fountain, aquariu or waterfall can add true magic to the atmosphere. Don Th Beachcomber, creator of the tiki bar, mimicked the sound of storm in his bar to convince customers that it was rainin outside, so they might as well have another drink. But water also integral to the experience – you can't have an island withou it – and the best places had elaborate networks of streams ar pools girdled with rock walls and spanned by bridges. The nov closed Kona Kai in Chicago was built almost entirely over wate while the recently gutted Islands restaurant in San Dieg featured water pouring from giant clam shells embedded rock walls and flowing under bridges through the dining roon

The Gemütlichkeit - This most closely translates to Englis as cosiness, but in German it additionally means tranquillit comfort, a lack of stress. I love this word because nothin sounds less cosy than the word gemütlichkeit, but also becaus it accurately describes the feeling I get in a good tiki ba Cosiness is very important to a good tiki bar, and this can b created in a number of ways. For me, it's important to keep intimate - low ceilings, booths or huts can ensconce and furthe "shelter" you from the "elements". Lots of twists and turns, a maze-like interior can add to this - a great example is th Bahooka in Rosemead, California.

That's not to say that dramatic interiors aren't striking a well - but they work best when least expected. Frank Lloy Wright was fond of having dark narrow entrances to his home so that when you reached the main area - often with a muc higher ceiling - you were more struck by the dramatic revea Entering the main room of the Mai Kai after coming through th low entryway, the sight of the peaked roof with its dozens lights is breathtaking. But the rest of its enormous interi houses a series of smaller rooms designed to make the dinir experience more personal.

My journey into the heart of tiki began in the early nineties the lost, lamented Trader Vic's outpost in Washington DC. Lure as I was by promises of "drinks as big as your head", I wa certainly intrigued to see what kind of cool watering hole cou possibly be found within the staid confines of the Washingto DC Hilton. Like many of the great Hilton Trader Vic's location this one was deep within the bowels of the hotel, a counter intuitive location for any kind of tropical paradise. Needless say, I was enchanted by the place - its look and its feel. (An yes, the drink was as big as my head.)

Sadly, this location is no more, but there are many oth wonderful tiki temples around the world - some large, othe tiny, but the great ones each have their own special qualitie Here are my top four:

Trailer Happiness

1. MAI-KAI – THE MOTHERSHIP

In the 1950s, two brothers from Chicago had a dream - to build a Polynesian restaurant that would become a landmark destination. They settled on the still sleepy but developing town of Fort Lauderdale, Florida, and set to work building the finest Polynesian supper club that has ever existed. They dreamed big, and their dream has grown with time: Mai-Kai now features eight dining rooms with seating for 489 people, a separate bar for 150, extensive tropical gardens, and an incredible nightly floorshow.

Travelling up North Federal Highway in Fort Lauderdale and gazing out at the anonymous big box retailers that dot the roadway, the last thing you are expecting are the lush grounds of the Mai-Kai. Surrounded by a series of waterfalls, rocky outcrops and the kind of dense vegetation that is only possible in the tropical climes of an area like South Florida, the enormous main A-frame is well hidden from view - a fact that makes the discoveries inside all the more dramatic.

After leaving your car with the valet, you enter the foyer and are directed into the Molokai Bar, one of the most beautifully appointed bars in the world, with miles of rigging, simulated rainstorms against the windows, and of course, the Mai-Kai's famous cocktails, which are among the best in the world. Returning to the main dining room, you're struck by the towering A-frame above you, and as you explore the many and varied dining rooms, and the rich, lush gardens, you can't help but wonder if life was really better 50 years ago when places like this were everywhere.

Well, they weren't exactly everywhere. In fact, the Mai-Kai was about the grandest place ever built, and we are incredibly fortunate to have it with us today. In many respects, it's almost too much – there's just so much to see that it usually overwhelms the first time visitor. Even the bathrooms are fantastic, and all the elements come together to create the ultimate tiki experience. In a rare bonus, some of the food is actually delicious - almost unheard of in a classic tiki bar.

2. TIKI-TI – THE LEGACY

Opened in 1961 by famed barman Ray Buhen, the postage-stamp sized Tiki-Ti in Los Angeles is a perfect window onto the glory of tiki in its heyday. Ray had tended bar at Don the Beachcomber's, China Trader, and many other legendary spots in Southern California. When he opened his own place, tiki was still in full swing, and Ray imagined starting a school to train bartenders in the art of mixing tropical drinks. While that never got off the ground, the Tiki-Ti continued to grow and prosper despite changes in tastes, the neighbourhood, and more. Today, it is run by Ray's son and grandson, both named Mike.

For me, the Tiki-Ti works so well for many reasons. It's both a convivial neighbourhood bar, and a direct connection to the past. I love their dedication to the traditions of the great tropical drink - all of their recipes are secret and most are poured from unmarked bottles. They're also cash only, have no beer or wine, and the drinks don't come cheap.

And yet, the place is packed nightly with a lively, friendly crowd. Where else could you find a neighbourhood bar where the regular patrons enjoy $15 goblets of rum and tropical juices just as a regular at an everyday bar would sup a beer and a shot? Everybody there gets it - they know what the place is about, why they came, and what to drink. It's packed with knickknacks collected over the years, tapa print walls that are beautifully caramelized by age and smoke, and, yes, there's even a little waterfall in the corner. It doesn't hurt that the only employees are the owners and, thanks to California's bizarre smoking laws, it's therefore perfectly legal to light up inside one of only a handful of places left in the state. So be sure to pay them a visit when you're next in LA. Go early, get comfy, and bring Mike Sr. a good cigar - he'll appreciate it!

3. HALA KAHIKI – THE STYLE

Wandering deep into the suburbs of Chicago, you'll find this gem of a place in the town of River Grove. Let your eyes adjust to the low lighting and feast upon a perfectly decorated slice of the tiki past. With each of its three rooms offering new delights at every turn, the Hala Kahiki creates a total escape. Much of the artwork comes from the Witco line of furnishings, which provided the décor for Elvis' Jungle Room at Graceland and Hef's Grotto at the Playboy Mansion. Soft hapa haole music plays gently as you lift a cocktail to your lips and – oh, sweet Jesus, is that nasty?! Sadly, yes, the drinks at the Hala Kahiki are terrible. Really, really terrible. But, as the old Chinese proverb says, "A diamond with a flaw is worth more than a pebble without imperfections."

4. TRAD'R SAM – THE NEIGHBOURHOOD

I am frequently criticized for my love of this wonderful little dump, but let me explain. Located in the Richmond district of San Francisco, Trad'r Sam opened its doors sometime in the 1930s - no one is quite sure when. In fact, no one is quite sure what happened to the "e" in Trader, either. Interestingly, there is a story, perhaps apocryphal, that suggests Sam sued Victor Bergeron for stealing the name "Trader" when he changed the name of his place in Oakland from Hinky Dink's to Trader Vic's. Obviously, Sam lost. No matter what, at the end of the day, Trad'r Sam carries the distinction of being the oldest tiki bar in its original location in the world.

It's a little salty, sure. Don't look too closely at the upholstery

But go in some afternoon and pull up a seat at the bar. Let the hobo next to you sleep on your shoulder. It's OK - he might drool a little, but he won't bite. Take a good look at the magnificent curved rattan bar in front of you. Notice the drop ceiling: you'd never find this in your average neighbourhood bar. Order a drink from the vast menu - you'll see that they all carry about the same description ("This one will knock you out"). Most are poor, but there are some gems - try the "Sabotage". Take your drink and retire to one of the "islands" around the bar. (Yes, the booths are named after South Pacific islands; you'll see it spelled out in rattan as you enter.) If you're with friends, try one of their famous Scorpion Bowls. Then leave before 9pm, when obnoxious college kids arise and pack the place.

I'm not selling you? Maybe you had to live in the neighbourhood. But maybe it's just a great reminder of a time when a desire to escape to a simple life in the tropics was a part of the American experience, and small neighbourhood tiki bars like this one dotted the landscape. Maybe it's because Trad'r Sam is a survivor: still selling escape, good times and potent potables after all those years.

When the time came to open my own place, I formulated my Scorpion Bowl as a blend of both the Trader and the Trad'r's recipes - to pay homage to the man who spread tiki around the world, as well as the scrappy guy down the street who just ran a great little tiki joint. Hopefully, in a cosmic way, it will help settle that lawsuit.

CITY DRINKING

The following pages feature our choice of the best hotels, restaurants and bars in six frequently visited cities. Our aim is to continually review and improve on these selections and share these discoveries through the pages of this quarterly magazine.

I've personally visited and reviewed all of the following bars but also greatly rely on the local knowledge of a network of friends who represent drinks brands in their respective home cities around the world. These brands also support this title and without their help and patronage its publication would not be possible.

While I believe we can dispassionately feature premium liquor brands I do not believe the same can be said about the hotels, restaurants and bars we recommend. Hence, we DO NOT accept payment from such establishments or run advertising of any type from them.

We all have likes and dislikes which shape our opinions. The following are my own but I'm also keen to hear what are your favourite hotels, restaurants and bars.

Cheers
Simon Difford
simon@diffordsguide.com

Sleeping

Tasked with selecting the best hostelries a city has to offer, I've inevitably tended toward four and five star hotels; but not necessarily so as I personally favour small and boutique over large and corporate. Whether modern and minimalist or traditional, rooms should be reasonably sized but above all clean, comfortable and homely.

Many hotel inspectors grade hotels on such things as having a night porter and 24-hour room service. While these luxuries are welcome I'm more worried about whether the hotel has a great bar that's open late, a knowledgeable and friendly concierge, serves breakfast till late and offers an even later check-out without additional charge. In sunny climes a pool and terrace are always appreciated. As for the perfect hotel room, that should have the following:

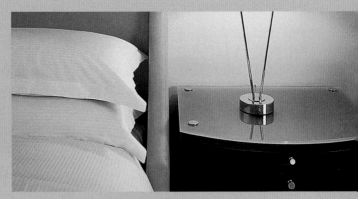

- **Mini bar** (after all this title is first and foremost about drink).

- **Safe** large enough to take a lap-top.

- **Wardrobe space** with plenty of hangers with proper hooks.

- **Tea & coffee** making facilities.

- **A separate bath** (for girlfriend) and powerful hot shower (for me).

- **A full length and well lit make-up mirror** (also for my girlfriend).

- **Air conditioning** - and windows that can be opened.

- **Dressing gowns** to aid the feeling of being at home.

- **Iron and ironing board.**

- **Free wi-fi internet access** and a desk with plenty of power sockets.

- **Hi-fi** to plug iPod into.

- **Quality, and spotlessly clean towels and linen.**

- **Duvets** rather than heavy old blankets on a large comfortable bed.

- **Drapes or blinds** that stop the sun waking me up a couple of hours after I've left the last bar.

Eating

Obviously we're looking for restaurants that serve great food in pleasant surroundings but while designer décor can help make the restaurant experience clean and simple with character can often be as good or better. A great restaurant should offer the following:

- **A bar** at which to sit and wait for late comers.

- **Attentive service,** but not overly so.

- **An aperitif drinks list.**

- **Great bread** or other nibbles.

- **An interesting and varied wine list.**

- **Friendly wait staff** with honest recommendations.

- **Choice of fish & vegetarian dishes** for the non-carnivorous.

- **Comfortable chairs and tables** well spaced apart.

- **Any music should be background**

- **Clean toilets** with hand towels (plus mirrors for the girls).

- **Atmospheric lighting** but sufficient to read the menu and see what you're eating.

- **Unpretentious menu** that conveys what's on offer without the use of a culinary dictionary.

- **Choice of dessert wines** and digestive spirits and liqueurs.

- **Time to relax** without being rushed away for the next sitting.

Drinking

We're not just looking for upscale cocktail lounge bars - a characterful pub or dive bar could be as good or better. However, we are after great drinks, be they wine, beer, spirits or cocktails. A truly great bar would have a superb range of all of these, but certainly a lounge should have great cocktails, a pub great beer and a wine bar great wines.

Décor needn't be designer chic and I've noticed the best looking bars improve as they wear over the decades. Conversely bad bars need a refit every two or three years.

Atmosphere is difficult to pin down but bars either have it or they don't. Really great bars manage to achieve this with relatively few people.

The distinction between a restaurant, bar or club can be blurred, but for the record anywhere where the music takes precedence over the drinks is a club, and anywhere where you have to order food in order to sit down is a restaurant.

The following contribute to a great bar.

Grades

After much discussion and visiting establishments (some several times) I've awarded each a grade out of five according its range of drinks, service, décor, and ambience. These grades reflect my own tastes and yours may be very different - please let me know. (simon@diffordsguide.com)

Disgusting ○ ○ ○ ○ ○   **Spectacular** ● ● ● ● ●

Recommendations

The following symbols appear at the foot of bar reviews where I consider the establishment reliably good at the following.

🍸 **Cocktails**

🍴 **Food**

🍷 **Wine**

🍺 **Beer**

▦ **Spirits**

🎚 **Music**

- **Friendly welcome on the door** even if from bouncer turning you away.

- **Plenty of bar counter space** and comfortable bar stools with backs and foot rests.

- **Hooks under the bar counter** for handbags and jackets.

- **A good and varied beer selection** served in suitable cold glassware.

- **An interesting and varied wine list** with tasting notes and plenty of wines by the glass.

- **A reasonable choice of premium liquor brands** across all categories - not just vodka.

- **A list of well-made classic cocktails** with some contemporary twists, made using fresh ingredients and not sour mix.

- **A cocktail list** - I'm sick of hearing "we can make any cocktail you ask for" – really?

- **Shapely clean glassware.**

- **Complementary iced water** offered with drinks.

- **Finger food, nibbles and fries.**

- **Good espresso coffee** (preferably Illy).

- **If music's played it should suit the mood and be at an appropriate volume.**

- **Comfy chairs and tables.**

- **Friendly, efficient table service.**

- **Atmospheric lighting.**

- **Good ventilation,** particularly where smoking is allowed.

- **Friendly and varied clientele** but not too crowded.

- **Clean toilets** with hand towels but without challenging gender signs - I don't want an initiative test before I can pee. And I don't want to have to tip a toilet attendant for the privilege either.

BARCELONA

Airport: Barcelona El Prat De Llobregat (BCN)
Time zone: Central European Time (GMT +1)

Balmy weather, great shops, world famous art galleries, a sandy Mediterranean beach and breathtaking architecture: Barcelona has all this and more besides. Its club scene is world famous, its restaurants are outstanding and there are more than a few cocktail bars and stylish lounges.

The capital of Catalunya, Barcelona lies sandwiched between the mountains and the Mediterranean coastline close to the border with France. The region, while part of Spain, has its own distinctive cuisine, dialect and culture.

Besides the architecture – and Antoni Gaudi's serpentine buildings continue to dazzle – shopping is one of Barcelona's great attractions. All the big international designer names are represented along Avenida Diagonal and the Passeig de Gràcia.

The climate is pleasant for most of the year and even in the winter it is rarely genuinely cold. In August the heat can be oppressive, and many bars and restaurants close for the entire month. Most shops also close between 1:30pm and 4pm but then stay open till 10pm.

Barcelona Hotels

ince hosting the Olympic Games in 992, Barcelona has become a popular ty break destination. Recent years have een a plethora of hotels open to meet is growing demand. The following are l upscale, luxury hotels and all, with the xception of Gran Hotel La Florida, are in e city centre.

rts Hotel

9-21 Carrer de la Marina, Barcelona, atalunya, 08005, Spain
el: +34 93 221 1000,
ww.ritzcarlton.com

his striking, contemporary hotel sits on e edge of the Port Olímpic yachting arbour and the Mediterranean beachfront. l 482 luxurious rooms have marble athrooms and high tech mod cons.

otel Casa Fuster

32 Passeig de Gràcia, Uptown, arcelona, Catalunya, 08008, Spain
l: +34 93 255 3000,
ww.hotelcasafuster.com
ooms: 96

his magnificent 1908 building in the opping district houses a traditional xury hotel that's big enough to offer five ar services but small enough to feel outique. Rooms are decorated to a 30s theme and embellished with art eco furnishings, and the hotel is owned by a rooftop pool.

laris Hotel

0 Pau Claris, Barcelona, Catalunya, 009, Spain. Tel: +34 93 487 6262, ww.derbyhotels.com
ooms: 124

though built in 1992, this 5* hotel ains a neo-classical facade. It is owned the art collector Jordi Clos and atures pre-Columbian artworks, yptian carvings, Hindu sculptures and ifth-century Roman mosaic. There is a nall rooftop pool but you will need to t up early to score a sunbed.

Hotel Cram

54 Carrer Aribau, Downtown,
Barcelona, Catalunya,
08011, Spain
Tel: +34 93 216 7700,
www.hotelcram.com
Rooms: 67

This slick, ultra-modern four star hotel was only completed in 2005 but sits behind an elegant 1892 façade. It is located just four blocks from the Passeig de Gràcia and offers a bar, the Michelin-starred Gaig restaurant and an outdoor swimming pool. Rooms boast 32-inch LCD televisions and wi-fi internet access.

Gran Hotel La Florida

83-93 Carrer Vallvidrera al Tibidabo,
Barcelona, Catalunya, 08035, Spain
Tel: +34 93 259 3000,
www.thesteingroup.com/florida
Rooms: 74 (inc. 22 suites)

This revamped five-star hotel lies a little way out of town in Tibidabo, but its hilltop perch offers sweeping views of the city and, traffic allowing, the free shuttle bus (daily 10am-6pm) will have you in town in 20 minutes. Rooms are lavish and amenities include a sun terrace and an impressive 37-metre indoor-outdoor infinity pool. The most romantic hotel in Barcelona.

Grand Hotel Central

30 Via Laietana, El Born, Barcelona,
Catalunya, 08003, Spain
Tel: +34 93 295 7900,
www.grandhotelcentral.com
Rooms: 147

In the centre of downtown, this slick, clean and modern hotel lies within an elegant building dating back to 1926. The good sized rooms brim with extras such as flat screen TVs, DVD and MP3 players, and internet access, while the lobby houses a Mediterranean restaurant - although you may prefer to snack beside the rooftop pool.

Neri Hotel

5 Carrer San Sever
(btwn cathedral & Placa de Sant
Jaume), Barcelona, Catalunya,
08002, Spain
Tel: +34 93 304 0655,
www.hotelneri.com
Rooms: 22

This romantic little hotel is set in an 18th century palace in Barcelona's Gothic quarter so is close to the city beach and the trendy El Born. Its high-impact design contrasts original features with very contemporary furnishings and finishes.

Omm Hotel

256 Rosselló,
Barcelona, Catalunya,
08008, Spain
Tel: +34 93 445 4000,
www.hotelomm.es
Rooms: 59

This modern hotel lies close to the shops on Passeig de Gràcia. Features include the Moo Restaurant and Moo Bar (see our reviews), plus an open air swimming pool. The rooms are spacious, well appointed and modern, while the combination of location, facilities and style make this our preferred Barcelona hotel.

Prestige Paseo de Gracia Hotel

62 Passeig de Gracia,
Barcelona, Catalunya,
08007, Spain
Tel: +34 93 272 4180,
www.prestigepaseodegracia.com
Rooms: 45

This designer, boutique 4* hotel lies behind a heavy, unmarked silver door on the busy Passeig de Gràcia, Barcelona's answer to Bond Street, a short stroll from Gaudi's whimsical La Pedrera. The bedrooms are high tech and well appointed and it is surely only the lack of a restaurant that stands before that extra star.

Barcelona Restaurants

Although Catalan cuisine does not have quite the same prestige as Basque cuisine, it is becoming increasingly recognised and Barcelona's best restaurants now have an international reputation.

Typical Catalan dishes include 'butifarra' (cured pork sausage), 'escalivada' (sliced, barbecued peppers and aubergines), 'olla barrejada' (meat stew) and 'botifarra amb mongetes' (sausage and beans). 'Allioli' (garlic mayonnaise) is found all over Spain but originated in Catalunya. My personal favourite is the simple 'pa amb tomàquet' (lightly toasted bread, rubbed with fresh tomato and sprinkled with olive oil and salt).

Spanish people eat late. Lunch is served between 2pm and 4pm and dinner usually well after 9pm. Restaurant kitchens stay open till around midnight. Spain is not a nation of tippers, although in upscale restaurants a tip of around 5% is customary.

Agut d'Avignon

3 Carrer de la Trinitat, Barri Gòtic, Barcelona, Catalunya, 08002, Spain
Tel: +34 93 302 6034
Cuisine: Catalan/Mediterranean

This upscale but intimate restaurant is set in a converted 19th-century mansion in the heart of Barcelona's Gothic Quarter (Barri Gòtic). The lengthy wine list covers Spain's key wine regions.

El Bulli

Cala Montjoi, Ap. 30, Roses, Girona, 17480, Spain
Tel. +34 972 150 457, www.elbulli.com
Cuisine: Molecular gastronomy

El Bulli is two hours' drive north of Barcelona in Roses on the Costa Brava but has three Michelin stars and is considered by many to be THE best restaurant in the world so I felt its inclusion here more than warranted. It's only open between April and September and you'll need to start calling for a reservation in mid-January when the phone lines open. During the six months when the restaurant is closed the chefs devise new recipes in their laboratory in Barcelona. The results are typically 27 course meals prepared using space age equipment, such as freeze-dried, shaved foie gras with consommé and tamarind. Make it your new year's resolution to start calling.

Ca l'Isidre

12 Carrer Les Flors, Barcelona, Catalunya, 08001, Spain
Tel: +34 93 441 1139
Cuisine: Catalan/Mediterranean

This well established, family run restaurant counts King Juan Carlos of Spain as a patron. It is noted for its traditional Mediterranean food, desserts and wine list.

Cal Pep

8 Plaça de les Olles (@ Carrer de Rera Palau), El Born District, Barcelona, Catalunya, Spain
Tel: +34 93 310 7961
Cuisine: Catalan/Mediterranean tapas

To experience this tiny tapas bar you'll probably have to line up outside for at least an hour or arrive before it opens (Mon 8pm-11:45pm, Tue-Sat 1:30pm-4pm & 8pm-11:45pm, closed Sun and August). The excellent seafood tapas justifies the wait.

Casa Jacinto

29-31 Gran Via Carlos III, Barcelona, Catalunya, 08028, Spain
Tel: +34 93 339 0023, www.casajacinto.com
Cuisine: Catalan/Mediterranean

This is a down to earth traditional, family ru restaurant which serves simply mac excellent food, particularly seafood. Nothin is fancy here, not even the prices, but expe warm, friendly service and lots of hams.

Casa Leopoldo

24 Carrer Sant Rafael, Barcelona, Catalunya, 08001, Spain
Tel: + 34 93 441 3014, www.casaleopoldo.com
Cuisine: Seafood/Catalan

Founded in 1929, Casa Leopoldo is wide regarded as serving the best tradition Catalan seafood in Barcelona.

Cerveceria Catalana

236 Carrer Mallorca
(@ Rambla de Catalunya), Barcelona,
Catalunya, 08008, Spain.
Tel: +34 93 216 0368
Cuisine: Catalan/Mediterranean tapas

If you simply want to wander into a traditional tapas bar and enjoy great Catalan bites, I recommend Cerveceria Catalana. It also serves some fine beers such as Chimay and good local wines.

Comerç 24

24 Comerç, El Born, Barcelona,
Catalunya, 08003, Spain
Tel: +34 93 319 2102,
www.comerc24.com/english
Cuisine: Cutting edge Spanish

Fans of molecular gastronomy will know of owner/chef Carles Abellan, who learnt his trade from Ferran Adrià of El Bulli. This restaurant and tapas bar will be an experience for your taste buds but you'll need to book well ahead.

Neichel Restaurant

1-5 Carrer Beltrán i Rózpide, Barcelona,
Catalunya, 08034, Spain
Tel: +34 93 203 8408
Cuisine: Mediterranean

Proprietor and chef Jean Louis Neichel's 'classic French meets Catalan' dishes make this one of Barcelona's top restaurants, with two Michelin stars to prove it. A contemporary, light dining room looks onto an attractive garden.

Cinc Sentits

58 Carrer Aribau,
Eixample, Barcelona,
Catalunya,
08011, Spain
Tel: +34 93 323 9490,
www.cincsentits.com
Cuisine: Modern Catalan

Named after the Catalan for 'five senses', this modern, minimalist restaurant is currently one of Barcelona's hottest. The gourmet tasting menu is recommended.

Ciudad Condal Cerveceria

18 Rambla Catalunya, Barcelona,
Catalunya, 08007, Spain
Tel: +34 93 318 1997
Cuisine: Catalan/Mediterranean tapas

This sits just behind Cerveceria Catalana in my Barcelona tapas bar league. It has a more formal restaurant behind but sit at the spacious tapas bar at the front and pick from the mouth-watering display laid

Restaurant Gaig

214 Carrer Aragón, Barcelona,
Catalunya, 08011, Spain Tel: +34 93 429
1017, www.restaurantgaig.com
Cuisine: Spanish

This family-run, Michelin-starred establishment has passed from generation to generation since 1869. Chef-owner Carles Gaig continues the tradition in these new, larger, modern premises, while the wine list is extensive and impressive.

Moo

Hotel Omm, 265 Calle Rosselló (@
Passeig de Gràcia), Eixample,
Barcelona, 08008, Spain
Tel: +34 93 445 4000, www.hotelomm.es
Cuisine: Modern Catalan

This lies at the back of the lobby area of one of Barcelona's 'hippest' hotels so expect a trendy crowd and higher prices than some. But Moo is not style over substance: when we've eaten here both service and food have been

El Racó d'en Freixa

22 Carrer Sant Elíes,
Barcelona, Catalunya,
08006, Spain
Tel: +34 93 209 7559,
www.elracodenfreixa.com
Cuisine: Catalan/Mediterranean

Chef Ramón Freixa Riera has inherited his father's talent for producing great traditional Catalan dishes.

El Racóde Can Fabes

6 Carrer Sant Joan,
Sant Celoni, Montseny,
Catalunya, Spain
Tel: +34 93 867 2851,
www.racocanfabes.com
Cuisine: Catalan/Mediterranean

Should you make the 30 mile drive out of Barcelona on the A7 (exit 7), you'll be rewarded by picturesque countryside and Catalan food that has been awarded the prestigious three Michelin stars. Better yet,

Barcelona Drinking

Barcelona's clubs have gained the city a reputation as one of Europe's great party cities. It also boasts a number of classic, old-school cocktail bars, as well as plenty of contemporary, designer lounge bars, but perhaps best of all are the tapas bars that lie on practically every corner.

The largest and most important wine region in Catalunya is Penedés, where a wide range of red and white grape varieties are grown. However, the area is most noted for its white wines. Cava, the sparkling wine, has its own denominación de origen and xampanyerías, bars which specialise in serving cava, are distinctive to Barcelona.

Barcelona has many small, intimate, classic cocktail bars. They feel like they should be off the lobby of a grand old five star hotel, but are in fact set among parades of normal shops. In these classic cocktails are king – particularly the Dry Martini and the Gimlet - to such an extent that these drinks have lent their names to a couple of Barcelona's best bars. ('Gimlet', incidentally, is pronounced 'Jim-Let' here.)

Many of the bars appear to open in shifts. Those that open early usually close relatively early, while late night bars usually stay open until 2am or 3am and the clubs party on till 5am or 6am. All the action starts a couple of hours later than in most other European cities so don't rush off the beach.

Young American readers may like to note that the legal drinking age in Barcelona is 16 years. Dress tends to the smarter side of casual. Should you seek that party atmosphere, head to the harbour areas of Port Olímpic and Maremagnum.

ABADIA

172 Carrer del Rosselló (btwn Carrers D'Enric Granados & D'Aribau), Barcelona, Catalunya, 08036, Spain

Tel: +34 93 454 9414
Hours: Mon-Sun 7pm-3am

Type: Beer bar
Alfresco: No
Entry: Most welcome
Highlights: Beer range
Atmosphere: Relaxed
Clientele: Local, after work crowd
Dress code: Casual
Price guide: €€
Bar snacks: Filled baguettes

The small pot still in the window of this narrow little bar could give the impression that it specialised in whisky or cognac. Once inside it becomes clear that Abadia is first and foremost a beer bar. Trappist beer memorabilia adorns the walls. The bar counter, which spans two-thirds of the long room, is lined with high bar stools and the glass display fridge behind it houses 50-odd different bottled beers. Belgian bottles, particularly Trappist brews, dominate but there are offerings from around the world, including local favourites such as Voll-Damm. The range is supplemented by a few draught offerings and all are dispensed in an appropriately shaped and branded glass.

Abadia's décor is plain and uncomplicated. This down-to-earth, friendly little place is very much a locals' joint and it is usual for the bar to be lined with men drinking a pint of Guinness – a sight more reminiscent of Dublin than Barcelona.

BAR ALMIRALL

33 Joaquin Costa, Raval, Barcelona, Catalunya, 08001, Spain

Tel: +34 93 318 9917
Hours: Mon-Sun noon-2am

Type: Lounge bar
Alfresco: No
Entry: Open door
Highlights: Art Nouveau decor
Atmosphere: Laid back
Clientele: Tourists
Dress code: Casual
Price guide: €€
Bar snacks: Eat elsewhere

Dating from 1860, this is Barcelona's second oldest bar (after the Marsella) and is worth visiting just to admire its Belle Epoque Art Nouveau interior. A bronze figurine holding a lamp sits at the end of the bar and the old bottles on the back bar are framed by carved wooden swirls and backed by antique mirrors. The floor is marble, the walls of wooden panelling and nicotine yellow plaster. Wood and glass panelling divides the space in two, creating a dimly lit, atmospheric area favoured by canoodling couples.

The overall feel is that of an old bar that's been locked up and forgotten for years, then opened up and stocked with cold beer earlier that day. And, despite the shelves of ancient spirits and liqueurs, beer rules in this classic space. Chimay and Damm dominate the small range of bottled beers but draught Estrella Damm is most popular.

OADAS COCKTAIL BAR

allers (@ Rambla), Barcelona, Catalunya, 08001,
ain

+34 93 318 9592
urs: Mon-Sat noon-2am (closed Sunday)

pe: Cocktail lounge bar
resco: No
try: Open door
ghlights: Cocktails
nosphere: Laid back
entele: Young lovers to ageing locals
ess code: Smart casual
ce guide: €€€
r snacks: Tapas

ng just off the bustling Rambla, this tiny,
angular place is one of Barcelona's
lest bars. It was opened in 1933 by
guel Boadas, who learnt his trade at the
nous Floridita bar in Cuba. He passed
ay in 1967 and his famous bar is now
ned by his daughter, Maria Dolores
adas. She has altered little of her
eritance and her father's memorabilia
adorns the panelled walls. Maria was
rn the year after her father opened this
and is practically part of the furniture.
sure to say hello – you'll usually find her
he far left of the bar.

The jolly team of bartenders
plendent in black jackets, white shirts
d black bow ties ply their trade with
nfidence and mix drinks by flamboyantly
uring the ingredients from one shaker
d aloft into another several feet below.

Cocktails are wonderfully old school
d Dry Martinis, Gimlets and Mojitos
pear most popular. We found their
rtini style drinks consistently better
n their long drinks. Try one of their
cellent Daiquiris or the 'Cocktail del
' (cocktail of the day) affixed to a sign
ind the bar.

BAR MARSELLA

65 Sant Pau, Raval, Barcelona, Catalunya, 08001, Spain

Tel: +34 93 442 7263
Hours: Mon-Sat 10pm-2:30am (closed Sunday)

Type: Café cum beer hall
Alfresco: No
Entry: Open door
Highlights: Few apart from spectacle
Atmosphere: Bohemian
Clientele: Local students & tourists
Dress code: Casual
Price guide: €€
Bar snacks: Not a place to eat

Antique bar meets cool grunge
Barcelona's oldest bar where the o
things that have changed in decades
the mismatched tiles on the patch
floor. Mirrors, panels and cabinets of
bottles cover the walls, and chandel
hang from the ceiling. The whole pl
has a rich tobacco haze to it – espec
the window, which would lose all th
character if properly cleaned.

Estrella Damm beer is the m
popular choice at the old marble
counter but Marsella is famed as a pl
to enjoy absinthe. This is served v
small forks on which to balance su
cubes and plastic bottles pierced v
holes through which to squirt water
inelegant but effective way to swee
and dilute your green fairy, which her
distinctly yellow.

Marsella is hardly a spot for upse
drinkers but its notoriety and specta
may draw you to visit. If you do, dr
down to fit in with the tourist and stud
crowd and guard your valuables w
walking the surrounding streets.

CAFÉ VIENNESE

● ● ● ○ ○

Hotel Casa Fuster, 132 Passeig de Gràcia, Uptown, Barcelona, Catalunya, 08008, Spain

Tel: +34 93 255 3000, www.hotelcasafuster.com
Hours: Mon-Sun noon-2am

Type: Hotel lounge bar
Alfresco: No
Entry: Via hotel lobby
Highlights: Vaulted ceiling
Atmosphere: Formal but relaxed
Clientele: International travelling set
Dress code: Nothing too casual
Price guide: €€€
Bar snacks: Tapas

Slightly inclined, the stunning floor of t
Casa Fuster hotel twists a path to t
hotel's spectacular lobby café bar l
Dorothy's Yellow Brick Road. Unl
in the Wizard of Oz, however, this path
a modernist mosaic of polish
black granite.

The Café Viennese is no less c
visual treat. Pink marble pillars rise fr
the black granite floor to a vaulted ceil
covered in gold leaf. The look is n
dissimilar to a luxury crypt but wa
lighting, wavy burgundy banquettes a
Paul Smith-style stripy chairs keep t
overall feel loungy.

This is a classic five star hotel and
café bar attracts the diverse upsc
international crowd you'd expect of su
an establishment. Expect old coupl
gorgeous girls, businessmen and yo
lovers splashing out on a glamoro
weekend away.

Sadly, the cocktails and drinks
don't match the splendour of the décor
stick to Martinis, Gimlets, Negronis and
like and you'll not be disappointed.

'HE CARIBBEAN CLUB

Carrer Sitges, Barcelona, Catalunya, 08001, Spain

l: +34 93 302 2182
ours: Tue-Sat 7pm-2am (closed August)

pe: Cocktail lounge bar
fresco: No
try: Open door if you can find it
ghlights: Cocktails
mosphere: Relaxed, subdued
ientele: Mixed bag of locals & odd tourist
ess code: Smart casual
ice guide: €€€
r snacks: Nibbles only

his tiny rum bar lies mid-way down a rrow back lane around the corner from adas in a 12th century building. It is sy to miss as its practically windowless ntage is only betrayed by a very subtle jn on the door. Don't confuse it with the arby pub - let your speakeasy instincts ide you.

Inside is a narrow, dimly lit room dicated to the Caribbean island of ıba. Its panelled walls are lined with ass display cases of antique cocktail akers and Cuban souvenirs. Ships' andlery such as brass portholes and mpasses adorn the walls and dot the ace, while the back section of the tiny ır boasts a serious rum collection. wever, if ordering a Daiquiri request at it is served 'classic style' or even in s most classic of bars you'll end up h a slushy blended affair.

Caribbean Club shares owners with adas and, as there, the bartenders ar black jackets and bow ties, and ow drinks from one half of the shaker the other when mixing.

Tirsa Cocktail Bar

The Caribbean Club

DRY MARTINI

162 Carrer Aribau, Barcelona, Catalunya,
08036, Spain

Tel: +34 93 217 5072, www.drymartinibcn.com
Hours: Mon-Sat 6:30pm-2:30am (closed Sunday)

Type: Cocktail lounge bar
Alfresco: No
Entry: No restrictions
Highlights: Cocktails
Atmosphere: Relaxed
Clientele: Tourists & local cocktail aficionados
Dress code: Smart casual
Price guide: €€€€
Bar snacks: Tapas

Dry Martini is something of a relic from
bygone era with its long wooden bar a
panelling. The service is also distinctly
school. Bartenders in white jackets prod
an array of classic cocktails with a touc
theatre and considerable style.

The bar's timewarp feel is enhanced
the collection of vintage gin and vermo
bottles which line the back bar and cram
wall-mounted cabinets. The shakers, strain
and other paraphernalia employed also l
like museum pieces. Yet modernity
recently come to Dry Martini, in the shap
an excellent range of infused vodkas such
truffle and jalapeño, served with an approp
morsel of a snack. Once you have whe
your appetite, just look for the door mar
'Speakeasy' and walk through the kitche
the excellent hidden restaurant beyond.

Dry Martini simply oozes classic sty
is large yet intimate with plentiful green lea
banquettes – similar in hue to the cherries w
garnish the Gimlets. Apart from the odd tou
you'll find yourself in the company of a cro
of older locals. They appreciate the Dry Mar
for which this bar is rightly named and fan

GIMLET BAR

4 Carrer Rec (btwn Passeig del Born & Carrer del Sabateret), Downtown, Barcelona, 08003, Spain

Tel: +34 93 310 1027
Hours: Mon-Sat 6:30pm-2am (closed Sunday)

Type: Cocktail lounge bar
Alfresco: No
Entry: No restrictions
Highlights: Cocktails
Atmosphere: Relaxed
Clientele: Local cocktail aficionados
Dress code: Casual
Price guide: €€€
Bar snacks: Tapas

Originally opened in 1979, this is the first of two Gimlet bars in Barcelona: one is uptown and one downtown. Originally they shared an owner. Now the only commonalities are the name and logo.

This downtown Gimlet is the original and more intimate that its estranged sibling. It lies in a zone of narrow streets where every other doorway appears to be a bar and the pavements heave with patrons well into the early hours. Gimlet sits on one of the quieter thoroughfares and is distinctly classical compared to its neighbours.

The small single room is dominated by a long, polished mahogany bar, lined with a broad cross-section of locals and the occasional foreigner. In this no messing cocktail bar classics are king. There is no menu yet discerning drinkers may order with confidence, since classics are always well made. Accordingly Gimlet is something of an oasis for cocktail aficionados in the area.

GIMLET

● ● ◐ ○

Carrer Santaló (btwn Maria Cubi & Laforia),
rcelona, Catalunya, 08021, Spain

: +34 93 201 5306, www.gimletbcn.com
urs: Mon-Sat 7pm-3am

pe: Cocktail lounge bar
fresco: No
try: Open door
ghlights: Gimlets & other classic cocktails
mosphere: Relaxed
entele: Youngish locals
ess code: Casual
ice guide: €€€
r snacks: Tapas from Casa Fernandez next door

is is the uptown estranged relation of
e famous downtown cocktail bar of the
me name. Both Gimlets maintain the
iginal logo but this one is now owned
the folk behind the famous Dry Martini
r on Aribau.

This Gimlet has a New York style
terior that is very modern in feel with
lished plaster, dark woods and lipstick
d booth seating. The uniforms are
so more contemporary than in other
assic Barcelona cocktail bars. Rather
an ye traditional bow ties, the staff sport
ck, gunmetal grey jackets with
andarin collars.

Despite the hip 'Martini lounge'
pearance, this Gimlet is still wonderfully
pretentious and locals of all ages pop
for classic cocktails, particularly
mlets and Dry Martinis. These are
onderfully made although the choice of
ns and vodkas is a little sparse. The
ecial Cocktail del Dia (cocktail of the
y) is worth considering, as are the tasty
as snacks from Casa Fernandez
xt door.

HARRY'S

143 Carrer Aribau, Barcelona, Catalunya, 08036, Spain

Tel: +34 93 430 3423,
Hours: Mon-Sat 6pm-3am

Type: Lounge bar
Alfresco: No
Entry: Open door
Highlights: Cocktails
Atmosphere: Relaxed but formally so
Clientele: Locals, business types
Dress code: Not too casual
Price guide: €€€
Bar snacks: Crisps, caviar, foie gras & salmon

Since Harry MacElhone acquired his n[...] famous Parisian bar in 1923, many othe[...] have been inspired to open their ow[...] Harry's around the world - most famou[...] the Venetian Giuseppe Cipriani in 193[...] The owner of this much more rece[...] Barcelona version decided on the nan[...] after a trip to Paris.

The décor of this wood panell[...] lounge is more refined than the Fren[...] original. The raised bar area house[...] highly polished mahogany counter a[...] shelves lined with Scotch whisky. H[...] height panels separate the bar area fro[...] two lower lounge spaces, one with[...] grand piano, and brown leather cl[...] chairs offer comfortable seating.

Bartenders in white dinner jack[...] and black bow ties mix well-ma[...] cocktails from a classically led list. Har[...] is situated opposite the Dry Martini a[...] so perfect for starting a Martini bar cra[...] although when quiet it can seem sligh[...] regimented and austere.

IDEAL COCKTAIL BAR

39 Carrer Aribau (@ Carrer de Mallorca), Barcelona, Catalunya, 08036, Spain

Tel: +34 93 453 1028
Hours: Mon-Sat noon-2:30am (closed Sunday)

Type: Cocktail lounge bar
Alfresco: No
Entry: No restrictions
Highlights: Cocktails
Atmosphere: Relaxed
Clientele: Tourists & local cocktail aficionados
Dress code: Smart casual
Price guide: €€€
Bar snacks: Tapas

Remember how doctors' waiting rooms used to be? All the furniture and artwork looked as if it had been salvaged, Shipman-style, from the drawing room of a recently deceased patient.

Imagine one of those old school surgeries crossed with the bar from a long forgotten hotel in the Scottish Highlands and you'll have an idea of this little place. In keeping with the Scottish theme, Ideal has a piper for its logo, and over sixty different malt whiskies, plus an excellent array of premium rums, cognacs and vodkas, line the back bar.

Ideal is down the road from Dry Martini and has a similar 'lost in time' feel with bartenders resplendent in white jackets. It is considerably smaller and lacks the pizazz of its better known rival but the cocktails and service are every bit as good.

MIRAMELINDO

15 Passeig del Born, Barcelona, Catalunya, 08003, Spain

Tel: +34 93 310 3727
Hours: Mon-Sun 7:30pm-3am

Type: Spanish pub
Alfresco: No
Entry: Open door but busy after midnight
Highlights: Cocktails
Atmosphere: Very relaxed, informal
Clientele: Tourists, few locals
Dress code: Casual
Price guide: €€
Bar snacks: Nuts and olives

Grand old wooden warehouse-style doors on Passeig del Born (a jousting ground for knights in medieval times) mark the entrance to Miramelindo. The small inset door leads to a dimly lit room with a high, slatted wood ceiling. The tunnel-like space is wonderfully atmospheric with toffee coloured walls, a bare wooden floor and an old upright piano in the fireplace. A cast iron spiral staircase leads to a gallery area with colonial-style wicker chairs.

Cocktails are listed on mirrors behind the bar illuminated by pink neon. Mojitos are lovingly assembled in a shallow marble sink under the glow of the pink light, while Miramelindo's three speciality cocktails are ladled into your glass from three large bowls nestled in ice on the bar counter. 'Coctel de Coca' is a thick Piña Colada style drink made with cognac and coconut milk. 'Zuma de Frutas Natural' is a non-alcoholic blend of orange, pineapple and banana which is great with a splash of rum. 'Coctel de Cava' is the local take on the Mimosa: Cointreau, orange juice and vodka topped up with cava. Otherwise just settle for a thirst quenching Voll-Damm Doble Malta beer.

MOO BAR

Hotel Omm, 265 Carrer Rosselló (@ Passeig de Gràcia), Barcelona, 08008, Spain

Tel: +34 93 445 4000, www.hotelomm.es
Hours: Mon-Sun noon-2am

Type: Cocktail lounge bar
Alfresco: Roof top bar
Entry: Subject to capacity
Highlights: Cocktails & lobby life
Atmosphere: Relaxed
Clientele: Tourists & hotel residents
Dress code: Designer casual
Price guide: €€€€
Bar snacks: Tapas

Hotel Omm is an ultra-modern, designer hotel which opened early in 2004, and Moo Bar is housed in its lobby. Actually, it would be more accurate to say that Moo Bar is the lobby, as the reception, bar and restaurant meld into each other in the open plan, contemporary design. Metal-mesh curtains, rough stone walls and Oriental-style fixtures are warmed by mellow lighting and comfy sofas.

The concise cocktail list centres on the classics: all are well made and delivered by friendly and efficient servers. The wine list is anything but concise and features some interesting bins as well as the expected, while food from the Roca brothers' Moo restaurant is simply superb.

Above all Moo is a great place to observe the rich tapestry of lobby life while sipping from a Martini glass.

TIRSA COCKTAIL BAR

174 Carrer Rafael de Campalans, L'Hospitalet,
Barcelona, 08903, Spain

Tel: +34 93 431 2302
Hours: Mon-Sat 6pm-2am

Type: Cocktail bar
Alfresco: No
Entry: Open door
Highlights: Cocktails
Atmosphere: Friendly, relaxed
Clientele: Locals & drinks industry
Dress code: Casual (not too tatty)
Price guide: €€€
Bar snacks: Nibbles only

This smashing little cocktail bar lies a little way out of the centre of town, toward the airport, but is worth the journey. Tirsa is owned by Manel Tirvió, who is also the president of 'El Club del Barman', the local bartenders' guild, so you are guaranteed excellent cocktails and often a crowd of drinks industry types. Few tourists make it over to this part of town so you'll find this series of intimate, wood panelled rooms frequented by friendly locals. Judging by our visit you'll end up sharing rounds of drinks with them till the early hours.

This is a great destination for any cocktail enthusiast and you'll find a good collection of spirits and even vintage cocktail shakers on display. The bijou private room upstairs would be great for a party booking.

LA VINYA DEL SENYOR

  ○

5 Plaça de Santa Maria, La Ribera, Barcelona,
Catalunya, 08003, Spain

Tel: +34 93 310 3379
Hours: Tue-Thu noon-1am, Fri-Sat noon-2am, Sun
noon-midnight

Type: Wine bar
Alfresco: Tables on Plaça de Santa Maria
Entry: Open door (but gets crowded)
Highlights: Wines and cheese
Atmosphere: Chilled, relaxed
Clientele: Locals & tourists
Dress code: Casual
Price guide: €€
Bar snacks: Great tapas and cheeses

The name of this superb but rustic and simple little wine bar translates as 'The Lord's Vineyard' and it lies across the square from the church of Santa Maria del Mar.

The international list changes regularly with an eclectic mix of wines, cavas and sherries to choose from. Much of the stock is piled up in cardboard boxes about the bar.

The décor lacks any pretensions and is delightfully tatty around the edges – like a well worn pair of jeans. Unless you're lucky enough to nab one of the stools at the marble bar counter then inside is pretty much standing room only. There are a handful of tables out in the square but perhaps the best table is the one at the top of the steep spiral staircase in front of the loos. This unromantic sounding spot is secluded and overlooks the square.

The tapas, and in particular the mixed plate of local cheeses, live up to the wines. When ordering, make allowances for the laid-back attitude of the chaps who serve here: you'll find they, and their wine recommendations, are top notch.

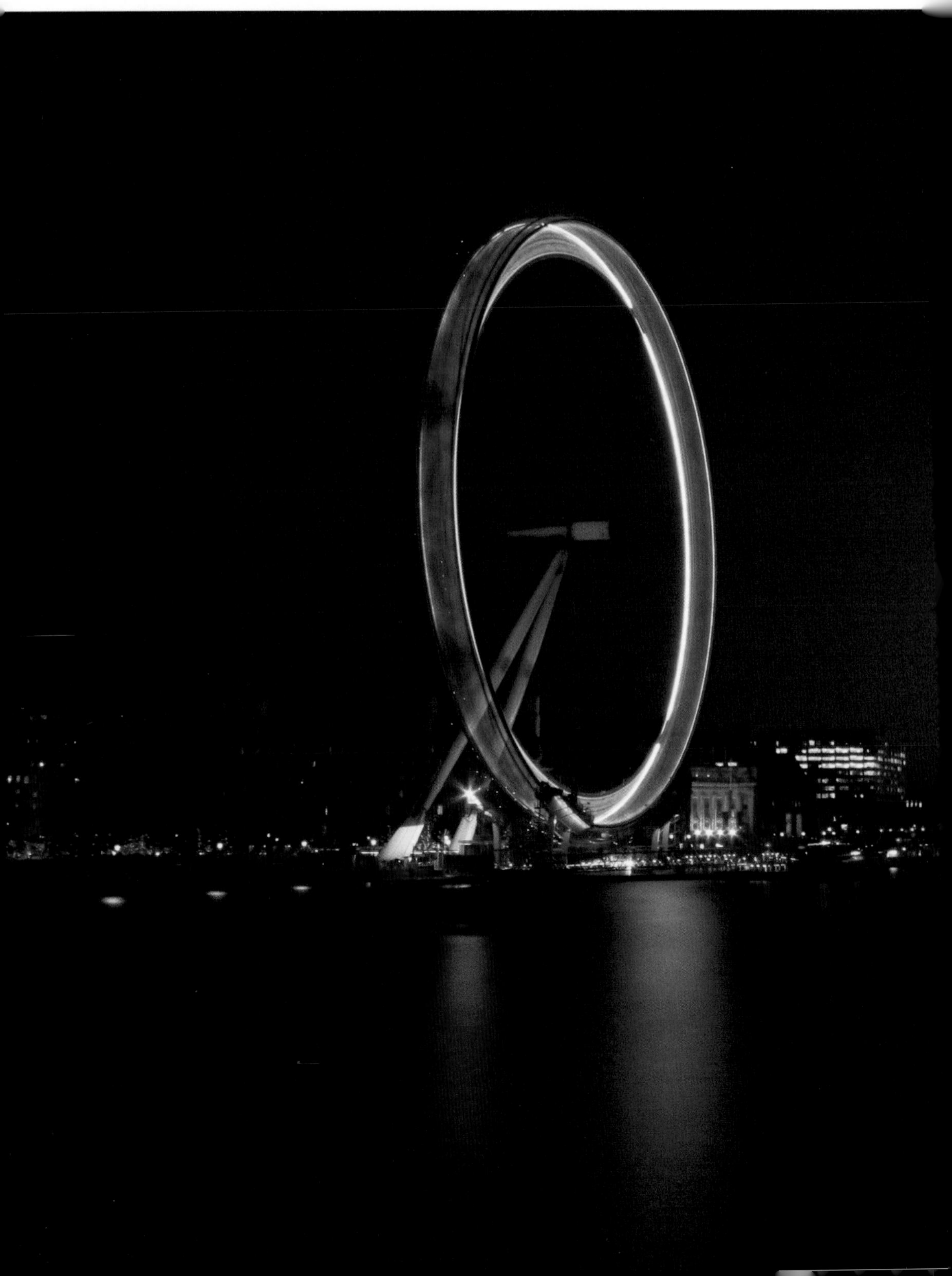

LONDON

Airport: Heathrow (LHR), Gatwick (LGW), City (LCY), Stansted (STN)
Time zone: Greenwich Mean Time (GMT)

London is Western Europe's biggest and, I believe, most vibrant city. And big it needs to be, as, even with its ancient, winding streets, there's one hell of a lot packed into its centre. I don't believe there's any city in the world that offers such a rich package of history, architecture, restaurants, theatres, galleries, museums, parks, shops and markets.

London also leads the world's bar scene. Its top cocktail Dublin's. Add to that the fact that London is one of the world's biggest centres for imported wine and spirits and you can see why I'm very happy to call it home.

London is so big, offering so much for diffordsguide readers, that we tackle one area of London in each edition of this quarterly guide. For a guide to city-wide London drinking please see our diffordsguide to Pubs & Bars which has reviews of 250 pubs and bars across the city's most important drinking

Trailer Happiness

NOTTING HILL & PADINGTON
(W2, W9-11)

Notting Hill and its surrounding environs of Maida Vale and Ladbroke Grove form an area of London with stark contrasts. Parts are affluent and fashionable with terraces of desirable, large Victorian townhouses populated by young and affluent stereotypical 'Notting Hillbillies' and 'Trustafarians'. However, turn the corner and there are ugly blocks of social housing. This has long been an area with a large immigrant community and past tensions have led to race riots. Thankfully, that appears in the past, replaced by Bohemian charm and the annual Notting Hill Carnival, which takes place in August.

Notting Hill is a great shopping district, with wares that appeal to a wide audience. From old record shops to fashion boutiques and niche bookstores to speciality food and drink purveyors, it really is a special place. As an added bonus, it is also home to the Portobello Road market on Saturdays - a strange hybrid of vintage clothing, ethnic froufrou, flash antiques and fruit 'n' veg stalls.

Notting Hill is a favourite with many American tourists, partly due to the 1999 Hollywood movie of the same name. The floppy-haired lothario sealed his link with the area when he returned in Bridget Jones. While Notting Hill is known for its carnival, Portobello Market, its style set and Hugh Grant, Paddington (to the North East) is perhaps best know for its lost bear and status as a transport intersection. Long before the Heathrow Express, the A40 flyover and even Paddington Station, this area had its waterways, and it's the redevelopment of the drained Paddington Basin which looks set to change its rather dowdy image.

Notting Hill & Paddington Hotels

Notting Hill's Victorian terraced architecture shapes the style of its hotels, which tend toward boutique. Consequently, room numbers are limited so early booking is imperative.

Paddington is a quite different scene with larger hotels such as the one we recommend below. If you are unable to secure a room in Notting Hill then the many hotels in Mayfair and Kensington are only ten minutes away by taxi.

Guesthouse West

163-164 Westbourne Grove, Notting Hill, London, W11 2RS, England
Tel: +44 (0)20 7792 9800,
www.guesthousewest.com
Rooms: 20

Situated in the heart of Notting Hill, this upmarket bed and breakfast occupies a former Edwardian family home. It's contemporary in style while retaining many period features. If available, opt for a "Terrace Room", although all rooms are elegant and well equipped with Wi-Fi, flat panel TV, Savoir beds, power showers and Molton Brown toiletries.

Hempel Hotel

31-35 Craven Hill Gardens, Lancaster Gate, London, W2 3EA, England
Tel: +44 (0)20 7298 9000,
www.the-hempel.co.uk
Rooms: 47 (inc. 5 suites)

Named after, and created by, British designer, Anouska Hempel, this 5 star luxury hotel is minimalist in style, blending ancient Eastern influences seamlessly with modern technology. An atrium provides natural light to the interior which, although boutique in size, feels spacious. The hotel nestles amongst highly desirable houses in a quiet residential garden square, just north of Hyde Park and between Lancaster Gate and Notting Hill.

The design ethos continues through the guest rooms which are all individually designed and luxurious. Amenities include CD/DVD player, mini bar, safe, bathrobes, slippers and turndown service. Wi-Fi is available throughout the hotel, its apartments and The Hempel Garden Square.

Hilton London Paddington Hotel

146 Praed Street, Paddington, London, W2 1EE, England
Tel: +44 (0)20 7850 0500,
www.hilton.co.uk
Rooms: 355

This five-storey Victorian building was built in 1854 but was completely renovated in 2002. While its location, smack on top of Paddington Station, is hardy idyllic, it makes it a mere fifteen minutes from Heathrow airport by the Heathrow Express train.

Traditionally furnished rooms are to the usual Hilton standard with marble bathrooms, Wi-Fi, air con, pay per view movies, PlayStations, tea and coffee facilities and laptop safes. Being a large hotel, facilities include a gym and sauna.

The Lennox Hotel

34 Pembridge Gardens, Notting Hill, London W2 4DX, England
Tel: +44 (0)20 7229 9977,
www.epoquehotels.com
Rooms: 20

Set in a privately owned stucco-fronted Victorian three storey townhouse, The Lennox lies moments from the top of Portobello Road on a very quiet, tree-lined street. The individually designed bedrooms are air conditioned with luxurious bathrooms, bathrobes, mini bar, laptop safe, Wi-Fi, satellite plasma TVs and CD/DVD players.

The Portobello Hotel

22 Stanley Gardens, Notting Hill, London, W11 2NG, England
Tel: +44 (0) 20 7727 2777,
www.portobellohotel.co.uk
Rooms: 24

Founded in 1971, The Portobello Hotel has become the preferred choice for many celebrities. This converted neo-classical mansion lies on a quiet back street, a short stroll from Portobello Road and Ladbroke Grove.

Rooms are lavish and famously bohemian in style with antiques, four-poster beds, freestanding Victorian baths and random items such as a Moroccan birdcage. They are also up to date with free internet access and free movies on eighteen-channel Bang and Olufsen televisions. Basement rooms have private patio gardens. Attentive service includes 24-hour meal availability should you get peckish in the middle of the night.

Although the hotel doesn't have its own gym facilities, these, including swimming pool, sauna and steam room, are available to guests just doors away. Although Health Club facilities come at a price, visitors do receive complimentary membership to the nearby Cobden Club.

The Royal Park

3 Westbourne Terrace, Bayswater, London, W2 3UL, England
Tel: +44 (0)20 7479 6600,
www.theroyalpark.com
Rooms: 48 (inc. 3 suites)

Part of the excellent Stein Group of hotels, The Royal Park is set in three mid 19th-century Grade II listed townhouses. The name is a reference to the hotel's location close to Hyde Park with Paddington and Lancaster Gate stations also only a short walk away.

The traditionally styled interior is cosy without being chintzy. Homely touches include two drawing rooms, furnished with comfy sofas and open fires. The rooms nod to a forgotten time, with antique Regency furniture and original paintings; many have canopied mahogany four-poster beds. Bathrooms came with bathrobes, slippers and power showers. Mod-cons include flat-screen fifteen-channel TVs and broadband internet access. The hotel does not have a restaurant so breakfast is served in your room. Sandwiches and snacks are available by room service.

Notting Hill & Paddington Restaurants

London is a cosmopolitan city and its cuisine is shaped by influences from the many different cultures it encompasses. Notting Hill and its environs reflect this.

London is also home to the gastro pub - spruced up old boozers that genrerally have a good wine selection and a chef turning out modern British fare, most often from an open kitchen. This particular area of London is well served by gastro pubs so when deciding where to eat you should also consider the pub and bar reviews over the page.

Assaggi

39 Chepstow Place, Notting Hill, London, W2 4TS, England
Tel: +44 (0)20 7792 5501
Cuisine: Italian

Not much more than a small room above a back street boozer but the Michelin-starred food that's served here makes securing one of the eleven tables challenging. The setting is relaxed, the service excellent and the food simply cooked and based on quality seasonal ingredients.

Bumpkin

209 Westbourne Park Road, Notting Hill, London, W11 1EA, England
Tel: +44 (0)20 7243 9818,
www.bumpkinuk.com
Cuisine: Traditional British

This four storey, rural themed restaurant starts rustic and casual on the ground floor with a relaxed all day dining room and gets more formal as you go up. The first floor offers more refined dishes in a slightly more formal atmosphere. The third floor is given over to private dining and the top floor houses two whiskey rooms, each seating around fifteen and equipped with poker tables and a sound system with iPod jack.

The kitchen uses organic produce where possible to make what are billed as home from home traditional British dishes. Bumpkin is from the folk who own Eclipse and Cocoon so also expect great cocktails and some well chosen wines.

E&O Restaurant

14 Blenheim Crescent (corner Kensington Park Rd), Notting Hill, W11 1NN, England. Tel: +44 (0)20 7229 5454, www.eando.co.uk
Cuisine: Pan-Asian

The name is short for Eastern and Oriental which hints at the Pan-Asian dishes on offer here. E&O is part of Will Ricker's stable that includes Great Eastern Dining Room, Eight Over Eight and Cicada. Like his other establishments, E&O attracts a good-looking crowd of fashionistas and the odd celebrity. The small, separate bar area is always bustling while the dining room is more relaxed. The menu includes faves such as salt & pepper squid and black cod.

Falafel King

274 Portobello Road, Notting Hill London, W11 1LR, England
Tel: +44 (0)20 8964 2279
Cuisine: Middle Eastern snack food

Walking from Notting Hill Gate tube up Portobello Road is hungry work on a Saturday morning and by the time you get to the Westway flyover you'll be ready for a spicy falafel sandwich from the Falafel King. There's always a queue and few seats but they are the best falafels in London. Extra chilis on mine, please.

Julie's Restaurant

135 Portland Road, Notting Hill, London, W11 4LW, England
Tel: +44 (0)20 7229 8331,
www.juliesrestaurant.com
Cuisine: Modern British

Celebrities have been coming here for over thirty years, attracted by the warren of eclectically decorated dining rooms and the garden room with its electric roof to allow alfresco eating. There is also a large front terrace with heaters.

Julie's opens at 9am to serve proper English breakfast. The brassiere style lunch and dinner menus may be of celerity standard but it should be mentioned that in December last year Julie's became what's thought to be the first restaurant in Britain to be fined for falsely claiming that certain dishes they were serving were organic when in fact they were not.

I-Thai

The Hempel Hotel, 31-35 Craven Hill Gardens, Lancaster Gate, London, W2 3EA, England. Tel: +44 (0)20 7298 9000, www.the-hempel.co.uk
Cuisine: Asian/modern European fusion

Set inside the designer Hempel hotel, t chic I-Thai's large, bright dining roc follows the hotel's minimalist modern sty The menu is a unique combination Modern European, Japanese and Thai w some superb flavour combination Surprisingly, for such a modern, fusion st restaurant, France dominates the wine li

The Ledbury

127 Ledbury Road, Notting Hill, London W11 2AQ, England
Tel: +44 (0)20 7792 9090,
www.theledbury.com
Cuisine: Modern French

This relatively new restaurant has pedigre being owned by the accomplished fc behind Chez Bruce, La Trompette and T Square. The dining room is modern a slick and the food by Australian chef, Br Graham, reliably good. The wine list ha good range, with many available by t glass and half bottle.

Levantine

26 London Street, Paddington, London, W2 1HH, England. Tel: +44 (0)20 7262 1111, www.levant.co.uk
Cuisine: Middle Eastern/Lebanese

The younger sibling of the establish Levant in Wigmore Street offers plenty spice in an Arabian Nights settir Wonderful mezze dishes should be wash down with Lebanese wine.

Notting Hill Brasserie

92 Kensington Park Road, Notting Hill, W11 2PN, England
Tel: +44 (0)20 7229 4481
Cuisine: Modern European

This is a cosy little place, right down to t mini armchairs at the tables and warn coloured walls. The Brasserie in the title a tad misleading as this is a serio restaurant with seriously good food a equally serious prices. The wine list equally grown-up, but fortunately incluc more sensibly priced bins.

Red Pepper

8 Formosa Street, Maida Vale, London, W9 1EE, England. Tel: +44 (0)20 7266 2708
Cuisine: Italian pizza/pasta

This tiny little restaurant with its cramped tables is always packed and consequently loud. You fare a little better upstairs or, weather permitting, out front if you can reserve a table. Once you have sampled the food here you'll warm to the buzzy atmosphere - and wonderful thin crust pizzas from the wood-fired oven and tasty pasta just like mama used to make. Wash it all down with a reasonably priced bottle from the short, all-Italian wine list.

Ribbands

147-149 Notting Hill Gate, Notting Hill, London, W11 3LF, England
Tel: +44 (0)20 7034 0301,
www.ribbandsrestaurants.com
Cuisine: Modern English/French

Named after partner/chef Paul Ribbands and opening at the end of 2006, Ribbands serves a modern fusion of British & French cuisine in a bright, modern setting where bare brick walls are juxtaposed crisp white tablecloths.

Drinking

Notting Hill is one of London's main pub and bar areas, partly driven by the numbers of wealthy, cool, young things that live there. The scene runs the gamut from old traditional boozers through to world-leading cutting edge cocktail lounge bars.

Smoking will be prohibited in most of the UK's enclosed public spaces, including restaurants, bars and nightclubs from 1 July this year. At the moment many have designated areas for smoking and non-smoking: very few are entirely non-smoking.

24-hour licensing was introduced last year, amid much fanfare and political debate but most pubs still close by midnight whilst bars tend to close between midnight and 3am. With a very few exceptions only clubs are open after 3am and do not serve alcohol.

The legal minimum age for buying alcohol is 18. In general, even if you are lucky enough to look under 21, you will only be asked for ID in pubs or bars which have a problem with under-age drinking.

BEACH BLANKET BABYLON

● ● ● ○ ○

45 Ledbury Road, Notting Hill, London, W11 2AA, England

Tel: +44 (0)20 7229 2907,
www.beachblanket.co.uk
Hours: Mon-Sun 10am-11pm

Type: Restaurant bar	
Alfresco: Small front terrace	
Entry: Subject to management and capacity	
Highlights: Decor	
Atmosphere: Relaxed	
Clientele: Moneyed local 30-somethings	
Dress code: Designer casual	
Price guide: £££	
Food: Full Mediterranean led menu	

BBB, as it's affectionately known, opened back in 1990 and is an established part of the Notting Hill bar scene. Set in an old Georgian house, it has undergone extensive renovation in recent years but retains its famously eclectic decor. Elements of Byzantine, Baroque and Gaudi blend with topiary, while out back the restaurant's interconnecting rooms continue the Baroque theme in an almost monastic setting.

The Mediterranean cuisine is as eclectic as the decor and of a reasonable standard. Sadly on our visits the cocktails have been disappointing. BBB still attracts local, moneyed 30-somethings and the spectacular interior remains an experience. However, there are now better places nearby to imbibe cocktails.

COBDEN CLUB

● ● ● ● ○

170 Kensal Road, Notting Hill, London, W10 5BN, England

Tel: +44 (0)20 8960 4222,
www.cobdenclub.co.uk
Hours: Mon-Sat 6pm-1:30am

Type: Members' club	
Alfresco: No	
Entry: Members & guests only	
Highlights: Cocktails, wines, food, atmosphere	
Atmosphere: Chilled to party	
Clientele: Record & film industry types	
Dress code: Designer casual	
Price guide: ££££	
Food: Full fusion menu or snacks	

This exclusive den occupies three floors of the old Cobden Working Men's Club, a wonderful, Grade II listed building. The ground floor, however, is only used for functions so head up the stairs to the cosy restaurant and lounge. With the inviting look and feel of a posh pub, and oodles of comfy sofas and chairs, this is the place to relax and chat. In the party space above, a magnificent Victorian hall with a stage at one end and a thirty foot bar at the other, well-known DJs entertain a mixture of public school escapees and record industry operators.

The two bars serve some of the best cocktails in London, while the food comes in homely proportions and should be consumed with a bottle from the well conceived wine list. Entry is tricky if you're not a member. But a mere £250 per year plus £100 joining fee could assure you a place at the heart of one of London's best kept secrets.

THE COW

● ● ● ● ○

89 Westbourne Park Road (opp. Westbourne Pk Villas), Notting Hill, London, W2 5QH

Tel: +44 (0)20 7221 5400
Hours: Mon-Sat noon-11pm,
Sun noon-10:30pm

Type: Gastro pub	
Alfresco: Few seats at front	
Entry: Open door (subject to space)	
Highlights: Food	
Atmosphere: Relaxed	
Clientele: Local moneyed set	
Dress code: Designer casual	
Price guide: £££	
Food: Fresh seafood to sausage & mash	

This is one of the most famous pubs in London – famous for being hip, rather than for some vague historical reference. In 1998 Tom Conran (son of Sir Terence) took over what was then a small boozer on its last legs and transformed it. It's still small and the design is delightfully un-Conranesque with light mustard walls, a red linoleum floor and rippled glass. While the décor is not sophisticated, the clientele is. They're drawn by the easy atmosphere and some seriously good food, particularly the seafood and oysters. The restaurant upstairs is equally low-key and echoes the high standards set downstairs.

This tiny pub is simply great, attracting an older and more considered audience than the Westbourne opposite. Its tiny proportions lead to much pavement drinking, particularly in the summer months.

Cobden Club

**BEEFEATER
ICED TEA**

2 MEASURES BEEFEATER
2 MEASURES COLD EARL GREY TEA
CHILLED 7-UP OR SPRITE

POUR BEEFEATER & EARL GREY
TEA INTO AN ICE-FILLED GLASS,
TOP UP WITH LEMONADE OR SPRITE

CRAZY HOMIES

127 Westbourne Park Road, Notting Hill, London, W2 5QL, England

Tel: +44 (0)20 7727 6771,
www.crazyhomieslondon.co.uk
Hours Mon-Sat 8am-11pm, Sun 9am-10pm

Type: Mexican restaurant & bar
Alfresco: No
Entry: Subject to capacity
Highlights: Food
Atmosphere: Better downstairs
Clientele: Attractive Notting Hillbillies
Dress code: Casual but stylish
Price guide: £££
Food: Authentic Mexican

Once a West Indian shebeen frequented by Christine Keeler and Stephen Ward of Profumo Affair fame, this is now a Mexican bar and restaurant owned by Tom Conran.

The bold décor, with lipstick red banquette seats and bar stools, makes the tiny ground floor space feel rather like the inside of a sweet jar. There is a second, larger bar in the basement, which is more atmospheric than the bright space above thanks to its low ceiling.

The food is inspired by Mexican taquerias and superb tacos, tostadas, burros and enchiladas are served on plastic trays, adding to their authenticity. Drinks arrive in chunky tumblers and follow the Mexican theme. Margaritas include the wonderfully named 'Sinful Cynthia's Cadillac Margarita', which is served with a Grand Marnier float, while the good range of premium tequilas should be chased with a spicy sangrita. Two wines are offered, a Petite Syrah and a Chardonnay, both from Baja California, Mexico.

Those in the know head downstairs where some superb bartenders operate and the lucky few get to sit at the bartender's table behind the bar counter itself.

ECLIPSE

186 Kensington Park Road, Notting Hill, London, W11 2ES, England

Tel: +44 (0)20 7792 2063, **www.**bareclipse.com
Hours: Mon-Fri 5pm-late,
Sat-Sun 4pm-late

Type: Lounge bar
Alfresco: Few pavement seats
Entry: Subject to capacity
Highlights: Atmosphere
Atmosphere: Often DJ driven party
Clientele: Notting Hill style set
Dress code: Stylishly relaxed
Price guide: £££
Food: Mediterranean/Moroccan

This Notting Hill outpost of the Eclipse bar chain lies only a stone's throw from Portobello Market. Its diminutive proportions are emphasized by the red brick walls, which, combined with the blazing log fire, make Eclipse a snug winter drinking hole. It is also a favourite with locals in summertime, as the front opens out and allows the atmosphere, along with the clientele, to spill out onto the pavement.

Thursdays and Saturdays see this laid-back lounge turn more clubby as DJs entertain a younger, up for it, party crowd. But cocktails are the mainstay here, whatever the night. There's an extensive list, shared with the other bars in the chain, and the house style leans towards fruity concoctions. In common with most Eclipse branches the most popular drink here is the Watermelon Martini.

ELECTRIC HOUSE

191 Portobello Road, Notting Hill, London, W11 2ED, England

Tel: +44 (0)20 7908 9696, **www.**electrichouse.com
Hours: Mon-Thu 8am-1am, Fri-Sat 8am-2am, Sun 10am-midnight.

Type: Private members' lounge bar/restaurant
Alfresco: No
Entry: Members & guests only
Highlights: Exclusive retreat feel
Atmosphere: Relaxed, laid back
Clientele: Celebs & moneyed media
Dress code: Stylish, designer casual
Price guide: ££££
Food: Full meals to snacks

Between the Electric Cinema and the Electric Brasserie hides the entrance to this Notting Hill sibling of Soho House. It is also owned by Nick Jones and also a private members' club.

A staircase wrapped around a lift shaft leads to the main members' bar and restaurant. This long, loft style room with its pitched ceiling and roof lights houses a lounge bar at the front and a dining room and open kitchen at the rear. The look is seventies, with white-washed walls, chunky pale teak tables and industrial style light fittings.

The stairs continue past the glass backed projection room of the cinema and The Study, a private dining or meeting room, to The Playroom. This has its own corner bar, plasma screen and door to a small roof terrace of wooden decking.

This haven attracts celebrities and moneyed media types who enjoy well made cocktails, well selected wines and modern British comfort food.

Lonsdale

THE FAT BADGER [NEW]

● ● ● ◐ ○

310 Portobello Road, Notting Hill, London, W10 5TA, England

Tel: +44 (0)20 8969 4500, **www**.thefatbadger.com
Hours: Mon-Fri noon-11pm, Sat 11am-11pm, Sun noon-10:30pm

Type:	Gastro pub
Alfresco:	No
Entry:	Open door
Highlights:	Food
Atmosphere:	Relaxed, laid back
Clientele:	Notting Hill set
Dress code:	Designer casual
Price guide:	£££
Food:	Rustic British upstairs & bar snacks downstairs

Originally a notorious Victorian boozer called The Caernarvon Castle and in more recent years Bed Bar, this pub, which lies at the less salubrious end of Portobello Road, has recently gone the way of so many others and been gastrofied. The Moroccan decor of Bed Bar has been replaced with the obligatory gastro pub mismatched old tables and chairs, huge chandeliers and loud wallpaper – in this case stamped with shocking pink scenes of London by Timorous Beasties.

Apart from a smattering of wines, the drinks selection seems to have progressed little from its Caernarvon days with Leffe Blonde as high as the drab beer selection reaches. But this is made up for by the excellent rustic British grub served in the upstairs dining room.

During its previous Bed Bar incarnation this place had a reputation for loud music, which seems to have continued. Perhaps loud music suits the wallpaper?

THE LADBROKE ARMS

● ● ● ● ○

58 Ladbroke Road (corner Wilby Mews), Notting Hill, London, W11 3NW, England

Tel: +44 (0)20 7727 6648, **www**.capitalpubcompany.com
Hours: Mon-Fri 11am-3pm & 5:30pm-11pm, Sat 11am-11pm, Sun noon-10:30pm

Type:	Gastro pub
Alfresco:	Front terrace
Entry:	Open door
Highlights:	Cask ales, food, atmosphere
Atmosphere:	Wonderfully relaxed
Clientele:	Locals & upmarket 30-somethings
Dress code:	Casual
Price guide:	£££
Food:	Eclectic gastro grub

Sat among the plants and hanging baskets on the front terrace of this pretty pub, it's easy to imagine you're in a quaint country village, not opposite a police station in downtown Notting Hill. The Ladbroke Arms rests on a back street away from the noise and traffic, and looks for all the world like a little cottage pub.

The theme continues inside with cream panelled walls and a plush dark green carpet. Tables, for both drinkers and diners, cram every last crevice but you'll find the Hillbilly regulars and staff a friendly bunch so sharing with new friends only adds to the appeal. The place stretches back and there are many hidden alcoves so venture beyond the small front bar in search of a space on one of the comfy banquette seats.

Expect as many as four well-kept real ales and a good wine list, including eight by the glass. However, it's the daily changing food menu which really excels.

LONSDALE

● ● ● ● ◐

44-48 Lonsdale Road, Notting Hill, London, W11 2DE, England

Tel: +44 (0)20 7727 4080
Hours: Mon-Fri 6pm-midnight, Sat noon-midnight Sun noon-11pm

Type:	Lounge bar
Alfresco:	No
Entry:	Subject to space & management
Highlights:	Cocktails, atmosphere & eye can
Atmosphere:	Chilled
Clientele:	Gorgeous, affluent locals & celebs
Dress code:	Casual but not cheap
Price guide:	££££
Food:	Tapas dishes

Originally a Truman's pub and mo recently Jac's Bar, this place, situated a residential street in deepest Notting H was a pretty ordinary local bar. But 2002 brothers Charles and Ada Breeden took the space over and open Lonsdale. It's been widely regarded one of London's best cocktail ba ever since.

It's not just the drinks that have wow factor. The interior, inspired Lenny Kravitz's Miami residenc impresses. Hemispherical bubbles li the walls - bronze in the downstairs and chromed spun aluminium upstairs 'Genevieve', so named in deference the Breedens' mother.

Phillip Jeffrey keeps a watchful e on both floors (and on the stylish loca who flock here), while the skilled Charl Vexenat is master of the bar. Lonsdale hard to fault – it's full of beautiful peopl drinking balanced, imaginative cockta and nibbling on tasty bar snacks, served by skilled, attentive staff.

CORPSE REVIVER NO. 2
BY JULIUS ELLIOTT

AVAILABLE @ LONSDALE

Glass: Marie Antoinette Coupette
Method: SHAKE all ingredients with ice and fine
strain into chilled glass.
22ml Beefeater gin
25ml Lillet blanc
22ml Freshly squeezed lemon juice
22ml Cointreau
1 dash Absinthe

BEEFEATER TRICOLORE
BY AGO PERRONE

AVAILABLE @ MONTGOMERY PLACE

Glass: Marie Antoinette Coupette
Garnish: Maraschino cherry & lime zest
Method: SHAKE all ingredients with ice and fine
strain into chilled glass.
40ml Beefeater gin
20ml Freshly squeezed lemon juice
15ml Tio Pepe sherry
10ml Pallini limoncello
1 barspoon Vanilla sugar

MONTGOMERY PLACE
● ● ● ● ◐

31 Kensington Park Road, Notting Hill, London,
W11 2EU, England

Tel: +44 (0)20 7792 3921,
www.montgomeryplace.co.uk
Hours: Mon-Fri 5pm-midnight, Sat 1pm-midnight,
Sun 1pm-11pm

Type: Cocktail lounge
Alfresco: No
Entry: Subject to space
Highlights: Classic cocktails & food
Atmosphere: Few pavement seats
Clientele: Discerning cocktail lovers
Dress code: Not shabby
Price guide: ££££
Food: Great tapas style dishes

If your favourite cocktail has recently
changed from a Caipirinha to a Mojito, this
bar is probably wasted on you. These are
indeed fine drinks, but this serious cocktail
bar offers a list of previously forgotten
Prohibition classics just waiting to be rediscovered. These short, very adult cocktails
are served with the reverence they deserve.

Fitted out in a refined forties style,
Montgomery Place is tiny. The long, narrow
space leads past a small bar lined with
stools to a cosy space with comfortable
banquette seating and wallpaper printed
with vintage string instruments. A group of
thirty pretty much fills the place.

Amazingly for such a tiny venue,
here is a full kitchen and a chef labours
in the basement to produce a range of
tasty, tapas style dishes that are all
beautifully presented.

Sheer economics dictates that food
and drink of this standard, served in such
tasteful and intimate surroundings, only
come at a price. Bring someone special
and treat your taste buds.

NEGOZIO CLASSICA
● ● ● ● ○

283 Westbourne Grove (corner Portobello Rd), Notting
Hill, London, W11 2QA, England

Tel: +44 (0)20 7034 0005,
www.negozioclassica.co.uk
Hours: Mon-Fri 11am-10pm, Sat 9am-10pm, Sun
11am-9pm

Type: Wine bar/liquor store
Alfresco: Few pavement tables
Entry: Open door
Highlights: Wine & food
Atmosphere: Relaxed
Clientele: Oenophiles
Dress code: Casual
Price guide: £££
Food: Italian specialties

Negozio Classica is the flagship
showroom for an Italian specialist food
and wine distributor. It combines the best
of an Italian delicatessen, wine bar and
wine merchants, and reflects the
company's skill in sourcing superb
products from artisanal producers.
There's a unique beer from Teo Musso,
whiskies, rums, cognacs, ports, some
superb grappas and a huge range of
Italian wines, most available by the glass,
the bottle, and, if you find you like them
enough, the case.

The delicatessen offers cheeses,
meats, cured hams, olive oils, balsamic
vinegars and handmade Gragnano
pasta. You can either buy and prepare
your meal at home or enjoy a prepared
meal here with a glass of wine.

Watch the world go by from one of
the pavement tables or sit inside at one
of the blond wood tables or the stainless
steel bar. Best of all retreat to an armchair
in the reading room out back.

THE PRINCE ALFRED
● ● ● ● ○

5A Formosa Street (@ Castellain Rd), Maida Vale,
W9 1EE, England

Tel: +44 (0)20 7286 3287
Hours: Mon-Sat 11am-11pm, Sun noon-10:30pm

Type: Traditional / gastro pub
Alfresco: Pavement tables / chairs
Entry: Open door
Highlights: Food
Atmosphere: Buzzy
Clientele: Notting Hillbillies
Dress code: Casual
Price guide: £££
Food: Excellent meals in Formosa Dining Room

Built in 1863, the beautiful façade of this
Victorian pub is graced with the original
curved and etched glass windows.
Inside, a tall mahogany centrepiece is
surrounded by a curved bar counter, the
area around which is split into five by
glazed partitions. Each zone has its own
entrance but they are connected by half-
height doors. Originally, the partitions
reflected divisions in Victorian society and
the areas are still known as the Public,
the Gentlemen's, the Ladies', the Private
and the Snug. Rotating, framed-glass
snob screens hide you from the prying
eyes of the bar staff. All this splendour is
protected by a Grade II listing.

This classic old pub attracts youthful
and exuberant up-market drinkers. The
excellent modern British cuisine served
in the attached conservatory restaurant,
known as 'The Formosa Dining Room',
draws a more mature crowd. There's
London Pride on draught and an
extensive wine list with plenty of gems
and bins by the glass.

THE PRINCE BONAPARTE

● ● ● ○ ○

80 Chepstow Road, Notting Hill, London, W2 5BE, England

Tel: +44 (0)20 7313 9491
Hours: Mon-Sat noon-11pm, Sun noon-10:30pm

Type: Traditional / gastro pub	
Alfresco: No	
Entry: Open door (gets packed)	
Highlights: Atmosphere	
Atmosphere: Buzzy to loud	
Clientele: Young Hillbillies to suits	
Dress code: Casually hip	
Price guide: £££	
Food: Modern British from open kitchen	

Formerly a workaday boozer called The Artesian, this large corner pub was bought by Beth Coventry and Phillip Wright who have succeeded in taking it stratospherically upmarket. Although popular with young Hillbillies the clientele is wide and varied. Suits and retired folk also enjoy the modern British food served from the open kitchen.

The large central bar is surrounded by old wooden chairs and tables. The back section, adjacent to the open kitchen and under a skylight, offers more of a restaurant feel. When busy, which is pretty much every evening, it can be raucous and the music system struggles to be heard over the bustle.

Real ale features and, while the wine list is not the longest, the reasonably priced selection covers most bases.

RUBY & SEQUOIA

● ● ● ○ ○

6-8 All Saints Road (Westbourne Park Rd end), Westbourne Park, London, W11 1HH,

Tel: +44 (0)20 7243 6363, **www.**ruby.uk.com
Hours: Mon-Thu 6pm-12:30am, Fri 6pm-2am, Sat 11am-2am, Sun 11am-12:30am

Type: Restaurant / lounge bar	
Alfresco: No	
Entry: Door policy on Fri & Sat	
Highlights: Atmosphere, food	
Atmosphere: Relaxed to party	
Clientele: Notting Hillbillies	
Dress code: Casual but designer	
Price guide: ££££	
Food: Snacks to full menu	

Once Mas Café, then Manor, this previously ill-fated site at the end of All Saints Road continues to be synonymous with hospitality and the good times continue to roll, particularly in the basement which goes off late in the week.

This latest incarnation, from the folk behind Ruby, uses the ground floor as a restaurant-cum-cocktail bar. The rounded walls and ceiling are covered in white and gold, space age, flock wallpaper and enclose a sea of tables surrounded by bottle-green and brown banquettes. The food, the cocktails and indeed the service are adequate but do not a destination make.

Although you'll probably have to wait till Friday or Saturday, it's the atmosphere sometimes achieved in the intimate, chocolate brown basement bar (Sequoia) that's worth seeking out. Here the DJ and mixologists shake things up amid snakeskin banquettes and tables that encase chandeliers.

Whether eating upstairs early in the week or partying in the basement later on, you'll be surrounded by young Hillbillies, implausibly blessed with both money and looks.

Trailer Happiness

Trailer Happiness

TRAILER HAPPINESS

Basement, 177 Portobello Road (corner of Elgin Crescent), Notting Hill, London, W11 2DY

Tel: +44 (0)20 7727 2700, **www.**trailerh.com
Hours: Tue-Sun 5pm-midnight

Type:	Lounge bar
Alfresco:	No
Entry:	Ring in advance and book
Highlights:	Cocktails & rums
Atmosphere:	Relaxed
Clientele:	Well spoken Notting Hillbillies
Dress code:	Casual
Price guide:	£££
Food:	Green Chilli Fireballs & much more

In November 2003 Jonathan Downey, the man behind Match bars, took over this tiny basement space in the heart of Notting Hill and created a very special den. To quote from his press release, Trailer H has the "e-z-boy feel of a low rent, mid-60s California valley bachelor pad... a retro-sexual haven of cosmo-politan kitsch and faded trailer park glamour – cork tiles and shag pile, love songs and vol-au-vents."

Those who appreciate Trader Vic's Tiki culture and drinks will no longer have to travel to Park Lane to find Zombies, Tiki mugs and volcano bowls. Kitsch is big here and flying ducks compete for wall space with prints by J.H. Lynch and Vladimir Tretchikoff.

The A-Team bar crew produce superb, rum laced cocktails. Imaginative bar snacks include "Alabama Black Snake Sesame Shrimp" and "Dr. Jay's Green Chilli Fireballs". All in all a theme bar with fun, style and a lot of rum – a crammed into a small basement.

Trailer Happiness

Trailer Happiness

WALMER CASTLE

3 Ledbury Road, Notting Hill, London, W11 2AJ,
ngland

el: +44 (0)20 7229 4620
ours: Mon-Sat 11am-11pm, Sun 11am-10:30pm

ype:	Traditional / gastro pub
lfresco:	Tables on pavement
ntry:	Open door
ighlights:	Thai food
tmosphere:	Can be loud
lientele:	Hillbillies
ress code:	Casual
rice guide:	£££
ood:	Thai snacks and meals

his narrow, Victorian pub is visually
nspectacular – a small, well lived in,
aditional boozer with mismatched
rooden tables and chairs sitting on bare
oorboards. The charming little lounge
ehind the bar is worth bagging early if
ou are looking to settle in for the night
rith a group.

The Walmer may not be the
uaintest of pubs but it is cosy enough
nd attracts plenty of goodlooking young
illbillies. Part of the attraction is the
andlelit Thai restaurant upstairs. Many
f the dishes are also served in the bar
nd spicy prawn crackers make a tasty
ternative to the usual salt 'n' vinegar
isps. The beer selection is distinctly bog
andard with London Pride on draught
nd the run-of-the-mill wine list features
1 by the glass.

The music can be loud and trashy,
nd two plasma screens show pop
deos.

Walmer Castle

Walmer Castle

Walmer Castle

MANCHESTER

Airport: Manchester Airport (MAN)
Time zone: Greenwich Meantime (GMT)

The home of Man United, Coronation Street and Oasis, this northern English city is very proud of its achievements. Yet a myriad of individuals have shaped Manchester's personality and drive its beating pulse.

Manchester Hotels

With a few exceptions, Manchester is short on classically luxurious accomodation, but some real gems are located outside the city centre: Didsbury is only a short taxi ride away, and a truly charming place to escape the pace of the city. Rooms can be in short supply, especially at weekends, so booking early is highly recommended.

Didsbury House Hotel

Didsbury Park, Didsbury Village, Manchester, Lancashire, M20 5LJ, England
Tel: +44 (0)161 448 2200
www.eclectic-hotel-collection.com
Rooms: 27

Situated in the well-heeled suburb of Didsbury, this former Victorian villa has been injected with New York style to create a glam boutique hotel. The facilities are on a par with its townie counterparts and the generously sized rooms are fitted out to extremely high standards.

Eleven Didsbury Park

11 Didsbury Park, Didsbury Village, Manchester, Lancashire, M20 5LH, England
Tel: +44 (0)161 448 7711
www.eclectic-hotel-collection.com
Rooms: 20

Not only do the standards of Eleven Didsbury Park match up to its aforementioned sibling, this relaxing bolthole provides a private garden and two lounges. Offers such as "Girls' Night In", with in-room chocolate fountain and beauty products, and "Secret Sunday" pampering sessions cater for the ladies.

Great John Street Hotel

Great John Street, Manchester, Lancashire, M3 4FD, England
Tel: +44 (0)161 831 3211
www.eclectic-hotel-collection.com
Rooms: 30

Heralded as one of the best new hotels in the world by Condé Nast this year, this really does pull out all the stops. The duplex rooms boast roll-top, freestanding baths and hand carved beds with hand sprung mattresses dressed in Egyptian cotton. A rooftop garden, complete with hot tub, allows guests to make the most of the cityscape, while an elegant, cosy bar keeps the palate wetted.

The Hilton Manchester Deansgate

Beetham Tower, 303 Deansgate, Manchester, Lancashire, M3 4LQ, England
Tel: +44 (0)161 870 1600
www.hilton.co.uk/manchester
Rooms: 279

This new kid on the block occupies the lower 23 floors of the recently constructed, 50 storey Beetham Tower. Besides all you'd expect from a Hilton, it offers magnificent views and plays host to quite possibly the chicest bar in Manchester, Cloud 23, which we've also reviewed here.

The Lowry Hotel

50 Dearmans Place, Chapel Wharf, Manchester, Lancashire, M3 5LH, England
Tel: +44 (0)161 827 4000
www.thelowryhotel.com
Rooms: 164

Part of the Rocco Forte Hotels group, the Lowry has played home to Manchester's most highbrow visitors and always has a celebrity or two within its walls. Its truly contemporary interior, fabulous cuisine and general dedication to the finer things in life saw it become Manchester's very first 5 star hotel.

Malmaison Hotel

1-3 Piccadilly, Manchester, Lancashire, M1 1LZ, England
Tel: +44 (0)161 278 1000
www.malmaison-manchester.com
Rooms: 167

From the wines and cocktails in the brasserie and bar, which are destinations in their own right, to the velvets and silks in the well-appointed rooms, the attention to detail makes this well-established, central hotel feel more intimate than its room count would suggest.

The Place Apartment Hotel

Ducie Street, Piccadilly, Manchester, M1 2TP, England
Tel: +44 (0)161 778 7500
www.theplacehotel.com
Rooms: 108

Formerly the "London Warehouse", this Grade II listed building is now an apartment-based hotel. Fully fitted kitchens and designated eating areas come as standard in all the accommodation, but the beautifully designed Cotton House downstairs offers both a restaurant and cocktail bar. Surely the best of both worlds?

Radisson Edwardian Hotel

Free Trade Hall, Peter Street, Manchester, Lancashire, M2 5GP, England
Tel: +44 (0)161 835 9929,
www.radissonedwardian.com/manchester
Rooms: 263

This outpost of the Radisson Edwardian brand offers contemporary, five-star luxe in the heart of the city centre. Amenities include complimentary high-speed internet, pool, fitness centre, spa, florist, restaurants and bar.

Rossetti Hotel

107 Piccadilly, Manchester, Lancashire, M1 2DB, England
Tel: +44 (0)161 247 7744,
www.aliashotels.com
Rooms: 61

Acclaimed as the ultimate city bolthole, Rossetti provides an eclectic alternative to the usual hotel experience. Classic Moltini furnishings rub shoulders with more contemporary pieces, while exposed brickwork and contemporary canvases grant the space a gritty, urban look.

Manchester Restaurants

While not yet a fine dining destination, Manchester offers a wealth of culinary styles. From "curry mile" in Rusholme to traditional British fayre at Sam's Chop House (which has been trading since 1872), there is something for everyone, and some of the most successful eateries offer great value for money amid relaxed surrounds.

Establishment

43 Spring Gardens, Manchester, Lancashire, M2 2BG, England
Tel: +44 (0)161 839 6300,
www.establishmentrestaurant.com
Cuisine: Modern & classic British & French

Establishment boasts a grand face and an even grander reputation. Formal in style, the restaurant is set in a Grade II listed Edwardian former banking hall which has been given a contemporary edge with modern furnishings and palette. It also has a serious cocktail offering.

The French

Midland Hotel, Peter Street, Manchester, Lancashire, M60 2DS, England
Tel: +44 (0)161 236 3333,
www.qhotels.co.uk
Cuisine: Classic French

This very traditional restaurant in the newly refurbished Midland Hotel is by some way Manchester's number one French eatery. If you're after Chateaubriand and Burgundy, this is your place.

The Grill on the Alley

5 Ridgefield, Manchester, Lancashire, M2 6EG, England
Tel: +44 (0)161 833 3465,
www.blackhousegrills.com
Cuisine: Grills

Dedicated to simply cooked, high calibre, fresh produce, the Grill features staples such as steaks, burgers (including a Kobe beef variation) and seafood. Guests can select their dinner directly from the lobster tank or cold fish display.

Juniper

21 The Downs, Altrincham, Cheshire, WA14 2QD, England
Tel: +44 (0)161 929 4008, www.juniper-restaurant.com
Cuisine: Very modern British

Chef Paul Kitching serves ever-changing and mindblowingly innovative dishes – from a line of cottage pie on a mirror to a strawberry dessert on a toothbrush – in a Michelin-starred gastronomic haven 25 minutes from Manchester city centre. On Tuesdays, five courses cost a mere £30.

Le Mont @ Urbis

Levels 5 & 6, Cathedral Gardens, Manchester, Lancashire, M4 3BG, England
Tel: +44 (0)161 605 8282,
www.urbis.org.uk
Cuisine: Modern French

Set in Manchester's museum of urban life, Le Mont offers fine dining in a unique setting with magnificent views of the city centre. The stark white interior sets the tone for this grown-up venue, which has the UK's first Bollinger Bar outside of London.

Lounge 10

10 Tib Lane, Manchester, Lancashire, M2 4JB, England
Tel: +44 (0)161 834 1331,
www.lounge10manchester.co.uk
Cuisine: Modern French

The exterior of this restaurant may appear modest, but behind its simple façade lies a truly decadent dining experience. Spanning three floors, Lounge 10 takes Moulin Rouge as its inspiration, with luxurious red velvet, lavish black tableware and provocative artworks adding to the seductive tone.

Market Restaurant

104 High Street, Manchester, Lancashire, M4 1HQ, England
Tel: +44 (0)161 834 3743,
www.market-restaurant.com
Cuisine: Modern British

One of Manchester's best-kept secrets, Market Restaurant is hidden away in the Northern Quarter. Open Wednesday through to Saturday, the snug establishment serves up the very best of British from fantastic local suppliers, alongside one of the finest beer selections in the city.

Restaurant Bar & Grill

14 John Dalton Street, Manchester, Lancashire, M2 6JR, England
Tel: +44 (0)161 839 1999,
www.individualrestaurants.co.uk
Cuisine: Global

This place is a real crowd-pleaser, and the varied menu in the bustling first floor restaurant offers great value for money. The ground floor bar, a destination in its own right, serves up great cocktails, giving it all-round appeal.

River Restaurant

Lowry Hotel,
50 Dearmans Place,
Chapel Wharf, Manchester, Lancashire, M3 5LH, England
Tel: +44 (0)161 827 4041,
www.thelowryhotel.com
Cuisine: Modern British

Chef Eyck Zimmer serves up interestir variations on British classics – check out h posh pie selection at £19.50 – in this upsca restaurant which was refurbed at th beginning of the year. The Terrace can b wonderfully sunny in fine weather.

Simply Heathcotes

Jacksons Row, Deansgate, Manchester, Lancashire, M2 5WD, England
Tel: +44 (0)161 835 3536,
www.heathcotes.co.uk
Cuisine: Modern British

Paul Heathcote takes pride in sourcir ingredients locally, and it is for this reason th his restaurant has remained a firm staple wi Manchester's foodies since its conception 1996. Consistently good, the relaxe atmosphere and friendly staff make eve meal a pleasure.

Stock

The Stock Exchange,
4 Norfolk Place, Manchester, Lancashire, M2 1DW, England
Tel: +44 (0)161 839 6644,
www.stockrestaurant.co.uk
Cuisine: Italian

Founder and executive chef Enzo Mauro ha created Manchester's "first premier Italia restaurant" in the luxurious setting of the cit former Stock Exchange. As well as th mouth-watering cuisine, it boasts an awa winning wine list and has become a favouri with the city's elite.

Yang Sing

35 Princess Street, Manchester, Lancashire, M1 4JY, England
Tel: +44 (0)161 236 2200,
www.yang-sing.com
Cuisine: Cantonese

Since 1977 Yang Sing has remained th most loved restaurant in China Town notwithstanding the fire that ravished interior in 1997. Now kitted out in 193 Shanghai glamour, it continues to off quite possibly the best Cantonese the region.

Restaurant Bar & Grill

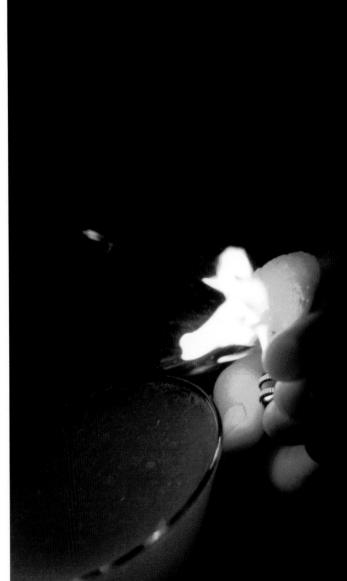

Manchester Drinking

Manchester's drinking circuits are clearly defined, both in location and in style.

For a touch of independence, head to the Northern Quarter, the city's equivalent of London's Shoreditch scene. Here, the bars on the whole are small, but with bags of personality. Only a couple of cocktail gems shine, but the musicians and creatives represent the cutting-edge of the city's social scene.

Deansgate, in the shopping district, is the cocktail capital of the city and where the most stylish sippers can be found. Expect to see footballers and soap stars in their droves – many of them at Manchester's latest headline grabber, Cloud 23.

Nearby 235 casino has also launched, so you can now sip cocktails whilst you lose your shirt. The drinks here were better than anticipated, but unless gambling's a major draw there are better bars elsewhere.

Canal Street is home to the gay village, which has proven constantly popular with both the gay and straight community, while Oxford Road attracts the city's large student population. Both offer a great night out.

Piccadilly has also seen many decent drinking establishments spring up, although beware the stack 'em high; sell 'em cheap mentality of some of the bigger operators here. Deansgate Locks and the Printworks host the city's more mainstream venues and are probably best avoided, especially at weekends. SL

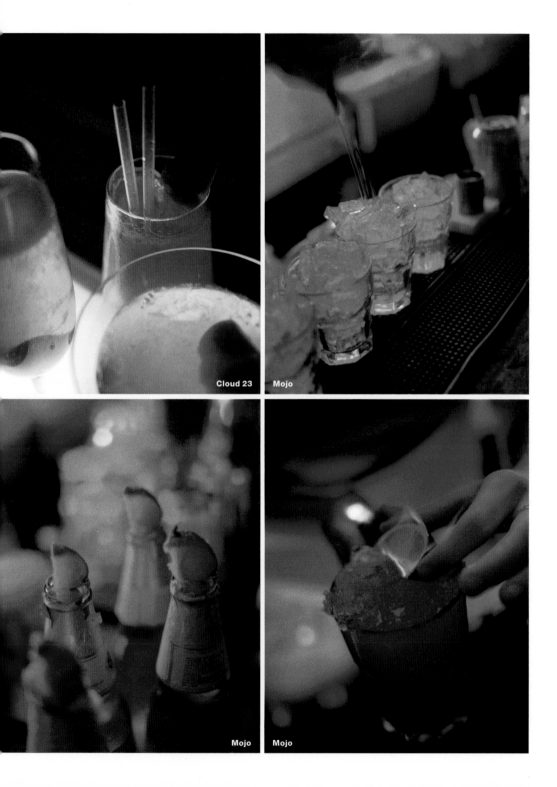

Cloud 23

Mojo

Mojo

Mojo

THE BAY HORSE

● ● ● ○ ○

35-37 Thomas Street, Northern Quarter, Manchester, Lancashire, M4 1NA, England

Tel: +44 (0)161 661 1040,
www.thebayhorsepub.co.uk
Hours: Mon-Sat 11am-11pm, Sun noon-10:30pm

Type: Urban pub
Alfresco: No
Entry: Most welcome
Highlights: Atmosphere
Atmosphere: Friendly, yet buzzy
Clientele: Gay and straight, hip urbanites
Dress code: Casually hip
Price guide: ££
Food: Bar nibbles

Tucked away in the riddle of side street that make up the Northern Quarter, Th Bay Horse is a small space with larg appeal. Taking the qualities favoured b a good, old fashioned boozer an instilling a healthy dose of kitsch appea owner Nicky Rybka-Goldsmith has mad this place a haven for those wanting more relaxed drinking experience in th heart of the city.

Drinkswise, the selection is fair compact; a modest choice of wines offered alongside a reasonable range beers, although cocktails are a little th on the ground. To make the most of th urban pub, check out the pool table the basement too. SL

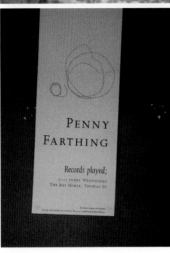

BLUU

● ● ○ ○

Smithfield Market, Thomas Street, Northern Quarter, Manchester, Lancashire, M4 1BD, England

Tel: +44 (0)161 839 7195, **www.**bluu.co.uk
Hours: Sun-Wed noon-midnight, Thu noon-1am, Sat-Sun noon-2am

Type: Lounge bar/restaurant
Alfresco: Terrace
Entry: Subject to management & capacity
Highlights: Decor
Atmosphere: Friendly, yet buzzy
Clientele: Young professionals and locals
Dress code: Funky, casual
Price guide: £££
Food: Modern British snacks and meals

Quite possibly the largest premises on the Northern Quarter circuit, Bluu still manages to convey the ethos of the local area through its decor. On street level, the space is relatively open plan, with exposed brickwork and columns reminding inhabitants of the area's links to industrial times. The basement zone has a more sensual side, and low lighting and suggestive canvases add an erotic edge.

Bluu boasts a comprehensive cocktail offering, with a mix of classic and contemporary libations. While drinkable, these are not a patch on its neighbouring competitor, Socio Rehab.

Towards the back, an 80-seat restaurant takes pride of place, and serves up local delicacies such as Bury black pudding and warm Eccles cakes: this seems the strongest area so far. SL

Cloud 23

Bluu

CLOUD 23
● ● ● ● ◐

23rd Floor, Hilton Manchester, Beetham Tower, 303 Deansgate, Manchester, Lancashire, M3 4LQ

Tel: +44 (0)161 870 1600,
www.hilton.co.uk/manchester
Hours: Mon-Thu 5pm-2am, Fri 5pm-3am, Sat 2:30pm-3am, Sun noon-midnight

Type: Hotel cocktail bar
Alfresco: No
Entry: Reservations recommended
Highlights: The view
Atmosphere: Super glamorous
Clientele: Pretty young things
Dress code: Well heeled and fabulous
Price guide: £££
Food: Nibbles – crisps etc.

The latest star to shine in Manchester's night time economy, Cloud 23 is located in the magnificent Beetham Tower, where the latest Hilton hotel also resides.

The experience begins before the bar is even in sight. Negotiate the red roped line-up to the express lift, and prepare to go from ground level to the 23rd floor is a mere fifteen seconds.

On entry, the panoramic view of the city and surrounding area is simply breath-taking. For those without a fear of heights, two portholes in the floor allow glimpses downwards too.

Drinks come courtesy of London consultancy, Gorgeous Group, who have made this place one of the best cocktail bars in Manchester overnight. And each of the libations on the list references Manchester's leading places and personalities, adding a touch of humour to the über-sophisticated environment. Ena Sparkles, anyone? SL

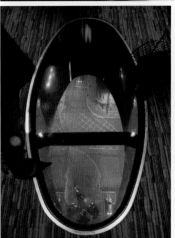

Cloud 23

COCOA ROOMS

1-6 Chapel Street, Cathedral Walks, Salford, Lancashire, M3 7NJ, England

Tel: +44 (0)161 834 3133, **www.**thecocoarooms.com
Hours: Tue-Wed 6pm-11pm, Thu-Fri 6pm-3am, Sat noon-3am, closed Sun-Mon

Type: Cocktail bar and restaurant
Alfresco: Riverside balcony, plus terrace and garden
Entry: £10 per head after 10pm
Highlights: Outdoor space
Atmosphere: Glitz and glamour
Clientele: Style set
Dress code: Strictly glamour
Price guide: £££
Food: Global restaurant

Out on a limb from the main circuits, Cocoa Rooms has had to scream loudly to get itself heard in the city. But this combination of bar, restaurant and club seems to have done the trick.

The archway setting has been given a softer edge with a muted colour palette and elegant furnishings. And in the summer months the outdoor terrace, complete with gardens, really does extend its charm.

On our visit, there was no real cocktail list, but with a decent selection of spirits at hand and some knowledgeable bartenders on the front line, we were not left lacking.

A global food offering and a range of club nights – including the local favourite, Peruvia – add extra points of interest. SL

THE LIVING ROOM

80 Deansgate, Manchester, Lancashire, M3 2ER, England

Tel: +44 (0)870 442 2537, **www.**thelivingroom.co.uk
Hours: Mon-Tue 10am-midnight, Wed-Thu 10am-1am, Fri-Sat 10am-2am, Sun 11am-midnight

Type: Cocktail bar and restaurant
Alfresco: No
Entry: Subject to management & capacity
Highlights: The atmosphere
Atmosphere: Always buzzy and busy
Clientele: Affluent
Dress code: Smart casual
Price guide: £££
Food: Separate dining space

Now seven years old, Manchester's Living Room was the original of what is now a successful nationwide chain. Sprawling over three floors, the colonially inspired venue incorporates a cocktail bar, where the upbeat bartenders keep the spirits raised in more ways than one, a packed restaurant and an exclusive top floor bar.

A wide range of wines and spirits is available, while a robust training programme ensures that the classic, contemporary and homegrown drinks on the menu are consistently well made.

Talk nicely to the staff and you may well find yourself invited up to the top floor. Christened The Study, this snug offers a laid-back sanctuary within this otherwise hectic establishment, and is often the stomping ground of the city's famous faces. SL

HARVEY NICHOLS SECOND FLOOR BAR

Harvey Nichols Store, Exchange Square, 21 New Cathedral Street, Manchester, Lancashire, M1 1AD, England

Tel: +44 (0)161 828 8898, **www.**harveynichols.com
Hours: Mon noon-6pm, Tue-Sat 10am-11pm, Sun 10am-6pm

Type: Cocktail bar
Alfresco: No
Entry: Open door
Highlights: Drinks selection
Atmosphere: Buzzy and busy
Clientele: Shoppers and the style set
Dress code: Designer smart-casual
Price guide: £££
Food: Modern British restaurant

Benefiting from its own entrance and lif Harvey Nichols Second Floor Ba appreciates the finer things in life ever bit as much as its namesake store.

Illuminated glass tanks and tinte ceiling lamps transform the white daytim look into a theatrical blaze of colour a night. Whether you are taking a respit from shopping or in search of a mor destinational drink, Second Floor has covered.

A wide range of spirits and wines a available, and a troop of well-trained sta are on hand to assist the uninitiated. Fc those who have trouble making up the mind, a set list of well-made cocktails thoughtfully provided.

With luck, should you fall in love wit a particular tipple, you will be able to bu it from the food hall conveniently situate next door. SL

The Living Room

MOJO

19 Back Bridge Street, Manchester, Lancashire, M3 2PB, England

Tel: +44 (0)161 839 5330, **www.**mojobar.co.uk
Hours: Mon-Thu 5pm-2am, Fri-Sat 5pm-3am

Type: Music-led cocktail bar
Alfresco: No
Entry: Subject to capacity
Highlights: Music
Atmosphere: Student party for grown-ups
Clientele: Mixed
Dress code: No
Price guide: £££
Food: No

Roger Needham and Mal Evans created the Mojo concept over ten years ago in Leeds, and the magic has finally worked its way to Manchester. Its discreet location on a hidden street in the Deansgate district hasn't prevented it from being an overnight success.

Spanning two floors, the venue is dominated by music. A rock & roll and indie soundtrack blares out each and every night, while memorabilia adorns most of the wall space. Decor is otherwise low-key and dominated by dark wood.

Behind the bar, rum is the spirit of choice, although the skilled bar crew offer a wide range of liquor and cocktails. There is no draught beer, although bottled variations are readily available.

While the drinks are great, it is the party atmosphere that really makes Mojo one of a kind. Loved as much by those who work in the trade as by the general public, this really is the cream of Manchester. SL

Mojo

Cocoa Rooms

Obsidian

OBSIDIAN BAR & RESTAURANT

● ● ● ◐ ○

Arora International Hotel, 18-24 Princess Street, Manchester, Lancashire, M1 4LY, England

Tel: +44 (0)161 238 4348
Hours: Mon-Thu noon-11pm, Fri-Sat noon-2am, Sun noon-10:30pm

Type: Hotel bar and restaurant
Alfresco: No
Entry: Subject to capacity
Highlights: Cocktails
Atmosphere: Friendly
Clientele: Affluent
Dress code: Designer smart-casual
Price guide: £££
Food: Modern European restaurant

Obsidian hopes to bring a taste of New York to Mancunians, and does so in style. With its clean, stark design, softened by clever lighting and deep leather booths, it sets out an aspirational stall yet retains an air of approachability too.

The restaurant has earned itself a strong reputation for its modern European cuisine, while after dark local DJ-ing talent like Hacienda veteran Dave Haslam transform the space into a popular clubbing environment.

And if that's not enough, the back bar positively groans under the weight of premium spirits, which the bartenders clearly know how to handle. The cocktail list is thorough, offering fruity options as well as natural and twisted classics. Most encouragingly, the team has also produced a large bespoke list, all of which are competitively priced. SL

THE OX

● ● ● ○ ○

71 Liverpool Road, Castlefield, Manchester, M3 4NQ,
England

Tel: +44 (0)161 839 7740, **www.**theox.co.uk
Hours: Mon-Thu 11am-2am, Fri-Sat 11am-midnight,
Sun noon-midnight

Type:	Gastro pub
Alfresco:	Mini beer garden
Entry:	No restrictions
Highlights:	Food
Atmosphere:	Relaxed and friendly
Clientele:	Locals
Dress code:	Casual
Price guide:	££
Food:	British dishes

Favoured by locals, The Ox has consistently had a great reputation for food, and deservedly so. It serves up the very best of British in a no nonsense manner, from Irish mussels to Scottish langoustines via steak and kidney pud, and has deservedly earned its mantle of 'best British pub'.

As befits a pub, The Ox boasts a good range of beers – both in bottles and on draught. More unusually, it also has a resident sommelier overseeing the wine side of things.

Should you fall for The Ox's substantial charms, rest safe in the knowledge that there are nine bedrooms upstairs. Well appointed and competitively priced, they offer a relaxed alternative to many of the city's larger hotels. SL

The Ox

The Ox

The Ox

PANACEA
● ● ● ● ○

14 John Dalton Street, Manchester, Lancashire, M2 6JR, England

Tel: +44 (0)161 839 9999,
www.panaceamanchester.co.uk
Hours: Sun 3pm-midnight, Mon-Tue noon-midnight, Wed noon-1am, Thu-Sat noon-2am

Type:	Cocktail bar and restaurant
Alfresco:	No
Entry:	Over 25s, no large single sex groups
Highlights:	Cocktails
Atmosphere:	Ultra glam
Clientele:	Affluent
Dress code:	Smart-casual in week, glam at weekends
Price guide:	£££
Food:	Global restaurant

Internationally, and for that matter in the south of England, the north of England has not traditionally been associated with sophistication. Panacea is one of those breakthrough venues which showed that style does not have to be limited to capital cities.

This is where Manchester's most glamorous come to play. Dress up to get down to the contemporary basement space, where cutting edge design reigns supreme. Panacea comes from the same stable as Restaurant Bar & Grill, and, as at its sibling, the global food menu is well done.

But it is the drinks offering that really has folk talking. From the lengthy wine and champagne list to the cutting edge cocktail selection, every aspect has been perfectly considered and delivered. SL

ROOM
● ● ● ● ○

81 King Street, Manchester, Lancashire, M2 4ST, England

Tel: +44 (0)161 839 2005
Hours: Mon-Wed 10am-11pm, Thu-Sat 10am-2am, Sun closed

Type:	Cocktail bar and restaurant
Alfresco:	No
Entry:	Open door
Highlights:	Decor
Atmosphere:	Refined but relaxed
Clientele:	Affluent
Dress code:	Smart casual
Price guide:	£££
Food:	Brasserie style restaurant

Located in a 19th century building which used to play host to Liberal politicians and their supporters, Room has a distinctly decadent feel. The Grade II listed structure has been ornately remodelled with spectacular attention to detail to house both a 70-cover bar and a 120-capacity restaurant.

But while the decor suggests grandeur, the down-to-earth attitude of the staff makes Room welcoming and relaxed. So does the brasserie style cuisine and effective drinks selection. All libations have earned their place on the list, and each, whether simple or complex, is perfectly balanced and served, making this one of the most classy but comfortable establishments in the city. SL

Socio-Rehab

SOCIO-REHAB

● ● ● ● ○

100-102 High Street, Northern Quarter, Manchester, Lancashire, M1 1HP, England

Tel: +44 (0)161 832 4529, **www.**sociorehab.com
Hours: Mon-Thu 5pm-midnight, Fri-Sat 5pm-1am, Sun 6pm-midnight

Type: Neighbourhood cocktail bar
Alfresco: No
Entry: Subject to capacity
Highlights: Cocktails
Atmosphere: Cosy and intimate
Clientele: Bartenders, urbanites & drinks fans
Dress code: Casually hip
Price guide: £££
Food: No

Many will say this little gem of a place
hard to find. Speakeasy-style, the o
indication of its location on this otherw
sparse street is a tiny sign with handwrit
script, while the rather concealed fronta
does little to attract passers-by. But i
certainly worth the effort.

The small but perfectly form
interior with its bachelor pad air acco
modates only 80 guests. Subdu
lighting and upholstered furnishings ma
it ideal for lounge lovers.

"A booze monkeys playgroup wh
stumbled upon", Socio Rehab is
handiwork of Beau Myers and
Morgan, two of Manchester's m
legendary bartenders. The pair ha
clearly demonstrated their credenti
when it comes to the calibre of spi
behind the bar and the reasonably pric
but well thought-out cocktail list. B
classic and contemporary libations co
creatively served and perfectly balanc

SAN FRANCISCO

Airport: San Francisco International (SFO)
Time zone: Pacific Standard Time (GMT -8 hours)

This East Coast city is as varied and as colourful as its history: a lurid melang
of goldmines, earthquakes, hippies and rockers. Its hilly streets form a mosa
of neighbourhoods, each with its own unique yet laidback vibe.

San Fran is a relaxed, liberal, artsy sort of place and its nightlife runs the gamut from loud str
joints to downbeat lounges and upscale restaurants. Even outside the Castro, the city is extreme
gay-friendly. No wonder, all in all, that it's Americans' favourite city destination.

San Fran Hotels

San Fran is a great place for the style-conscious traveller to stay. Options range from rock 'n' roll to classic luxury, but designer boutique is very much in vogue.

Hotel Adagio
550 Geary Street (btwn Jones & Taylor Sts), San Francisco, California, CA 94102, USA
Tel: +1 415 775 5000,
www.thehoteladagio.com
Rooms: 171

Perhaps better known for the Cortez tapas restaurant in the lobby, this modern hotel is just a few blocks from Union Square. The well sized, well priced rooms, while not as slick as others listed here, come with CD players, high definition TVs and complimentary internet and coffee.

Clift Hotel
495 Geary Street, San Francisco, California, CA 94102, USA
Tel: +1 415 775 4700,
www.clifthotel.com
Rooms: 373

This landmark hotel, which dates back to 1915, has been given a new, surrealist lease of life by Ian Schrager and Philippe Starck. Hardly cheap but still highly fashionable.

The Huntington Hotel
1075 California Street, San Francisco, California, CA 94108, USA
Tel: +1 415 474 5400,
www.huntingtonhotel.com
Rooms: 136

This classic luxury hotel, still family owned and operated, perches high on Nob Hill offering panoramic views of the bay. The individually decorated rooms feature antiques and Irish linen, the sumptuous bathrooms have terry robes and heavy bath towels, and a spa tops off the offer.

Hotel Monaco
501 Geary Street, San Francisco, California, CA 94102, USA
Tel: +1 866 622 5284,
www.monaco-sf.com
Rooms: 201 (inc. 24 suites)

Hotel Monaco dates back to 1910 and its Belle Epoque decor recently benefited from a multi-million-dollar facelift. It sits on Union Square close to the theatres and shops, while the spacious bedrooms offer canopied beds and complimentary high-speed internet. 'Tall' rooms feature longer beds and raised showerheads.

The Ritz-Carlton San Francisco
600 Stockton Street, San Francisco, California, CA 94108, USA
Tel: +1 415 296 7465, www.ritzcarlton.com
Rooms: 336

This landmark white stone building with its fluted columns was once home to an insurance company. It became a hotel in 1991, and the luxurious rooms offer cotton linens and oversize marble bathrooms with double basins. Spa and fitness facilities include an indoor pool and well-equipped gym.

Saint Regis Hotel
125 3rd Street, San Francisco, California, CA 94103, USA
Tel: +1 415 284 4000,
www.starwoodhotels.com/stregis
Rooms: 200 (inc. 60 suites)

This new hotel next to The San Francisco Museum of Modern Art offers contemporary rooms with state-of-the-art electronics and 42" plasma screens. Even the bathrooms have 32" LCD TVs to view as you soak in the deep tubs or enjoy a rainfall shower. The luxury continues in the 9,000 square foot spa.

Triton Hotel
342 Grant Avenue, San Francisco, California, CA 94108, USA
Tel: +1 415 394 0500,
www.hoteltriton.com
Rooms: 140

Stars including Jerry Garcia and Woody Harrelson designed the Celebrity Suites in this outré, eco-friendly boutique hotel. It's funkier than its competitors but also delivers comfort, service and even complimentary wireless Internet.

W San Francisco Hotel
181 Third Street, San Francisco, California, CA 94103, USA
Tel: +1 415 777 5300, www.whotels.com
Rooms: 423

The San Fran branch of the W chain is a contemporary, luxury hotel in the heart of downtown. Amenities include heated lap pool, terrace and spa.

San Fran Restaurants

This cosmopolitan city has recovered from the dot.com crash and it restaurant scene is back in full swing Here are some of our recommendation from the many eateries in town.

A16
2355 Chestnut Street (btwn Scott & Divisadero), Marina District, San Francisco, California, CA 94123, USA
Tel: +1 415 771 2216, www.a16sf.com
Cuisine: Southern Italian

Considered by many the best Italian in tow the wood-fired pizzas here are legendar among the best in the US. The décor a ambience are down to earth but the food heavenly.

Asia de Cuba
Clift, 495 Geary Street, San Francisco, California, CA 94102, USA
Tel: +1 415 929 2300,
www.morganshotelgroup.com
Cuisine: Asian-Latino fusion

The San Fran outpost of Jeffrey Chodorow Asia de Cuba brand offers reliably glam dinin Check out the spectacular, cross-shape sharing table made entirely of hand-etch Venetian mirror glass.

Aqua
252 California St (btwn Battery & Fron Sts), Financial District, San Francisco, California, CA 94111, USA
Tel: +1 415 956 9662, www.aqua-sf.co
Cuisine: Contemporary seafood

This fine dining restaurant serves Frenc influenced cuisine based on Bay Ar ingredients in the heart of the Financial Distri It is widely regarded as one of San Francisc top five restaurants so expect to lighten yc wallet and spot the odd celeb.

Bix
56 Gold Street (an alley off Montgome btwn Pacific & Jackson Sts), Financial District, San Francisco, California, CA 94133, USA
Tel: +1 415 433 6300,
www.bixrestaurant.com
Cuisine: Classic American/French

Live mellow jazz and bow tie clad servers s the scene in this art deco styled supper cl tucked away off a narrow alley. Also s review in bar section.

Boulevard Restaurant

Audiffred Building, 1 Mission Street (@ Steuart St), Embarcadero, San Francisco, California, CA 94105, USA
Tel: +1 415 543 6084,
www.boulevardrestaurant.com
Cuisine: Modern American /French

An elegant, Belle Epoque style dining room with views of the bay houses this regarded restaurant. Attentive servers deliver French influenced Californian dishes and can advise on the extensive and well considered wine list.

The Brazen Head

3166 Buchanan Street (@ Greenwich), Pacific Heights, San Francisco, California, CA 94123, USA
Tel: +1 415 921 7600,
www.brazenheadsf.com
Cuisine: American & international

This old-school neighbourhood restaurant and bar is intimate in both proportions and ambience. Food is served until 1am and the best seats are right at the bar: be sure to try the signature New York Strip Pepper Steak.

Chez Spencer Restaurant

82 14th Street (btwn Folsom & Harrison Sts), Mission, San Francisco, California, CA 94103, USA
Tel: +1 415 864 2191
Cuisine: French

This French gem is hidden behind a gate in an unlikely location close to Nihon bar. A covered patio gives onto the atmospheric dining room, which was once a hardware store. The pianist is a nice touch and stops the place being overly hip. Sadly not open lunchtimes or Sundays.

Le Colonial

20 Cosmo Place (off Taylor btwn Post & Sutter Sts), Theater District, San Francisco, California, CA 94109, USA
Tel: +1 415 931 3600,
www.lecolonialsf.com
Cuisine: French-Vietnamese

This noted French-Vietnamese restaurant moved into the former home of Trader Vic's in 1998, and the patchwork tile floors, shuttered windows, antique lamps, rattan furniture, palm fronds and ceiling fans keep the look suitably Colonial: there's even a veranda. This is a great place to take a date. If you're in a party mood, head to the cocktail lounge upstairs.

Gary Danko Restaurant

800 North Point Street (@Hyde St), Fisherman's Wharf, San Francisco, California, CA 94109, USA
Tel: +1 415 749 2060,
www.garydanko.com
Cuisine: Modern American

Reservations are legendarily hard to get – so book before you leave. You will be rewarded by chef-patron Danko's adventurous, yet balanced, modern Californian cooking.

Fleur de Lys

777 Sutter Street (btwn Jones & Taylor Sts), Nob Hill, San Francisco, California, CA 94109, USA
Tel: +1 415 673 7779,
www.fleurdelyssf.com
Cuisine: Modern French

Chef Hubert Keller serves inventive, modern, Southern French food in his highly regarded eatery, the original of the Vegas version.

Farallon

450 Post Street (btwn Mason & Powell Sts), Union Square District, Downtown, San Francisco, California, CA 94102, USA
Tel: +1 415 956 6969,
www.farallonrestaurant.com
Cuisine: Seafood

This regarded restaurant follows a whimsically over-the-top aquatic theme with blown-glass jellyfish chandeliers and a back bar covered in scales. Ask for a table in the pool room, which housed the Elk's Club swimming pool back in 1924, and has a magnificent arched ceiling covered with a mosaic of bathing beauties. The seafood is ocean fresh and wonderfully prepared.

French Laundry

6640 Washington Street, Yountville, California, CA 94599, USA
Tel: +1 707 944 2380,
www.frenchlaundry.com
Cuisine: Contemporary international

One of the world's top restaurants, this Napa Valley landmark has earned three Michelin stars for Thomas Keller's spectacularly inventive, French-influenced cuisine. The nine course tasting menus ($210) change daily, and reservations are almost impossible to come by. Jackets are required should you achieve one.

Globe

290 Pacific Avenue, Financial District, San Francisco, CA 94111, USA
Tel: +1 415 391 4132,
www.globerestaurant.com
Cuisine: Modern American

This friendly place has a bistro atmosphe which is enlivened by some tasty wines ar equally tasty cocktails. Food is served till 1ar

House Restaurant

1230 Grant Avenue (btwn Columbus Ave & Vallejo St), North Beach, San Francisco, California, CA 94133, USA
Tel: +1 415 986 8612, www.thehse.com
Cuisine: Asian-American

Larry Tse serves modern Asian fusion cuisi in an understated North Beach environmen

Jardinière Restaurant

300 Grove Street (@ Franklin St), Hayes Valley, San Francisco, CA 94102, USA
Tel: +1 415 861 5555, www.jardiniere.co
Cuisine: French-Californian

This glitzy restaurant has attracted San Fran moneyed crowd since 1997. Expect live ja and, unless you relish the vocal atmosphe below, request a table on the upstairs balcor Wherever you're perched, the Frenc Californian dishes live up to Jardinière formidable reputation.

Kokkari Estiatorio

200 Jackson Street (@ Front St), Downtown, San Francisco, California, CA 94111, USA
Tel: +1 415 981 0983, www.kokkari.con
Cuisine: Greek

Everything you'd expect of a brilliant Gre restaurant - exposed beams, classic Gre dishes and a sometimes boistero atmosphere.

Masa's Restaurant

648 Bush Street (btwn Powell & Stockton Sts), Downtown, San Francisco, California, CA 94108, USA
Tel: +1 415 989 7154,
www.masasrestaurant.com
Cuisine: Modern French

One of San Francisco's top fine dinin restaurants, the chocolate-hued roo features a whimsical bronze sculpture of lon limbed figures dancing with artichoke asparagus and grapes. The food is reliab superb while the wine list boasts over 90 selections: chaps will need a jacket.

Michael Mina Restaurant

Westin St. Francis Hotel,
335 Powell Street
(btwn Geary & Post Sts),
Downtown, San Francisco,
California, CA 94102, USA
Tel: +1 415 397 9222,
www.michaelmina.net
Cuisine: Modern American

Fine cuisine served in a modern dining room by a legendary chef. The 2,200 bin wine list is suitably extensive, the service is delightfully attentive and the excellence comes at a price.

Millennium Restaurant

580 Geary Street, Savoy Hotel,
Civic Center, San Francisco,
CA 94102, USA
Tel: +1 415 487 9800,
www.millenniumrestaurant.com
Cuisine: Vegetarian

This ethical, yet hardly sandal-clad, eatery serves inventive, high-end veggy food with a focus on organic produce, alongside sustainable, organic or even biodynamic wines.

Pesce Restaurant

2227 Polk Street
(btwn Green & Vallejo Sts),
Russian Hill, San Francisco,
California, CA 94109, USA
Tel: +1 415 928 8025
Cuisine: Venetian seafood

This simple, cosy neighbourhood restaurant serves the Venetian style of tapas – cicchetti – with an emphasis on seafood. The fish is superbly fresh and the atmosphere warm and casual. Sit at the zinc topped bar and enjoy some great drinks as you dine.

The Ritz-Carlton Dining Room

The Ritz-Carlton, 600 Stockton Street,
Nob Hill, San Francisco, CA 94108, USA
Tel: +1 415 773 6198,
www.ritzcarlton.com
Cuisine: Modern French

Chef Ron Siegel delivers superb French cuisine with a Japanese edge in a room that's as classically luxe as you'd expect from Ritz-Carlton. Be sure to order the tasting menu with wine pairing.

Swan's Oyster Dept

1517 Polk Street, San Francisco,
California, CA 94109, USA
Tel: +1 415 673 1101
Cuisine: Seafood

This San Fran institution is more snack bar than restaurant: diners eat shoulder to shoulder along the long marble bar counter. It is only open for lunch and the line stretches some way but the super-fresh seafood provides ample reward.

Tadich Grill

240 California Street,
(btwn Front & Battery Sts),
San Francisco, CA 94111, USA
Tel: +1 415 391 1849
Cuisine: Seafood

This classic restaurant can trace its roots back to a coffee stand established by three Croatian immigrants in 1849 and, although it moved to this site as recently as 1967, it still looks like something out of the 19th century. Old-school service delivers a bewildering range of seafood amid a vintage atmosphere. Tadich caters to the office crowd and so closes at 9:30pm.

Town Hall

342 Howard Street (@ Fremont St),
SoMa, San Francisco, California, CA
94105, USA
Tel: +1 415 908 3900,
www.townhallsf.com
Cuisine: Modern American

Town Hall is located in the historic Meco building and its warm interior has an almost colonial feel. The BBQ shrimp is worth the flight from London alone, and in general I can't praise the food enough. The short, classically led cocktail selection in the separate bar area matches the quality of the dishes.

Zuni Café

1658 Market Street (btwn Franklin &
Gough Sts), Hayes Valley, San
Francisco, California, CA 94102, USA
Tel: +1 415 552 2522
Cuisine: Mediterranean

Established back in 1979, this characterful, female-owned restaurant with its wood burning stove has become a Hayes Valley institution. The simple, homemade, organic food is celebrated, and the burgers are legendary. No need to dress up here.

San Fran Drinking

San Fran's bars are relaxed and laidback although, as in all of California, smoking is not permitted. Most restaurants, nightclubs and bars are open from 6pm until 2am and there are no casinos as gambling is illegal. Perhaps this goes some way to explaining why many of the better cocktail bars have a Casino cocktail on their list. The Journalist also seems strangely popular.

Laidback though they may be, each district of this great city has its own distinctive edge. Most upscale and classic venues are, of course, downtown. If you're looking for dance music and hip art bars, SoMa (South of Market) is a good option. For a more rock 'n' roll edge head to Mission district. Marina is great for style bars while North Beach is an eclectic mix of elegance and neon.

San Francisco is a site of pilgrimage for fans of Tiki culture as it was here, or rather just across the bay in Oakland, that Victor Jules Bergeron launched the first Trader Vic's 70-odd years ago. His influence is still felt and there are perhaps more Tiki bars per head in this part of California than anywhere else in the world. The most notable are Trader Vic's flagship branch in Emeryville and Forbidden Island in Alameda – both close to the site of the original.

Incidentally, I should warn fellow members of the drinks industry – or indeed anyone given to the laudable act of buying rounds of shots for hard-working bar staff – that the shooter of choice among San Francisco bartenders is Fernet Branca, a bitter Italian liqueur which is something of an acquired taste. The favourite after-work haunt of these folk is the R Bar (1176 Sutter St), which infamous dive is said to sell more Fernet Branca than anywhere in the world. You have been warned!

THE ALEMBIC

1725 Haight Street, San Francisco, California, CA
94117, USA

Tel: +1 415 666 0822, **www.**alembicbar.com
Hours: Mon-Fri 4pm-2am, Sat-Sun noon-2am

Type: Bar
Alfresco: No
Entry: Open door
Highlights: Cocktails, beer & spirits selection
Atmosphere: Chilled
Clientele: Hippies & drinks fans
Dress code: Casual
Price guide: $$$
Food: Mediterranean-style snacks & plates

The hippy location, a stone's throw away from the famous Amoeba Music store, suits this bar: its name is not just a type of still but a manufacturer of hand-made guitars and basses.

The Alembic only opened in summer 2006 but its interior gives it a well established, lived-in air. Bare filament lamps hang over a bar counter hewn from planks salvaged from the 49ers' stadium. A tin ceiling and mustard coloured walls add to the slightly rugged look.

Suspended blackboards announce a truly impressive range of bourbon, including some very rare bottles, plus rye whiskies and Scottish malts – and, with bottled brews from Europe and the US, plus draught offerings from The Alembic's sister brewpub, Magnolia (also reviewed), they certainly haven't stinted on the beers. The cocktail list changes regularly but always features 'Old School' drinks on one side and 'New School' the other. In my experience all are tasty, as is the Mediterranean style food.

BACAR

448 Brannan Street (btwn 3rd & 4th), SoMa, San
Francisco, California, CA 94107, USA

Tel: +1 415 904 4100, **www.**bacarsf.com
Hours: Sun 5:30pm-10pm, Mon-Wed 5:30pm-11pm,
Thu 4pm-11pm, Fri 11:30am-12pm, Sat 5:30pm-12pm

Type: Restaurant/wine bar
Alfresco: No
Entry: Dinner bookings take preference
Highlights: Wines, food
Atmosphere: Jazz fuelled
Clientele: Mature, office escapees
Dress code: Jeans to office attire
Price guide: $$$
Food: Northern Californian

Wine, jazz, a Californian led menu and some tasty cocktails make the scene at this warehouse styled bar and restaurant.

Despite the bare brick walls and raw timber, the feel is more designer than rustic, dominated by a three storey wall of wine that rises past dining room, mezzanine, private dining room and wine salon. This elegance, and the live jazz bands that play every evening apart from Sundays, draws a more mature crowd than elsewhere in the neighbourhood.

Hard-working barkeep Joselino knocks up some outstanding drinks, including his excellent Summer Smoke Margarita, while Two Below harvest ale and seasonal specials from Anchor on draught add beer appeal. But Bacar, whose name means 'wine goblet' in Latin, is predominantly about wine: choose a dish from the Northern Californian menu and pair it with one of 1,400 bottles from around the world, or opt for a glass or two from their choice of 63. The cheese plate is splendid with a big red.

BIRON

45 Rose Street (off Market Street btwn Gough & Frankl.
Hayes Valley, San Francisco, California, CA 94102, US

Tel: +1 415 703 0403, **www.**hotelbiron.com
Hours: Mon-Sun 5pm-2am

Type: Wine bar & art gallery
Alfresco: No
Entry: Open door
Highlights: Wine, cheese & atmosphere
Atmosphere: Relaxed, convivial
Clientele: 30-somethings
Dress code: Very casual
Price guide: $$$
Food: Superb cheese selection

This tiny wine bar cum art gallery lies a narrow street just off Market Stre. While at first glance it can appear a lit. grungy and rough around the edges, t. wonderfully down-to-earth space intimate and romantic - the kind of b. where couples open up and convers. tion flows.

The long, narrow room provid. plenty of nooks and crannies where l. sofas, high stools and low chairs m. Rows of spots beam down from t. ceiling to illuminate works by up-an. coming local artists (these chan. monthly), although the atmosphe. retains its candlelit feel.

The wine offering covers all sty. and origins and stretches to fifty by t. glass: the cheese selection is a. amazing, while the range of beers is go. and international. All in all, you'll proba. neither notice nor mourn the absence. spirits.

The Alembic

Biron

BIX

56 Gold Street (off Montgomery, Financial District, San Francisco, California, CA 94133, USA

Tel: +1 415 433 6300, **www.**bixrestaurant.com
Hours: Mon-Thu 4:30pm-midnight, Fri 11:30am-2pm, 5:30pm-1am, Sat 5:30pm-1am, Sun 6pm-midnight

Type: Restaurant & bar
Alfresco: No
Entry: Open door
Highlights: Décor & ambience
Atmosphere: Piano & singer enhanced
Clientele: Middle-aged professionals, younger at bar
Dress code: Dress for dinner
Price guide: $$$$
Food: Classic American/French

There are many things one might expect to find tucked halfway down a dark alley that is not much more than a car's width wide – but a grand converted banking hall packed with the city's elite is not one of them.

Once past the entrance – which must originally have been a back door - fluted columns topped with art deco embellishments rise to the soaring ceiling, while dinner jacketed folk dine at tables dressed in starched linen and a jazz trio plays.

This classic jazzy supper club is primarily a restaurant, yet the separate bar area makes a great place to stop for a drink and, despite the bartenders' white jackets and bow ties, operates a more casual dress code. A large punch bowl of crushed ice on the long mahogany bar chills Martini glasses in readiness for the excellent Sidecars, Manhattans, Negronis and Sazeracs, while a mural by Mindy Lehrman depicts a supper club filled with dancers in dinner wear.

BOURBON & BRANCH

501 Jones Street (@ O'Farrell Street), San Francisco, California, CA 94102, USA

Tel: register on website for number, **www.**bourbonandbranch.com
Hours: Tue-Sun 6pm-2am

Type: Speakeasy-style lounge bar
Alfresco: No
Entry: Register, then ring to reserve
Highlights: Cocktails
Atmosphere: Stylishly relaxed
Clientele: Cool 30-somethings
Dress code: Make an effort but casual
Price guide: $$$$
Food: No food or even coffee

Those familiar with Milk & Honey's speakeasy-style lounges will know the form here: unmarked door, reservations-only policy and unlisted number. You need to register on the bar's website to find the number, then ring to book – unless you fancy trying your luck at the unmarked, and often unlocked, back door next to the Coast Hotel on O'Farrell, which leads into the smaller 'Backroom' bar.

More conventional modes of entry allow access to two dimly lit rooms where candlelight flickers below a faux-vintage pressed tin ceiling. Intimate booths line the walls, quiet jazz fills the air and a small gallery area offers views over the bar. The wood-covered menu lists classic and contemporary cocktails which are made with care, premium spirits and freshly squeezed juices.

In true speakeasy style a bookcase in the second room forms a hidden door to the Backroom, where the cocktail list is shorter and the bar standing room only.

CORTEZ

Adagio Hotel, 550 Geary Street (@ Shannon St), San Francisco, California, CA 94102, USA

Tel: +1 415 292 6360, **www.**cortezrestaurant.com
Hours: Mon-Sun 5pm-1am

Type: Hotel lobby bar & restaurant
Alfresco: No
Entry: Via hotel lobby
Highlights: Cocktails
Atmosphere: Warm & buzzy
Clientele: Local 30-somethings & business typesi
Dress code: Not too casual
Price guide: $$$
Food: Global snacks and meals

Named after the Spanish conqueror c Mexico, this hotel bar cum restaurant popular with 30-something locals an international travellers alike.

The weirdly eclectic design blenc colonial elements such as the ric mahogany topped bar and wall plantation shuttered windows with full-c modernity in the form of the pastel glob lights that swing from black metal tubin like giant babies' mobiles. Come ear evening, as the office escapees flock to sup Martinis and discuss their day, th overall effect is both warm and appealin

Contemporary cocktails s alongside classics such as The Journalis and, judging by our experience, are we made even when the bar is busy. Th Italian-led wine selection includes 26 b the glass as well as flights.

The eclectic menu is predominant Mediterranean but also features oriental and American dishes. The 'small plates make interesting and tasty bar snacks.

EASTSIDE WEST
● ● ● ◑ ○

3154 Fillmore Street (@ Greenwich), Pacific Heights,
San Francisco, California, CA 94123, USA

Tel: +1 415 885 4000, **www.**eastsidewest.com
Hours: Mon-Wed 5pm-10pm, Thu-Fri 5pm-midnight,
Sat 10:30am-midnight, Sun 10:30am-10pm

Type: Neighbourhood restaurant bar
Alfresco: No
Entry: Relaxed door policy
Highlights: Food, atmosphere
Atmosphere: Friendly
Clientele: Mixed bag of locals
Dress code: Designer casual
Price guide: $$$
Food: Seafood-led contemporary American

Eastside West is very much a neigh-
bourhood affair. Locals use it as a
canteen, a bar and a routine meeting
point. The logo – a crab claw holding a
martini glass with a quaver in it - says
much about what to expect: great food,
good drinks, live music and DJs, all in a
casual café style. The wine and beer list
will satisfy the most discerning and the
cocktails will disappoint few. Seafood
and fresh oysters abound – even in the
cocktails. The house Bloody Mary, a
'Jumbo Mary', comes garnished with a
big juicy prawn.

The bar has its own distinct standing
(or leaning) area. There are tables for
diners beyond that but eating at the bar
is somehow cosier. By the way, this must
rank as one of the cleanest and tidiest bar
areas I've ever encountered – indicative
of the professional way this friendly place
is run.

FORBIDDEN ISLAND
TIKI LOUNGE
● ● ● ● ◑

1304 Lincoln Avenue (@ Sherman), Alameda,
California, CA 94501, USA

Tel: +1 510 749 0332,
www.forbiddenislandalameda.com
Hours: Tue-Thu 5pm-midnight, Fri-Sat 5pm-2am, Sun
2pm-midnight

Type: Tiki cocktail lounge
Alfresco: Back patio
Entry: Expect a line at weekends
Highlights: Interior & cocktails
Atmosphere: More fantasy than forbidden
Clientele: 30-something locals & Tiki fans
Dress code: Hawaiian shirts or casual
Price guide: $$$
Food: Deep fried tropical bites

This authentic Tiki paradise lies only a few
miles away from the original Oakland
Trader Vic's and just thirty minutes from
San Francisco proper. (Take the Alameda
ferry or the BART to Lake Merit, then a ten
minute cab ride.)

The entertaining menu might have you
believe that the site is the upturned hull of
HMS Spindrift but the prosaic reality
pinpoints it as a neighbourhood dive bar,
purpose-built in 1963.

The classic Tiki interior works the
naval island concept with vintage block
and tackle joining the obligatory bamboo,
thatch and puffer fish. The windowless
walls are lined with salvaged blackened
timber, the ceiling is covered with lauhala
mats and the bamboo booths are cosy and
warm. There is a grotto where a carved Tiki
stands proud – he also makes a cameo
appearance on the souvenir mugs.

The sixty rums which occupy the
bar's entire top shelf form the base for
tasty tropical cocktails made with freshly
squeezed juices.

THE IRISH BANK
● ● ● ○ ○

10 Mark Lane (off Bush Street), Downtown, San
Francisco, California, CA 94108, USA

Tel: +1 415 788 7152, **www.**theirishbank.com
Hours: Mon-Sun 11am-2am

Type: Irish pub
Alfresco: In lane outside
Entry: Almost everyone welcome
Highlights: Irish craic & Guinness
Atmosphere: Welcome to Ireland
Clientele: Locals & tourists
Dress code: Casual
Price guide: $$$
Food: Pub grub & better

No, this is not a US branch of an Irish financial
institution but a proper Irish pub (complete
with Guinness, natch), situated on a narrow
lane in downtown San Francisco.

Many people would think it hard to
confuse a bank with a bar (although I
suppose both have counters). Not,
apparently, the Bank of Ireland's lawyers,
who slapped an injunction on this pub as
soon as it opened under their client's
name, resulting in a relaunch as The Irish
Bank on Saint Paddy's day in 1996.

The setting is more rustic than
financial. Antique fripperies, including
church pews, sewing machines, barrels,
horse tackle and farm implements, adorn
the place, alongside the more obvious
photographs, posters and mirrors.

This is, in keeping with its rural
theme, an unsophisticated pub. The fun
and Guinness often spill out into the little
lane outside.

MAGNOLIA PUB & BREWERY

1398 Haight Street, Haight Ashbury, San Francisco, California, CA 94117, USA

Tel: +1 415 864 7468, **www.**magnoliapub.com
Hours: Mon-Thu noon-midnight, Fri noon-1am, Sat 10am-1am, Sun 10am-midnight

Type: Brew pub
Alfresco: No
Entry: Open door
Highlights: Food & beer
Atmosphere: Relaxed, laidback
Clientele: Locals – all ages
Dress code: Casual
Price guide: $$$
Food: Comfort food

Magnolia Pub & Brewery resides in a 1903 building which survived the earthquake of 1906. In the 1920s it became home to a pharmacy and the beautiful interior woodwork was installed; three different café incarnations followed, most notably one in the mid-1960s when the burlesque dancer Magnolia Thunderpussy created her celebrated desserts.

In November 1997 new owners squeezed a seven barrel brewing facility into the basement, installed booths and bars in the upstairs space and restored the historic tile floor and woodwork. A psychedelic mural by local artist, Jon Weiss, completes the place and helps give Magnolia a vibrancy which overrides its vintage.

Magnolia brews a number of cask conditioned ales and all beers are dispensed using British hand-drawn beer engines. I particularly like the bold, West Coast style 'Proving Ground IPA' (7% alc./vol.) but there is a beer for every palate here, including a chocolaty stout by the name of Cole Porter.

NIHON

1779 Folsom Street (corner 14th St), Mission, San Francisco, California, CA 94103, USA

Tel: +1 415 552 4400, **www.**nihon-sf.com
Hours: Mon-Sun 6pm-midnight

Type: Whisky lounge
Alfresco: No
Entry: Subject to capacity
Highlights: Whisky selection & food
Atmosphere: Chilled
Clientele: Discerning cool crowd
Dress code: Casual – but stylishly so
Price guide: $$$$
Food: Japanese cuisine

Bars that specialise in whisky tend to be rather staid places, attracting middle-aged and older men who venerate rare drams. Yet Nihon enhances its serious array of malts with a discerning crowd of cool, young professionals and decor far removed from the tartan-clad emporia of cliché.

Concrete lintels divide the petite, double height main room, while a backlit onyx bar creates a glow that highlights the white pebble floor. (Nihon is not kind to stilettos.) Stairs lead to a mezzanine level and a wonderfully atmospheric back room where diners enjoy excellent Japanese food.

The selection of Scotch malts and other whiskeys is strikingly comprehensive, and customers have the option to buy a bottle of their choice, which the bar then keeps for return visits. Should the water of life not float your boat, Nihon offers cocktails, sake and more mundane libations.

NOPA

560 Divisadero Street (corner Hayes St), San Francisco, California, CA 94117, USA

Tel: +1 415 864 8643, **www.**nopasf.com
Hours: Mon-Sun 6pm-1am

Type: Restaurant & bar
Alfresco: No
Entry: Open door
Highlights: Food, cocktails, beer
Atmosphere: Warm and relaxed
Clientele: Local professional 30-somethings
Dress code: Casual but not scruffy
Price guide: $$$
Food: Mediterranean/Californian comfort food

Once a banking hall, this site lay empt for years until gentrification worked it magic on the neighbourhood: it is now superb restaurant and bar.

Nopa's clean, contemporary interic impresses, as do the huge double heigh windows. Cartoonish murals of Sa Francisco grace the wall, while shoulder height panels divide the space.

Well executed cocktails are liste under 'Classics', 'Seasonal' and 'Spiritua - the latter all feature Highland Park 12-y o. The wine selection is positively inspire – fifteen are available by the glass, an twice that number as half bottles. Oh ye and there's a couple of local lagers o draught, a healthy spectrum of bottle brews (including Trappist ales) and a mor than decent range of spirits.

But the trendy 30-somethings wh crowd Nopa are mainly here for th excellent Mediterranean-influenced foo that emanates from the open kitchen a the back. Reserve a private table or ea at a communal table or the bar.

OOLA RESTAURANT & BAR

● ● ● ◐ ○

860 Folsom, San Francisco, California, CA 94107, USA

Tel: +1 415 995 2061, **www.**oola-sf.com
Hours: Sun-Mon 6pm-midnight, Tue-Sat 6pm-1am

Type: Restaurant & bar
Alfresco: No
Entry: Open door
Highlights: Food
Atmosphere: Laidback
Clientele: 30-somethings & off-duty bar staff
Dress code: Casual but not scruffy
Price guide: $$$
Food: American bistro

This long, narrow, double-height space belongs to the polished wing of the school of industrial design. The bare concrete floor and exposed brick walls are softened with gauzy curtains and paintings by Manny, one of the bartenders. Ambient music, low lighting and flickering tealights add to the warm, mellow atmosphere.

Oola has a better tequila offering than your average bar and an interesting, well-priced wine selection. From the small range of well made cocktails Mexico City (a Manhattan based on tequila) is the most popular.

The place takes its name from the chef Ola [sic] Fendert, who is not just hip – even by San Francisco's standards – but known for his cuisine. The organic baby back ribs are out of this world and, with food served until 1am, it's well worth joining the diners in the mezzanine level gallery.

ORBIT ROOM

● ● ● ◐ ○

1900 Market Street (corner Laguna St), San Francisco, California, CA 94102, USA

Tel: +1 415 252 9525
Hours: Sun 10am-2pm & 4pm-10pm, Mon 8am-2pm & 4pm-midnight, Tue-Sat 8am-2am

Type: Café bar
Alfresco: No
Entry: Open door
Highlights: Cocktails
Atmosphere: Laidback
Clientele: 30-somethings
Dress code: Casual
Price guide: $$$
Food: Café fare - pizza to pastry

Café bar by day and cocktail bar by night, this former ice cream parlour is retro in feel with that slight hint of scuzziness which seems a hipster must-have. Bronze coloured walls rise to an art deco patterned tin ceiling, while bar stools surround high concrete tables shaped like inverted cones.

The Orbit Room is famous for its star bartender, Alberta Straub, who plies her trade just two nights a week. Some years ago Alberta started her 'Trip Out Tuesdays' and decorated the bar to a travel theme with vintage airline flight bags, maps and the odd globe. More relevantly to you, dear reader, she also started creating her own cocktail recipes with homemade ingredients such as her own bitters, infused vodkas and bitter sugar.

If you're lucky enough to be at Orbit on a Tuesday or a Friday you may even find Alberta wearing one of her vintage stewardess uniforms but expect great contemporary drinks and well made classics even in her absence.

RANGE

● ● ● ● ◐

842 Valencia St (btwn 19th & 20th), Mission District, San Francisco, California, CA 94110, USA

Tel: +1 415 282 8283, **www.**rangesf.com
Hours: Sun-Thu 5:30pm-10pm, Fri-Sat 5:30pm-11pm

Type: Restaurant & bar
Alfresco: No
Entry: Subject to capacity
Highlights: Food, cocktails & atmosphere
Atmosphere: Very warm & friendly
Clientele: Friendly discerning locals
Dress code: Casual but stylish
Price guide: $$$$
Food: Innovative, interesting & incredibly tasty

This small neighbourhood restaurant and bar is owned and run by a husband and wife, assisted by a devoted team.

A central kitchen divides the long, narrow room into distinct bar and restaurant areas. Pastel yellow walls, polished wooden floor, granite bar counter and the large 'Blood Bank' refrigerator behind the bar create a modern yet warm interior, enlivened by art deco touches.

The succinct cocktail list offers nine regular cocktails along with daily specials – all are superb. The wine list is similarly to-the-point but presents a broad selection of well chosen bins including fifteen by the glass. There's a couple of local brews on draught and an international selection of quality bottled beers, while the food is, in my view, among the best in the city.

But it's not just this that makes Range one of my favourite San Fran venues for a few cocktails and a quick bite at the bar counter: the friendly clientele and staff give the place a real family feel.

THE REDWOOD ROOM

● ● ● ◐ ○

Clift Hotel, 495 Geary Street, Union Square, San Francisco, California, CA 94102, USA

Tel: +1 415 929 2383,
www.morganshotelgroup.com
Hours: Sun-Thu 5pm-2am, Fri-Sat 4pm-2am

Type: Hotel lounge bar
Alfresco: No
Entry: Surprisingly relaxed
Highlights: The energy & gorgeous people
Atmosphere: Chilled party
Clientele: Hotel guests and fashionistas
Dress code: Smart casual to downright chic
Price guide: $$$$
Food: Modern American snacks

The legendary Redwood nightclub in the historic Clift Hotel was established in 1934. But when Ian Schrager took it over, the vast, grand room was given the super-cool Starck treatment. The high ceiling, original redwood panelling, art deco fixtures and chandeliers combine with an illuminated Venetian bar counter and floor to ceiling light-box back bar to impressive effect. Plasma screens in classical frames often display portraits and other slowly moving artworks - seeing a painting's eyes move can be very disconcerting after a Martini or two.

Schrager has moved on but this remains a suitably glam destination where San Fran's party folk mingle with international hipster guests and the odd out of place suit. There are some reasonable beers and wines to choose from, and the back bar is loaded with premium spirits, but cocktails tend to be on the sweet side. If you are peckish, the local version of Jeffrey Chodorow's Asia de Cuba restaurant is next door.

RYE

● ● ● ◐ ○

688 Geary Street (@ Leavenworth St), Nob Hill, San Francisco, CA 94133, California, USA

Tel: +1 415 786 7803
Hours: Mon-Fri 5:30pm-2am, Sat-Sun 7pm-2am

Type: Lounge/party bar
Alfresco: Caged patio for smokers
Entry: Subject to management & capacity
Highlights: Cocktails
Atmosphere: DJ led
Clientele: Young but too cool to party
Dress code: Hip
Price guide: $$$
Food: Not a place to eat

Manhattan loft meets downtown San Francisco in this cool, industrial space. Mushroom coloured walls, chocolate browns, exposed brickwork, bare concrete floors, a huge, chalk city scene and an outsize mirror form the backdrop to a young and trendy crowd. The upper of the two split-level rooms houses the bar and a vintage pool table while the lower, more loungy space is dominated by a floor to ceiling rack of wine. Smokers congregate in a caged patio on the street like exhibits in an urban zoo.

Despite the slightly grungy look, Rye has upscale aspirations and the cocktails served here, particularly the classics, are consistently good: be sure to try the Basil Gimlet. Sadly the too-cool-to-party crowd seems happier with beer, although at least the choice includes Fat Tire and Trappist brews.

THE SLANTED DOOR LOUNGE

● ● ● ● ○

1 Ferry Building #3, San Francisco, California, CA 94111, USA

Tel: +1 415 861 8032, **www.**slanteddoor.com
Hours: Sun-Thu 11am-2:30pm & 5:30pm-10pm, Fri-Sat 11am-2:30pm & 5:30pm-10:30pm

Type: Restaurant & bar
Alfresco: No
Entry: Open door
Highlights: Food & cocktails
Atmosphere: Buzzy
Clientele: Upscale post-workers
Dress code: Business attire & fashionable
Price guide: $$$$
Food: Modern Vietnamese meals & snacks

The Phan family opened the original Slanted Door on Valencia Street in 1995: this new expression in the Ferry Building is considerably larger and slicker. While the modern, spacious restaurant is already well-renowned, the adjoining lounge is currently gaining a deserved reputation for its well made cocktails.

Here the long, bow-shaped bar is backed by a thick wall of layered glass which offers hints of the activity in the kitchen, and low-slung seating clusters around long, roughly fashioned and polished tree trunk tables. Cocktails are well made and very creative, an interesting beer selection proffers a number of less obvious Belgian brews and the range of teas is simply bewildering. The excellent food offering includes bar snacks such as spring rolls, oysters, dumplings and ribs.

Slanted Door is near the financial district and this, combined with its reputation, ensures that office escapees flock here of an evening.

Rye

TOMMY'S MEXICAN RESTAURANT & BAR

●●●●◑

5929 Geary Boulevard (btwn 24th & 23rd Aves), Outer Richmond, San Francisco, California, CA 94121, USA

Tel: +1 415 387 4747, **www.**tommystequila.com
Hours: Wed-Mon 6pm-11pm (closed Tuesdays)

Type: Mexican restaurant & bar
Alfresco: No
Entry: If there's room (arrive early)
Highlights: Margaritas & tequila range
Atmosphere: Relaxed
Clientele: Locals & tourists of all ages
Dress code: Casual
Price guide: $$$
Food: Authentic Mexican & Yucatecan food

Be careful not to confuse this Tommy's on Geary with Tommy's Joynt on Geary, which is miles downtown, for this authentic Mexican restaurant is also the self-proclaimed "premier tequila bar on earth". Barflies come buzzing from around the globe to sample some of the best Margaritas in the world, enhanced with agave syrup and hand-squeezed Persian limes, and accompanied by plentiful tortillas and salsa.

Tomas and Elmy Bermejo set up Tommy's in 1965 and all five of their children are now involved. From the red, diner-style banquette seating to the plain pine tables, little seems to have changed in 40 years.

Yet Julio Bermejo is now internationally acclaimed for his tequila knowledge and the bar shelves groan with the largest selection of 100% agave spirit in the USA. If you join Tommy's Blue Agave Club and work your way through 35 of his selection, you'll be awarded an oak-framed diploma and a T-shirt. Don't miss their amazing guacamole.

LIMES
LIMES
MAXIMUM SOFTENING TEMPERATURE
MINIMUM STORAGE TEMPERATURE

TORONADO

● ● ● ◐ ○

547 Haight (btwn Steiner & Fillmore Sts), Haight Ashbury, San Francisco, California, CA 94117, USA

Tel: +1 415 863 2276, **www.**toronado.com
Hours: Mon-Sun 11:30am-2am

Type: Beer bar
Alfresco: No
Entry: Open door policy
Highlights: Spectacular beer range
Atmosphere: Biker den
Clientele: Locals and beer aficionados
Dress code: Casual/grungy
Price guide: $$
Food: Sausage Grill next door

This rough and ready place serves beer and nothing but. The decor is utilitarian at its most basic and the service a refreshing antidote to the "have a nice day" school of etiquette. Toronado is, however, one of the best beer bars west of the Mississippi.

A board slung across the middle of the room displays over fifty different draught brews, while there are at least as many bottled beers on offer. Anyone who loves US craft brewing will appreciate the likes of Alaska Smoked Porter, Anchor Old Foghorn and other legendary beers.

The Sausage Grill next door serves what are best described as deluxe hot dogs. Stop off and place your order for wild boar, smoked lamb, veal or the sausage of your choice, return next door to get the beers in, then pop back and collect your meaty feast.

To enjoy the friendly local personalities who fill the room leave all your pretensions at the stable-like front door.

TOSCA CAFÉ

242 Columbus Avenue (btwn Broadway & Pacific Ave),
North Beach, San Francisco, California, CA 94133, USA

Tel: +1 415 986 9651
Hours: Mon-Sun 5pm-2am

Type: Café bar
Alfresco: No
Entry: No door policy
Highlights: Liquor-charged coffees
Atmosphere: Chilled
Clientele: Locals - all ages & walks
Dress code: Smart casual
Price guide: $$$
Food: Not a place to eat

This authentic, 40s bar is one of the city's oldest venues and a glamorous place to enjoy a late night bevvy or two. It is named after the Puccini opera and the vintage jukebox has a suitably classic playlist – Glenn Miller and Rat Pack standards or opera highlights. If you prefer hip hop to big band, you'd do better to end the night elsewhere.

Tosca's glamour is dated and well used but not faded. A print of Venice's Grand Canal and paintings depicting scenes from the eponymous opera look over an authentically elderly bar. Seating is diner style, in red vinyl booths. The espresso machine is aged and the cash register so antique that it does not accept cards. (Be sure to bring cash.)

Bartenders clad in white jackets make the house coffee for which Tosca is justly famous. Including steamed milk, chocolate and brandy, it makes a great nightcap for the local businessmen, arty Cisco types and scattered celebrities who frequent the bar.

TRADER VIC'S

9 Anchor Drive (off Powell St), Emeryville, California, CA 94608, USA

Tel: +1 510 653 3400, **www.**tradervics.com
Hours: Mon-Sun 11:30am-11pm

Type: Tiki lounge & restaurant
Alfresco: No
Entry: Open door
Highlights: Cocktails, food
Atmosphere: Slightly stuffy but relaxed
Clientele: Middle aged & older locals
Dress code: Not scruffy
Price guide: $$$$
Food: 'Tidbits', 'bar bites' & Polynesian fare

This flagship branch of the international Trader Vic's chain is the closest to Oakland, where it all began back in 1934. From San Francisco, it's a 30 minute schlep across the Bay Bridge on I-80 – take the first exit after the bridge, then turn left onto Powell Street at the lights and Trader Vic's is midway up on the right.

The large windows of the expansive dining room offer views over the masts of the Emeryville Marina and across the bay, and at sunset San Francisco and its bridges look spectacular. As you'd expect, the interior is Vic's trademark South Pacific with bamboo walls, fern patterned carpets and dugout canoes, plus shark's teeth, puffer fish and hand carved Tiki poles peeking out from every corner.

The Trader's take on Polynesian food is excellently prepared and presented, while you'll find excellent rum based cocktails and even (if you ask) the original Trader Vic's Mai Tai rather than the usual 'pre-mixed' Mai Tai.

TRES AGAVES

130 Townsend Street (@ Second St), SoMa, San Francisco, California, CA 94107, USA

Tel: +1 415 227 0500, **www.**tresagaves.com
Hours: Mon-Wed 11:30pm-10pm, Thu-Fri 11:30pm-11pm, Sat 10:30am-11pm, Sun 10:30am-10pm

Type: 'Mexican kitchen & tequila lounge'
Alfresco: Patio
Entry: Open door
Highlights: Tequila range & cocktails
Atmosphere: Lively
Clientele: 30-something office escapees
Dress code: Office attire to casual
Price guide: $$$
Food: Mexican plates & dishes

Housed in a former warehouse, this huge barn of a place is dedicated to tequila and the cocktails which can be made from it. Tres Agaves stocks thirty brands of tequila in well over 100 different expressions – all 100% agave. An incredible 85% of all liquor sold here is tequila, and the majority is lovingly made into Margaritas: the bar staff hand squeeze some 2,000 limes a day.

Industrial chic meets country style in the interior with its bare brick walls, exposed rafters and functional seating. A caged display of rare tequilas separates drinkers from diners.

A seemingly endless supply of freshly made hot tortilla chips, homemade salsas and guacamole follow the tequila theme, although for more substantial meals the menu is reassuringly traditional Jaliscan cuisine rather than Tex-Mex.

Tres Agaves draws a mixed crowd of 30-somethings from nearby offices and tequila nerds like me.

XYZ BAR

W Hotel, 181 Third Street (@ Howard), Downtown, San Francisco, California, CA 94103, USA

Tel: +1 415 777 5300, **www.**xyz-sf.com
Hours: Mon-Sun 5pm-2am

Type: Lounge/hotel bar
Alfresco: No
Entry: Hotel guests have preference
Highlights: Atmosphere
Atmosphere: Friendly
Clientele: Hotel guests & young professionals
Dress code: Chic/smart
Price guide: $$$$$
Food: Modern American snacks and plates

This upstairs venue in the hip W Hotel is like a magnet to young, successful Silicon Valley suits, local lawyers and anyone hoping to pull one of the above. Just don't make the mistake of settling into the lobby lounge downstairs and thinking you've made it to the party.

The long, narrow room with its curved ceiling looks rather as if it was built inside a large railway carriage. In fact, on my visit I enjoyed the hospitality so much that it felt as if the train had pulled away and was running over very uneven track.

The interior is stylish and the atmosphere is buzzy but the drinks are nothing special. XYZ is a place to meet a first date rather than to take one. And if you're past the stage of pulling dates in clubby bars then I'd recommend you head elsewhere.

BRAND NEW

The following pages feature some of the many new products available to discerning drinkers in markets around the world. New, in this context, can mean a range of things: some are simply brand new products, others have previously had limited availability and are now being more widely released, a few have just been tweaked with new packaging, name or blend. As with all the bottles that pass my desk I've rated them according to whether I consider them good, bad or just plain ugly.

I've personally never been to Mauritius, and in nearly twenty years in the drinks industry I'd never come across a bottle of rum that's escaped the island. Then suddenly, just before Christmas, my desk was littered with half a dozen Mauritian rums. They say rum is "the next big thing" so perhaps we'll be seeing a lot more bottles from the land of sun drenched beaches. Just in case we do, I've dredged up a few facts for you about Mauritius – and its rums – besides those you'll find in the following pages.

Officially 'The Republic of Mauritius', this tropical island nation lies off the coast of Africa in the southwest Indian Ocean. It was uninhabited until the Dutch colonised it at the end of the sixteenth century, and named it Mauritius after their prince before abandoning it in 1710. The French moved in five years later and established the first sugar plantations, manning them with slaves from Africa, Madagascar, China and India, before the British took the island from them in 1810. Mauritius gained independence in 1968 as a constitutional monarchy, with the British queen retained as nominal head of state, and became an independent republic in 1992.

The island was also the only habitat of the famously extinct dodo, a hapless creature which was, to be frank, fairly useless as birds go. The island's isolation and the absence of any natural predator meant the dodo hit an evolutionary brick wall: it was cumbersome, slow and flightless, meaning that when the Dutch arrived they could easily outrun it. Meanwhile, the rats which came on the Dutch ships feasted on the dodo's eggs, sealing its extinction by 1681 and subsequent fame. (Someone just has to produce a limited edition Mauritian dodo rum - this is a brand name crying out for exploitation.)

Mauritius has three rum distilleries: Grays, International and Cascade. Unusually both agricole rum (rum made from sugar cane juice) and rum made from molasses (a by-product of sugar production) are produced on the island, while both continuous and pot still distillation are used. The result is some varying rum styles.

L'AMITIÉ WHITE

Mauritian Rum
37.5% **alc./vol.** (75°proof)
Producer: Grays Inc. Ltd. Distillery, Beau Plan, Pamplemousses, Republic of Mauritius
UK agent: Green Island (UK) Ltd.
US agent: Not available

The Grays distillery which produces L'Amitié was founded in 1931 under the name of Mauritius OK Distillery Company and belongs to the group Harel Frères.

Pronounced 'lam-i-ti-ay', and meaning 'friendship' in French, this rum is made from fermented molasses put through a three column distillation process. It is unaged.
Comment: This is marketed as a 'well' rum, hence the low alcoholic strength and price point. Hints of sulphur and creamy mashed potato on the nose lead to a fresh, clean, initially sweet palate with a creamy mouth feel and notes of sugar and caramel. The finish is slightly bitter.

THE BITTER TRUTH ORANGE BITTERS

German Aromatic Bitters
37.5% **alc./vol.** (75°proof)
www.the-bitter-truth.com
Producer: The Bitter Truth, Munich, Germany
UK agent: Mail order from the-bitter-truth.com
US agent: Mail order from the-bitter-truth.com

The recent trend for rediscovering the classic cocktails has renewed interest in aromatic bitters due to their frequent use in old recipes. Sadly many of the brands old recipe books call for have long since disappeared so it is increasingly common for bartenders to attempt to recreate these extinct brands or create their own signature bitters by macerating botanicals in neutral alcohol.

It is against this background that two German bartenders have created their own range of bitters under the catchy 'The Bitter Truth' brand. Stephan Berg is a bartender of more than ten years experience, currently working in Munich, while his business partner, Alexander Hauck, is a graphics designer turned bartender based in Frankfurt. Alexander's background is evident on their packaging.

Their Orange Bitters is flavoured with bitter orange peel, herbs and spices.
Comment: The nose lacks the burst of zesty orange found in my Fee Brothers comparative sample. Similarly, the palate is dominated by bitter spice with orange flavour very much second, while Fee's is far more orangey and comparatively sweet. My own preference is for orange bitters to be predominantly orange and rather less spicy but I'm sure others will prefer The Bitter Truth. It also benefits from being clear rather than cloudy.

THE BITTER TRUTH OLD TIME AROMATIC BITTERS

German Aromatic Bitters
37.5% **alc./vol.** (75°proof)
www.the-bitter-truth.com
Producer: The Bitter Truth, Munich, Germany
UK agent: Mail order from the-bitter-truth.com
US agent: Mail order from the-bitter-truth.com

Old Time bitters are so named because they are based on recipes from the 19th century, containing aromatic spices such as cinnamon, cardamom and clove.
Comment: A slight powdery sediment is evident in these otherwise clear, golden bitters. Cinnamon immediately appears on the nose alongside more subtle nutmeg. The palate is bitter quinine spiced with cinnamon and nutmeg.

THE BITTER TRUTH LEMON BITTERS

German Aromatic Bitters
37.5% **alc./vol.** (75°proof)
www.the-bitter-truth.com
Producer: The Bitter Truth, Munich, Germany
UK agent: Mail order from the-bitter-truth.com
US agent: Mail order from the-bitter-truth.com

While orange bitters were overlooked for years, lemon bitters actually became extinct.
Comment: These clear golden bitters have a nose of cooked lemon juice and spice. The palate is intensely spicy and bitter with more subtle lemon zest flavours.

THE BITTER TRUTH ORANGE FLOWER WATER

German Aromatic Bitters
37.5% **alc./vol.** (75°proof)
www.the-bitter-truth.com
Producer: The Bitter Truth, Munich, Germany
UK agent: Mail order from the-bitter-truth.com
US agent: Mail order from the-bitter-truth.com

Flavoured using the fragrant petals of the bitter (Seville) orange tree, orange flower water is commonly used by chefs in pastries, puddings and cakes but until recently was forgotten by many bartenders. It is the make-or-break ingredient in revival classics such as the Ramos Gin Fizz.
Comment: Crystal clear with a soapy orange blossom nose. The palate is lightly bitter and delicately floral. I found this dilute and rather too subtle tasted against a sample from Star Kay White.

BOULARD GRAND SOLAGE

French Calvados
40% **alc./vol.** (80°proof)
www.calvados-boulard.com
Producer: Calvados Boulard S.A., Fécamp, Normandy, France
UK agent: Cellar Trends
US agent: Palm Bay Imports

The calvados house of Boulard was founded in 1825 by Pierre-August Boulard, and is still owned by his fifth generation descendant Vincent. Their calvados, all of which are Pays D'Auge Appellation Contrôlée, are the top selling calvados in the world.

The 'Pays d'Auge' appellation indicates that the apples used come from the heart of Normandy's Calvados region, around the villages of Orne and Eure, and law dictates that calvados labelled Pays d'Auge must be double-distilled in pot stills. (Pays d'Auge are generally the best calvados.)

Boulard use 120 different varieties of apple and source 20% of their needs from their own orchards: more than 500 local growers supply the balance. They produce all their own cider at their own plant, and double distil it in their eight copper pot stills before ageing in seasoned oak casks.

This VSOP equivalent calvados is blended from cider brandies aged for three to five years.
Comment: A rich cider and spice nose with hints of raisins, oak and linseed oil leads to an intensely flavoured palate that offers notes of old cider and stewed apple alongside a lightly oaky vanilla garnish and traces of minty freshness, cinnamon and pepper spice. Lighter, easier and more fruity than longer aged calvados, this is eminently suitable for cocktail use as well as for serving neat over ice.

ELEMENTS EIGHT [E]⁸ PLATINUM

St Lucian Rum
www.e8rum.com
40% **alc./vol.** (80°proof)
Producer: St Lucia Distillers, West Indies for Elements Eight Rum Company, London, England
UK agent: Elements Eight Rum Company
US agent: To be appointed

Elements Eight rums are the creation of Carl Stephenson and Andreas Redlefsen, both considerably experienced in marketing spirits, particularly rums. As the name suggests their rums are marketed around the concept of eight elements: 1/ environment (where the cane is grown), 2/ sugar cane, 3/ water, 4/yeast, 5/ distillation, 6/ tropical ageing, 7/ blending and 8/ filtration.

Carl and Andreas source their rums from the excellent St. Lucia distillery, which, as the island no longer has a sugar industry and so has no refinery, imports its molasses from Guyana.

Three distinct strains of yeast are used with purified water during fermentation of the molasses: each is individually batch fermented to allow it to impart its own flavour to the 'wash', and hence the rum. 'Hybrid Distillers Yeast' tends to produce lightly flavoured rums with sweet and buttery aromas. 'Killer Yeast' makes heavy rums with high levels of esters and alcohols, giving fruity and floral aromas.

The last strain is cultivated by St. Lucia Distillers and its attributes are a trade secret retained by the distillery.

Each batch of 'wash' is distilled individually using one of four stills – two 'John Dore' copper pot stills, one 'Coffey' column still and one Kentucky bourbon pot still. The column still produces light, more subtly flavoured rums; the bourbon still produces heavy, complex rums; and the John Dore stills produce the heaviest, most characterful rums. Elements Eight blends include varying amounts of rums distilled by all three still types, and based on wash fermented using all three yeast strains.

Elements Eight Platinum is a blend of rums aged for four years in American oak casks previously used to age Buffalo Trace bourbon. Charcoal and chill filtrations are used to remove the colour imparted during maturation and to purify the rum.
Comment: Fudge and sweet cinnamon dominate the nose and follow through to the palate which starts sweet and becomes drier as hints of bitter caramel and spice emerge. The long, spicy finish offers notes of white pepper and milky chocolate.

ELEMENTS EIGHT [E]⁸ GOLD

St Lucian Rum
www.e8rum.com
40% **alc./vol.** (80°proof)
Producer: St Lucia Distillery, West Indies for Elements Eight Rum Company, London, England
UK agent: Elements Eight Rum Company
US agent: To be appointed

Elements Eight Platinum is a blend of column and pot still rums aged for six years in American oak casks previously used to age Buffalo Trace bourbon.
Comment: The Demerara sugar and golden syrup nose delivers spicy hints of nutmeg and cinnamon and oily wafts of burnt plastic and overripe banana. The palate is rich yet dry with overripe banana, light mixed spice and more Demerara sugar; pot still notes precede a big, lightly spiced finish.

FEE BROTHERS LEMON BITTERS

American Bitters
alc./vol. (proof) not stated
www.feebrothers.com
Producer: Fee Brothers, Rochester, New York, USA
UK agent: Coe Vintners
US agent: Fee Brothers

Established in 1863, and still family-owned by the fourth generation, Fee Brothers takes its name from the four brothers depicted on the label - Owen, John, James and Joseph – who ran a winery and import business in Rochester, New York, in the latter half of the nineteenth century. The company survived a fire in 1908 and progressed through Prohibition by making altar wine, helping customers make their own wine at home (which was legal in small quantities), producing flavourings for bathtub alcohol and selling a malt extract drink which could be turned into beer by adding yeast. It survived the difficult years after Prohibition thanks to a premix called Frothy Mixer, and expanded steadily from 1964 onwards. The instantly recognisable design on the label dates back only to 1995, while the signature was first written by a James O'Rorke, bookkeeper for John and James Fee in the 1890s.

Like the other bitters in the Fee Brothers range this new, lemon flavoured bitters is packaged in the familiar 118ml paper wrapped bottle with a very user-friendly flip-open cap and dash dispensing top. According to its label it is "prepared from glycerine, a variety of carefully selected lemon oils, augmented with lemon grass and other natural flavours, water, and citric acid".

Comment: These slightly cloudy yellow bitters have an aroma of lemon zest, lemon meringue and lemon washing-up liquid. The palate features intense lemon zest and lemon grass flavours and is tart rather than bitter.

FLAMBOYANT VIEUX

Mauritian Rum
40% **alc./vol.** (80°proof)
Producer: International Distillers Mauritius Ltd, Republic of Mauritius
UK agent: Green Island (UK) Ltd
US agent: Not available

This blend of rums aged for up to seven years in casks previously used to aged bourbon is named for the 'flamboyant' or flame tree which is the national plant of Mauritius and depicted on the label. Flamboyant comes into flower around the time of Mauritian Independence Day in March and the trees lining the great avenues are ablaze with colour. The rum's golden hue comes from oak maturation: no colours are added.

Comment: An interesting nose with wafts of seaweed, toffee and fresh fennel leads to a dry palate with generous smoky oak, dry walnut and Brazil nuts. A suggestion of chewing on straw continues through the dry, slightly smoky finish.

GIFFARD ABRICOT DU ROUSSILLON

French Liqueur
25% **alc./vol.** (50°proof)
www.giffard.com
Producer: Giffard & Cie, Avrillé, France
UK agent: Coe Vintners
US agent: Christophe Barcat

Giffard traces its history back to Emile Giffard, a dispensing chemist in Angers, who developed a digestif liqueur based on mint and tested it on the customers of the adjoining Grand Hotel. So successful was his menthe pastille that he changed his store into a distillery: when his son Emile succeeded him in 1904, he expanded the company's product offer. Today Giffard produces a range of liqueurs and crèmes de fruits alongside its menthe pastille, and is owned by the fourth generation of the family.

Comment: Before even pouring, the natural appearance of this liqueur is striking compared to the other apricot brandies on my shelf. It is a light, slightly cloudy amber rather than bright orange. The nose is wonderfully perfumed with poached apricot, while the lightly syrupy palate is immediate and concentrated, dominated by clean, slightly cooked, almost jammy apricot flavours with subtle hints of almond.
The finish is clean and tangy, like good apricot jam.

GREEN ISLAND SUPERIOR LIGHT

Mauritian Rum
40% **alc./vol.** (80°proof)
www.greenislandrum.com
Producer: International Distillers Mauritius Ltd, Republic of Mauritius
UK agent: Green Island (UK) Ltd
US agent: Not available

Green Island rum was established in 1960 and is the best known and most widely exported Mauritian rum. It is distilled from molasses using a four column distillation process and is blended from rums aged for between three and five years. Charcoal filtration is used to remove the colour imparted by ageing and to purify the rum.

Comment: The clean nose offers a hint of grassiness. The dry, light, clean palate has subtle notes of fennel, coconut and toffee, and finishes with hints of peppermint and milk chocolate.

GREEN ISLAND SPICED GOLD

Mauritian Rum
37.5% **alc./vol.** (75°proof)
www.greenislandrum.com
Producer: International Distillers Mauritius Ltd, Republic of Mauritius
UK agent: Green Island (UK) Ltd
US agent: Not available

Given that Mauritius lies on the original spice route it is not surprising that Green Island also produce a spiced rum.

Comment: A vanilla rich nose has hints of cooked lime juice, cloves, cinnamon and fennel. Ginger heat and spice is immediately obvious on the palate, and builds and lasts right through the finish. Notes of lime cordial and mixed spice provide the backdrop.

MANDARINE NAPOLÉON

Belgian Liqueur
38% **alc./vol.** (76°proof)
www.mandarine-napoleon.com
Producer: Fourcroy SA, Brussels, Belgium
UK agent: Cellar Trends Ltd
US agent: Preiss Imports

While the bottle and, we are assured, the product remain unchanged, Mandarine Napoléon is now graced by a simpler, more modern label which emphasises the Mandarine part of the name over that of Napoléon.

Mandarine Napoléon is claimed to have been created in 1806 by Antoine-François de Fourcroy, a chemist and son of a pharmacist who served as a member of Emperor Napoléon's State Council. Antoine had frequent meetings with the emperor and used to make notes about these in his private diary. One such entry allegedly pertains to the recipe of Mandarine Napoléon.

Mandarin (a fruit we Brits refer to as a tangerine) was introduced to France in 1800 and was, at the time, considered exotic with special health properties. It became fashionable to steep the fruit in cognac and add sugar to produce a liqueur. Napoléon was partial to this combination and frequently invited Fourcroy to join him for a glass.

During the late 19th century, Louis Schmidt, a Belgian chemist interested in the work of Fourcroy, discovered the ingredients to Napoléon's liqueur in Fourcroy's diary. Schmidt had a small distillery in Brussels and launched a liqueur based on the recipe in 1892: his family continued production until they closed their distillery shortly after the Second World War. At this point members of the Fourcroy Company, which had coincidentally been in the wine and spirit trade since 1862, took over production of the liqueur, reconnecting Mandarine Napoléon with the Fourcroy name.

This liqueur's flavour comes from Mediterranean tangerine peel which is macerated in alcohol with a combination of twenty other botanicals (including green tea, clover, coriander and cumin) before being distilled. The distillate is then aged for a period of at least three years before being blended with cognac that has been aged for a minimum of six years.

Comment: Aromas of bitter orange zest burst out of the glass. The palate is rich and slightly syrupy, but not cloying, with zesty orange, bitter orange and citrus freshness.

MONIN POMEGRANATE

French Syrup
0% **alc./vol.** (0°proof)
www.monin.com
Producer: Georges Monin SA, Bourges, France & Clearwater, Florida, USA
UK agent: Bennett Opie Ltd
US agent: Monin Gourmet Flavoring Inc.

Monin, now the world leader in sugar based flavoured syrups, also make liqueurs. The company was established in 1912 by Georges Monin in Bourges, France, and is still family owned three generations on. Olivier Monin heads up the company, which has production facilities in the US as well as France.

Comment: A cooked raspberry nose leads to a richly flavoured raspberry and pomegranate palate. Interestingly, when compared to simply made homemade pomegranate syrup, this has a more concentrated nose and flavour. However, while the homemade version is more subtle the flavour is more recognisably pomegranate.

PARTIDA BLANCO

Mexican Tequila
40% **alc./vol.** (80°proof)
www.partidatequila.com
Producer: Partida Distillery (NOM: 1454), Amatitán, Jalisco, Mexico
UK agent: InSpirit Brands Ltd
US agent: Tequila Brands

The inimitable Gary Shansby, a private equity investor with 35 years consumer brand development experience, is a man who can spot a trend a mile off. A few years ago he noticed that, while premium vodka brands were big news, there was a premium tequila revolution brewing quietly. Market research confirmed his belief, yet he

quickly learnt that while he could build a new state of the art distillery and hire the best creative money could buy he needed genuine heritage, and an abundant supply of mature blue agave plants, to make his brand work.

Meanwhile over in Orange County, mother of two Sofia Partida, once a TV reporter and health club owner, was engaged in rediscovering her Mexican heritage. She had grown up in California, the youngest of eleven children, after her parents, Norberto and Elisa Partida, had left their hometown of Amatitán (ah-mah-tee-tawn) for California to become influential figures in the Cesar Chavez labour movement which provided organised camps offering homes, legal protection and educational services to Mexican farm workers.

After Norberto passed away in 1998 Sofia was compelled to visit his family and the small town where her parents grew up. Norberto's brother, Enrique, had also travelled to California as a young man but had returned to Amatitán some forty years before with enough money to buy land and begin growing blue agave. By the time Sofia arrived he was farming 5,000 acres and supplying many of Jalisco's top distillers, as well as distilling a little tequila himself. Sofia fell in love with the scenery and the tequila, and determined to create a family made, premium, 100% agave tequila brand.

Rather fortuitously, Sofia, who was looking for backing, was introduced to Gary Shansby. She offered family tequila heritage and the largest agave estate in Mexico; Gary had the marketing experience and access to funds to make her dream come true.

Partida Tequila was launched in June 2005. Sofia is the president, brand ambassador and a part owner, while Gary is the chairman, majority owner and marketer. The Mexican side of the operation is overseen by Vinicio Estrada, formerly an attorney who advised Gary during Partida's planning stages. However, it all starts in Enrique's agave fields.

The Partida family estate covers some 5,000 acres in the shadow of a dormant volcano, just outside the village of Amatitán. The rich, red volcanic soil is perfect for the cultivation of agave and those used to make Partida tequila are not harvested until they are at least ten years old. This is at least two years longer than the industry norm and ensures the natural sugars in the plant have developed sufficiently to produce sweet tequila.

The harvested and cut agave piñas (hearts) are slow roasted in two stainless steel ovens (autoclaves), which soften the fibres and transform the carbohydrates into fermentable sugars. The use of autoclaves allows a thorough clean between uses, important since analysis by the Partida team suggests that the coating of soot which forms on the walls of old-fashioned brick lined ovens gives tequila an overbearing smoky flavour. The cooked piñas are crushed to release the juice which is then fermented, before undergoing double distillation in stainless steel pot stills.

Partida's attention to detail is impressive. For example, they use stainless steel pipes as opposed to plastic ones to ensure against possible plastic taint. As you might expect, Partida is bottled without the additives such as glycerine or caramel that are often used to give mouthfeel and colour to lesser tequilas.

This 'blanco' unaged tequila is distinguished from others in the Partida range by its sky blue neck label and 'spirit bird' insignia.

Comment: A nose of green olives in herbal brine leads to a wonderfully clean, crisp, dry but not bone dry palate that is lightly peppered with hints of grapefruit, citrus and fresh herbs. The finish is satisfying, long and slightly smoky.

PARTIDA REPOSADO

Mexican Tequila
40% **alc./vol.** (80°proof)
www.partidatequila.com
Producer: Partida Distillery (NOM: 1454),
Amatitán, Jalisco, Mexico
UK agent: InSpirit Brands Ltd
US agent: Tequila Brands

Distinguished from the rest of the Partida range by its lime-green neck label and 'spirit bird' logo, this reposado tequila is aged for six months in French-Canadian oak barrels previously used to age Jack Daniel's. The empty casks are hot-washed twice with distilled water so only a little of the 'toast' and Jack Daniel's character is left to influence the tequila.
Comment: A spicy nose of caramel, fudge and vanilla leads to an initially incredibly smooth, almost creamy palate. The flavour and character quickly builds with the fudgy vanilla notes from the nose joined by warm, spicy, piny, drier elements. Hints of bitter dark chocolate and dry hazelnut and walnut lead into a bone dry finish that is strangely rewarding with hints of cigarette ash, nuts and smoke.

PARTIDA AÑEJO

Mexican Tequila
40% **alc./vol.** (80°proof)
www.partidatequila.com
Producer: Partida Distillery (NOM: 1454),
Amatitán, Jalisco, Mexico
UK agent: InSpirit Brands Ltd
US agent: Tequila Brands

This añejo tequila has a rust coloured neck label and 'spirit bird' insignia. It is aged for eighteen months in French-Canadian oak barrels previously used to age Jack Daniel's whiskey.
Comment: A slightly smoky, nutty nose with hints of maraschino cherry, ripe pear and oxidised, overripe pineapple leads to a very smooth palate with slightly woody, vanilla, caramel and Brazil/walnut notes. The initial experience is more akin to a mellow cognac than tequila thanks to the rich vanillins from the oak but agave notes emerge and build into the long, mellow, vanilla-ed finish. The pleasant subtle hints of tropical fruit last the distance.

ST. AUBIN BLANC

Mauritian Rum
50% **alc./vol.** (100°proof)
Producer: Cascade Ltd, St. Aubin, Rivière des
Anguilles, Republic of Mauritius
UK agent: Green Island (UK) Ltd
US agent: Not available

Pronounced 'sant-oh-bann', this has been a sugar plantation since 1819 but is a relative newcomer to rum production. The St. Aubin range are Mauritian agricole rums, made from the juice of freshly squeezed sugar cane. The fermented cane juice is distilled once only in an alembic still and the rum is bottled without ageing.
Comment: The huge 'green' nose displays grassy cane and icing sugar with hints of linseed oil. The palate is dry but, even when sampled neat, surprisingly mellow considering its strength. Fresh, sweet, grassy flavours are toned by an underlying peppery bitterness which is more evident in the finish.

ST. AUBIN VANILLE NATURELLE

Mauritian Rum
40% **alc./vol.** (80°proof)
Producer: Cascade Ltd, St. Aubin, Rivière des
Anguilles, Republic of Mauritius
UK agent: Green Island (UK) Ltd
US agent: Not available

This is simply St. Aubin agricole rum infused with vanilla (a pod lies at the bottom of each bottle) and sweetened and diluted with fresh sugar cane juice. The vanilla pods used come from St. Aubin's own plantations.
Comment: Surprisingly the nose is very oily, dominated by the character of agricole rum rather than the flavours of vanilla. The vanilla shines through on the sweet palate, although that underlying agricole rum oomph is still delightfully very much there. Just add lime juice for a spectacular Daiquiri.

ST. GERMAIN

French Liqueur
20% **alc./vol.** (40°proof)
www.stgermain.fr
Producer: La Maison St. Germain, Rue de Sèvres,
Saint-Germain-des-Prés, Paris, France
UK agent: Coe Vintners
US agent: Cooper Spirits Intl. LLC

If you read about my involvement with Rock & Rye in our last issue you will already be familiar with Rob Cooper, an American friend of mine and third generation distiller, entrepreneur and creator of liquor brands.

Rob has been working on making a high quality elderflower liqueur since 2002 when he realised what an important cocktail ingredient the non-alcoholic elderflower cordials were becoming in London. He believed that a liqueur would be a more stable medium to harness the delicate elderflower flavour than the existing sugar and water based cordials. My involvement in the project started in January last year when Rob sought my opinion on his latest formula. I've since tried literally dozens of samples and have seen the product steadily tweaked to arrive at the balanced and wonderfully floral product that is St. Germain.

Obviously the first thing you need to make an elderflower liqueur is elderflowers and Rob quickly discounted the freeze dried and frozen blossoms which are used in many other products. His quest took him to the French Alps where elder bushes grow abundantly and Hungarian and Romanian gypsies trawl the mountainsides to handpick the small white blossoms. They pedal their blossom laden bicycles to depots set up in the gardens of local homes where the flowers are weighed, the gypsies paid and the blossoms loaded into baskets ready for transportation to the distillery.

Speed is of the essence to capture the blossoms' delicate flavour as they quickly turn brown and lose their fragrance: conventional maceration methods yield little flavour while pressing causes unwanted bitterness. Much of the three years Rob spent working on St. Germain was spent developing the unique maceration process, which remains a closely guarded secret. The elderflower infused spirit is then blended with a hint of citrus, purified water and just enough sugar to enhance the natural flavour of the blossoms.

St. Germain's packaging reflects the artisan nature of its production - right down to the illustration of a bicycle carrying a gypsy and his flowers. The shapely eight-sided bottle was created as a tribute to the vibrant art deco period in St. Germain. Each is finished with a heavy, turned brass stopper and individually numbered and marked with the vintage year. (Due to the varying nature of the flowers the flavour will vary slightly with each vintage.)

Why the name? On his frequent trips to the Alps and distillery while developing the liqueur, Rob would fly in and out of Paris. On the way he fell in love with Saint-Germain-des-Prés and its cafés.
Comment: The clean floral nose has hints of pear, peach and grapefruit zest. The palate is syrupy but not cloying and is wonderfully fresh with rich elderflower and tropical fruit balanced by subtle lemon zest acidity.

SARTICIOUS

American Gin
47% **alc./vol.** (94°proof)
www.sarticious.com
Producer: Sarticious Spirits Inc., Santa Cruz, California, USA
UK agent: Not available
US agent: Sarticious Spirits Inc.

Sarticious is the product of two friends, Jeff Alexander and Mark Karakas, and their Californian micro distillery. Jeff is an experienced brewer, winemaker and distiller who has previously worked at Los Gatos Brewing Company, Savannah-Chanelle winery and St. George Spirits (makers of Hangar One vodka). Mark used to run the Mountain Winery in Saratoga. Today the two work together at their 120 gallon Jacob Carl alembic copper brandy still to produce craft spirits.

In case you are wondering, the word 'sarticious' is a new coinage. While not officially recognised as part of the English language, the partners assert it means 'well-dressed and desirable'. Botanicals used to flavour Sarticious include: juniper berries, organic orange and coriander, cardamom, cinnamon and pepper.
Comment: A powerful nose of wet Christmas tree and coriander is the precursor to an equally potent palate with piny coriander, fiery cracked black pepper and citrusy hints. The incredibly long finish starts with bursts of red chilli pepper heat and subsides to reveal its piny base. All the way through, however, the pine notes are wet and woody, not fresh and clean.

STARR

Mauritian Rum
40% **alc./vol.** (80°proof)
www.africanrum.com
Producer: Distiller unknown, Republic of Mauritius for Starr African Imports, Los Angeles, California, USA
UK agent: Not available
US agent: Starr African Imports

I've been able to find out very little about this rum, which is distilled and bottled on the island of Mauritius. According to Jeffrey Zarnow, the American brand owner, "Basically, we are pretty tight lipped about our distillation methods. Here is what I can tell you. Starr is made from world class Mauritian sugarcane. Like the top shelf vodkas, we filter out most of the impurities of the alcohol so it's as smooth if not smoother than any vodka. However, unlike the vodkas, we do not remove the wonderful flavour of the rum. The rum is a blend of aged rums that are aged up to six years." Starr's tall, triangular bottle is made in South Africa.
Comment: An earthy, chocolaty nose with hints of rosewater and cinnamon leads to a very light but spicy palate enlivened by touches of cinnamon, nutmeg, vanilla, cocoa and brown sugar.

VERMEER

Dutch Cream Liqueur
17% **alc./vol.** (34°proof)
www.vermeeruk.com
Producer: In the Netherlands for Vermeer Spirits Ltd.
UK agent: Vermeer Spirits Ltd
US agent: Skyy Spirits LLC

This Dutch chocolate cream liqueur is the creation of Maurice Kanbar, the man who originated Skyy vodka. Vermeer is named after the Dutch master, Johannes Vermeer, and this rounded, brown, stubby bottle's label depicts the artist's 'The Girl with a Pearl Earring'. However, given Maurice's past in cinema, you'll not be surprised, if you didn't already know, that it's also the title of a film starring Scarlett Johansson.
Comment: It's worth reinforcing the instructions on the bottle to shake this liqueur before opening. Obviously, I didn't, but fortunately I started on one of the sample miniatures prior to hitting the big bottle. A nose of powdered toffee hot chocolate with nose-tingling wafts of pepper leads to a creamy, dark chocolate palate that is slightly sweet, although the chocolate itself is slightly bitter. The chocolate tastes somehow powdery and artificial instead of smooth and natural.

VOLARE STRAWBERRY

Italian Liqueur
20% **alc./vol.** (40°proof)
www.volarecocktails.com
Producer: Rossi d'Asiago Distillers, Italy
UK agent: Hi-Spirits
US agent: Not available

My friend Jamie Stephenson, the multi-award and competition winning mixologist, helped design the ergonomic bottle in which the Volare range of liqueurs come packaged. It's perfectly weighted and ribs run around the bottle's belly and neck to make it easier to grip with wet hands.

Unscrew the capsule and you are in for a real surprise as a pourer pops up out of the bottle to allow you to effortlessly dispense without losing a drip. This natty system is branded 'Pro-pour' and although I worry it could get stuck due to the sugar in the liqueurs it certainly aids pouring in the short term.
Comment: The nose is of strawberry jelly – still in its cubed form and straight out the cellophane. The very light, clean palate also reminds me of strawberry jelly, rather than fresh luscious fruit, perhaps with a hint of watermelon. This is not in the same league as some of the wonderfully natural tasting French crèmes de fraise but pleasant enough poured over your fruit salad.

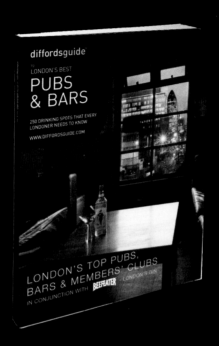

diffordsguide to

LONDON'S BEST PUBS & BARS

A POCKET-FRIENDLY GUIDE TO THE VERY BEST PUBS AND BARS IN LONDON:
MORE THAN 250 SPACES REVIEWED AND PHOTOGRAPHED.

AVAILABLE NOW

www.diffordsguide.com

ISSN: 0-9546174-9-5 **Cover price:** UK £4.97

VODKA

Vodka is a tricky subject - so tricky that its very definition is currently the subject of a range of legal challenges around the world. I will be covering flavoured vodkas in the next issue of this guide, so, for the purposes of this article, vodka is a clear spirit (Blavod aside) which can be produced from anything containing starch or sugar - including potatoes, molasses and, most commonly, grain.

Vodkas are generally regarded – by definition by the US Bureau of Alcohol, Tobacco & Firearms - as having little aroma and taste. Yet different brands do have their own identities, and their flavour profile varies greatly depending on what they are made from, how they are made, and the recipe they are made to. For example, a vodka made from rye grain will taste different from a vodka made from potatoes, and different again from a vodka made from grapes.

Just as with a wine, or any other spirit, the right style for you is a matter of personal taste.

HISTORY

ORIGINS

Vodka's origin is the source of a bitter dispute between Russians and Poles, both of whose national drink it is. Each argue that it originated in their country - the name 'vodka' derives from the Russian word for water, and the Polish word 'wódka' derives from the Polish word for water. In both cases, this is thought to be a reference to the alchemical idea that spirits were the water of life.

POLISH VODKA

The Polish word 'wódka' can be traced back to the 15th century and some allege that, during the period of Soviet dominance, evidence of vodka's Polish origin was covered up. Some also claim that Polish vodka was first produced in the eighth century – by freezing wine and skimming off the resulting harsh spirit – although to call this vodka would be stretching a point.

The first written record of a Polish spirit made from grain dates back to 1405, and these early vodkas, generally infused with herbs, spices or other flavourings, were used as medicines. In 1546, King Jan Olbracht passed a law which allowed every citizen to make and sell spirits. As a result, most families prepared vodkas, often flavouring them with fruits and herbs, which helped disguise the rough alcohols resulting from crude distillation in log stills. The tradition of flavouring vodka continues in Poland today.

The history of distilling in Poland is as long and complicated as the nation's own story of occupations, invasions and boundary changes, but commercial distillation began to take off at the end of the 18th century and column stills were in use by the late 19th century.

After the Second World War, the Soviet-backed government consolidated and nationalised the industry, leaving a total of six distilleries proper and 19 compounders. These organisations blended and bottled the raw spirits that the distilleries produced.

On nationalisation, both distilleries and compounders were each titled 'Polmos' followed by the name of the town in which they were located. The brands that the various businesses had made before the war were also nationalised so that each and any compounder could produce each and any vodka brand using the shared recipe. However, some compounders were better than others, so aficionados would look to buy their preferred brand from a particular one.

The collapse of the Iron Curtain saw capitalism wash over Poland and on 15th July 1999 the Polish government privatised the 19 Polmos compounders and their shared brands. The better compounders ended up with the better brands and the rest were given a year to cease production of the privatised spirits. (Global conglomerates such as V&S and Pernod-Ricard now own many of these businesses and their brands.)

A number of old Polmos vodka brands have yet to be purchased and these are still made under licence by some of the Polmos compounders. A second round of privatisation will no doubt follow and these too will eventually also be limited to one producer. In the meantime, however, there are around 1,000 brands of vodka in Poland but, bizarrely, many brands made in Poland for export to Europe and North America are not available in their homeland.

Rye is the most popular grain from which Polish vodka is produced, but Poland is also noted for the distillation of vodka from potatoes – Stobrawa are favoured as they have a high starch content and are easy to distil from. Contrary to popular belief, it is more expensive to produce vodka from potatoes than it is from grain.

Traditionally, unflavoured Polish vodka is not sweetened. Polish rye vodka usually has a slight natural sweetness and a hint of rye bread on the palate, while potato vodkas tend to be smooth and rounded with slight vegetable notes.

Polish vodkas were once graded into three categories according to purity: 'Luksusowy', meaning luxury, 'Wyborowy', meaning choice, and 'Zwykly', meaning standard. This nomenclature survives in some brands.

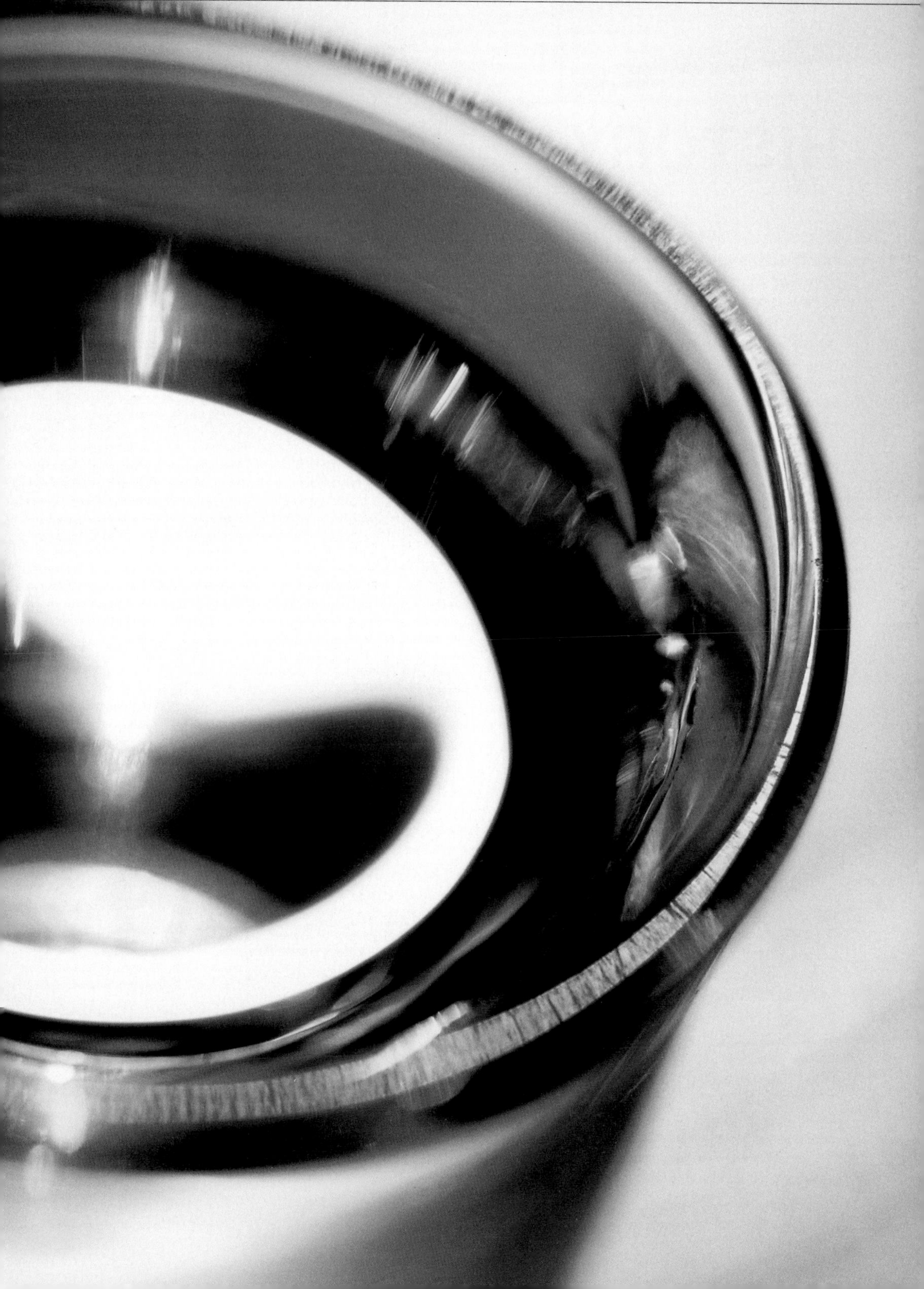

HISTORY

RUSSIAN VODKA

The Russians are believed to have been producing a kind of spirit as early as the end of the ninth century - like the Poles, probably by freezing wine or mead. Distillation appears to have reached the country in the mid-15th century, after a Russian delegation visited Italian monasteries to learn the secrets of the monks, and by 1700 vodka was well established. As in Poland, makers flavoured the spirit with fruits and herbs.

Russians attribute the invention of charcoal filtration to an 18th century chemist by the name of Theodore Lowitz who was hired to make the national drink more hygienic. His technique - a process to which a number of other nations lay claim – helped remove contaminants and produce cleaner vodka.

Whatever the impact of Lowitz's invention, vodka became an integral part of Russian life despite ongoing state taxation. In fact, some even consider the prohibition of alcohol during World War I one of the key motivating factors behind the Russian Revolution.

Under communism, the distilling industry, like every other industry, was nationalised and most Russian vodka was marketed through Sojuzplodoimport, the state-owned trading company. During the Cold War, exports to the West were extremely limited.

Yet, since the collapse of the communist Soviet Union, despite a challenging business environment that has seen armed standoffs between rival producers, several Western firms have invested in Russia, and home-grown entrepreneurs are also producing some excellent vodka. Sojuzplodoimport, of course, is now privatised – although the Russian government may be about to change that (but that's another story).

Russian vodkas tend to be distilled from wheat and consequently often have slight hints of aniseed. They are often sweetened with trace amounts of sugar or honey.

WESTERN VODKAS

The British and North American markets were, and, in volume terms, still are, dominated by Smirnoff, a Russian brand reinvented in the US in the 1930s that brought the category to the wider world. Consequently, until recent years, most Western vodkas borrowed their imagery from the romantic notion of Tsarist Russia, used Russian sounding names and decorated their labels with imposing crests. Little tended to be said about what they were produced from - often molasses neutral spirit rather than the more expensive grain neutral spirit.

But Sweden and Finland, due to their close proximity to Russia, also have a long-established vodka heritage and during the 1980s Absolut transformed the image of Western vodka thanks to spectacularly canny marketing and iconic advertising.

Another turning point came in the late 1990s when Sidney Frank launched Grey Goose, a French-made vodka, priced it high above the competition and marketed it as a luxury spirit. The Dutch-made pot still vodka Ketel One entered the new market around the same time, helping create the super-premium vodka category. Today Sweden, Finland, the Netherlands and France have established a reputation for quality vodka, supported by modern imagery emphasising purity. (While the Netherlands and France may be new to vodka, many distillers have been producing quality neutral spirits as the base for jenever and liqueurs for centuries, so were in prime position to benefit from vodka's growing popularity over the last decade or so.)

And, while Sidney Frank felt he had to go to France for an authentic luxury story, US distillers are using their country's grain and water – and even its grapes and potatoes – to produce an increasing number of boutique, small-batch vodkas alongside a number of brands that have behemoth aspirations.

As a result of the scale and disparate spread of production – brands are produced from Canada to New Zealand via Austria and Italy – it is hard to precisely characterise Western vodkas. They were traditionally considered relatively neutral in style due to modern distillation methods and state-of-the-art distillation columns. However, in recent years boutique and luxury producers have employed different types of still, particularly pot stills, to 'finish' rectified spirits and add a little of that character which vodka's detractors think it lacks. A trend for adding a barely discernable hint of flavour to what is marketed as a grain vodka has also emerged.

RAW INGREDIENTS

Vodka is most commonly made from molasses and grain, though grain is generally favoured for the production of premium or super-premium brands. The types of grain used will affect the taste of the finished vodka. Types of grain and the flavour associated include barley (lightly nutty, spicy sweetness), maize/corn (buttery), rye (nutty rye bread sweetness) and wheat (aniseedy).

Vodka can be made from anything that contains starch, as starch can be converted into sugar and alcohol is fermented from sugar. As well as using potatoes, made famous by Poland, vodka can be made from apples, bread, beetroots, carrots or even onions, and there are at least a couple of grape vodkas on the market.

The other important raw ingredient common to all vodka is water. The quality of the water used vastly affects the finished product and many brands pin their marketing story on the water they use. Most producers, however, are more vocal about the source of the water they use to distil their product than the purified tap water with which many still dilute it to bottling strength.

VODKA PRODUCTION

Like all spirits, vodka can only be distilled from a liquid that is already alcoholic. So before distillation the base ingredient must be mixed with water and yeast and then fermented. This produces a type of beer known as a 'wash' – generally around 8% alc./vol.

Distillation of the wash normally takes place in continuous (column) stills, ensuring that the final distillate is extremely pure and neutral tasting (it usually leaves its final distillation at 96% alc./vol.). However, an increasing number of top-end producers now choose to use pot stills, which leave more of the character and flavour of the raw material in the distillate.

Many producers filter the distillate through active charcoal or other substances. This process was originally designed to remove the bad fusel oils (toxic alcohols) from the distillate, which inefficient older stills could not remove. (While the Russians, the Poles and the Swedes claim credit for introducing charcoal filtration, little is said by the Irish who can rightly claim the invention of the continuous still in which most vodkas are still made.)

There is a trend among marketers to state on the label and in the literature that a vodka is 'triple distilled' or even 'quadruple distilled'. When, as often, this refers to distillation in a column still (or stills), such terms are meaningless. The purity of a column still distillate derives from the number of distilling plates the still houses – a 50-plate still will produce a much purer spirit than a 3-plate still – and has nothing to do with how many times, or in how many stills, the spirit has been rectified. (Pot still distillates, to which such terms originally referred, become purer and purer the more times they are distilled.)

Claims such as 'triple filtered' are almost equally laughable. The quality of a filtration depends on how long the spirit has been filtered, through what material and through what size filter. How many times it passes through the filter is irrelevant without this information.

In general, you should look for vodkas whose labels contain concrete information about the type of still used, the base ingredient – the kind of grain and where it comes from, for example - and the filtration method.

SERVING VODKA

In Eastern European and Nordic countries, vodka is drunk neat and ice-cold from small glasses, traditionally with salty and spicy preserved food. In Russia, long, thin stemmed glasses known as 'stopkis', rather like small champagne flutes, are preferred to 'shot' glasses as they allow drinkers to hold the glass by the stem, avoiding warming the vodka with their hands. But, whatever glass you decide to serve neat shots of vodka in, it should be frozen, as should the vodka itself.

Before the 1940s, vodka was hardly known outside of Eastern Europe and Scandinavia. Its worldwide success since then is mainly due to its marketing as a pure, clean, neutral spirit which can be mixed with anything. Although some argue that there is no cocktail that doesn't taste better made with another spirit altogether - or a flavoured vodka (taste a Cosmopolitan with grain vodka against one made with citrus vodka). Today, vodka is by far the most commonly used spirit base in cocktails.

Some bartenders now prefer to use different vodkas in different cocktails, depending on whether neutrality or flavour is required. Generally, however, it is true to say that neutral grain vodka adds alcohol to a mixed drink but little flavour or personality. That is unless it's really bad vodka.

EU VODKA DEFINITION

As I write this, the European Commission is considering a ruling on the definition of vodka. Countries including Poland, Finland and Sweden have been lobbying the commissioners to rule that vodka can only be made from grain or potatoes, while producers such as Diageo, which owns the grape-based Cîroc, are predictably attacking the proposal put forward. Apparently, the EC is now erring towards the more sensible ruling that vodka can be made from pretty much anything providing that its base ingredient is declared on the bottle.

While America remains the world's most important and influential market for vodka - and certainly for premium priced vodkas - it doesn't really matter what the bureaucratic money wasters in Brussels think as vodka will continue to be made from a number of different base ingredients, including grapes, and sold in the US as such. The most significant outcome would be a ludicrous situation where European drinkers were unable to buy products made in their countries for export to the US. This would be as idiotic as the ruling passed a decade ago requiring spirit bottles sold in the EU to be 70cl as opposed to the 75cl standard size favoured in most other parts of the world.

Ketel One Distillery

INFUSING VODKA

Back in the 1980s, bottles of 'Mars Bar vodka' dressed with floating fat globules were a common sight on the back bar. Thankfully, things have moved on and vodka now tends to be flavoured with herbs, spices and fresh fruit.

Should you wish to infuse your own vodka, simply put your choice of flavouring in a bottle, add vodka and leave to steep for a while, checking for taste regularly - fresh ingredients will generally only take a week or two to infuse.

The following tips may help:

- Warming the bottle and frequently turning or shaking it can help extract more flavour.
- Do-it-yourself flavouring will affect the strength of the finished product. European bars should not sell any drink below 37.5% alc./vol. as vodka.
- Favoured flavourings include blackberry, raspberry, strawberry, apple, melon, honey, chilli, vanilla pods, pepper, lemon, lime, orange, chocolate, toffee and cinnamon. But you can use almost any fruit, herb or spice that takes your fancy.
- If using toffee or sweets, break them up into small pieces to allow them to dissolve.
- Citrus fruit rinds should be used, not the pulp or flesh. Be sure to buy non-waxed fruit and scrub thoroughly before use.
- If using herbs or spices such as mint and vanilla, use only fresh leaves, pods and seeds. Always discard stems and larger, more bitter leaves.
- Try combinations of flavours and the addition of wine.
- Consider adding sugar to sweeten (boiled sweets and suchlike won't need any extra sugar).
- If you must go down the Mars Bar route, you should gently warm the combination in a saucepan and skim off the fat, before allowing to cool and straining back into the bottle.

●●●●○

ABSOLUT BLUE

Swedish Vodka
40% **alc./vol.** (80°proof)
www.absolut.com
Producer: Swedish Wine & Spirits Corporation
(Vin & Sprit), Stockholm, Sweden.
UK agent: Maxxium UK
US agent: Future Brands LLC

In 1879, Lars Olsson Smith introduced a vodka called 'Absolut rent brännvin', which translates as 'absolutely pure vodka'. The maverick entrepreneur circumvented a state-backed vodka producers' cartel by establishing a distillery on the island of Reimersholme (just outside the Stockholm city limits) and offering a free ferry service to his customers.

After Lars Olsson's death, the brand enjoyed little success under the ownership of the Swedish state liquor monopoly. Then, in 1979, the brand's centenary, Lars Lindmark, the new president of Vin & Sprit, decided to relaunch it. The bottle was redesigned in the style of an old Swedish medicine bottle found in an antique shop window in Stockholm's Old Town – appropriate, since vodka was sold in 16th & 17th century pharmacies as medicine.

The name 'Absolute Pure Vodka' could not be registered in the US because 'absolute' was a common adjective, so it was shortened to Absolut, the original Swedish spelling. The word 'Pure' in the original name also posed legal problems and was removed and the slogan 'Country of Sweden' was added, as was the silver medallion with an image of Lars Olsson Smith.

The now legendary minimalist advertising campaign was launched in 1980 with 'Absolut Perfection', which featured the bottle with a halo. The ads established the brand as a premium, fashionable vodka, leading to worldwide sales of 3.3 million cases at the end of its first decade and 6.7 million cases by 1999.

Absolut is still produced in the small southern Swedish town of Åhus, using winter wheat from the surrounding province, Skåne. The wash is distilled to a strength of around 90% alc./vol. then rectified through four different column stills to around 95% alc./vol. A little 'character' is added to this very pure and almost neutral spirit with the addition of a less pure, lower strength spirit. This flavouring spirit is made from specially selected grain that undergoes a different and separate wash process and is distilled more gently to a lower proof. Although it comprises only a low percentage of the finished vodka, it helps give Absolut its malty flavour. Unlike many other vodkas, Absolut has no added sugar, is not charcoal filtered and does not undergo any other form of chemical filtration.
Comment: A slightly doughy nose leads to a palate with lightly peppery, malty, bready notes followed by a slight hint of dried fruit and liquorice. Finishes bitter.

●●●●○

ALTAÏ

Russian Vodka
40% **alc./vol.** (80°proof)
Producer: Sokolovo Distillery (Group Pernod Ricard), Zmeinogorsk, Siberia, Russia.
UK agent: Pernod Ricard UK
US agent: Pernod Ricard US

Pronounced 'Aal-Tie', this vodka is the result of a cooperation agreement between the Siberian distillery Altaï and Pernod Ricard and was first produced in 1994 to Pernod's specifications after the French company invested in the Siberian plant. With Pernod Ricard's subsequent purchase of Wyborowa

and the distribution rights to Stolichnaya, Altaï's international future is now dubious.

Altaï is produced exclusively from Siberian raw materials. The region's short summer and long winter ensure an early grain harvest and it is claimed that this young 'winter' wheat produces a sweeter and mellower taste. The water used is drawn from the rivers of the Altaï mountains that straddle the borders of Mongolia, China and Kazakhstan - hence the name. Altaï is distilled using three continuous stills and filtered through silver birch charcoal.
Comment: The smooth, almost honeyed mouthfeel suggests added sugar but features an aggressive black pepper attack. Notes of citrus and vanilla give way to a grainy, citrus finish.

●●●●○

ARMADALE

Scottish Vodka
40% **alc./vol.** (80°proof)
www.armadalevodka.com
Producer: Girvan Distillery, Scotland
UK agent: William Grant & Sons
US agent: William Grant & Sons USA Inc.

Hip hop stars have featured liquor brands in their lyrics and videos for years, and cognac brands, in particular, have benefited from this trend. Armadale vodka takes the practice to its logical conclusion: a partnership between a distiller (William Grant) and an urban music label, Roc-A-Fella Records.

Roc-A-Fella, one of the largest urban record labels, was co-founded by hip hop moguls Damon 'Dame' Dash, Kareem 'Biggs' Burke and Shawn Carter (aka Jay-Z). It was Biggs who chose the vodka's name, apparently, after seeing Armadale Castle on the Scottish island of Skye.

Armadale is distilled from wheat and barley by a three column process at William Grant's Girvan distillery in Scotland. The clear bottle features a black banner wrapped horizontally around it, and a small red plaid tartan design.
Comment: A fairly neutral palate offers some spicy, aniseed grain character and a mild cracked black pepper burn that continues through the finish.

●●●●●

BELVEDERE

Polish Vodka
40% **alc./vol.** (80°proof)
www.belvederevodka.com
Producer: Polmos Zyrardów (CL Finance), Poland
UK agent: Moët Hennessy UK
US agent: Millennium Import LLC

Launched in 1996, a year before Grey Goose, Belvedere is widely regarded as the world's first super premium vodka. It is named after Poland's Presidential Palace in Warsaw and, like the building, translates as 'beautiful to see'. The tall, slender, frosted bottle has a drawing of the palace screen printed on the back, which appears through the clear window on the front magnified by vodka and framed by two snow-covered trees.

Belvedere hails from the small town of Zyrardów in the Mazovian plains, west of Warsaw. It is made from 100% Dankowskie

Zlote or 'Gold' Rye, a strain of rye grain that has been inter-crossed six times over a century and grows well in Mazovian soil. After distillation by a three column process - hence the claim that it is "quadruple distilled" - Belvedere is finished in a traditional copper pot still. It is filtered through charcoal and cellulose.
Comment: A pleasing faint vanilla-ed nose leads to a wonderfully clean, silky smooth palate with a creamy mouthfeel with hints of vanilla, white chocolate and prickly black pepper.

BLACK DEATH

English Vodka
40% **alc./vol.** (80°proof)
www.gjgreenall.co.uk
Producer: The Greenalls Group Plc, Warrington, England
UK agent: The Greenalls Group Plc
US agent: Cabo Distributing

Greenalls launched this vodka in 1992 and claim it "originated in Iceland in 1906, when the Sigurdsson family produced a clear, potent spirit which Icelanders called 'Svarta Daudi' or 'Black Death'".

Spirits have been distilled in Iceland almost since the Vikings colonised the island in 864AD. However, due to the strength of The Good Temperance Movement, prohibition was in effect for much of the modern era, and only began to come to an end in 1921 when the government legalised the sale of wine to enable Spain to pay for salt cod imports in kind and created a state-owned drinks monopoly. Spirits, in fact, remained banned until 1935 and due to an oversight in framing the legislation, the sale of beer over 2.2% alc./vol. remained illegal until 1st March 1989.

What many Icelanders know as 'Svarti Daudi' (pronounced Swat-D-Doli) is a type of brennivin, a cumin-flavoured aquavit. The black label, almost unchanged since the drinks monopoly created it - apparently as a warning of its effects - gained the drink its nickname, which translates as 'Black Death'.

Black Death's renown spread after 10th May 1940 when British troops set up bases in Iceland, and English and American forces based on the island started ordering Black Death in the local bars. (It was this or wine, since beer was still illegal.) This English vodka tastes very different to brennivin, which many consider the authentic Icelandic Black Death, and features a skull wearing a black top hat on the label.

BLAVOD

English Black Vodka
40% **alc./vol.** (80°proof)
www.blavod.com
Producer: Made & bottled in England by Hayman Distillers Ltd for Blavod Black Vodka Ltd, London, England
UK agent: Blavod Drinks Ltd
US agent: Blavod Extreme Spirits USA

Vodka is known for being clear, clean, relatively neutral in taste and so remarkably mixable. So what would lead someone to make a black vodka that combines with orange juice to produce something not dissimilar to a toxic spill? Well, dear readers, the PR story goes something like this:

One day Mark Dorman was drinking vodka in a bar in California's Napa Valley, when he overheard a customer ordering coffee and the bartender asking him whether he wanted black or white. He wondered why vodka drinkers were not offered a similar choice – and launched Blavod black vodka in 1996.

This supposed neutral vodka is distilled from molasses in England by Hayman Distillers Ltd. Its colour comes from black catechu, a Burmese herb.
Comment: The colour is more aquamarine than black, the white pepper nose proffers off-putting hints of coke and cigarette ash, and the rather jagged palate features hints of aniseed and liquorice with a white peppery edge. Black vodka is a great marketing gimmick, but it's hard to see a use for this apart from as an aquamarine float on gimmicky Halloween shots.

BOLS

Polish Vodka
40% **alc./vol.** (80°proof)
Producer: Unicom-Bols Group, Oborniki Wielkopolskie, Poland
UK agent: Not generally available
US agent: William Grant

Distilled from rye, this vodka is the result of a joint venture between Bols and Polish partner Unicom PZ. It became one of the top selling brands in its native Poland soon after its launch in 1995, partly due to a marketing campaign that cleverly bypassed the local laws against alcohol advertising.

Following ABN AMRO Capital's 2006 investment in Lucas Bols, the Dutch company acquired exclusive rights to Bols vodka everywhere outside its two key markets, Poland and Russia.
Comment: A clean neutral nose leads to a sweet and smooth palate with nutty peppery hints. Lacks character when compared to some other Polish vodkas.

BORU SILVER

Irish Vodka
40% **alc./vol.** (80°proof)
www.boruirishvodka.com
Producer: The Boru Vodka Co. (Castle Brands Inc.), Dublin, Republic of Ireland
UK agent: Castle Brands Spirits Group
US agent: Castle Brands Spirits Group

Boru is made from Irish barley and spring water at Carbery Distillers, County Cork, and is filtered through 10ft of Atlantic Irish oak charcoal. The name comes from the first high king of Ireland who defeated the Viking invasion of 1014, a date commemorated on every bottle with a raised motif.

The producers, who describe their brand as quadruple distilled, buy in barley-based neutral spirit then further rectify it before hydrating with locally sourced water. I am assured by the brand owner that there is "absolutely no glycerine or sugar added to the 40%". (A 37.5% alc./vol. version is also available.)
Comment: The smooth barley sweetness offers some citrus, peppery hints, and retains a certain perkiness throughout.

CAPE NORTH

European Vodka
40% **alc./vol.** (80°proof)
www.capenorth.se
Producer: Gabriel Boudier, France for Cape North
Vodka Company AB, Drottningholm, Sweden
UK agent: Emporia Brands Ltd
US agent: Soon to be appointed

Cape North is the latest European vodka to hit the
UK and US in a slick frosted bottle for a slice of the
lucrative premium vodka market. The bottle
suggests it is a Viking incursion, thanks to a
prominent Swedish flag and the boast that it is
"made from Swedish spring water".

Gabriel Boudier, a family-owned company
based in Dijon, France, and famous for producing
fruit liqueurs, take neutral spirit made from
French winter wheat and redistill it in small
copper pot stills. The resulting distillate is filtered
through diatomaceous soil using a Kieselguhr
filter. Finally, it is reduced to bottling strength with
water shipped from one of Sweden's most famous
springs.
**Comment: Subtle hints of raspberry and sucrose
on the nose lead to a clean, very smooth, almost
oily palate that suggests the addition of glycerine.
Subtle orange zest and malty notes add interest.
Clean, cracked black pepper finish.**

CHARBAY

American Vodka
40% **alc./vol.** (80°proof)
www.charbay.com
Producer: Domaine Charbay Distillers, St.
Helena, California, USA
UK agent: Not generally available
US agent: Domaine Charbay Distillers

Domaine Charbay is a small distillery atop Spring
Mountain in California's Napa Valley, owned and
operated by the Karakasevic Family. They distil
their vodka from American Midwest grain using a
stainless steel alembic Charentais still - the vodka
passes through the apparatus four times.
**Comment: Very subtle, minerally, grainy nose.
The clean, minerally palate has a very oily
mouthfeel (have they added glycerine?) with
subtle aniseedy, grainy notes. Very clean, soft,
lightly peppered finish.**

CHARODEI

Belarusian Vodka
Producer: Vseslav Charodei, Minsk, Belarus
UK agent: Not generally available
US agent: American Belarusian Import Export
Company Ltd

Pronounced 'Share-a-Day', Charodei is named
after the Belarus ruler Vseslav Charodei and his
picture adorns the frosted glass bottle. It is
distilled from Russian wheat and, unusually for a
Russian style vodka, is produced without charcoal
filtration.
**Comment: The grainy aniseed nose offers a minty
freshness with hints of citrus and spice. The
palate is clean, sweet and rounded, dominated by
aniseed with top notes of spearmint and vanilla.**

CHOPIN

Polish Vodka
40% **alc./vol.** (80°proof)
Producer: Podlaska Wytwórnia Wódek Polmos
S.A. (Moët Hennessy), Siedlce, Poland
UK agent: Not known
US agent: Millennium Import LLC

Despite initial opposition from the Polish Ministry
of Culture, this vodka is named after the great
composer. The frosted glass bottle has a window
on the front through which the Delacroix portrait
of Chopin on the rear of the bottle appears,
magnified by the vodka.

Launched in 1993, Chopin is based on
Stobrawa potatoes handpicked in the Mazovia
region of Poland and distilled using a four column
process. It requires approximately ten pounds of
potatoes to create just one bottle of Chopin vodka.
**Comment: A very subtle nose with a touch of
apple gives way to a smooth, slightly sweet palate
that offers vegetal, almost cabbagey hints,
alongside light pepper spice and nutty notes.**

CHRISTIANIA

Norwegian Vodka
40% **alc./vol.** (80°proof)
www.christianiavodka.com
Producer: Nordic Beverage AS, Norway

This Norwegian vodka is distilled using a six
column process from potatoes grown in
Trondelag, then filtered firstly through charcoal
and secondly using an air filtration process. It is
named after King Christian IV of Norway (reigned
1588-1648) – it's not clear if he was a vodka fan.
**Comment: The light, almost creamy, smooth
palate features mild pepper notes and hints of
vegetable.**

CÎROC

French Vodka
40% **alc./vol.** (80°proof)
www.cirocvodka.com
Producer: Moët Hennessy & Diageo, Courbevoie,
France
UK agent: Reserve Brands Group (Diageo GB)
US agent: Schieffelin & Somerset

Pronounced 'Si-Rock' and launched in the US in
February 2003, Cîroc is positioned as a luxury
vodka. It was the first vodka to be made
exclusively from grape spirit, and is based on and
marketed around an aromatic wine from the
Gaillac region of southwest France - known simply
as Mauzac wine. The main grape in the blend,
Mauzac Blanc, buds and ripens late, so is usually
picked well into autumn when early frosts are
common - hence the term 'Snap Frost' on the
bottle. Mauzac grapes grow in vineyards outside
the village walls of Cordes-sur-Ciel at elevations
of some 300m, and the name Cîroc combines two
French words: 'cîme', meaning summit and
'roche', meaning rock – in reference to their lofty
home.

The Mauzac Blanc grapes are cold macerated
and cold fermented. The wine is then held under a
vacuum at just above zero before being distilled
continuously; twice, through a specially adapted

copper pot still which forces the distillate through a small column before passing through a long swan neck.

Quite separately, in another distillery in Cognac, neutral spirit made from Ugni Blanc grapes is rectified through four column stills to produce an extremely pure spirit. This refined grape neutral spirit is then taken to the distillery where the Mauzac spirit was produced and blended with small amounts of it. The blend is twice distilled through the custom-built copper pot still, blended with a hint of sugar and reduced to bottling strength.

Cîroc's tall slender bottle is embossed with a cockerel perched on a cluster of grapes to symbolise the Gaillac region and its grape growing heritage.
Comment: A dusty, lightly citrus nose leads to a fresh, clean palate that combines lemon zest flavours with a light peppery burn. The finish is dominated by pepper, and the whole tastes rather like a very subtle citrus vodka.

CRISTALL

Russian Vodka
40% **alc./vol.** (80°proof)
www.cristall.com
Producer: Cristall Distillery, Moscow, Russia
UK agent: Not known
US agent: Frank Pesce International

One of a range of vodkas in the Cristall Moscow Signature Series, this Russian vodka is twice filtered through carbon granules made from the wood of Russia's native birch.
Comment: Although thin, the vodka maintains a nicely rounded wheatyness, while aniseed and caramel hints add depth. The finish is spicy pepper.

CITADELLE

French Vodka
40% **alc./vol.** (80°proof)
www.citadellevodka.com
Producer: Cognac Ferrand, Ars, France
UK agent: Eaux de Vie
US agent: Not known

Citadelle is produced from Capet, a variety of wheat, using a five column distillation process. Unusually, this includes what Cognac Ferrand describes as a "micro oxygenation process", which involves passing oxygen bubbles through the distillate. The finished spirit is then blended with fresh spring water from the tiny village of Gensac in the Grande Champagne area to reduce it to bottling strength.
Comment: A nose of boiled fruity sweets and poached pear leads to an oily, smooth palate (added glycerine?) that starts with sweet pear drop and builds with black pepperspice. Oily pear notes continue through the peppery spicy finish.

DANZKA RED

Danish Vodka
40% **alc./vol.** (80°proof)
www.danzka.com
Producer: Belvédère Scandinavia A/S, Herlev, Denmark
UK agent: Not known
US agent: Not known

Packaged in a distinctive aluminium bottle, Danzka was developed in 1985 for the US market and is made from Danish wheat using a continuous six-column distillation process. After diluting with demineralised water, the spirit is triple filtered through activated carbon and membrane filters.
Comment: Quite a rich aniseed flavour is balanced by sweetness that emerges mid-palate and light, fresh citrus top notes. Aniseed lingers in the finish.

CRACOVIA CLASSIC

Polish Vodka
40% **alc./vol.** (80°proof)
www.polmos.krakow.pl
Producer: Destylernia Polmos w Krakówie S.A., Kraków, Poland
UK agent: Malcolm Cowen Ltd
US agent: Not known

Launched in 1996 and pronounced 'Crack-Ov-Ya', this premium Polish vodka is named after the city of Kraków (which was once the capital of Poland) and the city's coat of arms features on the label. Cracovia is distilled from rectified potato spirit filtered through carbon. Production takes place close to the historic salt mines, which have been in operation for over six centuries.
Comment: A somewhat burnt candy nose leads to a sweet but rather jagged palate where creamy potatoes are served with butter, vanilla and a dusting of black pepper.

DIVA

Scottish Vodka
40% **alc./vol.** (80°proof)
www.divavodka.com
Producer: Blackwood Distillers, Lerwick, Shetland, Scotland
UK agent: Blackwood Distillers
US agent: Blackwood USA

Diva is distilled from wheat using a three column process and filtered through Nordic birch charcoal. It then travels through a dense column of gems, including diamonds, rubies and emeralds, for a final filtration before bottling. The distinctive bottle contains a column of gemstones including cubic zirconia, Scottish smoky topaz, pink tourmaline, sky blue topaz, London blue topaz, amethyst, citrine and peridot.
Comment: A minerally, dusty nose leads to a soft, slightly sweet palate (perhaps with the help of glycerine/sugar?), with a cracked black pepper garnish and faint hints of citrus and berry fruits.

DOVGAN ADMIRAL

Russian vodka
40% **alc./vol.** (80°proof)
www.dovgan.co.uk
Producer: Deyros, Buturlinovka, Voronezh, Russia
UK agent: Blue Planet Spirits
US agent: Not known

The Buturlinovskiy distillery is Russia's oldest working distillery and dates back to 1901. The recipe to which Dovgan Admiral is made is also said to be old, and apparently dates back to 1885. Dovgan is produced in only one distillery – Dovgan's owners rectify their own neutral wheat spirit rather than buying it in from another distiller. This undergoes a sand column purification process before being hydrated with water drawn from the distillery's own well.
Comment: Subtle aniseed features in a clean, cracked black pepper palate with a hint of vanilla. The peppery finish is clean and lasting.

EFFEN

Dutch Vodka
40% **alc./vol.** (80°proof)
www.effenvodka.com
Producer: Hooghoudt Distillers B.V., Groningen, The Netherlands
UK agent: Hi-Spirits
US agent: Planet 10 Spirits

Launched in the US in 2003 and then in the UK in September 2006, Effen is named after a Dutch term meaning 'smooth, even and balanced'. The vodka is distilled from wheat grown in Northern Holland using a continuous distillation process. Its makers claim their vodka "is distilled at much lower temperatures than other luxury vodkas to avoid 'caramelisation' of the distillate". They apparently also use a 'bottom-up' filtration process which forces the liquid through peat rather than the more usual charcoal.
 Effen is stylishly presented in a rubber sleeve-covered bottle. Each seamless rubber sleeve is handmade and hand-applied one bottle at a time by spraying with water and then slipping over the bottle. No adhesive is required as the rubber sleeve sits in a ridge in the bottle.
Comment: A neutral nose gives little away. The palate is very clean with a silky mouthfeel. For those who like their vodka clean and neutral in style this is almost impossible to fault. I have to admit to finding the grippable, rubber-coated bottle strangely appealing.

ERISTOFF

French Vodka
37.5% **alc./vol.** (75°proof)
Producer: Bacardi-Martini, Beaucaire, France
UK agent: Not generally available
US agent: Bacardi-Martini

Allegedly created for Nikolai Alexandrovich Eristoff, a Georgian prince, in 1806. The story goes after the Russian revolution the prince took the recipe to Europe where production later resumed in Milan. In 1960, the brand was taken over by Martini & Rossi. It enjoys volume sales in mainland Europe where it is positioned as a standard vodka.
Comment: Very neutral nose gives little away. The palate is raw alcohol with little character or finesse though, equally, there is nothing actually unpleasant in what is a very clean, highly rectified spirit.

FINLANDIA

Finnish Vodka
40% **alc. /vol.** (80°proof)
www.finlandia-vodka.com
Producer: Rajamäki Distillery, Finland for Brown-Forman
UK agent: Bacardi Brown-Forman UK
US agent: Bacardi Brown-Forman

The Finns learned the art of vodka distillation from their Russian neighbours and by the mid-1800s practically every household owned some kind of distillation apparatus. This inevitably led to regulations outlawing DIY distillation, and, in 1919, two years after Finland declared its independence from Russia, distillation all but ceased with the onset of Finnish Prohibition. When this was finally lifted on 5th April 1932, the state took over exclusive control of distillation. Alko, the state-owned company, established Finlandia in 1970 and a year later the brand became the first Scandinavian vodka to be sold in the US. It is now owned by the giant American Brown Forman Corporation.
 Finlandia is distilled from Finnish six-row barley (a variety of barley found in Nordic countries that gives a lower yield than two-row barley) using seven state-of-the-art, 30m-high stainless steel distillation columns in the Koskenkorva distillery. The distilled spirit is then transported by rail to the historic distillery in Rajamäki (originally established in 1888 as a yeast factory for bread manufacture).
 Here it is blended with water drawn from nearby glacial springs that are so pure their water requires no filtration or chemical purification. To protect this precious water source from contamination, the company owns vast tracts of unspoiled wilderness in the vicinity of the well.
 During the Winter War (1939-1940) with the Russians, the Rajamäki distillery contributed to the Finnish war effort by producing Molotov cocktails responsible for putting hundreds of soviet tanks out of commission. Over half-a-million bottles containing the volatile concoction of alcohol, paraffin, gasoline and tar were produced at Rajamäki.
 The red sun and the white reindeer on the front of Finlandia's bottle owe their origin to a Finnish legend that goes something like this: One winter night, a spell was cast on a beautiful young girl transforming her into a fearsome

43,000 RUSSIANS DIED FROM DRINKING BOOTLEG VODKA IN 1997. FAKE BOOZE CAPTURED BY OFFICIALS IS TURNED INTO BRAKE FLUID OR WINDOW CLEANER.

white reindeer. Many men hunted the beast due to its valuable white hide including the girl's boyfriend who had no idea what had become of his lover. He, like many other hunters before him, fell victim to her antlers and received a fatal wound. He, in turn, inflicted a lethal gash to the reindeer's neck. The blood broke the spell, the reindeer became a girl again and the couple died in each other's arms. The legend goes on to say that any wish you make will be granted if you are lucky enough to see the sun, the moon and a white reindeer at the same time.

Comment: An almost neutral nose is the precursor to an extremely clean palate with sweet barley notes balanced by lightly spicy, nutty hints. Long, lightly black peppery finish.

FLAGSHIP BLUE LABEL

Russian Vodka
40% **alc. /vol.** (80°proof)
www.flagshipvodka.co.uk
Producer: Russian Wine & Vodka Company, Chernogolovka Distillery, Moscow, Russia
UK agent: Flagship Vodka Ltd
US agent: Not known

Created in 1998, the Russian name of this vodka transliterates as 'flag man'. Tsar Peter I was the first Russian Admiral and became respectfully known as 'Mister Flagship of Russian Fleet'. Flagship Vodka is made at the Chernogolovka Distillery near Moscow from Russian wheat using a three column distillation process and is hydrated with refined natural spring water.
Comment: Lots of wheat on the nose, very characterful vodka with full bodied palate and hints of aniseed.

42 BELOW

New Zealand Vodka
42% **alc. /vol.** (84°proof)
www.42below.com
Producer: Pacific Dawn Distillers (Bacardi Martini), Wellington, New Zealand.
UK agent: Bacardi Martini
US agent: Bacardi Martini

42 Below is named due to New Zealand, its country of origin, lying on the 42nd parallel. It was created in 1996 by Geoff Ross who first started distilling in his garage with a still his wife bought him. Hooked, he made the move from the advertising industry to set up his 42 Below vodka brand and sold the first bottling in 1999. Christmas 2006 brought Geoff a very lucrative buyout deal from Bacardi. I bet his wife is happy she bought him that still.

42 Below's marketing centres on its location and the purity of the spring water used. It is distilled from GM-free wheat using a four column distillation process and undergoes 35 levels of filtration.
Comment: Hints of aniseed emerge from a clean nose. The clean palate sees initial sweetness quickly followed by a strong cracked black pepper burn which dominates subtle hints of aniseed. Black pepper lasts through the fiery finish.

FRÏS

Swedish Vodka
40% **alc. /vol.** (80°proof)
www.frisvodka.com
Producer: Frïs Skandia A/S (V&S Group), Stockholm, Sweden
UK agent: Maxxium UK
US agent: The Absolut Spirits Company (Shaw Ross)

Pronounced 'Freeze', this vodka's name comes from the Danish word meaning 'frost and ice', a reference to its unusual production method. It is distilled from wheat grain using a six column distillation process and a freeze distillation process unique to Frïs. This patented process is applied in the second column, named the 'Lutter Column'. Here, very low temperatures are used to freeze unwanted fusel oil impurities into solids so they can be removed from the alcohol, which remains liquid. The finished spirit is hydrated with softened water drawn from artesian wells in Northern Jutland. Finally, this vodka is infused with minerals before filtration.
Comment: Very neutral on both the nose and the palate, this vodka is very clean with fresh grated black pepper alcohol.

GRAFFITI

Scottish Vodka
40% **alc./vol.** (80°proof)
www.graffitispirit.com
Producer: Graffiti Spirit, Bellshill, Scotland
UK agent: Lombard Brands Ltd
US agent: Wein-Bauer Inc.

Launched in 2002, Graffiti is made in Scotland from wheat and malted barley using an eight column distillation process. Graffiti is bottled without carbon filtration, which is considered unnecessary due to the high standard of distillation.
Comment: Bran and cereal nose leads to a palate with notes of dry nuts, aniseed, roasted pine nuts and hints of dry malt extract. Peppery, nutty finish.

GREY GOOSE

French Vodka
40% **alc./vol.** (80°proof)
www.greygoosevodka.com
Producer: H Mounier (Bacardi-Martini), Cognac, France.
UK agent: Bacardi Brown-Forman
US agent: Grey Goose Importing Co (Bacardi-Martini)

Launched in the US in 1997, Grey Goose enjoyed immediate success, but we Brits had to wait until August 2000 before it crossed the English Channel from Cognac where it's made. Grey Goose was made for the American market by an American. It was the idea of Sidney Frank, a legendary drinks marketer and boss of his eponymous drinks importing company. His vision was to create a vodka that his fellow Americans would be only too happy to pay a premium for. France, particularly Cognac, is perceived by Americans as being a place where quality spirits are produced, so that's where he sourced his new vodka.

Sidney Frank died a contented billionaire in January 2006 at the age of 86, as a couple of years earlier he had sold Grey Goose to Bacardi for $2.2 billion, the highest price ever paid for a single liquor brand.

Originally, I, and many others, were led to believe that this was a multi-grain vodka, a blend of four different grains - rye, wheat, barley and corn. However, after Bacardi took over the brand in August 2004 it emerged that Grey Goose was made from 100% wheat from La Beauce, France and is distilled using a five column distillation process in France's Cognac region. (In the beginning, stories of traditional copper pot stills abounded.)

Grey Goose is hydrated with artesian spring water originating in the French Massif Central and passing through Champagne limestone to emerge in the Gensac spring in Cognac. The limestone makes the water soft and slightly sweet and this is said to lie at the heart of Grey Goose's character.

However, its real heart and soul came courtesy of Sidney Frank.

Comment: A very neutral nose with the merest whiff of nuts and fennel. The clean palate has a slightly creamy mouthfeel and a grainy cracked pepper sweetness with delicate hints of citrus and aniseed. Clean, sweet peppered finish.

HANGAR ONE STRAIGHT

American Vodka
40% **alc./vol.** (80°proof)
www.hangarone.com
Producer: St. George Spirits, Alameda, California, USA
UK agent: Not yet available
US agent: Craft Distillers Portfolio

Hangar One is named after the distillery's rented space at the old Alameda Naval Air Station in California. The huge hangar sits on the edge of a disused runway (now a bird sanctuary) overlooking the Bay with panoramic views of the Bay Bridge and San Francisco. The colossal space offers plenty of scope for expansion and Frisbee-throwing, as St. George Spirits is very much a boutique distiller with its bottling line and stock barely occupying a quarter of the available space. Still, they've used the space wisely and installed a massage parlour and a dinky Arnold Holstein state-of-the-art still.

Established in 2001, Hangar One is the brainchild of two revered Californian craft distillers, Jörg Rupf of St. George Spirits and Ansley Coale of Germain-Robin brandy. They, aided by the enthusiasm and care of Lance Winters, use eaux de vie distilling techniques to create a straight vodka with real character and flavoured vodkas with genuine distilled flavour rather than flavoured by use of essences.

To make their straight vodka they use neutral spirit distilled in the Midwest from Great Plains wheat as a backdrop and blend this with a distillate of Viognier grapes made in their own tiny Holstein alembic still. This beautiful little still has a large boil ball to encourage reflux and a three bladed paddle to keep the wine moving in the pot and prevent burning. The vapour passes through two short columns, the first with twelve plates and the second with four plates. Between 10% and 25% Viognier distillate is blended with the wheat neutral spirit depending on the wine distillation and careful blending ensures consistency between batches.

The good folk at Hangar One rightly shun the idea of adding sugar, glycerine or anything else to their vodka.

Comment: Clean nose with only the merest hint of cereal, violet and pear. The palate is rounded and soft with pleasant grainy notes and hints of red pepper, cracked black pepper, pear, violet and toasted aniseed bagel. The finish is long and clean.

HEAVY WATER

Norwegian Vodka
40% **alc./vol.** (80°proof)
www.heavy-water.com
Producer: Heavy Water International AS, 42 Oscarsgt, 0258 Oslo, Norway
UK agent: Not generally available
US agent: Heavy Water International AS

Launched in October 2005, this vodka derives its name from the rare isotope, D20, which scientists call 'heavy water'. Heavy Water Vodka is blended and bottled by J&J Nordic at the Bloomberg estate, near Källby in southwest Sweden, on the shore of Northern Europe's largest lake, Lake Vänern. It is made from Scandinavian-grown winter wheat that is fermented and blended with water from a deep artisian well, then continuously distilled.

Heavy Water vodka is packaged in a very distinctive, almost Action Man-like squat bottle with a chunky, ridged plastic closure. A rod bearing the brand name hangs inside the bottle - a reference to the use of heavy water in nuclear reactors.

Comment: A dusty nose with hints of fennel leads to a bran cereal palate with aniseedy notes, chased by more subtle toasted almond notes and the merest hint of citrus zest. The mouthfeel is surprisingly creamy. The finish is black pepper followed by a subtle but lingering taste of cream soda.

HUZZAR

Irish Vodka
37.5% **alc. /vol.** (75°proof)
Producer: Irish Distillers Group Plc (Group Pernod-Ricard), Midleton Distillery, County Cork, Republic of Ireland.
UK agent: Pernod Ricard UK
US agent: Pernod Ricard USA

Launched in 1969, this vodka takes its name from the Huzzars, 15th century cavalry officers famous for their sword skills. Although in the past it has sported fake Russian imagery, it is very much an Irish vodka, being distilled using a three column process at Midleton Distillery, County Cork, Ireland.

ICEBERG

Canadian Vodka
40% **alc. /vol.** (80°proof)
www.icebergvodka.net
Producer: Canadian Iceberg Vodka Corp., St. John's, Newfoundland, Canada.
UK agent: Drinks Company Ltd
US agent: Cabo Distributing

First produced in September 1995, Iceberg vodka comes in a unique bottle designed to resemble a chiselled piece of ice. Ice is harvested by former cod fishermen from 12,000 year-old icebergs off the northeast coast of Newfoundland as they float south from the Canadian Arctic (they are licensed to harvest 72,000 metric tonnes per year). This is melted and filtered, then blended with neutral spirit which is sourced from Ontario where it is distilled using a three-column process from Canadian sweetcorn.

Comment: A clean nose with hints of buttery corn leads to a clean, fairly neutral palate where the corn notes found in the nose emerge mid-palate. Slight underlying sweetness on the palate leads to a finish that starts dry and ends slightly bitter.

IDÔL

French Vodka
40% **alc. /vol.** (80°proof)
www.idolvodka.com
Producer: L'Heriter-Guyot, Burgundy, France
UK agent: Not generally available
US agent: Boisset America

First launched in 1999, Idôl is made from small, hand-picked Chardonnay and Pinot Noir grapes from Burgundy, France. It is distilled seven times and filtered five times and hydrated with water from a spring in the Côte d'Or, which is filtered using reverse osmosis. The result is a very neutral vodka which Boisset, its owners, claim has "zero measurable impurities".

The purple colour of the brand name is apparently meant to emphasise its grape-based origins.

IMPERIA

Russian Vodka
40% **alc. /vol.** (80°proof)
www.russianstandard.com
Producer: Russian Standard Company, St Petersburg, Russia
UK agent: Iceberg CL
US agent: Rémy Cointreau USA

Launched in the US in Autumn 2005, this is the super premium flagship vodka of the Russian Standard Company. It is distilled at Russian Standard's new US$60 million distillery on the outskirts of St Petersburg from Russian winter wheat using an eight column distillation process. It is then filtered through quartz crystals.

The 1894 date statement on the tall hexagonal bottle refers to a decree given that year by Tzar Alexander III that vodka must meet minimum requirements for his seal of approval. The specifications which a vodka had to meet were determined by Dimitri Mendeleev, the scientist famed for creating the Periodic Table of elements.
Comment: A grainy nose with hints of cream soda leads to a palate with buttery grainy notes garnished with aniseed, fennel and slightly bitter cracked black pepper. Long, creamy, but bitter, slightly peppered finish. Refined and rich in character this vodka is typically Russian in style.

IVAN THE TERRIBLE

Russian Vodka
40% **alc. /vol.** (80°proof)
www.ivantheterriblevodka.com
Producer: Ladoga Distillery, St. Petersburg, Russia
UK agent: DTN Brands Ltd
US agent: Not generally available

Named after Tzar Ivan the IV, better known under his nickname of Ivan the Terrible (Ivan Grozny in Russia), Ivan may be better known for decapitating his enemies and killing his own son but he also makes it into the history books for establishing a government vodka monopoly. In 1540, he issued distilling licenses to the boyars (the nobility) and outlawed distillation by any unlicensed distillery.

The Ivan the Terrible vodka bottle is a copy of a Russian decanter called Romanoff's Schtof and is finished with a hand-made glass stopper (so careful how you rip of the plastic sleeve which seals it in place).

Comment: Rich toasted grain flavours with cracked black pepper spice and hints of aniseed neatly sums up the nose, palate and finish of this typically Russian-style vodka. Big bold flavours - none of your wimpy Western neutrality here.

JEAN-MARC XO

French Vodka
40% **alc./vol.** (80°proof)
www.jeanmarcxovodka.com
Producer: Daucourt, Cognac, France
UK agent: Not generally available
US agent: Daucourt Martin Imports, LLC

Named after him and made by him in Cognac in France, Jean-Marc makes his vodka from four different French wheat grains: Ysengrain, Orvantis, Azteque, and Chargeur. He separates the grain from its chaff before fermentation in order to eliminate any bitterness and then distils nine times using small traditional French copper elambic stills. Jean-Marc uses only Gensac spring water from the Cognac area and is charcoal-filtered through Limousin oak.

JEWEL OF RUSSIA CLASSIC

Russian Vodka
40% **alc./vol.** (80°proof)
www.jewelofrussia.com
Producer: Chernogolovka Distillery (Ost-alco Ltd), Moscow, Russia
US agent: BMC Imports
UK agent: Jewel of Russia Ltd

Jewel of Russia is packaged in a distinctive square-shaped, decanter-style bottle with silk cord and red wax seal, which, according to its makers, replicates a 300 year-old bottle design. It is made from Russian winter wheat and rye and undergoes a special five-step slow-flow filtration process.
Comment: Neutral style nose, which exudes only a hint of black pepper and aniseed. Palate starts silky smooth with cracked black pepper spice building. Clean and fresh with a hint of aniseed and good grain notes. Clean, peppery finish.

JEWEL OF RUSSIA ULTRA

Russian Vodka
40% **alc./vol.** (80°proof)
www.jewelofrussia.com
Producer: Chernogolovka Distillery (Ost-alco Ltd), Moscow, Russia
US agent: BMC Imports
UK agent: Jewel of Russia Ltd

According to its makers, this vodka is made from winter wheat and rye using "ancient recipes", but due to modern rectification "special proprietary techniques are used to restore the original historic taste of Russian vodka". The square decanter-style bottle is something of a work of art, with a traditional Russian hand-painted miniature scene on each bottle, individually signed and numbered by the artist.
Comment: A whiff of lemon zest and peppery spice and aniseed on the nose. The palate starts oily and gains peppery spice. I find what I can only describe as artificial lemony notes amongst the pepper.

KAUFFMAN LUXURY 2002 VINTAGE

Russian Vodka
40% **alc./vol.** (80°proof)
www.vodkakauffman.com
Producer: WH Import Company, Moscow, Russia
UK agent: Eaux de Vie Ltd
US agent: Not generally available

This super luxury priced vodka was self-named and created in 2002 by Dr. Mark Kaoufman, President of the National Wine & Food Association and author of a series of wine books. His vodkas are vintage releases, made from wheat of a single harvest only, it is claimed, " in the years when the finest wheat grains are identified". The water used to make Kauffman Vodka is double filtered through Sodium-cation filters. The vodka itself is filtered through birch-coal columns and quartz sand.

The distinctive, perfume-style bottles were designed by Saint Gobaine in France. Two vintage styles are produced: 'Selected Russian' vodka (tall bottle) and 'Luxury Russian' vodka (squat bottle). Only 25,000 bottles per vintage are made and each bottle carries a limited-edition number. The vintage is indicated by a clear sticker on the back of the bottle with the year visible by looking through the bottle from the front.
Comment: A delicate nose with hints of peachy rye leads to a very soft palate with an oily mouthfeel. Delicately flavoured with very subtle toasted rye bread and apple. Did the designers of this over-the-top bottle intend it to be used to stuff codpieces? Please let's reserve this style of packaging for the perfume shelves. I'd have scored this higher if it wasn't in a comedy bottle.

KETEL ONE

Dutch Vodka
40% **alc./vol.** (80°proof)
www.ketelone.com
Producer: Nolet Distillery, Schiedam, The Netherlands.
UK agent: InSpirit Brands Ltd
US agent: Nolet Spirits USA

Ketel One vodka is the creation of one of Holland's oldest distilling dynasties. The Nolet family of Schiedam has been distilling since 1691 when Joannes Nolet started his distillation business in Schiedam, Holland, near the mouth of the great river Maas, on the North Sea. The Nolet family were one of the first of many distillers to establish themselves in Schiedam; attracted to the area due to its accessibility to shipping and its close proximity to one of Holland's largest grain actions. By 1882 the Nolet distillery was one of 394 distilleries operating there. Today there are only four.

The Dutch refer to their pot stills as 'ketels', thus this vodka is named after the Nolets' original 'Distilleerketel #1', which dates back to 1864. The spirit produced in this hand-stoked, coal-fired alembic copper pot still is blended with that produced at the distillery's other, similar, but gas fired copper pot stills. This wheat-based spirit is then rested in tanks before being charcoal filtered to ensure its purity.

Ten generations after Joannes, Carolus Nolet now runs the company with his two sons, Carl and Bob. They introduced Ketel One to the US in 1992 where it has since enjoyed phenomenal growth. This success story is being repeated in the UK where the brand launched in 1999.
Comment: Lightly spicy nose. Smooth, moderately sweet, clean palate with aniseed wheat character, subtle hints of citrus, sweet liquorice and overripe banana. Lightly spiced black pepper and caramel finish.

KOSKENKORVA

Finnish Vodka
40% **alc. /vol.** (80°proof)
Producer: Primalco OY, Helsinki, Finland
UK agent: Not generally available
US agent: Not generally available

This is a Finnish vodka made from barley and named after the distillery of the same name where it is produced. Built in 1938 and modernised in 1987, this is also where the neutral spirit that is the base of Finlandia vodka is distilled. Pronounced 'Cross-Ken-Corr-Va', this state-owned vodka was launched in July 1953 and is the best selling vodka in Finland.
Comment: An extremely clean vodka with a sweet grainy edge.

KRÓLEWSKA (RED CAPSULE)

Polish Vodka
40% **alc. /vol.** (80°proof)
www.vsluksusowa.pl
Producer: V&S Luksusowa Zielona Góra S.A., Zielona Góra, Lubuski, Poland
UK agent: Marblehead Brand Development Ltd
US agent: Not generally available

Pronounced 'Crewe-Lev-Ska', literally meaning 'king', this 'Royal Vodka' is packaged in a tall, ecclesiastical-style bottle depicting a stained glass window from the medieval church of Mariacki in Kraków, once capital of Poland and the place of residence of the Polish kings. The three panes printed on the back of the bottle are viewed through the vodka, which has a magnifying effect, and feature the crowned eagle of Poland, the royal coat of arms and the three turrets of the city of Kraków. Launched in 1994, this vodka is triple distilled from rye grain and heavily rectified and filtered (but not charcoal filtered). A blue capped version at 42% alc./vol. is also available.
Comment: A nose with hints of grape and swimming pool leads to a sweet, grainy palate with an oily mouthfeel. Subtle nutty, cracked black pepper spicy notes. Oily, slightly aggressive finish.

KRYSHTAL ETALON

Belarusian Vodka
40% **alc. /vol.** (80°proof)
www.kristal.by
Producer: Minsk Kryshtal Distillery, Oktyabrskaya St, Minsk, Republic of Belarus
UK agent: The Real Vodka Company
US agent: Not known

Launched in 2003, Kryshtal Etalon is the flagship vodka of the Minsk Kryshtal distillery, the oldest (established 1893) and the biggest distiller in Belarus. Kryshtal Etalon is made from a blend of winter wheat and rye using a four column distillation process and is filtered through flint. It is hydrated with water drawn from the distillery's own 293m deep well. According to the distillery's own very informative website, "the formula of vodka Kryshtal Etalon contains high quality grain ethyl rectified alcohol 'Super-Lux', softened flint-processed drinking water, bicarbonate sodium, ascorbic acid, crystalline glucose, iodinated salt".
Comment: An almost neutral nose leads to a palate with silky, creamy mouthfeel and good grain character. The finish is jagged, bitter and peppery.

LEVEL

Swedish Vodka
40% **alc./vol.** (80°proof)
www.levelvodka.com
Producer: Swedish Wine & Spirits Corporation, Stockholm, Sweden.
UK agent: Maxxium UK
US agent: Future Brands

Launched in the US in March 2004, this 'spirit of Absolut' comes in a bottle that's more model-like, being both taller and thinner, than its older sibling Absolut. In deference to its family heritage, Level is graced with a small silver silhouette of the original Absolut bottle sitting like a medallion just under its neck. Its contents are also more sophisticated, being made using both continuous and batch distillation.

Level is distilled from winter wheat grown in Southern Sweden and hydrated using spring water from the same region. It is distilled in the same historic distillery as Absolut in the Swedish town of Åhus.
Comment: A smooth, clean vodka with subtle hints of citrus zest and freshly grated black pepper – good grain character.

LUKSUSOWA SILVER

Polish Vodka
40% **alc./vol.** (80°proof)
www.vsluksusowa.pl
Producer: V&S Luksusowa Zielona Góra S.A., Zielona Góra, Lubuski, Poland
UK agent: Marblehead Brand Development Ltd
US agent: Adamba Imports

Pronounced 'Looks-Uhs-Over', its name literally means 'luxury vodka', a reference to the best of the three grades of vodka traditionally produced in Poland. First made in 1928, Luksusowa is one of the oldest trademarks amongst Polish vodka brands.

It was originally made at Polmos Warsaw and became one of the vodka brands produced by several of the old Polmos compounding plants. In 1999, when the Polmos brands, distilleries and compounders were privatised the brand was bought by Polmos Zielona Góra in Western Poland. Then, in May 2003, the Swedish conglomerate Vin & Sprit AB bought both the brand and Polmos Zielona Góra from the Polish government. Although the label has changed over the years, the bottle has always remained tall and square.

The spirit used to make Luksusowa is produced from potatoes grown along the Baltic Sea coast where the soil is loamy and said to produce potatoes superior in quality. The base spirit is distilled from potatoes at several locations and shipped to Zielona Góra by rail where the potato spirit is blended with water drawn from three deep wells under the plant before being bottled on site. Luksusowa is not charcoal filtered and is naturally sweet without added sugar.

Luksusowa was originally made at 45% alc./vol and a red label version at this strength is still produced. A Black Label variant at 50% alc./vol. is also marketed.
Comment: Subtle mineral grassy nose. Clean palate with creamy mouthfeel and sweet grassy, mineral notes and faint hints of creamy mashed potatoes. The finish is also sweet with hints of aniseed.

MEDOFF ROYAL

Ukrainian Vodka
40% **alc./vol.** (80°proof)
www.medoff.co.uk
Producer: Soyuz-Victan Ltd, Simferopol, Crimea, Ukraine
UK agent: Gary Magan & Company
US agent: Soyuz-Victan USA

Ilya Sergeyevich Voskresensky (1856-1932), a Russian doctor and dietician from St. Petersburg, is credited with pioneering the adding of honey to vodka to 'smooth' its flavour. In 2003, Ilya Voskresensky's descendants (who live in London) met with the Ukrainian distiller Soyuz Viktan and an agreement was forged to create Medoff vodka. Royal is one of a range of four vodkas sold under the Medoff brand and is sweetened using the bee secreatian, known as royal jelly.
Comment: Dusty, peppery nose. The bold grainy, peppery spirity palate is also strangely smooth and oily. Clean, oily, cracked black pepper finish.

MEDOYEFF

American Vodka
40% **alc./vol.** (80°proof)
www.medoyeff.com
Producer: House Spirits Distillery, 7th Avenue, Portland, New Oregon, USA
UK agent: Not generally available
US agent: McClaskey's Wine Distributors

Medoyeff was created in 2002 by partners Lee Medoff and Christian Krogstad at their House Spirits Distillery in Portland, Oregon. Previously, Medoff had had 14 years' experience brewing and distilling at McMenamins, while Krogstads brought brewing experience and business acumen.

Medoyeff vodka is distilled from rye and filtered through charcoal and limestone. It is named after Medoff's original Russian family name, which was changed when his grandfather emigrated to the US. It is packaged in a tall slender, frosted bottle with a screen-printed, military-inspired capital 'M' on the bottle with a star over it, giving it a slightly Russian appearance.
Comment: Neutral-style nose with faint nutty and fruity notes. The palate, which is slightly oily and sweet with good grain character, starts clean and develops dusty peppery notes.

MOSKOVSKAYA OSOBAYA

Russian Vodka
40% **alc./vol.** (80°proof)
www.moskovskaya.com
Producer: Sojuzplodimport (S.P.I), Russia (bottled in Riga, Latvia)
UK agent: Pernod-Richard UK
US agent: Pernod-Ricard USA

Moskovskaya Osobaya literally translates as 'Special Muscovite' and is a reference to its originally being made at the famous Cristall distillery in Moscow. The distillery was founded in 1901 as the Moscow State Wine Distillery No. 1., and supplied the Kremlin elite with Cristall brand vodkas.

Moskovskaya is one of 43 previously state-owned vodka brands brought in 1997 by Sojuzplodimport (S.P.I.) and has since been subject to the same legal wrangles as its better known sibling, Stolichnaya. As a result, Moskovskaya destined for the international market, is distilled in Russia and then shipped in bulk for bottling in Latvia.

NEMIROFF ORIGINAL

Ukrainian Vodka
40% **alc./vol.** (80°proof)
www.nemiroff.ua
Producer: Nemiroff Ukrainian Vodka Company,
Nemirov, Vinnitsa Region, Ukraine
UK agent: Alcomm Ltd
US agent: Medco Atlantic Inc.

The Nemiroff distillery takes its name from the
small town in which it's located, not far from the
Ukrainian city of Vinnitsa. The surrounding
countryside is a wheat farming area, so providing
the distillery with a local source of grain.
Nemiroff Original was launched in September
1999 and is better known by some as 'Nemiroff
Black' due to the colour of its label. This vodka is
distinctive due to a composition that includes
caraway and honey.
Comment: Quite a light palate, with aniseed, soured
cream hints, laced with sweetness in the finish.

NEMIROFF LEX

Ukrainian Vodka
40% **alc./vol.** (80°proof)
www.nemiroff.ua
Producer: Nemiroff Ukrainian Vodka Company,
Nemirov, Vinnitsa Region, Ukraine
UK agent: Alcomm Ltd
US agent: Medco Atlantic Inc.

Meaning 'Law' in Latin and launched in November
2003, Lex is Nemiroff's super premium vodka. It is
presented in an arching bottle designed by French
Design Studio 'Version Originale'. It features a rip-
pull tab which breaks a plastic seal on the skirted
capsule allowing the bottle to be opened. While
this may secure against tampering, it leaves a
jagged, less than premium looking capsule to
reseal the open bottle.
  I understand that the base grain neutral spirit
used to make this vodka is 'aged' (possibly rested
in stainless steel tanks rather than oak casks) for
six months prior to being blended with alcohol and
distilled from oat flakes and lime blossoms.
Comment: A nose with wafts of fennel-laced
toasted wheat bread leads to a sweet and creamy
palate with strong notes of cracked black pepper
garnished with more subtle candied citrus peel,
fennel, violet and doughy notes. Long, clean,
vanilla-ed, peppery finish.

**WHEN PABLO PICASSO WAS
ASKED TO NAME THE
THREE MOST IMPORTANT
FEATURES OF POST-WAR
FRENCH CULTURE, HE
REPLIED, 'MODERN JAZZ,
BRIGITTE BARDOT AND
POLISH VODKA'.**

VODKA O2

English Vodka
40% **alc./vol.** (80°proof)
www.sparklingvodka.com
Producer: International English Distillers Ltd,
Langley Green, Warley, West Midlands, England
UK agent: St. Austell Brewery
US agent: Not generally available

Not the UK cellular phone network but the
world's first sparkling vodka, Vodka O2 is
made in Warley, England, from wheat with a
small amount of malted Barley. It is triple
distilled in traditional copper pot stills and
then filtered through activated carbon and
titanium micro-mesh. Lastly, O2 is given
some sparkle with an oxygen infusion.
Comment: A fairly neutral nose with the
merest hint of lemon doesn't prepare you
for the far from neutral palate where the
lemon bursts through. The taste is strangely
reminiscent of vodka and flat bitter lemon.
O2 may be sparkling but champagne it is
not, and far from worrying about a potential
spray when opening, you'd barely notice the
tiny bubbles if you weren't looking for them.

PAN TADEUSZ

Polish Vodka
40% **alc./vol.** (80°proof)
www.vsluksusowa.pl
Producer: V&S Luksusowa Zielona Góra S.A.,
Zielona Góra Lubuski, Poland
UK agent: Not generally available
US agent: Not generally available

This rye-based vodka is named after a book
by the famous Polish writer Adam
Mickiewicz. There is a reprint of the book's
title page on the vodka's frosted bottle. Pan
Tadeusz is mainly sold in the Polish home
market.
Comment: Light palate but with a rich grain
character and hints of cracked black pepper.

PARLIAMENT

Russian Vodka
40% **alc./vol.** (80°proof)
www.parliament-vodka.com
Producer: Urozhay Distillery, Nikolsko-
Archangelskoje, Balashika, Moscow, Russia.
UK agent: ISF GmbH
US agent: Not generally available

Parliament is produced by the Moscow-
based Urozhay company established in 1991.
It is made from multiple column distilled
Russian grown rye and hydrated using the
250m-deep Urozhay spring. Milk is added
prior to filtration, which coagulates around
impurities that are then removed in a
multistage filtration process.

PEARL

Canadian vodka
40% **alc./vol.** (80° proof)
www.pearlvodka.com
Producer: Luxco, St. Louis, Missouri, USA
UK agent: Not generally available
US agent: Pearl Spirits Inc.

Launched in 1999, this vodka is made from Canadian winter wheat using a five column distillation process and is hydrated with Canadian Rocky Mountain spring water.

●●●●●◖

POLSKA WODKA

Polish Vodka
40% **alc./vol.** (80°proof)
www.vsluksusowa.pl
Producer: V&S Luksusowa Zielona Góra S.A., Zielona Góra, Lubuski, Poland
UK agent: Marblehead Brand Development Ltd
US agent: Adamba Imports

This rye grain vodka is compounded at V&S Luksusowa. It is not charcoal filtered and contains no added sugar or flavouring. Pronounced 'Pol-Sca', it's proudly nationalistic name means 'Polish vodka'.
Comment: Very characterful, grain-rich palate with hints of cracked black pepper. Clean and flavoursome rather than richly flavoured.

●●●●◖○

PÖLSTAR

Icelandic Vodka
40% **alc./vol.** (80°proof)
www.polstarvodka.com
Producer: William Grant & Sons, Borgarnes, Iceland
UK agent: William Grant & Sons
US agent: Not generally available

Launched in the UK in June 1997, Pölstar is made in Iceland from rectified grain spirit blended with Icelandic water drawn from the Seleyri spring. The brand was acquired in December 2002 by William Grant as part of an ongoing diversification of its traditional Scotch portfolio. As we go to press I understand that Pölstar is being discontinued in favour of the company's new Icelandic Reyka vodka, which is also produced at Borgarnes.
Comment: Upfront sweetness with a light peppery tingle and a hint of aniseed coming through.

●●●●●

POTOCKI WÓDKA

Polish Vodka
40% **alc./vol.** (80°proof)
www.potockivodka.com
Producer: Potocki Spirits (Poland) Ltd, Poland
UK agent: Potocki Spirits (Europe) Ltd
US agent: Potocki Spirits America

Pronounced 'Pot-Ot-Ski', this vodka is a mark of one man's fight for the memory of his family. Jan-Roman Potocki, an ex-banker, is a direct descendant of one of Poland's once most aristo

cratic families who lost their lands and assets twice. Once in 1917 during the Russian Revolution and again in 1944 when the Soviet armies forced the Potockis to leave the country.

The Potocki family originally rose to prominence through military prowess at the service of Polish Kings and from the 15th century they successfully defended what's now called the Ukraine from invading Russians, Tartars, Cossacks and Turks. Their two-and-a-half cross symbol, the 'Pilawa', was originally a battlefield standard and now proudly graces Potocki Wódka bottles. It can also still be seen on the Potocki Palace in Warsaw, now a museum.

The Potocki estates at Lancut (pronounced 'Wine-Suit') in southern Poland were visited by eminent guests, including the Hapsburg Emperor, and were famed for horse breeding and hunting. Jan-Roman Potocki's great grandfather was a keen hunter and it is his hunting diary signature that is today embossed on the side of every bottle of Potocki Wódka.

The Potocki estate at Lancut was also renowned for its distillery, which produced vodka and liqueurs. Established in 1784, this was Poland's second oldest distillery, missing out on being the oldest by just two years. Jan-Roman has revitalised an old family vodka recipe from this distillery to produce today's Potocki Wódka. This ultra premium vodka is double distilled in Poland from rye to Jan-Roman's exacting specifications and is so pure when it leaves the still that charcoal filtration is not required. It is also naturally smooth and slightly sweet and so no sugars or other additives are used.

Jan-Roman has also gone to considerable time and expense in the presentation of his vodka. Beautiful bottles from Italy are hand-filled and labelled by hand with labels from a specialist in Bordeaux, and finished with capsules from Spain.
Comment: Incredibly smooth with a hint of sweetness and a rich grainy, light, zingy spiced flavour. Subtle hints of nuts (mainly Brazil) and rye bread. Good long finish with hints of almond emerging.

●●●●●

PRAVDA

Polish Vodka
40% **alc./vol.** (80°proof)
www.pravdavodka.com
Producer: Jobert, Poland
UK agent: Not generally available
US agent: La Maison Delan et Cie

Pravda is made from late harvest rye grain, the majority is grown organically in the Wielkopolska fields of Southern Poland. It is distilled using a five column distillation process, hydrated using filtered spring water from the Carpathian Mountains and filtered though white birch charcoal before final purification by chill filtration.

Pravda is packed in a shapely, etched bottle with simulated ice fissions and bejewelled with a blue crystal mounted on the bottle's shoulder.
Comment: A clean nose with hints of toasted bread and charcoal leads to an almost neutral styled clean soft palate with a creamy mouthfeel and hints of toasted rye bread and almonds.

RAIN

American Vodka
40% **alc./vol.** (80°proof)
www.rainvodka.com
Producer: Buffalo Trace Distillery (Sazerac Company), Frankfort, Kentucky, USA.
UK agent: Not known
US agent: Sazerac Company

Launched in 1996 and packaged in a frosted teardrop-shaped bottle, this is one of the original organic vodkas.

Rain is distilled seven times in four separate stills from organically grown sweet white corn sourced from a single farm (Fizzle Flat Farm in Yale, Illinois). It is filtered through charcoal and, before further filtration, through fine diamond dust.
Comment: A nose with a hint of spice leads to a peppery, corn-on-the-cob palate with buttery and aniseed hints. Light apple, toffee and nutty notes and slightly sweet.

REYKA

Icelandic Vodka
40% **alc./vol.** (80°proof)
www.reykavodka.com
Producer: The Reyka Distillery (William Grant & Egils), Borgarnes, Iceland.
UK distributor: First Drinks Brands
US agent: William Grant

William Grant & Sons constructed Iceland's first and only distillery in the small fishing village of Borgarnes, on the island's west coast. Operated in partnership with Egils, a local company with a bottling facility on the same site, the Reyka Distillery launched this vodka in September 2005. Reyka is powered by environmentally friendly, geothermal energy and the name derives from the old Icelandic word for 'steam'. The vodka is made in small batches from barley grain spirit using a Carter-Head still, built specially by the copper-smiths Forsyth's of Rothes, Scotland. The distillate is passed through lava rock, which has a filtering effect.

Reyka is hydrated with spring water direct from the Grábrók Spring, which is located under a 4,000 year-old lava field near the distillery. The water is so pure and low in minerals that it does not require any industrialised demineralising treatment before blending with the spirit.

Reyka is packaged in a heavy-based glass bottle with a cork stopper. The label features Mt. Hekla, an Icelandic volcano that last erupted in 1845, spreading volcanic ash as far as Scotland.
Comment: Clean, cracked black pepper spice on the palate with subtle hints of fennel.

ROBERTO CAVALLI

Italian Vodka
40% **alc./vol.** (80°proof)
robertocavalli.com
Producer: Fratelli Francoli S.p.A., Ghemme, Corso Romagnano, Italy
UK agent: Not generally available
US agent: Dorado-Pizzorni & Sons LLC

Sadly, the success of a vodka brand, more than any other spirit, is about fashion, packaging and marketing rather than what's inside the bottle. So it shouldn't be surprising that a fashion designer has put his name to a vodka brand in addition to his lines of clothing, sunglasses, shoes and handbags. To quote Cavalli: "The art of hospitality has always been one of my greatest passions, that's why creating this vodka felt very natural and spontaneous to me – it's limpid, pure and brilliant as my perfect woman."

Cavalli is known for using wild animal prints in his design and his vodka sees animal prints and a serpent wrapped around a frosted bottle. This vodka is not run up in some sweatshop but crafted by Distillerie Francoli in Ghemme, Italy. It is made from Italian-grown grain, hydrated with water from the peaks of Monte Rosa and filtered through crushed Carrera marble.
Comment: A fairly neutral nose with hints of nuts and dried fruit, the creamy palate starts soft and quickly builds with peppery spice turning dry with nutty, raisin notes. The finish is dry and peppery.

RODNIK

Russian Vodka
40% **alc./vol.** (80°proof)
www.vodkarodnik.ru
Producer: JSC Rodnik, Samara Alcohol & Liquor Distillery, Samara, Russia
UK agent: Euronest Limited
US agent: Silver Comet Inc

The Rodnik Distillery is situated by the Volga River in the old eastern Russian town of Samara on the Volga River. The name is a transliteration of the Russian word for spring. The distillery was established in 1895 and now produces over 40 million bottles of vodka per year. Rodnik is made using multi-column distillation from Russian wheat and filtered through Birchwood charcoal.
Comment: Palate opens with aniseed notes and builds peppery notes. Sweet, peppery finish.

ROTH

American Vodka
40% **alc./vol.** (80°proof)
www.rothvodka.com
Producer: Roth Vodka LLC, San Jose, California, USA
UK agent: Not generally available
US agent: Beam Wine Estates

Roth vodka is made from six varieties of grape grown in Sonoma County, California, including French Colombard and Chardonnay. The grape juice is blended and fermented for about six days before being passed through a continuous copper still five times over a ten-day period. The distillate is reduced to bottling strength and charcoal-filtered.

1 OF EVERY 4 DRINKS CONSUMED IN THE WORLD IS VODKA (OR CONTAINS VODKA).

Launched in late 2005, Roth is the brainchild of Ted Simpkins, co-proprietor of Lancaster Estate, a winery in Sonoma County, and an executive with Southern Wine and Spirits, one of the country's leading distributors. Roth is marketed as a Californian vodka distilled from grapes and is particularly aimed at wine lovers, with $1 for every case of Roth vodka sold donated to the American Guild of Sommeliers Education Foundation. **Comment: There is more damp cardboard than discernible grape aroma to Roth's nose. The palate starts silky and slightly sweet but a peppery burn quickly dominates. The finish is dry and peppered.**

SERIOUSLY

Swedish Vodka
40% **alc./vol.** (80°proof)
www.seriously.com
Producer: Facile & Company AB, Stockholm, Sweden
UK agent: Boutique Brands
US agent: Not known

British-born Swedish businessman Philip Diklev and his friend Henrik Facile launched Seriously in 2000. It is made with grain neutral spirit, distilled from winter wheat then blended with flavourings and Swedish lake water.
Comment: A slight hint of boiled sweets on the nose leads to a medium-bodied, wheaty palate with hints of aniseed and curdy lemon zest.

RUSSKY STANDART ORIGINAL

Russian Vodka
40% **alc./vol.** (80°proof)
www.russianstandard.com
Producer: Russian Standard Company, Livitz Distillery, St Petersburg, Russia
UK agent: Iceberg CL
US agent: Rémy Cointreau USA

Russky Standart (aka Russian Standard) was created in 1998 by the Russian billionaire Roustam Tariko. It is made at Russian Standard's new $60 million distillery on the outskirts of St Petersburg using wheat from Russia's heartlands and pure glacier water from the frozen North. Russky Standart is distilled to the Tsar's premium quality standard of 1894, as set by Professor Dmitri Mendeleev, and the bottle references that date, and carries Mendeleev's signature. The bottle's shape is inspired by the 200 tonne bell commissioned by Tsarina Anna which stands at the foot of the Ivan the Great Bell Tower in Moscow. Russky Standart is filtered once through charcoal and once through quartz crystal.

Russky Standart is targeted at the super premium segment of the market, and in its native country the price is so prohibitive that only very affluent people can afford it.
Comment: A clean nose with wafts of wheat leads to an equally wheaty palate with notes of freshly ground black pepper and hints of aniseed. An underlying sweetness smoothes over what could otherwise be a slightly jagged palate. Lots of character.

SEAGRAM'S EXTRA SMOOTH

American Vodka
40% **alc./vol.** (80°proof)
www.seagramsvodkalive.com
Producer: Joseph E Seagram & Sons (Pernod Ricard), Lawrenceburg, Indiana, USA
UK agent: Not generally available
US agent: Pernod Ricard USA

This is made from American Indiana grain using a five column distillation process. A number of flavoured line extensions are also available, including black cherry and orange.

SIBIRSKAYA

Russian Vodka
42% **alc./vol.** (84°proof)
Producer: Topaz Distillery (Russian Alcohol) under licence from Zao 'Sojuzplodimport', Moscow, Russia
UK agent: Not known **US agent:** Not Known

Sibirskaya is one of 17 government-owned Russian vodka brands controlled by federal company ZAO Soyuzplodoimport. Sibirskaya was formerly produced by a number of different distilleries in Russia but is exclusively licensed by Soyuzplodoimport to produce and develop the brand.

Sibirskaya is distilled from Siberian winter wheat using continuous stills and filtered through silver birch charcoal and quartz sand.
Comment: A nose of cracked pepper alcohol with a hint of aniseed. Quite an aggressive palate, with black pepper attack and aniseed garnish. Labelled 'Genuine Russian Vodka', it has the character of traditional Russian vodka.

SIWUCHA

Polish vodka
40% **alc./vol.** (80°proof)
www.vsluksusowa.pl
Producer: V&S Luksusowa Zielona Góra S.A., Zielona Góra, Poland
UK agent: Marblehead Brand Development Ltd
US agent: Adamba Imports

Pronounced 'She-Voo-Ha', this potato vodka is a contemporary reproduction of a 16th century Polish vodka – both in flavour and packaging. It was developed in 1996 by master vodka blender Elzbieta Goldynka to celebrate the 50th anniversary of the Zielona Góra Polmos.

Siwucha is an unusually complex vodka. It is based on two quite different rectified rye grain spirits, which are blended and then subtly flavoured by an extraction of wild berry. The blend is matured in old oak casks for 30 days to allow the flavours to marry and the oak to faintly flavour and colour the vodka. It is then hydrated with water from Zielona Góra's own wells, packaged in an old-fashioned bottle and finished with a driven cork and a hand stamped wax seal.

Siwucha is not charcoal-filtered and has no added sugar or glycerine.
Comment: This remarkably smooth vodka has a sweet edge and a soft finish. The earthy rye bread palate offers hints of artichoke, green tea and asparagus.

SKYY

American Vodka
40% **alc./vol.** (80°proof)
www.skyy.com
Producer: Skyy Spirits Inc. (Campari), San Francisco, USA
UK agent: Fior Brands Ltd
US agent: Skyy Spirits LLC

Maurice Kanbar, a San Francisco-based inventor and entrepreneur, suffered when he drank alcohol and attributed this to congeners (impurities) in spirits. Thus began his quest to create the purest vodka possible - he launched Skyy, which he claims has the "fewest impurities" of any vodka (at 0.8mg per litre), in 1991.

Skyy is made from wheat using four column distillation and filtered through calcium carbonate, cellulose plates and granular carbon.
Comment: The lack of any desirable nose warns of this vodka's neutrality. The slightly sweet palate offers subtle grainy hints and barely perceptible wafts of liquorice, black pepper, mint and lime.

SKYY90

American Vodka
45% **alc./vol.** (90°proof)
www.skyy90.com
Producer: Skyy Spirits Inc., San Francisco, USA.
UK agent: Fior Brands Ltd
US agent: Skyy Spirits LLC

The name of this super premium Skyy vodka line extension refers to its alcoholic proof. It is made from Amber winter wheat in a five column, seven stage distillation process and hydrated using Sierra Mountain water.
Comment: Very smooth and slightly sweet, this is a minerally, biscuity vodka with a good, clean simplicity.

SMIRNOFF NO 21 (RED LABEL)

American Vodka
40% **alc./vol.** (80°proof)
www.smirnoff.com
Producer: The Pierre Smirnoff Company (Diageo), Stamford, Connecticut, USA
UK agent: See below for UK version
US agent: Diageo North America

Smirnoff Red commemorates the Smirnovskaya Vodka No 21, which was originally supplied to the Tsar's armed forces. In 1815, Moscow was rebuilding itself after the ravages of the Napoleonic wars and Ivan Smirnov (the original transliteration of the Russian family name) was building a distillery on the bank of the Moskva River.

Ivan registered Societé Ivan Smirnov in 1818 and bequeathed the company to his nephew Piotr Arsenyevitch Smirnov on his death. During the second half of the 19th century, Piotr Smirnov Fils (as the company became known) became the largest producer of vodka in Russia, thanks to Piotr's use of charcoal filtration and continuous distillation

to create a very pure spirit. Piotr's sons continued the business after their father's death. In 1917, however, the Russian Revolution transformed the national landscape. The Bolsheviks confiscated all private industries in Moscow, including the Smirnov distillery (which became a state garage). Nicolai Smirnov died penniless in Moscow, while his brother, Vladimir, escaped the firing squad and fled the country. He ended up in France where he established a small distillery close to Paris and gave his last name a French twist, creating the brand we know today as Smirnoff.

Then, in 1934, Vladimir was forced to sell his vodka to a fellow émigré, Rudolph Kunett, who had supplied the Smirnov family with grain before the Revolution under his former name of Kukhesh. Rudolph acquired the exclusive rights to sell Smirnoff vodka in the US and Canada and established a distillery to produce Smirnoff vodka in Connecticut, USA.

The company changed hands again in the late 1930s when Kunett sold out to John Martin of Heublein Co, then a small liquor firm based in Connecticut. Heublein acquired the world rights to Smirnoff from Vladimir's widow in 1951 and on 15th August 1952 W&A Gilbey Ltd (now part of Diageo) agreed to manufacture and sell Smirnoff vodka in Britain. In 1983, Heublein was purchased by the group that is now Diageo.

Today, Smirnoff is made mostly from grain neutral spirit; a term that suggests some molasses spirit could be involved. The spirit is rectified using continuous distillation in a process that takes 24 hours, then blended with demineralised water to reduce it from 95% alc./vol. to 57% alc./vol.. Although modern stills remove the impurities that would have remained in Piotr's vodka, Smirnoff is still filtered through charcoal, which modern environmental sensibilities dictate is sourced from sustainable hardwood trees. The spirit is filtered for up to eight full hours, using seven tons of charcoal, and finally reduced to bottling strength with more demineralised water. Smirnoff's present packaging was introduced in 2003 and features a red and silver logo and a double-headed eagle inspired by the Imperial coat of arms.

Smirnoff is Diageo's highest volume brand and achieved sales of 26.9 million bottles in the year ending 30 June 2006. It is ranked, by volume, as the number one premium vodka and the number one premium spirit brand in the world.
Comment: The spicy nose leads into a spicy peppery palate with hints of aniseed. Pepper prickles through the finish.

SMIRNOFF RED NO 21

Scottish Vodka
37.5% **alc./vol.** (75°proof)
www.smirnoff.com
Producer: The Pierre Smirnoff Company (Diageo), Cameron Bridge Distillery, Windygates, Leven, Fife, Scotland
UK agent: Diageo UK
US agent: See above for US version

The British version of Smirnoff Red has a lower alcoholic strength than its US counterpart - its new packaging arrived in 2004.
Comment: Slightly dusty/spicy nose leads to a fiery peppered palate (seemingly more fiery than the US sample that's 2.5% alc./vol. stronger). The temperature rises through to the finish.

SMIRNOFF BLACK NO 55

Scottish Vodka
40% alc./vol. (80°proof)
www.smirnoff.com
Producer: The Pierre Smirnoff Company (Diageo),
Cameron Bridge Distillery, Windygates, Leven,
Fife, Scotland
UK agent: Diageo UK
US agent: Diageo North America

Diageo launched Smirnoff Black in the US in 1995,
and the UK two years later, declaring with some
fanfare that it was distilled and bottled in Moscow,
Russia. Production quietly moved to Scotland not
long thereafter and this vodka was subsequently
relaunched with new packaging in June 2006.
　　Smirnoff Black is still made in Scotland.
Copper pot stills are used to 'finish' grain neutral
spirit, which is then filtered through Siberian
silver birch charcoal.
**Comment: A hint of dark liquorice on the nose
suggests this vodka is going to live up to its black
title. Add water and a hint of new make spirit (unaged Scotch whisky) emerges on the nose. A hint
of that liquorice comes through on the robust
cracked black pepper palate, which has generous
malted barley notes. A good deal of Scottish
character seems to find its way into this 'Russian'
vodka.**

SMIRNOFF BLUE NO 57

Vodka (produced in various countries)
45% alc./vol. (90°proof)
Producer: The Pierre Smirnoff Company (Diageo),
various countries
UK agent: Diageo UK
US agent: Diageo North America

This high strength version of Smirnoff was
launched in 1958. Today it is mostly sold in travel
retail (duty free).

SMIRNOFF PENKA

Polish Vodka
40% alc./vol. (80°proof)
www.smirnoff.com
Producer: Polmos Józefów, Józefów, Mazowsze,
Poland
UK agent: Reserve Brands (Diageo)
US agent: Diageo North America

Launched in 2003 as a super premium Smirnoff
line extension, Penka is distilled in two column
stills from rye grain. The spirit then undergoes a
final distillation in a small custom-made copper
pot still, which is said to boast a unique heating
element to extract only the finest cut.
　　Penka is made in the small Polish town of
Józefów, close to Warsaw, which seems a little
sad given the brand's Russian heritage.
**Comment: A strange nose of candied
orange/creamy chocolate confectionary with
peppery, angelica spice. The palate has a strange
creaminess to it with notes of white chocolate,
lemon pie and nutmeg spice. A tad exotic – not
what I'd expect from a Polish rye.**

SMIRNOV

Russian Vodka

During the 19th century, Piotr Arsenyevitch
Smirnov built the largest brand of vodka in
Imperial Russia and his sons ran the business
until the Bolsheviks seized the distillery
during the Russian Revolution. Only one
brother, Vladimir Smirnov, escaped Russia
and established a distillery in his new home of
Paris, France, giving his name a French twist
with the spelling 'Smirnoff'. He sold his vodka
in 1934, and the brand is now owned by
Diageo.
　　In 1991, as Russia transitioned from a
state-run to a capitalist economy, the two
great-grandsons of Piotr Smirnov, Andrei and
Boris Smirnov, founded the Trading House of
P.A. Smirnov and started producing vodka
under the Smirnov brand. UDV (as Diageo then
was) protested against this, registered the
Smirnoff brand with the Russian patent
agency and, in 1996, signed a contract with a
local distillery to make Smirnoff vodka in
Russia. The battle lines between Smirnov and
Smirnoff were drawn.
　　As Smirnov's direct descendants, the
Smirnovs believed they had a right to use their
family name. Diageo, however, argued that it
had brought the Smirnoff brand to international fame over the preceding decades and
was entitled to benefit from its efforts. So the
brands sat side by side in Russian liquor
stores while the lawyers battled on.
In 2004, a deal was cut. Smirnoff agreed to
remove the Cyrillic script and Russian coat of
arms from its bottle while Smirnov agreed to
Smirnoff's presence in the Russian
marketplace.
　　However, while Smirnoff was fighting it
out with Smirnov, the Smirnovs were struck by
internecine strife. Andrei Smirnov sold his 50%
share of the business to Alfa Group, a major
Russian consortium, which is purported to
have squeezed Boris Smirnov out of the
business. Boris, who had inherited over 280 of
Piotr Smirnov's original vodka recipes from his
great-grandmother, then established his own
vodka under the 'Boris Smirnov' name.
The latest twist in the saga of Smirnoff v.
Smirnov was Diageo's acquisition of the P.A.
Smirnov brand through a company in which
Diageo holds a 75% stake and Alfa Group 25%.

SNOW LEOPARD

Polish Vodka
40% alc./vol. (80°proof)
www.snowleopardvodka.co.uk
Producer: Polmos Lublin, Poland
UK agent: Snow Leopard Vodka Ltd
US agent: Not known

The brainchild of a former vice president of
Allied Domecq, Stephen Sparrow, this vodka
is named after an endangered cat native to the
mountain ranges of central and southern
Asia. The Snow Leopard has a beautiful soft
grey coat with ringed spots, which turn white
in the winter, and 15% of any profits from
Snow Leopard vodka is donated to the Snow
Leopard Trust which works to protect the
feline and its habitat.
　　Unusually, this vodka is made from spelt
(Triticum spelta), a grain that had gone out of

fashion before being rediscovered by the health food industry. I understand it is distilled in small batches through a four stage distillation process.

Comment: All very nice and philanthropic but a strange name for a Polish vodka. Surely there is a more appropriate Asian liquor to name after a mountain cat from central and south Asia? Almost neutral, minerally, damp nose with hints of aniseed, the palate is clean and dry with peppery spice but with creamy mouthfeel and subtle hints of vanilla. Clean, minerally finish with pepper spice.

SNOW QUEEN

Kazakh Vodka
40% **alc./vol.** (80°proof)
www.snowqueenvodka.com
Producer: Geom, Kazakhstan
UK agent: Kazakh Vodka Ltd
US agent: Peerless Importers Inc.

It seems like only yesterday that Kazakhstan was known for being oil-rich and anti-democratic but then came Borat and now a luxury vodka. Actually, Snow Queen arrived in the UK before Borat, in May 2006, while it is being rolled out in the US this Spring (2007). Snow Queen is made from organic wheat (I'm not sure who, if anybody, accredits its organic status) using a five column distillation process. It is hydrated using artesian spring water from the foothills of the Himalayas which is purified using reverse osmosis and sand filtration. The finished vodka is filtered using Kazakh birch charcoal.

Snow Queen's website mentions use of 100% natural honey so it seems fair to deduce that, like many Russian vodkas, this is used to slightly sweeten and soften the vodka.

Comment: There is a slight hint of aniseed on the clean, cracked black pepper nose. The palate is also clean and richly grainy with cracked black pepper spice and a hint of sugar and aniseed. Clean, grainy, spicy finish.

SOBIESKI

Polish Vodka
40% **alc./vol.** (80°proof)
www.sobieskivodka.pl
Producer: Alco Pegro Sp (Belvedere Groupe), Kolaczkowie, Witkowo, Poland
UK agent: Paragon Vintners Ltd
US agent: Sobieski USA

Named after the Polish King, Jan III Sobieski (1629-1696), and made from Dankowski rye grain harvested from the Polish fields of Mazowsze, this vodka is said to be distilled following traditional recipes kept since the 19th century at the Radziejowice Mansion.

Comment: A minerally, faintly herbal nose with wafts of charcoal. The slightly sweet palate has a creamy mouthfeel and satisfying, cleansing peppery spice and a hint of creamy vanilla. Long, clean, lightly peppered finish. A well-rounded, characterful vodka.

SOLIDARNOSC

Polish Vodka
40% **alc./vol.** (80°proof)
www.solidarnosc.co.uk
UK agent: Solidarnosc UK (Ltd)
US agent: Not generally available

This vodka is named after and carries the livery of Solidarnosc (Solidarity), the Polish trade union founded in the 1980s at the then Lenin Shipyards, and originally led by Lech Walesa. Solidarity helped oppose the communist government, leading to elections in 1989 and a Solidarity-led coalition government with Walesa elected president.

Unusually for a Polish vodka, Solidarnosc is distilled from wheat rather than rye.

Comment: Living in London with its strong Polish community I am aware that the branding of this vodka has upset some who remember what Solidarnosc stood for in the 1980s struggle against the repression of communism. The vodka itself has a nose with burnt rubber notes that mask more subtle wafts of aniseed. Given this, the palate is surprisingly clean and slightly sweet with pleasant grainy notes and an oily mouthfeel.

SPIRYTUS REKTYFIKOWANY

Polish Vodka
79.9% **alc./vol.** (159.8°proof)
Producer: Produced by several different Polmos distilleries in Poland.
UK agent: Hakts et Cie Ltd
US agent: Not generally available

In Polish, 'spirytus rektyfikowany' literally means 'rectified spirit' and that's exactly what this is – high strength ethyl alcohol. Often labelled for export 'Polish Pure Spirit', it is sold in three strengths: 'blue label' at 57.1% alc./vol., 'yellow label' at 79.9% alc./vol. and 'green label' at 96% alc./vol.

Comment: At a whopping 79.9% **alc./vol.** this powerful spirit is surprisingly creamy and sweet on the palate. There is, of course, plenty of alcohol peppery burn but it also has a grainy sweetness with hints of fruit, vanilla and a touch of aniseed. The purity and strength of this vodka makes it ideal for home infusions.

IN 17TH CENTURY POLAND, COMMUNAL GLASSES HOLDING AS MUCH AS A GALLON OF VODKA WERE USED FOR TOASTING.

● ● ● ● ○

SQUARE ONE

American Vodka
40% **alc./vol.** (80°proof)
www.squareonevodka.com
Producer: Square One Organic Spirits LLC, Rigby,
Idaho, USA
UK agent: Not generally available
US agent: Square One Organic Spirits

Square One Organic Spirits was founded in 2006 by
Allison Evanow, a drinks industry veteran who is
also an environmentalist. As CEO, she believes in
running her company ethically and is committed to
maintaining its female majority ownership.
Allison's vodka is made with 100% organic
American rye grown in North Dakota. This is
fermented using only organic yeasts and natural
nutrients in a process certified by the US
Department of Agriculture's (USDA) National
Organic Program (NOP). (By contrast, standard fermentation processes allow GMO yeasts, chemical
additives and synthetic de-foaming agents.)
The water used in Square One is drawn from the
nearby Snake River watershed of the Teton mountain
range in Wyoming. Four column continuous distillation produces a spirit which is hydrated with more
Teton water, carbon filtered and bottled.
**Comment: An almost completely neutral nose
that yields only subtle toasted notes leads to a
clean palate with dry hints of toasted rye bread
balanced by a hint of creamy sweetness and rose
water. Long, clean, toasted finish.**

● ● ● ● ○

SPUTNIK

Russian Vodka
40% **alc./vol.** (80°proof)
www.sputnikvodka.com
Producer: Distilled in Russia and bottled in
Ukraine
UK agent: Russian Vodka House Ltd
US agent: Not generally available

Sputnik is named after and commemorates the
launch of the first satellite to attain Earth's orbit.
It is distilled in a three column process from
Russian winter wheat then hydrated with purified
spring water. Finally, it is filtered through birch
charcoal prior to bottling.
**Comment: A clean, fairly neutral nose leads to
grainy peppery palate with a hint of sweetness
and aniseed. Cracked black pepper dominates
the buttery finish.**

● ● ○ ○ ○

STARKA

Polish Vodka
50% **alc./vol.** (100°proof)
Producer: Polmos Szczecin,
Szczecin, Poland

Pronounced 'Star-Ka', this is made according to a
16th century recipe using unrectified rye spirit
that is blended with Malaga wine then aged for ten
years in small oak casks. The style may have
originated from the tradition of pouring vodka into
an old wine barrel at the birth of a baby girl and
leaving it to mature until her wedding.
**Comment: This style of vodka is something of an
acquired taste. The palate is oaky and tannic with
muddy flavours alongside the more appealing
caramel, black pepper and vanilla. The bitter
finish is actually unpleasant.**

● ● ● ● ○

STOLICHNAYA RED

Russian Vodka
40% **alc./vol.** (80°proof)
www.stoli.com
Producer: Sojuzplodimport (S.P.I), Russia (bottled
in Riga, Latvia)
UK agent: Pernod Ricard UK
US agent: Pernod Ricard USA

Fondly known as 'Stoli', Stolichnaya's name
comes from the Russian word 'Stolitsa', which
means 'capital city', and the very Cyrillic label
depicts Moscow's famous Moscova Hotel.
The official formula for Stolichnaya is said to
have been first documented in 1938 but the
brand was not launched until the 1950s. During
the Soviet years, the version of Stolichnaya
exported to the West was considered far
superior to that made for the domestic market.
Today, Stoli is believed to be distilled from
winter wheat using two column stills. The
elaborate filtration process is supposed to
include filtering through charcoal made from
young silver birch trees, twice through quartz
sand and finally through a fine cloth.
Stolichnaya is no stranger to legal
wrangles. In 1997, a private company,
Sojuzplodimport, which is part of S.P.I.,
purchased the rights to use all 43 previously
state-owned vodka brands, including
Stolichnaya, for the sum total of $300,000. After
five years of litigation from the ministry which
had handled the brand during the Soviet era, a
Moscow court ruled that all the vodka brands
should return to state ownership as the
company which had sold the rights to S.P.I. was
not the brand's legal owner, making the sale
invalid. While that ruling has no international
jurisdiction, it means that S.P.I. can no longer
sell Stolichnaya in Russia or even export vodka
branded from Russia. So S.P.I. now exports bulk
vodka from Russia to Latvia where it is bottled as
Stolichnaya for international markets.
Confusingly, Stolichnaya in Russia is now
owned by the government and is handled by the
similarly named Soyuzplodoimport Federal
State Company (F.K.P.), established in
December 2001. Today, Pernod Ricard and Yury
Shefler, a former Russian compatriot who
created S.P.I. and is a major shareholder, own
the rights to distribute Stolichnaya in all world
markets other than Russia. Pernod Ricard
continues negotiations over settlement of the
dispute with F.K.P. in the hope they will
eventually also have access to Stolichnaya's
huge domestic market.
Since October 2006, Stolichnaya has also
seen trauma in the United States. Roustam
Tariko, billionaire owner of competitor vodkas
Russian Standard and Imperia, has alleged that
claims of Stolichnaya's Russian authenticity are
misleading. He is quoted as saying: "If
Stolichnaya vodka comes from Latvia rather than
Russia, it should be honest about that". But
according to Pernod Ricard, the brand's international distributor, Stolichnaya is "truly Russian,
being distilled and produced in Russia (Talvis
alcohol-producing association in Tambov, Central
Russia and the Kaliningrad S.P.I.-RVVK distillery)
using Russian grain and water. It is then shipped
in bulk and bottled (at the S.P.I.-owned Riga
Latviyas Balsams distillery) in Latvia."
**Comment: Given all the hassle that continues to
plague this brand why doesn't Pernod Ricard
concentrate more on the rather better and less
contentious Wyborowa? Stolichnaya has an oily,
charcoal nose which leads to a peppery palate
with a creamy mouthfeel and hints of aniseed
and sweet citrus.**

●●●●●●

STOLICHNAYA ELIT

Russian Vodka
40% **alc./vol.** (80°proof)
www.stoli.com
Producer: (S.P.I) Soyuzplodoimport, Russia
(bottled in Latvia)
UK agent: Pernod Ricard UK
US agent: Pernod Ricard USA

This premium line extension was first launched in California, USA, in mid-2004. Elit is distilled from Russian winter wheat using three column stills and filtered through a column of Siberian birch charcoal. Next it undergoes a freeze filtration process, which involves flash-chilling the vodka to −18°C and passing it through two additional charcoal filtration steps. Thus Elit is said to be triple filtered vodka.

Elit is packaged in a tall, slim, clear bottle with Cyrillic print. The black, tapered neck is crowned with a heavy metal screw-cap.
Comment: A cracked black pepper nose is the precursor to a smooth, rich, grainy, mineral palate with faint hints of aniseed and lemon zest. The finish is sweet with peppery notes.

SVEDKA

Swedish Vodka
40% **alc./vol.**
www.svedka.com
Producer: Spirits Marque One, Sweden
US agent: Spirits Marque One LLC
UK agent: Not generally available

Svedka was created in 1998 by Guillaume Cuvelier, previously an executive with Moet Hennessy (LVMH Group). Cuvelier's co-partner is the Belgium-based Alco Group. The brand has quickly grown over recent years in the US, partly due to a clever advertising campaign. Set in 2033, and featuring a robot (or 'Femme Bot') with a voluptuous breast plate as the unlikely star and 'the future of adult entertainment', these ads carry the strap line 'voted #1 vodka of 2033'.

Svedka is made from Swedish winter wheat using a five column distillation process.

SVENSK

Swedish Vodka
40% **alc./vol.** (80°proof)
www.fondberg.se
Producer: Fondberg & Co, Stockholm, Sweden
UK agent: Not widely available
US agent: Svensk Export Vodka

This is a Swedish vodka launched in the UK in April 1999. The company behind Svensk (the first privately-owned spirits company to be launched in Sweden since 1917) was established in 1996 when Sweden entered the European Union and the government monopoly was dismantled. Unfortunately, all did not go well for the new company and it went bankrupt. The brand was purchased in November 2001 by prominent Swedish wine and spirit importer Fondberg & Co. The labelling on the bottle is now royal blue and two new flavours, lemon and wild strawberry, have been launched alongside the standard vodka.

Svensk is based on spirit distilled from Scandinavian wheat and water drawn from Lake Vättern, one of the largest natural water sources in the world.

SYMPHONY

Czech Vodka
40% **alc./vol.** (80°proof)
www.symphonyvodka.com
Producer: Kafka & Partners, Prague, Czech Republic
US agent: Kafka & Partners
UK agent: Kafka & Partners Ltd

Symphony vodka is distilled from potatoes in the Czech Republic. Each bottle features one of 12 different figurines representing a member of the orchestra, such as a conductor, violinist, trumpeter, drummer etc.

TANQUERAY STERLING

British Vodka
40% **alc./vol.** (80°proof)
www.tanqueray.com
Producer: Charles Tanqueray & Co. (Diageo), Cameron Bridge Distillery, Windygates, Leven, Fife, Scotland
UK agent: Not generally available
US agent: Diageo North America

This vodka shares its brand name and distinctive bottle shape with the better-known gin - the boar's head symbol on the label is taken from the escutcheon of the Clan Gordon. No longer available in the UK but popular in the US, Tanqueray Sterling vodka is made from grain neutral spirit which is redistilled in an old copper pot still.

●●●●○

TETON GLACIER

American Vodka
40% **alc./vol.** (80°proof)
www.glaciervodka.com
Producer: Silver Creek Distillery, Rigby, Idaho, USA
US agent: Worldwide Wines & Spirits Importers
UK agent: None known

Teton Glacier is made using four-column, continuous distillation from Idaho Russet potatoes. It is filtered through charcoal and garnet crystals before bottling in a French-made, square glass decanter.
Comment: Neutral nose and a smooth and slightly sweet, almost oily (glycerine possibly?) palate with clean pepper, piny notes. Slight hints of cabbage water, vegetable notes, pine and vanilla. The clean finish has lasting cracked black pepper notes. I find the viscosity of the palate off-putting.

●●●●○

THREE OLIVES

English Vodka
www.threeolives.com
Producer: (under licence) Gilbert & John Greenall, Warrington, England
UK agent: Not available
US agent: White Rock Distillery

This wheat-based vodka is quadruple distilled and quadruple filtered in Warrington England. The type of still and filtration are not specified.
Comment: Slightly syrupy mouthfeel but, nevertheless, a very neutral and clean tasting vodka. Lacks character, but then, on the other hand, it says so little that it's hard to find anything truly nasty.

●●○○○

3 VODKA

American Vodka
40% **alc. /vol.** (80°proof)
www.3vodka.com
Producer: 3 Vodka Distilling Co. (Sovereign Brands LLC), Chicago, USA
UK agent: Not generally available
US agent: Sovereign Brands LLC

Vodka can be made from anything that contains starch, which, when converted to sugar, is the foodstuff for yeast which makes alcohol. Grain is a common ingredient, as is potato. However, the two brothers, Brian and Brett Berish, with a little help from father Barry, who's a former Jim Beam Brands CEO, are the first to make vodka from soybeans. Reading the company's literature it would appear that select grains also form a base ingredient along with the highly publicised 'soy isolates'.

Distinguished by its ring-like cap, which also doubles as a shot measure, 3 Vodka is certified and recommended by the American Vegetarian Association and, apparently, contains zero carbohydrates. A vodka to appeal to diet-crazed vegetarians?
Comment: The nose has an unfortunate whiff of sterilising solution. The palate is strangely creamy, slightly sweet and yet aggressive. Nutty, white chocolate notes do little to redeem this. Sod the vegetarians, this vodka needs meat!

●●●●○

TITO'S HANDMADE

American Vodka
40% **alc. /vol.** (80°proof)
www.titosvodka.com
Producer: Fifth Generation Inc., Austin, Texas, USA
US agent: Fifth Generation Inc
UK agent: Not generally available

A vodka entitled 'Tito's Handmade' with a front label that states "Crafted in an old-fashioned pot still by Texas' first & only distillery" will grab the attention of most spirit aficionados. Rightly so as it turns out.

Tito's is made by a Texan called Burt Butler Beveridge II who goes by the nickname 'Tito' and is a geologist by trade. He ferments his own corn and distils it using a pot still a full six times. He then filters the distillate through activated carbon.

Tito's far from understated label also has the reassuring statement, "No sugar or gelatine added".
Comment: An almost neutral nose, it has the merest hint of creamy corn. The clean palate is slightly sweet with a creamy mouthfeel and faint hints of tinned sweet corn. The clean finish is not as long as some vodkas with mild peppery notes.

●●●●○

TRIPLE EIGHT

American Vodka
40% **alc./vol.** (80° proof)
www.888vodka.com
Producer: Triple Eight Distillery, Nantucket, MA 02584, USA
US agent: Cisco Brewers
UK agent: Not generally available

Triple Eight (888) Vodka is produced on Nantucket Island by the Triple Eight micro distillery, part of the Cisco Brewery (known for their Whale's Tale Pale Ale microbrew). The distillery, Nantucket's first legal spirits producer, gets its name from Nantucket Well #888.

Triple Eight vodka is suitably triple distilled in a small pot still from organically grown corn and hydrated using water from the afore-mentioned well.
Comment: Relatively sweet with hints of aniseed, a syrupy mouthfeel and a cracked black pepper finish.

●●●●○

TÜRI

Estonian Vodka
40% **alc./vol.** (80° proof)
www.turivodka.com
Producer: Bacardi-Martini, Onistar, Tallinn, Estonia
US agent: Monsieur Henry (Sazerac)
UK agent: Not available

This Estonian vodka is packaged in a bottle with rugged looks that wouldn't look out of place amongst the wrenches in a mechanic's tool chest. It is distilled from Estonian rye using a four column distillation process and then charcoal filtered.
Comment: Sweet and honeyed with faint hints of raspberry amongst the grainy palate. The 'burn' and finish are surprisingly harsh considering the sweetness of the palate.

●●●●○

U.K. 5 ORGANIC

English Vodka
37.5% **alc. /vol.** (75°proof)
www.uk5.org
Producer: The Organic Spirits Company, Tannery Lane, Bramley, Surrey, England
UK agent: The Organic Spirits Co.
US agent: Executive Imports

U.K. 5 Organic vodka is produced using organic grain and is certified by the Soil Association. It is marketed as being free of the stabilisers and softeners used in some vodkas, has a low methanol content of 3.8g/ltr, and a high ethyl acetate content of 11.5g/ltr.
Comment: A nose with hints of soft plastic leads to a smooth and supple palate with some aniseed, and a wheaty note. Sweet, grainy finish.

ULTIMAT

Polish Vodka
40% **alc. /vol.** (80°proof)
www.ultimatvodka.com
Producer: Belska Polmos, Poland.
UK agent: Amathus
UK agent: Adamba Imports

This is a truly luxury vodka presented in a hand-made crystal decanter that combines two bottles; a clear bottle outside and a lead-free, hand-blown cobalt blue bottle inside. The vodka itself is made from a blend of three different grain vodkas – 70% potato, 15% wheat and 15% rye. Each of these is separately distilled to 96% alcohol by volume. They are then diluted to 30% with demineralised water and then redistilled to achieve maximum purity. The final distillate is then filtered through ceramic filters.
Comment: An unpromising, slightly rubbery nose leads to a very clean palate, which, although fairly neutral in style, has subtle hints of buttery mashed potato, sherbet, aniseed and lightly nutty, spicy rye. Very long, clean, slightly sweet finish.

U'LUVKA

Polish Vodka
40% **alc. /vol.** (80°proof)
www.uluvka.com
Producer: V&S Luksusowa Zielona Góra S.A. (under contract from The Brand Distillery Ltd), Zielona Góra, Lubuski, Poland.
UK agent: The Brand Distillery Ltd (70cl £24.67)
US agent: Not known

Pronounced 'You-Love-Ka', this vodka benefits from clever British branding and packaging design, but the spirit itself comes courtesy of the blending experts at Zielona Góra in Poland. They have adapted a long-forgotten recipe based on Polish grains (50% rye, 25% wheat and 25% barley) to create a naturally-smooth vodka without added sugar, honey or suchlike.
The teardrop-shaped bottle with its twisted neck stands out. The different elements of the symbol on the bottle represent spirit (the 'T' shape with the curved tail), soul (the question mark without the dot), sun (the circle) and moon (the central dot). All in all, the bottle is well designed and the vodka brilliantly made.
Comment: A subtle nose leads to a smooth, rounded and clean palate. The result is slightly sweet with subtle hints of aniseed, Brazil nuts and spicy, salted butter.

URSUS CLASSIC

Dutch Vodka
40% **alc./vol.** (80°proof)
www.ursusvodka.com
Producer: Ursus Vodka Company (Diageo), Atoomweg, Le Hoorn, The Netherlands
UK agent: Diageo
US agent: World Wide Liquors Inc.

Named after the Latin word for 'bear', this Dutch vodka is distilled from grain and is said to be based on an Icelandic recipe. In November 2004, Diageo plc acquired this and Ursus Roter brands at a cost of €45 million.

VAN HOO

Belgian Vodka
40% **alc. /vol.** (80°proof)
www.fourcroy.com
Producer: Fourcroy-Renglet SA, Brussels, Belgium.
UK agent: Not generally available
US agent: Preiss Imports

Launched in 1997, Van Hoo takes its name from the Van Hoorebeke family who started distilling gin in the middle of the 18th century. Their distillery in the village of Eeklo, Belgium, is the country's oldest distillery and is now owned by Fourcroy, famous for producing Mandarine Napoleon liqueur. Produced from grain, this vodka is distilled using a four step process in continuous and pot stills before being charcoal filtered and packaged in a sarcophagus-shaped cobalt blue bottle.
Comment: Soft, subtle texture on the palate with smoky, aniseed hints, a lightly caramelised sweetness and fresh citrus hints. Liquorice finish.

VERTICAL VODKA

French Vodka
40% **alc. /vol.** (80°proof)
www.verticalvodka.com
Producer: Chartreuse Diffusion, Voiron, France.
UK agent: John E Fells
US agent: Frederick Wildman & Sons

This French vodka is formulated and produced under the supervision of the Carthusian monks, famous for making Chartreuse liqueur. It undergoes four separate distillations, the first two in stainless steel stills; the latter two in tin-lined copper pot stills.
Comment: A mild, lightly aniseedy palate with a tinge of black pepper to tickle the tongue and some spicy heat towards the finish.

VILLA LOBOS

Mexican Vodka
45% **alc. /vol.** (90°proof)
www.wineandspirit.com
Producer: Licores Veracruz Distillers, Cordoba, Mexico
UK agent: Wine & Spirit International
US agent: Not generally available

This Mexican vodka comes in a bottle complete with a gun wielding bandito and a sombrero. Inside each bottle is an agave worm, actually the larva of the Night Butterfly and more commonly found in bottles of mezcal.
Villa Lobos is distilled five times from three different cereal grains and hydrated using water taken from a deep artesian well.
Comment: A mellow palate, considering the strength, but perky with fresh graininess, it has a light spice and wafts of smoky sweetness. Fresh, lightly peppered finish.

VINCENT VAN GOGH

Dutch Vodka
40% **alc. /vol.** (80°proof)
www.vangoghvodka.com
Producer: Royal Dirkzwager Distilleries,
Schiedam, The Netherlands
UK agent: Not generally available
US agent: Luctor International

Van Gogh vodka is aimed at the US Martini market, and, like its namesake, this vodka heralds from the Netherlands. Van Gogh is available in a bewildering range of flavours including melon, pineapple, orange, coconut, apple, citroen, vanilla, raspberry and chocolate.

Word has it that Van Gogh is a multi-grain vodka – predominantly wheat with a little corn and barley. These grains are distilled using a two column process and then redistilled in a copper pot still.

VLADIVAR

Scottish Vodka
37.5% **alc./vol.** (75°proof)
www.vladivar.com
Producer: Whyte & Mackay, Glasgow, Scotland.
UK agent: Whyte & Mackay
US agent: Not available

Vladivar is the number two vodka brand in the UK market, with the majority of its sales being in the north of England and Scotland. Vladivar was originally made in Warrington by Greenalls, until 1990 when the brand was sold to Whyte & Mackay and production moved to Scotland.

VOX

Dutch Vodka
www.voxvodka.com
Producer: The Netherlands for Jim Beam Brands Co.
UK agent: Not generally available
US agent: Jim Beam Brands Co.

Vox is made in the Netherlands from wheat using a five column distillation method. It is hydrated with demineralised water and filtered through screens made of inert material.

IN EASTERN EUROPE EVERYTHING FROM NUCLEAR REACTORS TO POLICE STATIONS HAVE BEEN TURNED INTO VODKA DISTILLERIES.

WOKKA SAKI

English Vodka
40% **alc./vol.** (80?proof)
www.wokkasaki.com
Producer: Extreme Spirits, Steeple Bumpstead, Suffolk, England
UK agent: Extreme Spirits, Suffolk
US agent: Pasternak Wine Imports

A blend of vodka, sake and fruit essence, Wokka Saki launched in the US in 2004. And, although it is made in the UK, it was only launched here in Spring 2006.

Rectified wheat grain spirit is redistilled in a 400l stainless steel pot still known as 'Tom Thumb' by Thames Distillers in London. The resulting spirit is then blended with 20% Japanese honjozo-shu sake and a touch of fruit essence.

The label claims inspiration from "the snow monsters of Mt. Zao". These are giant conifer trees on the slopes of Mount Zao in Japan that are covered with ice during winter and form distorted shapes that stick out of the frozen landscape.
Comment: A waft of peach essence precedes a clean, slightly sweet, creamy palate that has the same peachiness evident in the nose – like a few drops of peach schnapps liqueur in a glass of potato vodka. The sake content is hard to distinguish over the fruit essence and the spirit's peppery burn, and I find the finish strangely aggressive. Wokka Saki should really sit in the flavoured vodka camp – albeit subtly.

WYBOROWA BLUE

Polish Vodka
40% **alc./vol.** (80°proof)
www.polmos.poznan.pl
Producer: Polmos Poznan (Pernod-Ricard), Pozan, Poland
UK agent: Pernod Ricard UK
US agent: Pernod Ricard USA

Pronounced 'Vee-Bor-Ova', Wyborowa claims to be "the world's oldest brand of vodka" with its origins going back to 1823 when Hartwig Kantorowicz established his new distillery in the Polish town of Poznan. In 1927, Wyborowa became the world's first vodka to register its brand name internationally. Wyborowa is produced from hardy winter strains of rye (which tend to grow in the northwest of Poland). These are planted in the autumn and harvested the following summer, meaning that the grain is high in starch and so is easier to break down into sugar and ferment into alcohol.

The rye is sent to privately-owned, small-scale agricultural distilleries, where it is mashed and distilled once in a copper column still, yielding a raw spirit at around 90%. It takes 100kg of rye to produce around 35-37l of spirit. Wyborowa has contracts with 30 such distilleries, which produce this raw spirit according to a stipulated recipe. This spirit is then transferred to Wyborowa's distillery plant for rectification using a three column continuous distillation process. The rectified spirit is then reduced to bottling strength by diluting it with water from the distillery's own deep well. Once diluted, the vodka is passed twice through mesh filters before bottling.
Comment: A nose with nutty hints of rye bread and subtle cracked black pepper leads to a clean and soft but full-flavoured palate where the dry, nutty rye bread notes found on the nose are balanced by an almost creamy sweetness. Nutty (Brazil, walnut and almond) hints extend long into the rounded, clean finish.

●●●●●◐

WYBOROWA EXQUISITE

Polish Vodka
40% **alc./vol.** (80°proof)
www.polmos.poznan.pl
Producer: Polmos Poznan (Pernod-Ricard),
Pozan, Poland
UK agent: Pernod Ricard UK
US agent: Pernod Ricard USA

According to Pernod Ricard's marketing department, legend has it that in 1823, the same year Hartwig Kantorowicz established his new distillery in the Polish town of Poznan, he entered his new vodka into a competition held by a Polish newspaper to find the finest clear vodka in Poland. The head of the judging panel proclaimed it "Wyborowa!" meaning exquisite in English and it was named the best vodka in Poland. Delighted by the result, Kantorowicz decided to name his vodka after the word the panel agreed best described his vodka. Thus, this super premium offering from Wyborowa is 'Exquisite'.

The iconic bottle was designed by architect Frank Gehry, creator of Bilbao's Guggenheim museum, who also happens to be of Polish descent. Those with good memories (or original bottles) will recall that when this line extension was first launched in mid 2004 it was actually named 'Wyborowa Single Estate' with the word 'Exquisite' being relegated to the bottom of the bottle. This new pack reverses this with 'Single Estate' now being in the small print at the foot of the unchanged, shapely Gehry bottle.

Exquisite is distilled from a single rye variety, Dankowskie Zlote, with the 'Single Estate' declaration referencing the fact that it is only made using raw spirit made at a distillery in Turew, Poland. Here, the Dankowskie Zlote is fermented and distilled using a single copper column still. In common with Wyborowa Blue, this raw spirit is then taken to Wyborowa's main distillery where it is rectified and reduced to bottling strength using water from the distillery's own well. Some (including me) gripe that 'Single Estate' should mean that ALL production and even bottling takes place at the one location.
Comment: A delicate, subtly nutty, biscuity, rye bread nose leads to a wonderfully smooth and rounded palate that bursts with flavour. Bone dry, slightly burnt hints of Brazil nuts and rye are softened by subtle sweet hints of French marshmallow. It has a drier and more character-ful palate and a bolder finish than Wyborowa Blue. Surprisingly, in many respects, I find myself preferring the Blue, especially when the slightly false (in my opinion) 'Single Estate' claim and the price is taken into account.

Xellent Swiss vodka is made using two types of bread-quality Swiss rye: Matador and Picasso (Picasso being dominant). Distillerie Willisau source rye grown in the alpine foothills at altitudes of 500-800m and have contracts with farmers there to help control the quality of the rye used.

The fermented mash is distilled in 17 l traditional, small copper alembic stills, each with a 500l capacity. The raw spirit produced by this first distillation is then redistilled using a tall 45-plate column still. The spirit is then further rectified by a second pass through the column still to produce a 96% alc./vol. distillate. This is rested in vats for a couple of months before being diluted with water from the Titlis glacier in Engelberg (Mountain of Angels) at the heart of central Switzerland. The vodka is then rested for a further six months prior to filtration through active carbon and an additional secret filtering technique is performed before it is ready for bottling.
Comment: The nose is minerally with subtle hints of cherry and dark chocolate. The soft, enveloping palate continues the theme with grainy mineral and green tea notes accompanied by hints of bitter chocolate and maraschino cherry. The lightly spiced finish ends with a bitter chocolate dryness. A most unusual vodka.

It's worth pointing out that, judging by my bottle, once the seal is cracked on the silver plastic screw cap it seems ineffectual at properly resealing the bottle so I wouldn't advise laying a bottle in the drawer of your freezer.

●●●●●◐

XELLENT

Swiss Vodka
40% **alc./vol.** (80°proof)
www.xellent.com
Producer: DIWISA (Distillerie Willisau) SA,
Willisau, Switzerland
UK agent: Rubicon Trading Ltd
US agent: The Spirit of Hartford LLC

This is claimed to be the first Swiss vodka - under-standable, because until 1999 it was illegal to distil a vodka like this in Switzerland. The Affentranger family, who own the distillery that produces Xellent, helped lobby for the law to be changed. Their distillery, Distillerie Willisau, was founded in 1918 and lies in the town of Willisau, north of Lake Lucerne.

'MOST RUSSIANS DON'T CARE WHETHER THEY ARE RULED BY FASCISTS OR COMMUNISTS OR EVEN MARTIANS AS LONG AS THEY CAN BUY SIX KINDS OF SAUSAGE IN THE STORE AND LOTS OF CHEAP VODKA.'

RUSSIAN POLITICIAN ALEXANDER LEBED.

●●●●○

YOURI DOLGORUKI

Russian Vodka
40% **alc./vol.** (80°proof)
www.youridolgoruki.com
Producer: Kristall Distillery, Moscow, Russia (for Belvédère S.A. & Vremena Goda)
UK agent: Paragon Vintners Ltd
US agent: Sobieski USA

Distilled and bottled at Moscow's famous Kristall distillery, this super premium vodka is named after the founder of the Russian capital, Youri Dolgoruki and was first produced in 1997 to the celebrate the 850th anniversary of the city of Moscow.

The back of the bottle is silkscreen printed in six colours with an image of the famous St. Basil's Cathedral, which is visible through a clear window in the front of the frosted glass.

Distilled using a four column process and filtration through Russian birch charcoal, I believe that a small amount of sugar and food additives are used to soften and add taste to the vodka.
Comment: Clean neutral style mineral nose, possibly yields some notes of fudge. Clean palate with smooth mouthfeel and light peppery spice. Grainy notes are accompanied by subtle lemon zest. Very, clean, lightly peppered finish.

●●●●◐

ZYTNIA EXTRA

Polish Vodka
40% **alc./vol.** (80°proof)
www.extrazytnia.com.pl/
Producer: Polmos Silesian, Bielsko Bia, Poland.
UK agent: Hakts et Cie Ltd
US agent: Stanley Stawski Imports

Pronounced 'Zhit-Nee-Ya', the name comes from a Polish word used to describe the smile of a village elder or mayor. Extra Zytnia is a traditional, dry, aromatic Polish rye vodka. After distillation, small amounts of apple spirit and aromatic fruit are added to the vodka, giving a subtle, but interesting flavour. A premium version called Specjalna Zytnia is also produced.
Comment: Incredibly smooth rye with hints of pear, and lightly spicy cooked fruit and apple. Cinnamon and pepper spice emerge mid-palate. Mellow but quite vivacious white pepper finish.

'CALL ME WHAT YOU LIKE, ONLY GIVE ME SOME VODKA.'

RUSSIAN PROVERB

Ketel One distillery

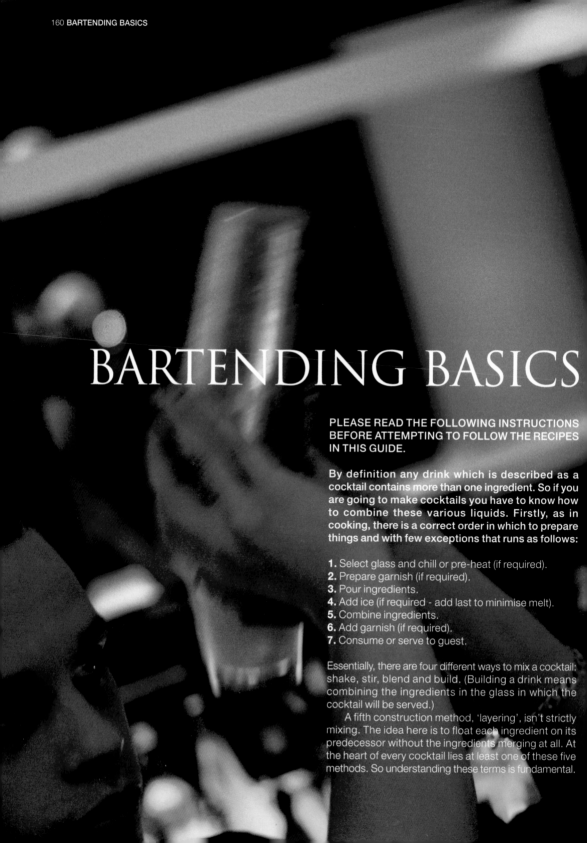

BARTENDING BASICS

PLEASE READ THE FOLLOWING INSTRUCTIONS BEFORE ATTEMPTING TO FOLLOW THE RECIPES IN THIS GUIDE.

By definition any drink which is described as a cocktail contains more than one ingredient. So if you are going to make cocktails you have to know how to combine these various liquids. Firstly, as in cooking, there is a correct order in which to prepare things and with few exceptions that runs as follows:

1. Select glass and chill or pre-heat (if required).
2. Prepare garnish (if required).
3. Pour ingredients.
4. Add ice (if required - add last to minimise melt).
5. Combine ingredients.
6. Add garnish (if required).
7. Consume or serve to guest.

Essentially, there are four different ways to mix a cocktail: shake, stir, blend and build. (Building a drink means combining the ingredients in the glass in which the cocktail will be served.)

A fifth construction method, 'layering', isn't strictly mixing. The idea here is to float each ingredient on its predecessor without the ingredients merging at all. At the heart of every cocktail lies at least one of these five methods. So understanding these terms is fundamental.

SHAKE

When you see the phrase 'shake with ice and strain', you should place all the necessary ingredients with cubed ice in a cocktail shaker and shake briskly for about twenty seconds. Then you should strain the liquid into the glass, leaving the ice behind in the shaker.

Shaking not only mixes a drink. It also chills and dilutes it. The dilution is as important to the resulting cocktail as using the right proportions of each ingredient. If you use too little ice it will quickly melt in the shaker, producing an over-diluted cocktail - so always fill your shaker at least two-thirds full of fresh ice.

Losing your grip while shaking is likely to make a mess and could result in injury, so always hold the shaker with two hands and never shake fizzy ingredients.

Although shakers come in many shapes and sizes there are two basic types.

STANDARD SHAKER

A standard shaker consists of three parts and hence is sometimes referred to as a three-piece shaker. The three pieces are **1.** a flat-bottomed, conical base or 'can', **2.** a top with a built-in strainer and **3.** a cap.

I strongly recommend this style of shaker for amateurs due to its ease of use. Be sure to purchase a shaker with a capacity of at least one pint as this will allow the ice room to travel and so mix more effectively.

TO USE:

1. Combine all ingredients in the base of the shaker and fill two-thirds full with ice.
2. Place the top and cap firmly on the base.
3. Pick up the closed shaker with one hand on the top and the other gripping the bottom and shake vigorously. The cap should always be on the top when shaking and should point away from guests.
4. After shaking briskly for a count of around 20 seconds, lift off the cap, hold the shaker by its base with one finger securing the top and pour the drink through the built-in strainer.

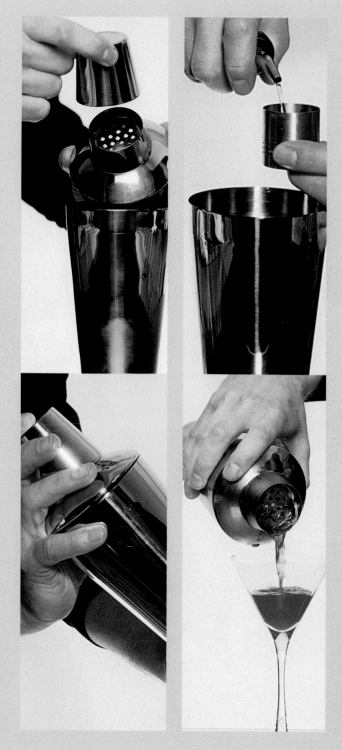

BOSTON SHAKER

A Boston shaker comprises two flat-bottomed cones, one larger than the other. The large cone, or 'can', is made of stainless steel while the smaller cone can be either glass or stainless steel. I prefer glass as this allows both mixer and guest to see the drink being made.

Avoid Boston shakers that rely on a rubber ring to seal. I use Alessi Boston tins as I find these seal without a thump and open with the lightest tap. However good your Boston shaker, these devices demand an element of skill and practice is usually required for a new user to become proficient.

TO USE:

1. Combine ingredients in the glass or smaller of the two cans.

2. Fill the large can with ice and briskly upend over the smaller can (or glass), quickly enough to avoid spilling any ice. Lightly tap the top with the heel of your hand to create a seal between the two parts.

3. Lift shaker with one hand on the top and the other gripping the base and shake vigorously. The smaller can (or glass) should always be on the top when shaking and should point away from guests.

4. After shaking for around 20 seconds, hold the larger (base) can in one hand and break the seal between the two halves of the shaker by tapping the base can with the heel of your other hand at the point where it meets the upper can (or glass).

5. Before pouring place a strainer with a coiled rim (also known as a Hawthorne strainer) over the top of the can and strain the mixture into the glass, leaving the ice cubes behind.

STIR

If a cocktail recipe calls for you to 'stir with ice and strain', stir in a mixing glass using a bar spoon with a long, spiralling stem. If a lipped mixing glass is not available, one half of a Boston shaker, or the base of a standard shaker, will suffice.

Combine the ingredients in the mixing glass, adding the ice last. Slide the back of the spoon down the inside of the mixing glass and stir the drink. Then strain into a glass using a strainer (or the top of a standard shaker if you are using a standard shaker base in place of a mixing glass).

Some bartenders (and I'm one) prefer to use the flat end of a bar spoon to stir a drink. Simply place the flat end on top of the ice in the mixing glass and start to stir, working the spoon down the drink as you go.

FINE STRAIN

Most cocktails that are served 'straight up' without ice benefit from an additional finer strain, over and above the standard strain which keeps ice cubes out of the drink. This 'fine strain' removes small fragments of fruit and fine flecks of ice which can spoil the appearance of a drink. All you need to do is strain a cocktail through the strainer you would normally use while holding a fine sieve, like a tea strainer, between the shaker and the glass. Another popular term for this method is 'double strain'.

BLEND

When a cocktail recipe calls for you to 'blend with ice', place ingredients and ice into a blender and blend until a smooth, even consistency is achieved. Ideally you should use crushed ice, as this lessens wear on the blender's blades. Place liquid ingredients in the blender first, adding the ice last, as always. If you have a variable speed blender, always start slowly and build up speed.

FLAME

The term ignite, flame or flambé means that the drink should be set alight. Please exercise extreme care when setting fire to drinks. Be particularly careful not to knock over a lit drink and never attempt to carry a drink which is still alight. Before drinking, cover the glass so as to suffocate the flame and be aware that the rim of the glass may be hot.

MUDDLE

Muddling means pummelling fruits, herbs and/or spices with a muddler (a blunt tool similar to a pestle) so as to crush them and release their flavour. (You can also use a rolling pin.) As when using a pestle and mortar, push down on the muddler with a twisting action.

Only attempt to muddle in the base of a shaker or a suitably sturdy glass. Never attempt to muddle hard, unripe fruits in a glass as the pressure required could break the glass. I've witnessed a bartender slash his hand open on a broken glass while muddling and can't over-emphasize how careful you should be.

...AYER

...the name would suggest, layered ...nks include layers of different ...redients, often with contrasting ...ours. This effect is achieved by ...refully pouring each ingredient ...o the glass so that it floats on ...predecessor.

...e success of this technique is ...pendent on the density (specific ...vity) of the liquids used. As a rule of ...mb, the less alcohol and the more ...gar an ingredient contains, the ...avier it is. The heaviest ingredients ...ould be poured first and the lightest ...t. Syrups are non-alcoholic and ...ntain a lot of sugar so are usually the ...aviest ingredient. Liqueurs, which ...high in sugar and lower in alcohol ...an spirits, are generally the next ...aviest ingredient. The exception to ...s rule is cream and cream liqueurs, ...ch can float.

One brand of a particular liqueur may ...heavier or lighter than another. The ...ative temperatures of ingredients may ...o affect their ability to float or sink. ...nce a degree of experimentation is ...vitable when creating layered drinks. ...ering can be achieved in one of two ...ys. The first involves pouring down ...spiral handle of a bar spoon, keeping ...flat, disc-shaped end of the spoon ...r the surface of the drink. Alternatively ...u can hold the bowl end of a bar ...oon (or a soup spoon) in contact with ...side of the glass and over the surface ...he drink and pour over it.

The term 'float' refers to layering ...final ingredient on top of a cocktail.

ICE

A plentiful supply of fresh ice is essential to making good cocktails. When buying bagged ice avoid the hollow, tubular kind and the thin wafers. Instead look for large, solid cubes of ice. I have a Hoshizaki ice machine which produces large solid cubes, and thoroughly recommend it.

When filling ice cube trays, use bottled or filtered water to avoid the taste of chlorine often apparent in municipal water supplies. Your ice should be dry, almost sticky to the touch. Never use 'wet' ice that has started to thaw.

When serving a drink over ice, always fill the glass with ice, rather than just adding a few cubes. This makes the drink much colder, the ice lasts longer and so melting ice does not dilute the drink.

Never use ice in a cocktail shaker twice, even if it's to mix the same drink as last time. You should always throw away ice after straining the drink and use fresh ice to fill the glass if required.

Unless otherwise stated, all references to ice in this guide mean cubed ice. If crushed ice is required for a particular recipe, the recipe will state 'crushed ice'. This is available commercially. Alternatively you can crush cubed ice in an ice-crusher or simply bash a bag of it with a rolling pin.

If a glass is broken near your ice stocks, melt the ice with warm water, clean the container and re-stock with fresh ice. If this occurs in a busy bar and you are not immediately able to clean the ice well, mark it as being contaminated with a liberal coating of red grenadine syrup and draw ice from another station.

MEASURING

Balancing each ingredient within a cocktail is key to making a great drink. Therefore the accuracy with which ingredients are measured is critical to the finished cocktail.

In this guide I've expressed the measures of each ingredient in 'shots'. Ideally a shot is 25ml or one US fluid ounce (29.6ml), measured in a standard jigger. (You can also use a clean medicine measure or even a small shot glass.) Whatever measure you use should have straight sides to enable you to accurately judge fractions of a shot. Look out for measures which are graduated for quarter and half shots.

The measure 'spoon' refers to a bar spoon, which is slightly larger than a standard teaspoon.

Some bartenders attempt to measure shots by counting time and estimating the amount of liquid flowing through a bottle's spout. This is known as 'free-pouring' and can be terribly inaccurate. I strongly recommend the use of a physical measure.

GARNISHES

Garnishes are used to decorate cocktails and are often anchored to the rim of the glass. Strictly speaking, garnishes should be edible, so please forget about paper parasols. Anything from banana chunks, strawberries or redcurrants to coffee beans, confectionery, basil leaves and slices of fresh ginger can be used as a garnish. The correct garnish will often enhance the aroma and flavour as well as the look of a drink.

Fruit should be unblemished and washed prior to use. Olives, in particular, should be washed thoroughly to prevent oil from spoiling the appearance of a drink. Cut citrus fruits have a maximum shelf life of 24 hours when refrigerated. Cherries and olives should be stored refrigerated and left in their own juices.

Olives, cherries, pickled onions and fresh berries are sometimes served on cocktail sticks. A whole slice of citrus fruit served on a cocktail stick 'mast' is known as a 'sail': this is often accompanied by a cherry.

Celery sticks may be placed in drinks as stirring rods while cinnamon sticks are often placed in hot drinks and toddies.

To sprinkle chocolate on the surface of a drink you can either shave chocolate using a vegetable peeler or crumble a Cadbury's Flake bar. The instruction 'dust with chocolate' refers to a fine coating of cocoa powder on the surface of a drink. (When dusting with nutmeg it is always best to grate fresh nutmeg as the powdered kind lacks flavour.)

Citrus peels are often used as a garnish. Besides the variations listed under 'zest twist' overleaf, thin, narrow lengths of citrus peel may be tied in a 'knot'. A 'Horse's Neck' is the entire peel of either an orange, a lemon or a lime, cut in a continuous spiral and placed so as to overhang the rim of the glass.

Wedges of lemons and limes are often squeezed into drinks or fixed to the glass as a garnish. A wedge is an eighth segment of the fruit. Cut the 'knobs' from the top and bottom of the fruit, slice the fruit in half lengthwise, then cut each half into four equal wedges lengthwise.

Mint sprigs are often used to garnish cups and juleps.

ZEST TWIST

This term refers to flavouring a drink by releasing the aromatic oils from a strip of citrus zest. Using a knife or peeler, cut a half inch (12mm) wide length of zest from an unwaxed, cleaned fruit so as to leave just a little of the white pith. Hold it over the glass with the thumb and forefinger of each hand, coloured side down. Turn one end clockwise and the other anticlockwise so as to twist the peel and force some of its oils over the surface of the drink. Deposit any flavoursome oils left on the surface of the peel by wiping the coloured side around the rim of the glass. Finally, drop the peel onto the surface of the drink. (Some prefer to dispose of the spent twist.)

A flamed zest twist is a dramatic variation on this theme which involves burning the aromatic oils emitted from citrus fruit zest over the surface of a drink. Lemons and limes are sometimes treated in this way but oranges are most popular. Firm, thick-skinned navel oranges, like Washington Navels, are best.

You will need to cut as wide a strip of zest as you can, wider than you would for a standard twist. Hold the cut zest, peel side down, between the thumb and forefinger about four inches above the drink and gently warm it with a lighter flame. Then pinch the peel by its edges so that its oils squirt through the flame towards the surface of the drink - there should be a flash as the oils ignite. Finally, wipe the zest around the rim of the glass.

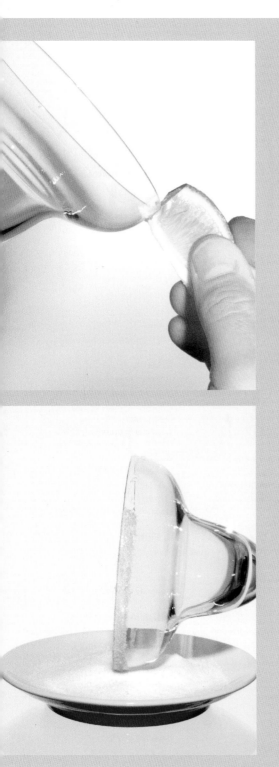

SALT/SUGAR RIM

Some recipes call for the rim of the glass to be coated with salt, sugar or other ingredients such as desiccated coconut or chocolate: you will need to moisten the rim first before the ingredient will hold. When using salt, whip a cut wedge of lime around the outside edge of the rim, then roll the outside edge through a saucer of salt. (Use sea salt rather than iodised salt as the flavour is less biting.) For sweet ingredients like sugar and chocolate, either use an orange slice as you would a lime wedge or moisten a sponge or paper towel with a suitable liqueur and run it around the outside edge of the glass.

Whatever you are using to rim the glass should cling to the outside edge only. Remember, garnishes are not a cocktail ingredient but an optional extra to be consumed by choice. They should not contaminate your cocktail. If some of your garnish should become stuck to the inside edge of the glass, remove it using a fresh fruit wedge or a paper towel.

It is good practice to salt or sugar only two-thirds of the rim of a glass. This allows the drinker the option of avoiding the salt or sugar. If you rim glasses some hours prior to use, the lime juice or liqueur will dry, leaving a crust of salt or sugar crystals around the rim. The glasses can then be placed in a refrigerator to chill ready for use.

A professional piece of equipment with the unfortunate title of a 'rimmer' has three sections, one with a sponge for water or lime juice, one containing sugar and another containing salt. Beware, as this encourages dipping the glass onto a moist sponge and then into the garnish, and so contaminating the inside of the glass.

GLASSWARE

Cocktails are something of a luxury. You don't just ping a cap and pour. These drinks take time and skill to mix so deserve a decent glass.

Before you start, check your glassware is clean and free from chips and marks such as lipstick. Always handle glasses by the base or the stem to avoid leaving finger marks and never put your fingers inside a glass.

Ideally glassware should be chilled in a freezer prior to use. This is particularly important for martini and flute glasses, in which drinks are usually served without ice. It takes about half an hour to sufficiently chill a glass in the freezer.

If time is short, you can chill a glass by filling it with ice (ideally crushed, not cubed) and topping it up with water. Leave the glass to cool while you prepare the drink, then discard the ice and water once you are ready to pour. This method is quicker than chilling in the freezer but not nearly so effective.

To warm a glass ready for a hot cocktail, place a bar spoon in the glass and fill it with hot water. Then discard the water and pour in the drink. Only then should you remove the spoon, which is there to help disperse the shock of the heat.

There are thousands of differently shaped glasses, but if you own those mentioned here you have a glass to suit practically every drink and occasion. Failing that, a set of Collins, Martini and Old-fashioned or Rocks glasses, and possibly flutes if you fancy champagne cocktails, will allow you to serve the majority of drinks in this guide. Use a Martini in place of a Coupette and a Collins as a substitute for Hurricane and Sling glasses.

1. Martini

Those in the old guard of bartending insist on calling this a 'cocktail glass'. It may once have been! But to most of us today a V-shaped glass is a Martini glass. Anything bigger than 7oz is ridiculous, as a true Martini warms up too much in the time it takes to drink such a large one. Chill before use.
Capacity to brim: 7oz / 20cl

2. Sling

This elegant glass has recently become fashionable again – partly due to the popularity of long drinks such as the Russian Spring Punch.
Capacity to brim: 11oz / 32cl

3. Shot

Shot glasses come in all shapes and sizes. You'll need small ones if you're sensible and big ones if you're not!
Capacity to brim (pictured glass): 2oz / 6cl

4. Flute

Flutes are perfect for serving champagne cocktails as their tall, slim design helps maintain the wine's fizz. Chill before use.
Capacity to brim: 6oz / 17cl

5. Collins

In this guide I refer to a tall glass as a 'Collins'. A hi-ball is slightly squatter than a Collins but has the same capacity. A 12oz Collins glass will suffice for cocktails and is ideal for a standard 330ml bottle of beer. However, I favour 14oz glasses with the occasional 8oz for drinks such as Fizzes which are served tall but not very long.
Capacity to brim: 14oz / 40cl or 8oz / 24cl

6. Coupette

This is commonly referred to as a 'Margarita glass' since it is used to serve the hugely popular cocktail of the same name. Its rim cries out for salt.
Capacity to brim: 8oz / 24cl

7. Goblet

Not often used for cocktails, but worth having, if for no other reason than to enjoy your wine. An 11oz glass is big enough to be luxurious.
Capacity to brim: 11oz / 32cl

8. Boston

A tall, heavy conical glass with a thick rim, designed to be combined with a Boston tin to form a shaker. It can also be used as a mixing glass for stirred drinks.
Capacity to brim: 17oz / 48cl

9. Hurricane

Sometimes referred to as a 'poco grande' or 'Piña Colada' glass, this big-bowled glass is commonly used for frozen drinks. It screams out for a pineapple wedge, a cherry and possibly a paper parasol as well. Very Del Boy.
Capacity to brim: 15oz / 43cl

10. Old-fashioned

Another glass whose name refers to the best-known drink served in it. It is also great for enjoying spirits such as whiskey. Choose a luxuriously large glass with a thick, heavy base. Alternatively, the similarly shaped 'Rocks' glass has a thick rim and is usually made from toughened glass so better suited to drinks that require muddling in the glass.
Capacity to brim: 11oz / 32cl

11. Snifter

Sometimes referred to as a 'brandy balloon'. The bigger the bowl, the more luxurious the glass appears. Use to enjoy cocktails and deluxe aged spirits such as Cognac.
Capacity to brim: 12oz / 35cl

12. Toddy

Frequently referred to as a 'liqueur coffee glass', which is indeed its main use, this glass was popularised by the Irish Coffee. Toddy glasses have a handle on the side, allowing you to comfortably hold hot drinks.
Capacity to brim: 8.5oz / 25cl

13. Sour

This small glass is narrow at the stem and tapers out to a wider lip. As the name would suggest, it is used for serving Sours straight-up. I favour serving Sours over ice in an Old-fashioned but any of the recipes in this guide can be strained and served 'up' in this glass.
Capacity to brim: 4oz / 12cl

14. Rocks

Like an Old-fashioned with a thick rim, this is usually made from toughened glass - perfect for drinks that require muddling in the glass. A hardy glass, if there is such a thing.
Capacity to brim: 9oz / 27cl

THE 14 KEY INGREDIENTS

MAKE MORE THAN 100 COCKTAILS IN THIS GUIDE WITH JUST THE 14 KEY ALCOHOLIC INGREDIENTS.

LOOK FOR THE ⚷

You don't need a fully stocked bar to start mixing cocktails. After all, many of the greatest cocktails require few ingredients: a Martini is made with just two and a Margarita three ingredients.

With just the fourteen Key Ingredients opposite, a few mixers, some fresh fruit, copious amounts of ice and a handful of kitchen basics you will be able to make more than a hundred cocktails (listed overleaf).

Add your favourite spirits and liqueurs to these fourteen and then refer to our full ingredients appendix on page 272 to find yet more fantastic drinks.

**KETEL ONE
VODKA**

**PLYMOUTH
GIN**

**LIGHT WHITE
RUM**

PARTIDA TEQUILA

BOURBON

**BLENDED SCOTCH
WHISKY**

COGNAC

**COINTREAU
LIQUEUR**

**COFFEE
LIQUEUR**

**GRAND MARNIER
LIQUEUR**

**GIFFARD
APRICOT
BRANDY**

**RICH BERRY
LIQUEUR**

**DRY
VERMOUTH**

CHAMPAGNE

ESSENTIAL JUICES & MIXERS

CRANBERRY JUICE   ORANGE JUICE   PRESSED APPLE JUICE   PINK GRAPEFRUIT JUICE   PINEAPPLE JUICE   SODA WATER   COLA   GINGER ALE & GINGER BEER   TONIC WATER

FRIDGE & LARDER ESSENTIALS

SUGAR (GOMME) SYRUP   GRENADINE SYRUP   LIME CORDIAL   ANGOSTURA AROMATIC BITTERS   FRESH LEMONS   FRESH LIMES

FRESH MINT   STRAWBERRIES   RASPBERRIES   MARASCHINO CHERRIES   VANILLA PODS   DOUBLE CREAM

MILK   EGGS   SUGAR CUBES   RUNNY HONEY   FILTER & ESPRESSO COFFEE   EARL GREY TEA

NOT FORGETTING... ICE - THE MOST IMPORTANT COCKTAIL INGREDIENT

IF YOU HAVE THE 14 KEY ALCOHOLIC INGREDIENTS LISTED ON THE PREVIOUS PAGE ALONG WITH THE FRIDGE AND LARDER ESSENTIALS FEATURED OPPOSITE THEN YOU HAVE ALL YOU NEED TO MAKE THE FOLLOWING COCKTAILS.

WE MARK ALL COCKTAILS WHICH CAN BE MADE USING THESE BASIC INGREDIENTS WITH OUR KEY ALCOHOLIC INGREDIENT LOGO ⚷

ABSOLUTELY FABULOUS ●●●●○
ACAPULCO DAIQUIRI ●●●●○
ACE ●●●●○○
ADIOS ●●●○○
ADIOS AMIGOS COCKTAIL ●●●○○
AGENT ORANGE ●●●●○
AGGRAVATION ●●●●○
ALAN'S APPLE BREEZE ●●●○○
ALICE FROM DALLAS ●●●○○
ALICE IN WONDERLAND ●●●○○
AMERICANA ●●●○○
ANITA'S ATTITUDE ADJUSTER ●●●○○
APPLE DAIQUIRI ●●●●○
APPLE MARTINI #1 (SIMPLE VERSION) ●●●●○
APPLE VIRGIN MOJITO (MOCKTAIL) ●●●●○
APPLILY MARRIED CCCCE
APRICOT FIZZ ●●●○○
APRICOT LADY SOUR ●●●●○○
APRICOT MARTINI ●●●○○
ARIZONA BREEZE ●●●●○
ARNAUD MARTINI ●●●●○
ARNOLD PALMER ●●●●○
ATTITUDE ADJUSTER ●●●○○
BACARDI COCKTAIL ●●●●○
BALALAIKA ●●●●○
BALD EAGLE ●●●●○
BALLET RUSSE ●●●○○
BARNUM (WAS RIGHT) ●●●●○
BATANGA ●●●●○
BAY BREEZE ●●●○○
BEACH ICED TEA ●●●○○
BEBBO ●●●●○
BEE'S KNEES #2 ●●●●○
BEE'S KNEES #3 ●●●●○
BERMUDA ROSE COCKTAIL ●●●●○
BETWEEN DECKS ●●●○○
BETWEEN THE SHEETS #1 (CLASSIC FORMULA) ●●●○○
BETWEEN THE SHEETS #2 (DIFFORD'S FORMULA) ●●●●○
BEVERLY HILLS ICED TEA ●●●○○
BIARRITZ ●●●●○
BINGO ●●●○○
BITTER SWEET SYMPHONY ●●●○○
BLACK CHERRY MARTINI ●●●●○
BLACK FEATHER ●●●●○
BLACK RUSSIAN ●●●○○
BLINKER ●●●●○
BLUE BLAZER ●●●○○
BORA BORA BREW (MOCKTAIL) ●●●○○
BOSTON ●●●●○
BOULEVARD ●●●●○
BOURBON SMASH ●●●○○
BRADFORD ●●●●○
BRANDY BUCK ●●●○○
BRANDY FIZZ ●●●●○

BRANDY FLIP ●●●●○
BRANDY SMASH ●●●●○
BRANDY SOUR ●●●●○
BREAKFAST MARTINI ●●●●●
THE BUCK ●●●●○
BUCK'S FIZZ ●●●○○
BUENA VIDA ●●●●○
BULLDOG ●●●●○
BULL'S BLOOD ●●●●○
C C KAZI ●●●●○
CACTUS BANGER ●●●●○
CAIPIRISSIMA ●●●●○
CAIPIROVSKA ●●●●○
CAJUN MARTINI ●●●○○
CALIFORNIAN MARTINI ●●●●○
CALL ME OLD-FASHIONED ●●●●○
CANCHANCHARA ●●●○○
CAPE CODDER ●●●●○
CAPPERCAILLE ●●●●○
CARROL COCKTAIL ●●●○○
CASSINI ●●●●○
CELTIC MARGARITA ●●●●○
CHAMPAGNE COCKTAIL ●●●○○
CHAMPAGNE CUP ●●●○○
CHARLIE CHAPLIN ●●●○○
CHELSEA SIDECAR ●●●●○
CHIMAYO ●●●●○
CHIN CHIN ●●●●○
CINDERELLA ●●○○○
CLARIDGE COCKTAIL ●●●●○
CLIPPER COCKTAIL ●●●○○
CLOCKWORK ORANGE ●●●○○
CLOVER LEAF COCKTAIL #1 (CLASSIC FORMULA) ●●●●○
CLOVER LEAF COCKTAIL #2 (MODERN FORMULA) ●●●○○
COFFEE & VANILLA DAIQUIRI ●●●●○
COFFEE BATIDA ●●●○○
COLONEL COLLINS ●●●●○
COLONEL T ●●●○○
COLONEL'S BIG OPU ●●●○○
COLORADO BULLDOG ●●○○○
CORDLESS SCREWDRIVER ●●●○○
COSMOPOLITAN #4 (1934 RECIPE) ●●●●○
COUNTRY BREEZE ●●●●○
COWBOY MARTINI ●●●○○
CRANBERRY DELICIOUS ●●●○○
CRANBERRY & MINT MARTINI ●●●○○
CREAMSICLE ●●●○○
THE CROW COCKTAIL ●●●○○
CUBA LIBRE ●●●○○
CUBA PINTADA ●●●●○
CUBAN ISLAND ●●●○○
CUBAN MASTER ●●●○○
CUBAN SPECIAL ●●●○○

cocktails a-c

A

ABACAXI RICAÇO UPDATED ●●●●○

Glass: Pineapple shell (frozen)
Garnish: Cut a straw sized hole in the top of the pineapple and replace it as a lid.
Method: Cut the top off a small pineapple and carefully scoop out the flesh from the base to leave a shell with 12mm ('/2 ") thick walls. Place the shell in a freezer to chill. Remove the hard core from the pineapple flesh and discard; roughly chop the remaining flesh, add other ingredients and **BLEND** with one 12oz scoop of crushed ice. Pour into the pineapple shell and serve with straws. (The flesh of one pineapple blended with the following ingredients will fill at least two shells.)

1	fresh	Pineapple
3	shot(s)	Mount Gay golden rum
3/4	shot(s)	Freshly squeezed lime juice
1/2	shot(s)	Sugar syrup (2 sugar to 1 water)

Origin: Adapted from David A. Embury's 1948 'Fine Art of Mixing Drinks'. Pronounced 'Ah-bah-Kah-shee Rich-kah-S0', the Portuguese name of this Brazilian drink literally translates as 'Extra Delicious Pineapple'.
Comment: Looks and tastes great but a load of hassle to make.

ABACI BATIDA ●●●●○

Glass: Collins
Garnish: Pineapple wedge on rim
Method: SHAKE all ingredients with ice and strain into glass filled with crushed ice.

2'/2	shot(s)	Cachaça
3	shot(s)	Freshly extracted pineapple juice
1/2	shot(s)	Sugar syrup (2 sugar to 1 water)
1/2	shot(s)	Freshly squeezed lemon juice

Origin: The Batida is a traditional Brazilian drink and 'Abaci' means pineapple in Portuguese, the official language of Brazil.
Comment: Unfortunately, this excellent drink has not transferred as quickly from its homeland as the Caipirinha.

ABBEY MARTINI ●●●●○

Glass: Martini
Garnish: Orange zest twist
Method: SHAKE all ingredients with ice and fine strain into chilled glass.

2	shot(s)	Plymouth gin
1	shot(s)	Sweet vermouth
1	shot(s)	Freshly squeezed orange juice
3	dashes	Angostura aromatic bitters

Origin: This 1930s classic cocktail is closely related to the better known Bronx.
Comment: A dry, orangey, herbal, gin laced concoction.

A.B.C. ●●●○○

Glass: Shot
Method: Refrigerate ingredients then **LAYER** in chilled glass by carefully pouring in the following order.

1/2	shot(s)	Luxardo Amaretto di Saschira
1/2	shot(s)	Baileys Irish cream liqueur
1/2	shot(s)	Rémy Martin cognac

Comment: A stripy shooter with almond, whiskey, cream and cognac.

ABSINTHE COCKTAIL #1 ●●●●○

Glass: Martini
Garnish: Mint leaf
Method: SHAKE all ingredients with ice and fine strain into chilled glass.

1	shot(s)	La Fée Parisian 68% absinthe
1	shot(s)	Chilled mineral water
1/4	shot(s)	Sugar syrup (2 sugar to 1 water)

Variant: If grenadine (pomegranate syrup) is substituted for the sugar syrup this becomes a Tomate.
Origin: Dr. Ordinaire perfected his recipe for absinthe in 1792 and from day one it required the addition of water and sugar to make it palatable.
Comment: Absinthe tamed and served up.

ABSINTHE COCKTAIL #2 ●●●○○

Glass: Martini
Garnish: Lemon zest twist
Method: SHAKE all ingredients with ice and fine strain into chilled glass.

1	shot(s)	La Feé Parisian (68%) absinthe
1/4	shot(s)	Almond (orgeat) syrup
1/4	shot(s)	Anisette liqueur
1	dash	Angostura aromatic bitters
3/4	shot(s)	Chilled mineral water (reduce if wet ic

Variant: Absinthe Frappé - served over crushed ic
Origin: My adaptation of a classic recipe.
Comment: This aniseed flavoured mix tastes sur prisingly tame but includes a shot of the notorio green fairy.

FOR MORE INFORMATION SEE OUR

**INGREDIENTS
APPENDIX
ON PAGE 272**

ABSINTHE DRIP COCKTAIL #1 (FRENCH METHOD) NEW

●●●○○

Glass: Old-fashioned or absinthe glass
Method: POUR absinthe into glass. PLACE cube of sugar on a slotted absinthe spoon resting across the top of the glass. Using a bottle of chilled mineral water with a small hole in the cap, DRIP water over the sugar so it dissolves and drips into the glass. Traditionally the same amount of sugar is added as water but I find full strength absinthe requires more dilution. Add ice, stir and serve.

1½	shot(s)	La Feé Parisian (68%) absinthe
1	large	Sugar cube
2	shot(s)	Chilled mineral water (reduce if wet ice)

Origin: This is the traditional method of serving absinthe. It was common until shortly before the First World War, when the drink was banned in most countries.
Comment: Patience is a virtue. Slow dripping of the water is essential to dissolve the entire sugar cube and give the drink enough sweetness to balance the absinthe.

ABSINTHE DRIP COCKTAIL #2

(CZECH METHOD) NEW

●●●○○

Glass: Old-fashioned or absinthe glass
Method: PLACE sugar cube on a slotted absinthe spoon resting across the top of the glass. POUR absinthe over the sugar cube into the glass. LIGHT the absinthe soaked cube and leave to burn and caramelise. Using a bottle of chilled mineral water with a small hole in the cap, DRIP water over what's left of the sugar so it dissolves and drips into the glass. Add ice, stir and serve.

1½	shot(s)	La Feé Parisian (68%) absinthe
1	large	Sugar cube
2	shot(s)	Chilled mineral water

Comment: More about the theatrics involved in its making than the taste of the finished drink.

ABSINTHE FRAPPÉ UPDATED

●●●●○

Glass: Old-fashioned
Garnish: Mint sprig
Method: SHAKE all ingredients with ice and fine strain into glass filled with crushed ice. CHURN (stir) and serve with straws.

1½	shot(s)	La Fée Parisian (68%) absinthe
½	shot(s)	Marie Brizard anisette liqueur
1½	shot(s)	Chilled mineral water
¼	shot(s)	Sugar syrup (2 sugar to 1 water)

Origin: Created in 1874 by Cayetano Ferrer at Aleix's Coffee House, New Orleans, which consequently became known as The Absinthe Room. Today the establishment is fittingly known as the Old Absinthe House but sadly US law prevents it from actually serving absinthe.
Comment: Aniseed and the fire of absinthe are moderated by sugar and ice but still a dangerous combination.

ABSINTHE ITALIANO COCKTAIL NEW

●●●○○

Glass: Martini
Garnish: Lemon zest twist
strain into chilled glass.

1	shot(s)	La Fée Parisian (68%) absinthe
½	shot(s)	Marie Brizard anisette liqueur
¼	shot(s)	Luxardo maraschino liqueur
1½	shot(s)	Chilled mineral water (reduce if wet ice)

Origin: A long lost classic.
Comment: Liqueurs sweeten and tame the absinthe burn in this milky green concoction.

ABSINTHE SOUR

●●●●○

Glass: Old-fashioned
Garnish: Lemon zest twist
Method: SHAKE all ingredients with ice and strain into ice-filled glass.

1	shot(s)	La Fée Parisian 68% absinthe
1	shot(s)	Sugar syrup (2 sugar to 1 water)
1	shot(s)	Freshly squeezed lemon juice
½	fresh	Egg white

Variant: Served 'up' in sour glass.
Comment: A touch of the sours for absinthe lovers.

ABSINTHE SPECIAL COCKTAIL NEW

●●●○○

Glass: Martini
Garnish: Lemon zest twist
Method: SHAKE all ingredients with ice and fine strain into chilled glass.

1	shot(s)	La Fée Parisian (68%) absinthe
¼	shot(s)	Plymouth gin
¼	shot(s)	Marie Brizard anisette liqueur
1	dash	Fee Brothers orange bitters
2	dashes	Angostura aromatic bitters
1½	shot(s)	Chilled mineral water (reduce if wet ice)

Origin: A long lost classic.
Comment: Tongue numbingly strong in flavour and alcohol.

ABSINTHE SUISESSE

●●●○○

Glass: Old-fashioned
Garnish: Mint sprig
Method: SHAKE all ingredients with ice and strain into glass filled with crushed ice.

1½	shot(s)	La Fée Parisian (68%) absinthe
½	shot(s)	Orgeat (almond) sugar syrup
1	fresh	Egg white
½	shot(s)	Double (heavy) cream
½	shot(s)	Milk

Origin: New Orleans 1930s.
Variant: Also spelt 'Suissesse' and sometimes made with absinthe, vermouth, sugar, crème de menthe and egg white shaken and topped with sparkling water.
Comment: Absinthe smoothed with cream and sweet almond.

ABSINTHE WITHOUT LEAVE

Glass: Shot
Method: Refrigerate ingredients then **LAYER** in chilled glass by carefully pouring in the following order.

¾	shot(s)	Pisang Ambon liqueur
¾	shot(s)	Baileys Irish cream liqueur
½	shot(s)	La Fée Parisian (68%) absinthe

Origin: Discovered in 2003 at Hush, London, England.
Comment: This green and brown stripy shot is easy to layer but not so easy to drink.

ACE

Glass: Martini
Garnish: Maraschino cherry on rim
Method: SHAKE all ingredients with ice and fine strain into chilled glass.

2	shot(s)	Plymouth gin
½	shot(s)	Pomegranate (grenadine) syrup
½	shot(s)	Double (heavy) cream
½	shot(s)	Milk
½	fresh	Egg white

Comment: Pleasant, creamy, sweetened gin. Add more pomegranate syrup to taste.

ABSOLUTELY FABULOUS UPDATED

Glass: Flute
Garnish: Strawberry on rim
Method: SHAKE first two ingredients with ice and strain into glass. **TOP** with champagne.

1	shot(s)	Ketel One vodka
2	shot(s)	Cranberry juice
Top up with		Brut champagne

Origin: Created in 1999 at Monte's Club, London, England, and named after the Absolutely Fabulous television series where Patsy consumed copious quantities of Stoli and Bolly – darlings.
Comment: Easy to quaff – Patsy would love it.

ACE OF CLUBS DAIQUIRI

Glass: Martini
Garnish: Dust with cocoa powder
Method: SHAKE all ingredients with ice and fine strain into chilled glass.

2	shot(s)	Mount Gay Eclipse golden rum
½	shot(s)	Giffard White crème de cacao
½	shot(s)	Freshly squeezed lime juice
⅛	shot(s)	Sugar syrup (2 sugar to 1 water)

Origin: A long lost classic thought to have heralded from the Bermudian nightclub of the same name.
Comment: A Daiquiri with a hint of chocolate.

ACAPULCO

Glass: Collins
Garnish: Pineapple wedge on rim
Method: SHAKE all ingredients with ice and strain into ice-filled glass.

1	shot(s)	Partida tequila
1	shot(s)	Mount Gay Eclipse golden rum
1	shot(s)	Freshly squeezed grapefruit juice
2½	shot(s)	Pressed pineapple juice
½	shot(s)	Sugar syrup (2 sugar to 1 water)

Comment: An innocuous, fruity mixture laced with tequila and rum.

ACHILLES HEEL

Glass: Collins
Garnish: Apple slice
Method: SHAKE all ingredients with ice and strain into ice-filled glass.

2	shot(s)	Zubrówka bison vodka
¼	shot(s)	Chambord black raspberry liqueur
¼	shot(s)	Peach schnapps liqueur
1	shot(s)	Pressed apple juice
½	shot(s)	Freshly squeezed lemon juice

Origin: Created in 2005 at Koba, Brighton, England.
Comment: If you like French Martinis you'll love this semi-sweet Tatanka with knobs on.

ACAPULCO DAIQUIRI

Glass: Martini
Garnish: Lime wedge on rim
Method: SHAKE all ingredients with ice and fine strain into chilled glass.

1½	shot(s)	Light white rum
½	shot(s)	Cointreau triple sec
¾	shot(s)	Freshly squeezed lemon juice
¾	shot(s)	Rose's lime cordial
½	fresh	Egg white

Comment: A smooth, yet citrus-rich Daiquiri.

ADAM & EVE

Glass: Old-fashioned
Garnish: Lemon zest twist
Method: SHAKE all ingredients with ice and strain into ice-filled glass.

2	shot(s)	Bourbon whiskey
½	shot(s)	Galliano liqueur
¼	shot(s)	Sugar syrup (2 sugar to 1 water)
3	dashes	Angostura aromatic bitters

Comment: Lovers of the Sazerac will appreciate this herbal, bourbon-laced concoction.

●●●●○

ADELAIDE SWIZZLE NEW

Glass: Collins
Garnish: Lime slice
Method: POUR all ingredients into glass filled with crushed ice and SWIZZLE.

2	shot(s)	Light white rum
1/2	shot(s)	Freshly squeezed lime juice
3/4	shot(s)	Velvet Falernum liqueur
2	dashes	Peychaud's aromatic bitters

Origin: This is the signature cocktail at Café Adelaide's Swizzle Stick Bar, New Orleans, USA. There it is made with a liquid poured from a plain bottle marked 'top secret' but, having tried a drop, I think it is Falernum.
Comment: A slightly pink, dry, spicy long drink with rum and a hint of cloves and lime.

●●●◐○

ADIOS

Glass: Shot
Method: Refrigerate ingredients then LAYER in chilled glass by carefully pouring in the following order.

3/4	shot(s)	Kahlúa coffee liqueur
3/4	shot(s)	Partida tequila

Comment: Surprisingly tasty with a potent agave reminder of what you've just knocked back.

●●●◐○

ADIOS AMIGOS COCKTAIL NEW ⌐

Glass: Martini
Garnish: Lemon zest twist
Method: SHAKE all ingredients with ice and fine strain into chilled glass.

1	shot(s)	Light white rum
1/2	shot(s)	Dry vermouth
1/2	shot(s)	Rémy Martin cognac
1/2	shot(s)	Plymouth gin
1/4	shot(s)	Freshly squeezed lime juice
1/4	shot(s)	Sugar syrup (2 sugar to 1 water)
1/2	shot(s)	Chilled mineral water (omit if wet ice)

Origin: Adapted from Victor Bergeron's 'Trader Vic's Bartender's Guide' (1972 revised edition).
Comment: To quote Vic, "You know that adios means good-bye. You drink two or three of these, and it's adios, believe me, it's adios."

●●●●○

ADONIS

Glass: Martini
Garnish: Orange zest twist
Method: STIR all ingredients with ice and strain into chilled glass.

2	shot(s)	Tio Pepe fino sherry
1	shot(s)	Sweet vermouth
2	dashes	Fee Brothers orange bitters

Origin: Thought to have been created in 1886 to celebrate the success of a Broadway musical.
Comment: Surprisingly delicate, dry, aromatic oldie.

●●●●◐○

AFFINITY

Glass: Martini
Garnish: Lemon zest twist
Method: STIR all ingredients with ice and strain into chilled glass.

2	shot(s)	Scotch whisky
1	shot(s)	Sweet vermouth
1	shot(s)	Dry vermouth
3	dashes	Angostura aromatic bitters

AKA: Scotch Manhattan
Variant: Rob Roy & Violet Affinity
Comment: This classic cocktail may be something of an acquired taste for many modern drinkers.

●●●○○

AFTER EIGHT

Glass: Shot
Method: SHAKE all ingredients with ice and fine strain into chilled glass.

1/2	shot(s)	Ketel One vodka
1/2	shot(s)	Giffard White crème de cacao
1/2	shot(s)	Giffard Giffard green crème de menthe

Comment: Looks like mouthwash but tastes like liquid After Eight chocolates.

●●○○○

AFTER SIX SHOT

Glass: Shot
Method: Refrigerate ingredients then LAYER in chilled glass by carefully pouring in the following order.

1/2	shot(s)	Kahlúa coffee liqueur
1/2	shot(s)	Giffard white crème de Menthe Pastille
1/2	shot(s)	Baileys Irish cream liqueur

Comment: A layered, creamy, coffee and mint shot.

●●●●○

AFTERBURNER

Glass: Snifter
Method: POUR all ingredients into glass, swirl to mix, FLAMBÉ and then extinguish flame. Please take care and beware of hot glass rim.

1	shot(s)	Giffard white crème de Menthe Pastille
1	shot(s)	Kahlúa coffee liqueur
1/2	shot(s)	Wray & Nephew overproof rum

Comment: A surprisingly smooth and moreish peppermint-laced drink.

DRINKS ARE GRADED AS FOLLOWS:

● DISGUSTING ●○ PRETTY AWFUL ●● BEST AVOIDED
●●○ DISAPPOINTING ●●● ACCEPTABLE ●●●○ GOOD
●●●● RECOMMENDED ●●●●◐ HIGHLY RECOMMENDED
●●●●● OUTSTANDING / EXCEPTIONAL

A

AGED HONEY DAIQUIRI

Glass: Martini
Garnish: Lime wedge on rim
Method: STIR honey with rum in base of shaker until honey dissolves. Add lime juice and water, SHAKE with ice and fine strain into chilled glass.

2	shot(s)	Aged rum
1½	spoons	Runny honey
½	shot(s)	Freshly squeezed lime juice
½	shot(s)	Chilled mineral water (omit if wet ice)

Comment: Sweet honey replaces sugar syrup in this natural Daiquiri. Try experimenting with different honeys. I favour orange blossom honey.

AGENT ORANGE

Glass: Old-fashioned
Garnish: Orange zest twist
Method: SHAKE all ingredients with ice and strain into ice-filled glass.

1	shot(s)	Ketel One vodka
½	shot(s)	Grand Marnier
½	shot(s)	Cointreau triple sec
2	shot(s)	Freshly squeezed orange juice

Comment: Fresh orange is good for you. This has all of the flavour but few of the health benefits.

AGGRAVATION

Glass: Old-fashioned
Garnish: Dust with freshly grated nutmeg
Method: SHAKE all ingredients with ice and strain into ice-filled glass.

2	shot(s)	Scotch whisky
¾	shot(s)	Kahlúa coffee liqueur
¾	shot(s)	Double (heavy) cream
¾	shot(s)	Milk
¼	shot(s)	Sugar syrup (2 sugar to 1 water)

Comment: If you like Scotch and enjoy creamy drinks, you'll love this.

FOR MORE INFORMATION SEE OUR
INGREDIENTS APPENDIX ON PAGE 272

AIR MAIL

Glass: Martini
Garnish: Mint leaf
Method: STIR honey with rum in base of shaker until honey dissolves. Add lemon and orange juice, SHAKE with ice and fine strain into chilled glass. TOP with champagne.

1	shot(s)	Mount Gay Eclipse golden rum
2	spoons	Runny honey
½	shot(s)	Freshly squeezed lime juice
½	shot(s)	Freshly squeezed orange juice
Top up with		Brut champagne

Origin: This old classic is basically a Honeysuckle topped up with champagne.
Comment: Rum, honey and a touch of citrus freshness make this one of the better champagne cocktails.

A.J.

Glass: Martini
Garnish: Dust with cinnamon powder
Method: SHAKE all ingredients with ice and fine strain into chilled glass.

2	shot(s)	Boulard Grand Solage Calvados
2	shot(s)	Freshly squeezed grapefruit juice
½	shot(s)	Sugar syrup (2 sugar to 1 water)

Comment: Amazingly simple and beautifully balanced. I hope you like apple brandy as much as I do.

AKU AKU NEW

Glass: Large Martini (10oz)
Garnish: Pineapple wedge & cherry on rim
Method: BLEND all ingredients with 12oz scoop crushed ice. Serve with short straws.

1	shot(s)	Light white rum
½	shot(s)	Peach schnapps liqueur
1½	shot(s)	Pressed pineapple juice
½	shot(s)	Sugar syrup (2 sugar to 1 water)
¾	shot(s)	Freshly squeezed lime juice
10	fresh	Mint leaves

Origin: Adapted from Victor Bergeron's 'Trader Vic's Bartender's Guide' (1972 revised edition).
Comment: This Tiki classic looks a little like frozen stagnant pond water but tastes minty fresh and rather good.

ALABAMA SLAMMER #1 UPDATED

Glass: Martini
Garnish: Orange zest twist
Method: SHAKE all ingredients with ice and fine strain into chilled glass.

1½	shot(s)	Ketel One vodka
¾	shot(s)	Southern Comfort
1	shot(s)	Freshly squeezed orange juice
¼	shot(s)	Pomegranate (grenadine) syrup

Comment: None of the ingredients come from Alabama and the drink is served too long to slam. However, it's a good, rhythmic, rhyming name, if a little naff these days.

●●●○○

ALABAMA SLAMMER #2 UPDATED

Glass: Old-fashioned
Garnish: Peach wedge on rim
Method: SHAKE all ingredients with ice and strain into ice-filled glass.

1¹/₂	shot(s)	Southern Comfort
¹/₂	shot(s)	Plymouth sloe gin liqueur
¹/₂	shot(s)	Luxardo Amaretto di Saschira
2	shot(s)	Freshly squeezed orange juice
³/₄	shot(s)	Freshly squeezed lemon juice

Comment: Rich in flavour and quite sweet with a citrus bite. Surprisingly peachy!

●●●●◐

THE ALAMAGOOZLUM COCKTAIL UPDATED

Glass: Martini
Garnish: Pineapple wedge on rim
Method: SHAKE all ingredients with ice and fine strain into chilled glass.

1	shot(s)	Jonge jenever
³/₄	shot(s)	Yellow Chartreuse
³/₄	shot(s)	Wray & Nephew overproof white rum
¹/₄	shot(s)	Grand Marnier liqueur*
³/₄	shot(s)	Sugar syrup (2 sugar to 1 water)
1	shot(s)	Chilled mineral water
¹/₄	shot(s)	Angostura aromatic bitters
¹/₄	fresh	Egg white

Origin: Adapted from David A. Embury's 1948 'Fine Art of Mixing Drinks', where he writes, "This cocktail is supposed to have been a speciality of the elder Morgan of the House of Morgan, which goes to prove as a bartender he was an excellent banker."
Comment: Even Mr Embury would approve of this version. Overproof Jamaican rum and copious amounts of bitters make this drink.

●●●◐○

ALAN'S APPLE BREEZE 🗝

Glass: Collins
Garnish: Apple wedge on rim
Method: SHAKE all ingredients with ice and strain into ice-filled glass.

2	shot(s)	Light white rum
³/₄	shot(s)	Giffard apricot brandy du Roussillon
2	shot(s)	Pressed apple juice
2	shot(s)	Cranberry juice
¹/₂	shot(s)	Freshly squeezed lime juice
¹/₂	shot(s)	Sugar syrup (2 sugar to 1 water)

Origin: Created in 2002 by Alan Johnston at Metropolitan, Glasgow, Scotland.
Comment: A sweet, tangy version of the Apple Breeze.

●●●●○   A

B

ALASKA MARTINI UPDATED

Glass: Martini
Garnish: Orange zest twist
Method: SHAKE all ingredients with ice and fine strain into chilled glass.

2¹/₂	shot(s)	Plymouth gin
³/₄	shot(s)	Yellow Chartreuse
1	shot(s)	Tio Pepe fino sherry
3	dashes	Fee Brothers orange bitters

AKA: Nome
Origin: In his 1930 'The Savoy Cocktail Book', Harry Craddock writes, "So far as can be ascertained this delectable potion is NOT the staple diet of the Esquimaux. It was probably first thought of in South Carolina – hence its name." The addition of dry sherry is recommended in David Embury's 1948 'Fine Art of Mixing Drinks'.
Comment: If you like gin and Chartreuse, you'll love this strong and complex Martini.

●●●●○

ALASKAN MARTINI NEW

Glass: Martini
Garnish: Lime zest twist discarded & mint leaf
Method: STIR all ingredients with ice and strain into chilled glass.

2¹/₂	shot(s)	Plymouth gin
³/₄	shot(s)	Yellow Chartreuse

Origin: Modern version of the Alaska.
Comment: Stir long and well – this needs dilution. The result will appeal to gin and Chartreuse fans.

●●●○○

ALESSANDRO UPDATED

Glass: Martini
Garnish: Lemon zest twist
Method: SHAKE all ingredients with ice and fine strain into chilled glass.

1¹/₂	shot(s)	Opal Nera black sambuca
³/₄	shot(s)	Plymouth gin
³/₄	shot(s)	Double (heavy) cream
³/₄	shot(s)	Milk

Comment: Hints of aniseed, elderflower and gin emerge from this grey, creamy drink.

●●●◐○

ALEXANDER

Glass: Martini
Garnish: Dust with freshly grated nutmeg
Method: SHAKE all ingredients with ice and fine strain into chilled glass.

1¹/₂	shot(s)	Plymouth gin
1	shot(s)	Giffard White crème de cacao
³/₄	shot(s)	Double (heavy) cream
³/₄	shot(s)	Milk

AKA: Gin Alexander or Princess Mary
Comment: A Prohibition favourite – white, smooth and better than you'd imagine.

ALEXANDER

The original Alexander, a mix of gin, crème de cacao and cream, came into existence early in the twentieth century, certainly before 1917. It became a Prohibition favourite as the cream and nutmeg garnish disguised the rough taste of homemade 'bathtub' gin. While the original, gin based Alexander has slipped from popularity, its successors, particularly the Brandy Alexander, have an enduring place on the world's cocktail lists.

Alexander variations include
Alessandro
Alexander the Great
Alexander's Big Brother
Alexander's Sister
Alexandra
Bird of Paradise
Brandy Alexander
Cherry Alexander
Irish Alexander

●●●●○○

ALEXANDER THE GREAT UPDATED

Glass: Martini
Garnish: Dust with freshly grated nutmeg
Method: SHAKE all ingredients with ice and fine strain into chilled glass.

1½	shot(s)	Ketel One vodka
½	shot(s)	Kahlúa coffee liqueur
½	shot(s)	Giffard White crème de cacao
¾	shot(s)	Double (heavy) cream
¾	shot(s)	Milk

Comment: A tasty combination of coffee, chocolate and cream, laced with vodka.

●●●●○○

ALEXANDER'S BIG BROTHER

Glass: Martini
Garnish: Physalis (Cape gooseberry) on rim
Method: SHAKE all ingredients with ice and fine strain into chilled glass.

1½	shot(s)	Plymouth gin
¼	shot(s)	Cointreau triple sec
¾	shot(s)	Bols Blue curaçao liqueur
¾	shot(s)	Double (heavy) cream
¾	shot(s)	Milk

Comment: Orangey in taste and creamy blue in colour - mildly better than pink for the macho out there.

●●○○○

ALEXANDER'S SISTER

Glass: Martini
Garnish: Mint leaf
Method: SHAKE all ingredients with ice and fine strain into chilled glass.

1½	shot(s)	Plymouth gin
¾	shot(s)	Giffard white crème de Menthe Pastille
¾	shot(s)	Double (heavy) cream
¾	shot(s)	Milk

Comment: A green minty thing for dairy lovers.

●●●●○○

ALEXANDRA

Glass: Martini
Garnish: Dust with freshly grated nutmeg
Method: SHAKE all ingredients with ice and fine strain into chilled glass.

1½	shot(s)	Pusser's navy rum
1	shot(s)	Kahlúa coffee liqueur
¾	shot(s)	Double (heavy) cream
¾	shot(s)	Milk

Comment: Surprisingly potent and spicy, despite the ladylike name.

ALFONSO

Glass: Flute
Garnish: Twist of lemon
Method: Coat sugar cube with bitters and drop into glass. **POUR** Dubonnet and then champagne into chilled glass.

1	cube	Sugar
4	dashes	Angostura aromatic bitters
½	shot(s)	Dubonnet Red
Top up with		Piper-Heidsieck brut champagne

Origin: Named after the deposed Spanish king Alfonso XIII, who first tasted this drink while exiled in France.
Comment: Herbal variation on the classic Champagne Cocktail.

ALFONSO MARTINI NEW

Glass: Martini
Garnish: Orange zest twist
Method: SHAKE all ingredients with ice and fine strain into chilled glass.

½	shot(s)	Plymouth gin
1	shot(s)	Grand Marnier liqueur
½	shot(s)	Dry vermouth
¼	shot(s)	Sweet vermouth
2	dashes	Angostura aromatic bitters
½	shot(s)	Chilled mineral water (omit if wet ice)

Origin: Adapted from Victor Bergeron's 'Trader Vic's Bartender's Guide' (1972 revised edition).
Comment: Dry yet slightly sweet with hints of orange, gin and warm spice.

ALGERIA NEW

Glass: Martini
Garnish: Orange zest twist
Method: SHAKE all ingredients with ice and fine strain into chilled glass.

2	shot(s)	Pisco
½	shot(s)	Cointreau triple sec
½	shot(s)	Giffard apricot brandy du Roussillon
¾	shot(s)	Chilled mineral water (reduce if wet ice)

Origin: Modern adaptation of a classic.
Comment: Pisco, apricot and orange combine wonderfully in this medium dry, balanced cocktail with a tangy bite.

ALGONQUIN

Glass: Old-fashioned
Garnish: Cherry on stick
Method: SHAKE all ingredients with ice and strain into ice-filled glass.

2	shot(s)	Rye whiskey
1¼	shot(s)	Dry vermouth
1¼	shot(s)	Pressed pineapple juice
2	dashes	Peychaud's aromatic bitters

Origin: One of several classic cocktails accredited to New York City's Algonquin Hotel in the 1930s. Its true origins are lost in time.
Comment: Pineapple juice adds fruit and froth, while Peychaud's bitters combine subtly with the whiskey in this dry, aromatic drink.

ALICE FROM DALLAS

Glass: Shot
Method: Refrigerate ingredients then **LAYER** in chilled glass by carefully pouring in the following order.

½	shot(s)	Kahlúa coffee liqueur
½	shot(s)	Grand Marnier
½	shot(s)	Partida tequila

Comment: Coffee and orange spiked with tequila.

ALICE IN WONDERLAND

Glass: Shot
Garnish: Lime wedge
Method: Refrigerate ingredients then **LAYER** in chilled glass by carefully pouring in the following order.

1	shot(s)	Grand Marnier
½	shot(s)	Partida tequila

Comment: Brings a whole new dimension to tequila and orange.

ALIEN SECRETION NEW

Glass: Collins
Garnish: Pineapple wedge & cherry
Method: SHAKE all ingredients with ice and strain into ice-filled glass.

2	shot(s)	Ketel One vodka
½	shot(s)	Midori melon liqueur
½	shot(s)	Malibu coconut rum
3	shot(s)	Pressed pineapple juice

Origin: One of many 80s cocktails with a dodgy name.
Comment: Lime green and fruity but all too drinkable, with a distinct bite despite its mild sweetness.

ALL FALL DOWN

Glass: Shot
Method: Refrigerate ingredients then **LAYER** in chilled glass by carefully pouring in the following order.

½	shot(s)	Kahlúa coffee liqueur
½	shot(s)	Partida tequila
½	shot(s)	Pusser's Navy (54.5%) rum

Comment: Too many of these and you will.

DRINKS ARE GRADED AS FOLLOWS:

● DISGUSTING   ●● PRETTY AWFUL   ●● BEST AVOIDED
●●○ DISAPPOINTING   ●●● ACCEPTABLE   ●●●○ GOOD
●●●● RECOMMENDED   ●●●●○ HIGHLY RECOMMENDED
●●●●● OUTSTANDING / EXCEPTIONAL

A

ALL WHITE FRAPPÉ

Glass: Old-fashioned
Garnish: Lemon zest
Method: BLEND ingredients with 6oz scoop of crushed ice. Pour into glass and serve with short straws.

1	shot(s)	Luxardo Sambuca dei Cesari
1	shot(s)	White crème de cacao liqueur
1	shot(s)	Giffard white creme de menthe pastille
1	shot(s)	Freshly squeezed lemon juice

Comment: Aniseed, chocolate, peppermint and lemon juice are an unlikely but tasty combination for summer afternoons.

ALLEGROTTINI NEW

Glass: Martini
Garnish: Orange zest twist
Method: SHAKE all ingredients with ice and fine strain into chilled glass.

1½	shot(s)	Ketel One Citroen vodka
¾	shot(s)	Cointreau triple sec
¼	shot(s)	Dry vermouth
¾	shot(s)	Freshly squeezed orange juice
¼	shot(s)	Freshly squeezed lime juice

Origin: Discovered in 2005 at the Four Seasons Hotel, Prague, Czech Republic.
Comment: Strongly citrus but dry rather than bitter.

ALMOND MARTINI #1

Glass: Martini
Garnish: Sink three roasted almonds
Method: SHAKE all ingredients with ice and fine strain into chilled glass.

2	shot(s)	Ketel One vodka
½	shot(s)	Freshly squeezed lemon juice
½	shot(s)	Almond (orgeat) sugar syrup
1	shot(s)	Pressed apple juice
2	dashes	Fee Brothers peach bitters (optional)

Origin: Created in 2004 by Matt Pomeroy at Baltic, London, England.
Comment: Almond inspired with hints of apple and lemon juice.

ALMOND MARTINI #2 [UPDATED]

Glass: Martini
Garnish: Sink three almonds
Method: SHAKE all ingredients with ice and fine strain into chilled glass.

2	shot(s)	Almond flavoured vodka
¾	shot(s)	Luxardo Amaretto di Saschira
¼	shot(s)	Dry vermouth
¾	shot(s)	Chilled mineral water (omit if wet ice)

Origin: Created in 2005 by yours truly.
Comment: A delicate, almond flavoured Vodka Martini.

ALMOND OLD FASHIONED

Glass: Old-fashioned
Garnish: Orange zest twist
Method: STIR one shot of tequila with two ice cubes in a glass. Add amaretto, agave syrup, bitters and two more ice cubes. Stir some more then add another two ice cubes and the remaining tequila. Stir lots more so as to melt ice then add more ice. The melting and stirring in of ice cubes is essential to the dilution and taste of the drink.

2	shot(s)	Partida tequila
¼	shot(s)	Luxardo Amaretto di Saschira
¼	shot(s)	Agave syrup
3	dashes	Fee Brothers orange bitters

Origin: Created in 2005 by Mark Pratt at Maze, London, England.
Comment: One to please fans of both tequila and the Old Fashioned drinks genre.

AMARETTO SOUR

Glass: Old-fashioned
Garnish: Cherry & lemon slice sail
Method: SHAKE all ingredients with ice and strain into ice-filled glass.

2	shot(s)	Luxardo Amaretto di Saschira
1¼	shot(s)	Freshly squeezed lemon juice
½	fresh	Egg white
2	dashes	Angostura aromatic bitters

Comment: Sweet 'n' sour – frothy with an almond buzz

AMBER

Glass: Collins
Garnish: Apple wedge & nutmeg dust
Method: MUDDLE ginger in base of shaker. Add other ingredients, SHAKE with ice and strain into glass filled with crushed ice.

4	slices	Fresh root ginger (thumbnail sized)
1½	shot(s)	Zubrówka bison vodka
4	shot(s)	Pressed apple juice
½	shot(s)	Sugar syrup (2 sugar to 1 water)
½	shot(s)	Apple schnapps liqueur

Origin: Created in 2001 by Douglas Ankrah for Akbar at the Red Fort, Soho, London, England.
Comment: A fantastic combination of adult flavours in a long, thirst-quenching drink. Also great served up.

AMBROSIA

Glass: Flute
Method: SHAKE first four ingredients with ice and strain into glass. TOP with champagne.

1	shot(s)	Rémy Martin cognac
1	shot(s)	Boulard Grand Solage Calvados
¼	shot(s)	Freshly squeezed lemon juice
¼	shot(s)	Cointreau triple sec
Top up with		Brut champagne

Comment: Dry, fortified champers with a hint of apple.

AMBROSIA COCKTAIL

Glass: Martini
Garnish: Dust with freshly grated nutmeg
Method: SHAKE all ingredients with ice and fine strain into chilled glass.

3/4	shot(s)	Rémy Martin cognac
2	shot(s)	Advocaat liqueur
1	shot(s)	Cuarenta Y Tres (Licor 43) liqueur
1/2	shot(s)	Yellow Chartreuse

Origin: I created this drink and named it after the Greek for 'elixir of life, the food of the gods'. In Britain Ambrosia is a brand of custard, so advocaat seemed appropriate, while, if there is a God, he/she/it surely drinks Chartreuse.
Comment: Easy-drinking but complex with a herbal edge.

AMERICAN BEAUTY #1 UPDATED

Glass: Large (10oz) Martini
Garnish: Float rose petal
Method: SHAKE first six ingredients with ice and fine strain into chilled glass.
Use the back of a spoon to FLOAT red wine over drink.

2 1/2	shot(s)	Rémy Martin cognac
1/2	shot(s)	Dry vermouth
1/2	shot(s)	Giffard White crème de menthe Pastille
1/2	shot(s)	Freshly squeezed orange juice
1/2	shot(s)	Pomegranate (grenadine) syrup
3/4	shot(s)	Chilled mineral water (reduce if wet ice)
1/4	shot(s)	Red wine

Origin: Adapted from David A. Embury's 1948 'Fine Art of Mixing Drinks'.
Variant: When served in a tall glass with crushed ice this is called an American Beauty Punch.
Comment: Both fresh and refreshing - a subtle hint of peppermint gives zing to this cognac cocktail.

AMERICAN BEAUTY #2 NEW

Glass: Martini
Garnish: Mint leaf
Method: SHAKE first five ingredients with ice and fine strain into chilled glass. Use the back of a soup spoon to FLOAT port over drink.

1	shot(s)	Rémy Martin cognac
1	shot(s)	Dry vermouth
1/4	shot(s)	White crème de menthe
1	shot(s)	Freshly squeezed orange juice
1/2	shot(s)	Pomegranate (grenadine) syrup
1/2	shot(s)	Tawny port

Origin: Adapted from Victor Bergeron's 'Trader Vic's Bartender's Guide' (1972 revised edition).
Comment: Invigorating and peppermint fresh yet sophisticated and complex.

AMERICAN PIE MARTINI

Glass: Martini
Garnish: Apple wedge on rim
Method: SHAKE all ingredients with ice and fine strain into chilled glass.

1 1/2	shot(s)	Bourbon whiskey
1/2	shot(s)	Apple schnapps liqueur
1/2	shot(s)	Giffard crème de myrtille
3/4	shot(s)	Cranberry juice
1/2	shot(s)	Pressed apple juice
1/4	shot(s)	Freshly squeezed lime juice

Origin: Adapted from a recipe discovered at Oxo Tower Restaurant & Bar, London, England.
Comment: This berry and apple pie has a tangy bite.

AMERICANA

Glass: Flute
Garnish: Peach slice
Method: Coat sugar cube with bitters and drop into glass. POUR bourbon and then champagne into chilled glass.

1	cube	Sugar
4	dashes	Angostura aromatic bitters
1/2	shot(s)	Bourbon whiskey
Top up with	Brut	champagne

Comment: The Wild West take on the classic Champagne Cocktail.

AMERICANO

Glass: Collins
Garnish: Orange slice
Method: POUR Campari and vermouth into ice-filled glass and TOP with soda. Stir and serve with straws.

2	shot(s)	Campari
2	shot(s)	Sweet vermouth
Top up with	Soda water (club soda)	

Origin: First served in the 1860s in Gaspare Campari's bar in Milan, this was originally known as the 'Milano-Torino' as Campari came from Milano (Milan) and Cinzano from Torino (Turin). It was not until Prohibition that the Italians noticed an influx of Americans who enjoyed the drink and so dubbed it Americano.
Comment: A bitter, fizzy, long refreshing drink, which you'll love if you like Campari.

AMSTERDAM COCKTAIL NEW

Glass: Martini
Garnish: Orange zest twist
Method: SHAKE all ingredients with ice and fine strain into chilled glass.

2	shot(s)	Egte Oude Jenever
1	shot(s)	Cointreau triple sec
1	shot(s)	Freshly squeezed orange juice
3	dashes	Fee Brothers orange bitters

Origin: Adapted from Victor Bergeron's 'Trader Vic's Bartender's Guide' (1972 revised edition).
Comment: Seriously orange, dry but wonderfully smooth.

A
B
C
D
E
F
G
H
I
J
K
L
M
N
O
P
Q
R
S
T
U
V
W
X
Y
Z

A

ANGEL FACE NEW

● ● ● ● ◗

Glass: Martini
Garnish: Apple wedge on rim
Method: SHAKE all ingredients with ice and fine strain into chilled glass.

1	shot(s)	Plymouth gin
1	shot(s)	Boulard Grand Solage Calvados
1	shot(s)	Giffard apricot brandy du Roussillon

Origin: Adapted from Harry Craddock's 1930 'The Savoy Cocktail Book'.
Comment: Rich apricot and apple with a backbone of botanical gin. Balanced rather than dry or sweet.

ANGEL'S SHARE #1 NEW

● ● ● ● ◗

Glass: Martini
Garnish: Orange zest twist
Method: STIR heaped spoon of orange marmalade with cognac in base of shaker until marmalade dissolves. Add other ingredients, SHAKE with ice and fine strain into chilled glass.

1	spoon	Orange marmalade
2	shot(s)	Rémy Martin cognac
1/4	shot(s)	Cuarenta Y Tres (Licor 43) liqueur
1/2	shot(s)	Freshly squeezed lemon juice
1/4	shot(s)	Sugar syrup (2 sugar to 1 water)

Origin: Created in 2005 by Milo Rodriguez, London.
Comment: Tangy citrus fruit and cognac smoothed with a sweet hint of vanilla.

ANGEL'S SHARE #2 NEW

● ● ● ● ◗

Glass: Snifter
Method: POUR the Chartreuse into glass and coat the inside of the glass with the liqueur by tilting and rotating it. DISCARD excess liqueur. Carefully set the liqueur on the interior of the glass alight and allow it to BURN for a few seconds. Extinguish flame by placing a saucer over the glass, add other ingredients and SWIRL to mix. Beware of hot glass rim.

1/4	shot(s)	Green Chartreuse
1 1/2	shot(s)	Rémy Martin cognac
3/4	shot(s)	Nocello walnut liqueur
1/2	shot(s)	Tawny port

Origin: Adapted from a recipe created in 2005 by Jacques Bezuidenhout at Harry Denton's Starlight Room, San Francisco, USA.
Comment: A fabulous drink, especially when VEP Chartreuse, family reserve cognac and 20 year old tawny port are used as per the original Starlight Room recipe.

DRINKS ARE GRADED AS FOLLOWS:

● DISGUSTING ● ◐ PRETTY AWFUL ● ● BEST AVOIDED
● ● ◐ DISAPPOINTING ● ● ● ACCEPTABLE ● ● ● ● GOOD
● ● ● ● RECOMMENDED ● ● ● ● ◐ HIGHLY RECOMMENDED
● ● ● ● ● OUTSTANDING / EXCEPTIONAL

ANIS'TINI

● ● ● ● ○

Glass: Martini
Garnish: Star anise
Method: MUDDLE star anise in base of shaker. Add other ingredients, SHAKE with ice and fine strain into chilled glass.

2	dried	Star anise
1	shot(s)	Ketel One vodka
3/4	shot(s)	Luxardo Sambuca dei Cesari
1/2	shot(s)	Pernod anis
1 1/2	shot(s)	Chilled mineral water (reduce if wet ice)

Origin: Discovered in 2002 at Lot 61, New York City, USA.
Comment: Specks of star anise are evident in this aniseedy Martini.

ANITA'S ATTITUDE ADJUSTER ⚷

● ● ● ○ ○

Glass: Sling
Garnish: Lemon slice
Method: SHAKE first seven ingredients with ice and strain into ice-filled glass. TOP with champagne and gently stir.

1/2	shot(s)	Cointreau triple sec
1/2	shot(s)	Partida tequila
1/2	shot(s)	Light white rum
1/2	shot(s)	Plymouth gin
1/2	shot(s)	Ketel One vodka
1/2	shot(s)	Freshly squeezed lime juice
1/2	shot(s)	Sugar syrup (2 sugar to 1 water)
Top up with		Brut champagne

Comment: Anita has a problem – she's indecisive when it comes to choosing base spirits.

ANTE NEW

● ● ● ● ○

Glass: Martini
Garnish: Orange zest twist
Method: STIR all ingredients with ice and strain into chilled glass.

2	shot(s)	Boulard Grand Solage Calvados
1	shot(s)	Dubonnet Red
1/2	shot(s)	Cointreau triple sec
2	dashes	Angostura aromatic bitters

Origin: Recipe adapted from one discovered in 2006 on drinkboy.com.
Comment: Medium dry, complex spiced apple with hints of orange.

APACHE

● ● ● ○ ○

Glass: Shot
Method: Refrigerate ingredients then LAYER in chilled glass by carefully pouring in the following order.

3/4	shot(s)	Kahlúa coffee liqueur
1/2	shot(s)	Midori melon liqueur
1/2	shot(s)	Baileys Irish cream liqueur

AKA: Quick F.U.
Comment: A coffee, melon and whiskey cream layered shot.

A

APHRODISIAC

Glass: Collins
Garnish: Apple slice on rim
Method: MUDDLE ginger in base of shaker. Add other ingredients, SHAKE with ice and fine strain into ice-filled glass.

2	slices	Fresh root ginger (thumbnail sized)
2	shot(s)	Vanilla-infused vodka
1/2	shot(s)	Green Chartreuse
2 1/2	shot(s)	Pressed apple juice
1 1/2	shot(s)	Sauvignon Blanc wine

Origin: Created in 2002 by Yannick Miseriaux at The Fifth Floor Bar, London, England.
Comment: As strong in flavour as it is high in alcohol.

APPLE & BLACKBERRY PIE UPDATED

Glass: Martini
Garnish: Cinnamon dust & blackberry
Method: MUDDLE blackberries in base of shaker. Add vodka and apple juice, SHAKE with ice and fine strain into chilled glass. FLOAT cream on the surface of the drink by pouring over the back of a spoon and swirl to form a thin layer. Depending on the sweetness of your blackberries, you may need to add a touch of sugar syrup.

7	fresh	Blackberries
2	shot(s)	Ketel One vodka
1	shot(s)	Pressed apple juice
Float		Double (heavy) cream

Origin: Created in 2005 by yours truly.
Comment: A dessert in a glass, but not too sweet.

APPLE & CRANBERRY PIE UPDATED

Glass: Martini
Garnish: Dust with cinnamon powder
Method: SHAKE first three ingredients with ice and fine strain into chilled glass. FLOAT cream on surface of drink by pouring over the back of a spoon and swirl to form a thin layer.

1 1/2	shot(s)	Ketel One vodka
3/4	shot(s)	Apple schnapps liqueur
1	shot(s)	Cranberry juice
Float		Double (heavy) cream

Origin: Created in 2003 by yours truly.
Comment: Sip apple and cranberry through a creamy cinnamon layer.

FOR MORE INFORMATION SEE OUR

INGREDIENTS APPENDIX ON PAGE 272

APPLE & CUSTARD COCKTAIL

Glass: Martini
Garnish: Apple wedge on rim
Method: SHAKE all ingredients with ice and fine strain into chilled glass.

2	shot(s)	Advocaat liqueur
1 1/2	shot(s)	Boulard Grand Solage Calvados
1/2	shot(s)	Apple schnapps liqueur
1/4	shot(s)	Vanilla sugar syrup

Origin: I created this in 2002 after rediscovering advocaat on a trip to Amsterdam.
Comment: Smooth and creamy, this tastes like its name.

APPLE & ELDERFLOWER COLLINS UPDATED

Glass: Collins
Garnish: Lemon slice
Method: SHAKE first four ingredients with ice and strain into ice-filled glass. TOP with soda, stir and serve with straws.

1 1/2	shot(s)	Plymouth gin
1	shot(s)	St Germain elderflower liqueur
1	shot(s)	Apple schnapps liqueur
1	shot(s)	Freshly squeezed lime juice
Top up with		Soda water (club soda)

Origin: Formula by yours truly in 2004.
Comment: A John Collins with lime in place of lemon and sweetened with apple and elderflower liqueurs.

APPLE & ELDERFLOWER MARTINI
(FRESH FRUIT) NEW

Glass: Martini
Garnish: Float wafer thin apple slice
Method: SHAKE all ingredients with ice and fine strain into chilled glass.

1 3/4	shot(s)	Vodka
1	shot(s)	St Germain elderflower liqueur
1 1/4	shot(s)	Pressed apple juice

Origin: Created in 2006 by yours truly.
Comment: Light and easy - apple and elderflower laced with vodka.

APPLE & MELON MARTINI

Glass: Martini
Garnish: Apple wedge on rim
Method: SHAKE all ingredients with ice and fine strain into chilled glass.

2	shot(s)	Ketel One vodka
1	shot(s)	Sour apple liqueur
1/2	shot(s)	Midori melon liqueur
1/2	shot(s)	Freshly squeezed lime juice

Comment: The ubiquitous Green Apple Martini with extra colour and flavour thanks to a dash of melon liqueur.

B C D E F G H I J K L M N O P Q R S T U V W X Y Z

A

APPLE & SPICE ●●●○○

Glass: Shot
Garnish: Dust with cinnamon powder
Method: Refrigerate ingredients then LAYER in chilled glass by carefully pouring in the following order.

¾ shot(s)	Boulard Grand Solage Calvados
¾ shot(s)	Double (heavy) cream

Comment: Creamy apple shot.

APPLE BLOSSOM COCKTAIL NEW ●●●●◐

Glass: Martini
Garnish: Orange zest twist
Method: SHAKE all ingredients with ice and fine strain into chilled glass.

2 shot(s)	Boulard Grand Solage Calvados
2 shot(s)	Sweet vermouth

Origin: Adapted from Victor Bergeron's 'Trader Vic's Bartender's Guide' (1972 revised edition).
Comment: Stupidly simple to mix but complex to taste – spiced and concentrated apple juice.

APPLE BRANDY SOUR UPDATED ●●●●◐

Glass: Old-fashioned
Garnish: Lemon sail (cherry & lemon slice)
Method: SHAKE all ingredients with ice and strain into ice-filled glass.

2 shot(s)	Boulard Grand Solage Calvados
1 shot(s)	Freshly squeezed lemon juice
¾ shot(s)	Sugar syrup (2 sugar to 1 water)
3 dashes	Angostura aromatic bitters
½ fresh	Egg white

Comment: Sour by name - balanced sweet and sour apple by nature.

APPLE BREEZE UPDATED ●●●●○

Glass: Collins
Garnish: Apple wedge on rim
Method: SHAKE all ingredients with ice and strain into ice-filled glass.

2 shot(s)	Zubrówka bison vodka
2½ shot(s)	Pressed apple juice
1½ shot(s)	Cranberry juice

Variant: Substitute vodka for Zubrówka bison vodka.
Comment: A lot more interesting than the better known Sea Breeze.

APPLE BUCK ●●●●○

Glass: Collins
Garnish: Apple wedge
Method: SHAKE first four ingredients with ice and strain into ice-filled glass. TOP with ginger ale.

1½ shot(s)	Boulard Grand Solage Calvados
½ shot(s)	Sour apple liqueur
1 shot(s)	Pressed apple juice
½ shot(s)	Freshly squeezed lime juice
Top up with	Ginger ale

Origin: Adapted from a drink created in 2004 by Wayne Collins.
Comment: A refreshing long number with a taste reminiscent of cider.

APPLE CART UPDATED ●●●○○

Glass: Martini
Garnish: Apple wedge on rim
Method: SHAKE all ingredients with ice and fine strain into chilled glass.

1½ shot(s)	Boulard Grand Solage Calvados
1 shot(s)	Cointreau triple sec
1 shot(s)	Freshly squeezed lemon juice
½ shot(s)	Chilled mineral water (omit if wet ice)

AKA: Calvados Sidecar
Variant: Deauville
Origin: This classic cocktail is an adaptation of the even older Sidecar.
Comment: A serious combination of apple with orange and sweet with sour.

APPLE CRUMBLE MARTINI #1 ●●●●○

Glass: Martini
Garnish: Apple wedge on rim
Method: SHAKE all ingredients with ice and fine strain into chilled glass.

2 shot(s)	Scotch whisky
¼ shot(s)	Butterscotch schnapps liqueur
1 shot(s)	Pressed apple juice
½ shot(s)	Freshly squeezed lemon juice
¼ shot(s)	Sugar syrup (2 sugar to 1 water)

Comment: That's the way the apple crumbles - in this case enhancing the flavour of the Scotch.

APPLE CRUMBLE MARTINI #2 ●●●●○

Glass: Martini
Garnish: Dust with cinnamon powder
Method: SHAKE all ingredients with ice and fine strain into chilled glass.

2 shot(s)	Tuaca Italian liqueur
½ shot(s)	Freshly squeezed lemon juice
2 shot(s)	Pressed apple juice

Origin: Created in 2002 by Eion Richards at Bond's Bar, London, England.
Comment: Easy to make and equally easy to drink.

A

APPLE DAIQUIRI 🗝

Glass: Martini
Garnish: Apple wedge on rim
Method: SHAKE all ingredients with ice and fine strain into chilled glass.

2	shot(s)	Light white rum
1¹/₂	shot(s)	Pressed apple juice
¹/₂	shot(s)	Freshly squeezed lime juice
¹/₄	shot(s)	Sugar syrup (2 sugar to 1 water)

Origin: Formula by yours truly in 2004.
Comment: A classic Daiquiri with a very subtle hint of apple.

APPLE MAC

Glass: Martini
Garnish: Float apple slice
Method: SHAKE all ingredients with ice and strain into ice-filled glass.

2	shot(s)	Scotch whisky
1¹/₂	shot(s)	Pressed apple juice
¹/₂	shot(s)	Stone's Original green ginger wine

Variant: Also suits being served over ice in an old-fashioned glass.
Origin: I created this twist on the classic Whisky Mac in 2004.
Comment: Scotch, ginger and apple are a threesome made in heaven.

APPLE MANHATTAN #1 UPDATED

Glass: Martini
Garnish: Apple slice on rim
Method: SHAKE all ingredients with ice and fine strain into chilled glass.

2	shot(s)	Bourbon whiskey
1¹/₂	shot(s)	Apple schnapps liqueur
¹/₂	shot(s)	Sweet vermouth

Origin: My take on a drink created by David Marsden at First on First in New York City and latterly popularised by Dale DeGroff. Traditionalists may want to stir it.
Comment: Rusty gold in colour, this is a flavoursome number for bourbon lovers.

APPLE MANHATTAN #2 NEW

Glass: Martini
Garnish: Apple wedge on rim
Method: STIR all ingredients with ice and strain into chilled glass.

2	shot(s)	Bourbon whiskey
³/₄	shot(s)	Apple schnapps liqueur
¹/₄	shot(s)	Cointreau triple sec
¹/₂	shot(s)	Sweet vermouth

Origin: Created in 2005 by Åsa Nevestveit and Robert Sörman at Grill, Stockholm, Sweden.
Comment: Exactly as billed – a Manhattan with a hint of apple.

APPLE MARTINI #1 (SIMPLE VERSION) 🗝

Glass: Martini
Garnish: Cherry in base of glass
Method: SHAKE all ingredients with ice and fine strain into chilled glass.

2¹/₂	shot(s)	Ketel One vodka
2	shot(s)	Pressed apple juice
¹/₄	shot(s)	Sugar syrup (2 sugar to 1 water)

Variant: Sour Apple Martini, Caramelised Apple Martini
Origin: Formula by yours truly in 2004.
Comment: This is subtitled the simple version for good reason but, if freshly pressed juice is used, it's as good if not better than other Apple Martini recipes.

APPLE MARTINI #2

Glass: Martini
Garnish: Apple wedge on rim
Method: SHAKE all ingredients with ice and fine strain into chilled glass.

2	shot(s)	Ketel One vodka
³/₄	shot(s)	Apple schnapps liqueur
2	shot(s)	Pressed apple juice

Comment: There are as many different recipes for this drink as there are varieties of apple and brands of apple liqueur: this is one of the more popular.

APPLE MOJITO UPDATED

Glass: Collins
Garnish: Mint sprig
Method: Lightly MUDDLE (just to bruise) mint in base of glass. Add other ingredients, half fill glass with crushed ice and CHURN (stir) with bar spoon. Fill glass to brim with more crushed ice and churn some more. Serve with straws.

12	fresh	Mint leaves
2	shot(s)	Light white rum
1	shot(s)	Freshly squeezed lime juice
1	shot(s)	Apple schnapps liqueur

Origin: Recipe by yours truly in 2005.
Comment: An enduring classic given a touch of apple. Those with a sweet tooth may want to add more apple liqueur or even a dash of sugar syrup.

FOR MORE INFORMATION SEE OUR

INGREDIENTS
APPENDIX
ON PAGE 272

B
C
D
E
F
G
H
I
J
K
L
M
N
O
P
Q
R
S
T
U
V
W
X
Y
Z

A

APPLE OF ONE'S EYE

●●●●○○

Glass: Collins
Garnish: Apple wedge on rim
Method: SHAKE first three ingredients with ice and strain into ice-filled glass. TOP with ginger beer.

2	shot(s)	Rémy Martin cognac
1/2	shot(s)	Freshly squeezed lime juice
1 1/2	shot(s)	Pressed apple juice
Top up with		Ginger beer

Comment: This spicy concoction is long and refreshing.

APPLE PIE MARTINI

●●●●○

Glass: Martini
Garnish: Apple wedge on rim
Method: SHAKE all ingredients with ice and fine strain into chilled glass.

1 1/2	shot(s)	Zubrówka bison vodka
1/2	shot(s)	Goldschläger cinnamon schnapps
2	shot(s)	Pressed apple juice
1	shot(s)	Cranberry juice

Origin: Created in 2000 by Alexia Pau Barrera at Sand Bar, Clapham, England.
Comment: There's a good hit of cinnamon in this apple pie.

APPLE PIE SHOT

●●●○○

Glass: Shot
Garnish: Dust with cinnamon powder
Method: SHAKE first two ingredients with ice and strain into chilled glass. FLOAT cream on drink by carefully pouring over the back of a spoon.

1	shot(s)	Apple schnapps liqueur
1/2	shot(s)	Hazelnut (crème de noisette) liqueur
1/4	shot(s)	Double cream

Comment: Nuts, apple, cinnamon and cream – pudding, anyone?

APPLEISSIMO

●●●●○

Glass: Collins
Garnish: Apple slice on rim
Method: SHAKE first three ingredients with ice and strain into ice-filled glass. TOP with anis and serve with straws.

1 1/2	shot(s)	Apple schnapps liqueur
2	shot(s)	Pressed apple juice
1 1/2	shot(s)	Cranberry juice
1 1/2	shot(s)	Pernod anis

Comment: Stir the anis in with straws before drinking. Anis is best added last as it reacts on contact with ice.

APPLE SPRITZ

●●●●●○

Glass: Flute
Garnish: Peach or apple slice on rim
Method: POUR first two ingredients into glass and top with champagne.

3/4	shot(s)	Apple schnapps liqueur
1/4	shot(s)	Peach schnapps liqueur
Top up with		Brut champagne

Origin: Discovered in 2003 at Paramount Hotel, New York City, USA.
Comment: Sweet, fruity champagne – oh yeah, baby.

APPLE STRUDEL #1

●●●○○

Glass: Martini
Garnish: Dust with cinnamon powder
Method: SHAKE first five ingredients with ice and fine strain into chilled glass. Carefully FLOAT cream by pouring over the back of a spoon.

1	shot(s)	Apple schnapps liqueur
1/2	shot(s)	Goldschläger cinnamon schnapps
1/2	shot(s)	Giffard White crème de cacao
1/2	shot(s)	Giffard brown crème de cacao
1	shot(s)	Pressed apple juice
3/4	shot(s)	Double (heavy) cream

Variant: May also be served as a shot.
Origin: Created in 1999 by Alex Kammerling, London, England.
Comment: This sweet dessert cocktail tastes just like mum's home-made apple pie with cream.

APPLE STRUDEL #2 UPDATED

●●●●◑

Glass: Martini
Garnish: Coat half rim with cinnamon and sugar
Method: SHAKE all ingredients with ice and fine strain into chilled glass.

1 1/2	shot(s)	Vanilla-infused Ketel One vodka
1/2	shot(s)	Scotch whisky
1/2	shot(s)	Apple schnapps liqueur
1/2	shot(s)	Dry vermouth
1	shot(s)	Pressed apple juice

Origin: Recipe by yours truly in 2006.
Comment: Apple, vanilla and a hint of Scotch – reminiscent of the dessert but a good deal drier.

APPLE SUNRISE

●●●○○

Glass: Collins
Garnish: Apple slice
Method: SHAKE all ingredients with ice and strain into ice-filled glass.

2	shot(s)	Boulard Grand Solage Calvados
1/2	shot(s)	Giffard Cassis Noir de Bourgogne
3 1/2	shot(s)	Freshly squeezed orange juice

Origin: Created in 1980 by Charles Schumann, Munich, Germany.
Comment: A pleasing blend of fruits with the apple punch of Calvados.

APPLE VIRGIN MOJITO (MOCKTAIL) ⚷

Glass: Collins
Garnish: Mint sprig
Method: MUDDLE mint in base of glass. Add apple juice, sugar and lime juice. Half fill glass with crushed ice and CHURN (stir) with bar spoon. Fill glass to brim with more crushed ice and churn some more. Continue adding crushed ice and churning until glass is filled. Serve with straws.

12	fresh	Mint leaves
2	shot(s)	Pressed apple juice
1	shot(s)	Freshly squeezed lime juice
1/4	shot(s)	Sugar syrup (2 sugar to 1 water)

Variant: Add three dashes of Angostura aromatic bitters.
Comment: As non-alcoholic cocktails go this is one of the best.

APPLESINTH

Glass: Old-fashioned
Garnish: Apple wedge on rim
Method: SHAKE all ingredients with ice and strain into glass filled with crushed ice.

1	shot(s)	La Fée Parisian (68%) absinthe
1	shot(s)	Apple schnapps liqueur
2	shot(s)	Pressed apple juice
3/4	shot(s)	Freshly squeezed lime juice
1/2	shot(s)	Passion fruit sugar syrup

Origin: Created in 1999 by Alex Kammerling, London, England.
Comment: Hints of apple and liquorice combine to make a very moreish cocktail.

APPLES 'N' PEARS

Glass: Martini
Garnish: Apple or pear slice on rim
Method: SHAKE all ingredients with ice and fine strain into chilled glass.

1	shot(s)	Pear flavoured vodka
1	shot(s)	Boulard Grand Solage Calvados
3/4	shot(s)	Xanté pear brandy liqueur
1 1/2	shot(s)	Pressed apple juice

Origin: Created in 2005 by yours truly.
Comment: 'Apples and pears' means stairs. Well worth climbing.

APPLILY MARRIED UPDATED ⚷

Glass: Martini
Garnish: Coat half rim with cinnamon and sugar
Method: STIR honey with vodka in base of shaker until honey dissolves. Add apple juice, shake with ice and fine strain into chilled glass.

2	spoons	Runny honey
2 1/2	shot(s)	Ketel One vodka
1/2	shot(s)	Pressed apple juice

Origin: Created in 2005 by yours truly.
Comment: Apple and honey are indeed a marriage made in heaven, especially when laced with grainy vodka notes.

APRICOT COSMO

Glass: Martini
Garnish: Apricot slice
Method: STIR apricot preserve with vodka until preserve dissolves. Add other ingredients, SHAKE with ice and fine strain into chilled glass.

2	shot(s)	Ketel One vodka
1	spoon	Apricot preserve (St. Dalfour)
1	shot(s)	Cranberry juice
1/4	shot(s)	Passion fruit sugar syrup
1/2	shot(s)	Freshly squeezed lime juice
2	dashes	Fee Brothers orange bitters

Origin: Created in 2004 at Aura Kitchen & Bar, London, England.
Comment: The apricot preserve adds a flavoursome tang to the contemporary classic.

APRICOT FIZZ UPDATED ⚷

Glass: Collins (8oz max)
Garnish: Lemon wedge
Method: SHAKE first three ingredients with ice and strain into ice-filled glass. TOP with soda water.

2	shot(s)	Giffard apricot brandy du Roussillon
1	shot(s)	Freshly squeezed orange juice
1/2	shot(s)	Freshly squeezed lime juice
Top up with		Soda water (from siphon)

Comment: This low-alcohol, refreshing cocktail is perfect for a summer afternoon.

APRICOT LADY SOUR ⚷

Glass: Old-fashioned
Garnish: Lemon sail (lemon slice & cherry)
Method: SHAKE all ingredients with ice and strain into ice-filled glass.

1 1/2	shot(s)	Light white rum
1	shot(s)	Giffard apricot brandy du Roussillon
1	shot(s)	Freshly squeezed lemon juice
1/4	shot(s)	Sugar syrup (2 sugar to 1 water)
1/2	fresh	Egg white

Comment: This seemingly soft and fluffy, apricot flavoured drink hides a most unladylike rum bite.

APRICOT MANGO MARTINI

Glass: Martini
Garnish: Mango slice
Method: MUDDLE mango in base of shaker. Add other ingredients, SHAKE with ice and fine strain into glass.

1	cupful	Fresh diced mango
2	shot(s)	Plymouth gin
1/2	shot(s)	Giffard apricot brandy du Roussillon
3/4	shot(s)	Freshly squeezed lemon juice
1/2	shot(s)	Sugar syrup (2 sugar to 1 water)

Variant: Use one-and-a-half shots of mango purée in place of fresh mango and halve amount of sugar syrup.
Comment: A simple, great tasting variation on the fresh fruit Martini.

A

APRICOT MARTINI

Glass: Martini
Garnish: Lemon zest twist
Method: SHAKE all ingredients with ice and fine strain into chilled glass.

1½	shot(s)	Plymouth gin
1	shot(s)	Giffard apricot brandy du Roussillon
¼	shot(s)	Freshly squeezed lemon juice
⅛	shot(s)	Pomegranate (grenadine) syrup
3	dashes	Angostura aromatic bitters
¾	shot(s)	Chilled mineral water (omit if wet ice)

Comment: This scarlet cocktail combines gin, apricot and lemon juice.

APRIL SHOWER UPDATED

Glass: Martini
Garnish: Orange zest twist
Method: SHAKE all ingredients with ice and fine strain into chilled glass.

2	shot(s)	Rémy Martin cognac
½	shot(s)	Bénédictine D.O.M. liqueur
1½	shot(s)	Freshly squeezed orange juice

Comment: This mustard coloured, medium dry, cognac-based drink harnesses the uniquely herbal edge of Bénédictine.

APRICOT SOUR

Glass: Old-fashioned
Garnish: Lemon zest twist
Method: STIR apricot jam (preserve) with bourbon until it dissolves. Add other ingredients, SHAKE with ice and fine strain into ice-filled glass.

2	spoons	Apricot jam (preserve)
1½	shot(s)	Bourbon whiskey
½	shot(s)	Giffard apricot brandy du Roussillon
1	shot(s)	Pressed apple juice
½	shot(s)	Freshly squeezed lemon juice

Origin: Created in 2005 by Wayne Collins for Maxxium UK.
Comment: Short and fruity.

A

Glass: Old-fashioned
Method: SHAKE all ingredients with ice and strain into ice-filled glass.

2	shot(s)	Scotch whisky
1	shot(s)	Cherry (brandy) liqueur
1½	shot(s)	Cranberry juice

Comment: A sweet cherry edge is balanced by the dryness of cranberry and Scotch.

THE ARGYLL NEW

Glass: Martini
Garnish: Orange zest twist
Method: STIR all ingredients with ice and strain into chilled glass.

2	shot(s)	Southern Comfort
1	shot(s)	Sweet vermouth
1	dash	Fee Brothers orange bitters

Comment: Southern Comfort lovers only need apply.

ARIZONA BREEZE

Glass: Collins
Garnish: Grapefruit wedge on rim
Method: SHAKE all ingredients with ice and strain into ice-filled glass.

2½	shot(s)	Plymouth gin
3	shot(s)	Cranberry juice
2	shot(s)	Freshly squeezed grapefruit juice

Comment: A tart variation on the Sea Breeze – as dry as Arizona.

ARMILLITA CHICO NEW

Glass: Martini (large 10oz)
Garnish: Lime wedge on rim
Method: BLEND all ingredients with 12oz scoop crushed ice.

2	shot(s)	Partida tequila
1	shot(s)	Freshly squeezed lime juice
½	shot(s)	Pomegranate (grenadine) syrup
2	dashes	Orange flower water

Comment: Similar to a frozen Margarita but more subtle and dry.

ARMY & NAVY NEW

Glass: Martini
Garnish: Lemon zest twist
Method: SHAKE all ingredients with ice and fine strain into chilled glass.

2	shot(s)	Plymouth gin
½	shot(s)	Freshly squeezed lemon juice
¼	shot(s)	Almond (orgeat) syrup
½	shot(s)	Chilled mineral water (omit if wet ice)

Origin: This old classic was originally made to an 8:4:4 formula but I have borrowed this 8:2:1 formula from David A. Embury's 1948 'Fine Art of Mixing Drinks' (he describes the original formulation as "horrible"). The addition of water is a Difford touch.
Comment: Almond and lemon flavoured gin. Subtle, citrusy and dry.

●●●●○

ARNAUD MARTINI UPDATED

Glass: Martini
Garnish: Blackberry on rim
Method: STIR all ingredients with ice and strain into chilled glass.

1	shot(s)	Plymouth gin
1	shot(s)	Dry vermouth
1	shot(s)	Giffard Cassis (or Chambord)

Origin: A classic cocktail named after the pre-war stage actress Yvonne Arnaud.
Comment: An interesting balance of blackcurrant, vermouth and gin. Sweet palate and dry finish.

●●●●○

ARNOLD PALMER (MOCKTAIL) NEW

Glass: Collins
Garnish: Lemon slice
Method: SHAKE all ingredients with ice and strain into ice-filled glass.

2	shot(s)	Freshly squeezed lemon juice
1	shot(s)	Sugar syrup (2 sugar to 1 water)
3	shot(s)	Cold breakfast tea

Variants: Tom Arnold, John Daly
Origin: A popular drink throughout the United States. Named after and said to be a favourite of the legendary golfer.
Comment: Real lemon iced tea. Balanced and wonderfully refreshing.

●●●○○

ARTLANTIC

Glass: Collins
Garnish: Orange wedge
Method: SHAKE all ingredients with ice and strain into ice-filled glass.

1	shot(s)	Spiced rum
1/2	shot(s)	Luxardo Amaretto di Saschira
1/2	shot(s)	Bols Blue curaçao liqueur
1/2	shot(s)	Freshly squeezed lime juice
3	shot(s)	Pressed apple juice

Origin: Atlantic Bar & Grill, London, England.
Comment: This sea green cocktail tastes much better than it looks.

●●●●○

ASIAN GINGER MARTINI

Glass: Martini
Garnish: Ginger slice on rim
Method: MUDDLE ginger in base of shaker. Add other ingredients, SHAKE with ice and fine strain into chilled glass.

2	slices	Fresh root ginger (thumbnail sized)
1 1/2	shot(s)	Ketel One vodka
2 1/4	shot(s)	Sake
1/4	shot(s)	Sugar syrup (2 sugar to 1 water)

Origin: Adapted from a recipe created in 2004 by Chris Langan of Barnomadics.
Comment: Lightly spiced with ginger, distinctly oriental in character.

●●●●○ A

ASIAN MARY

Glass: Collins
Garnish: Lemongrass
Method: MUDDLE ginger in base of shaker and add vodka. Squeeze wasabi paste onto bar spoon and STIR with vodka and ginger until dissolved. Add other ingredients, SHAKE with ice and fine strain into ice-filled glass.

3	slices	Fresh root ginger (thumbnail sized)
3	peas	Wasabi paste
2	shot(s)	Ketel One Citroen vodka
1	spoon	Soy sauce
4	shot(s)	Tomato sauce
1/2	shot(s)	Freshly squeezed lemon juice

Comment: An aptly named Bloody Mary with plenty of Asian spice.

●●●●○

ASIAN PEAR MARTINI

Glass: Martini
Garnish: Pear slice on rim
Method: SHAKE all ingredients with ice and fine strain into chilled glass.

2	shot(s)	Sake
1/4	shot(s)	Xanté pear brandy liqueur
1/2	shot(s)	Poire William eau de vie
1 1/2	shot(s)	Freshly extracted pear juice
1/4	shot(s)	Freshly squeezed lemon juice

Origin: Created in 2002 by yours truly.
Comment: Sake and pear juice with a kick.

●●●●○

ASSISTED SUICIDE

Glass: Shot
Method: SHAKE first two ingredients with ice and strain into chilled glass. TOP with cola.

1	shot(s)	Wray & Nephew overproof rum
1/2	shot(s)	Jägermeister
Top up with		Cola

Comment: Not for the faint-hearted.

●●●○○

ASYLUM COCKTAIL NEW

Glass: Old-fashioned
Method: POUR ingredients into glass without ice and STIR. Gently add ice and do NOT stir again. Consume once drink has turned cloudy.

1 1/2	shot(s)	Plymouth gin
1 1/2	shot(s)	Pernod anis
1/4	shot(s)	Sonoma Pomegranate (grenadine) syrup

Origin: Created by William Seabrook, famous for his account of eating human flesh, and first published in a 1935 book, 'So Red the Nose, or Breath in the Afternoon'.
Comment: Seabrook said of this drink, "look like rosy dawn, taste like the milk of Paradise, and make you plenty crazy." He must have been a Pernod lover!

A

ATHOLL BROSE ●●●●○

Glass: Martini
Garnish: Dust with freshly grated nutmeg
Method: Prepare oatmeal water by soaking three heaped tablespoons of oatmeal in half a mug of warm water. Stir and leave to stand for fifteen minutes. Then strain to extract the creamy liquid and discard what's left of the oatmeal.

To make the drink, **STIR** honey with Scotch until honey dissolves. Add other ingredients, **SHAKE** with ice and fine strain into chilled glass.

2	spoons	Runny heather honey
2	shot(s)	Scotch whisky
1½	shot(s)	Oatmeal water
¼	shot(s)	Drambuie liqueur
¼	shot(s)	Luxardo Amaretto di Saschira
½	shot(s)	Double (heavy) cream

Origin: My adaptation of a Scottish classic. Legend has it that Atholl Brose was created by the Earl of Atholl in 1475 when he was trying to capture Iain MacDonald, Lord of the Isles and leader of a rebellion against the king. Hearing rumours that MacDonald was drawing his drinking water from a small well, the Earl ordered it to be filled with honey, whisky and oatmeal. MacDonald lingered at the well enjoying the concoction and was captured.
Comment: Forget the porridge and kick start your day with a Atholl Brose.

ATLANTIC BREEZE ●●●○○

Glass: Collins
Garnish: Orange slice
Method: SHAKE all ingredients with ice and strain into ice-filled glass.

1½	shot(s)	Light white rum
½	shot(s)	Giffard apricot brandy du Roussillon
¼	shot(s)	Galliano liqueur
2½	shot(s)	Pressed pineapple juice
½	shot(s)	Freshly squeezed lemon juice

Comment: A fruity, tropical cocktail finished with herbal and citrus notes.

ATOMIC COCKTAIL ●●●○○

Glass: Martini
Garnish: Orange zest twist
Method: SHAKE first three ingredients with ice and fine strain into chilled glass. **TOP** with champagne.

1¼	shot(s)	Ketel One vodka
1¼	shot(s)	Rémy Martin cognac
½	shot(s)	Amontillado sherry
Top up with		Brut champagne

Origin: Created in the early 50s in Las Vegas. A-bomb tests were being conducted in Nevada at the time.
Comment: Golden and flavoursome – handle with care.

ATOMIC DOG ●●●○○

Glass: Collins
Garnish: Pineapple wedge on rim
Method: SHAKE all ingredients with ice and strain into ice-filled glass.

1½	shot(s)	Light white rum
¾	shot(s)	Midori melon liqueur
¾	shot(s)	Malibu coconut rum liqueur
2½	shot(s)	Pressed pineapple juice
¾	shot(s)	Freshly squeezed lemon juice

Comment: A long, refreshing tropical drink with melon, coconut and pineapple juice.

ATTITUDE ADJUSTER ⚷ ●●●○○

Glass: Hurricane
Garnish: Orange sail (orange slice & cherry)
Method: SHAKE first three ingredients with ice and strain into ice-filled glass. **TOP** with cola then **DRIZZLE** orange and coffee liqueurs.

2	shot(s)	Plymouth gin
1	shot(s)	Cointreau triple sec
¾	shot(s)	Freshly squeezed lime juice
Top up with		Cola
¼	shot(s)	Grand Marnier
¼	shot(s)	Kahlúa coffee liqueur

Comment: I've simplified and tried to improve this somewhat dodgy but popular cocktail – sorry, I failed!

THE ATTY COCKTAIL NEW ●●●●○

Glass: Martini
Garnish: Lemon zest twist
Method: SHAKE all ingredients with ice and fine strain into chilled glass.

2¼	shot(s)	Plymouth gin
¾	shot(s)	Dry vermouth
¼	shot(s)	La Feé Parisian (68%) absinthe
¼	shot(s)	Benoit Serres violet liqueur

Origin: Adapted from Harry Craddock's 1930 'The Savoy Cocktail Book'.
Comment: Dry and aromatic with floral hints and aniseed notes.

AUNT AGATHA ●●●●○

Glass: Old-fashioned
Garnish: Orange zest twist
Method: SHAKE first three ingredients with ice and strain into glass filled with crushed ice. **DRIP** bitters over surface.

1½	shot(s)	Pusser's navy rum
2	shot(s)	Freshly squeezed orange juice
1	shot(s)	Pressed pineapple juice
3	dashes	Angostura aromatic bitters

Origin: Aunt Hagatha was one of Samantha's aunts in the 1960s TV series 'Bewitched'; Aunt Agatha was Bertie Wooster's terrifying aunt in P.G. Wodehouse's books.
Comment: A most unusual looking, tropical tasting concoction.

A

AUNT EMILY

Glass: Martini
Garnish: Apricot wedge on rim
Method: SHAKE all ingredients with ice and fine strain into chilled glass.

1½	shot(s)	Plymouth gin
1½	shot(s)	Boulard Grand Solage Calvados
¾	shot(s)	Giffard apricot brandy du Roussillon
¾	shot(s)	Freshly squeezed orange juice
⅛	shot(s)	Pomegranate (grenadine) syrup

Origin: A forgotten classic.
Comment: Aunt Emily is onto something as these ingredients combine to make a stylish fruity Martini.

AUNTIE'S HOT XMAS PUNCH

Glass: Toddy
Garnish: Cinnamon stick in glass
Method: POUR all ingredients into glass and stir. MICROWAVE for a minute (vary time depending on your microwave oven), stir again and serve.

¾	shot(s)	Freshly squeezed lemon juice
1½	shot(s)	Pedro Ximénez sherry
2¼	shot(s)	Rémy Martin cognac
3	shot(s)	Pressed apple juice
4	dashes	Peychaud's aromatic bitters

Origin: I created this drink to serve live on Christmas Eve 2002 during a broadcast on BBC radio. 'Auntie' is a nickname for the BBC and the drink uses the traditional punch proportions of 1 sour, 2 sweet, 3 strong and 4 weak.
Comment: A fruity seasonal warmer.

AUTUMN MARTINI

Glass: Martini
Garnish: Orange zest twist
Method: Cut passion fruit in half and scoop out flesh into shaker. Add other ingredients, SHAKE with ice and fine strain into chilled glass.

1	fresh	Passion fruit
2	shot(s)	Zubrówka bison vodka
1	shot(s)	Pressed apple juice
½	shot(s)	Passion fruit sugar syrup
½	fresh	Egg white

Origin: Created in 2004 by yours truly, inspired by Max Warner's excellent Autumn Punch.
Comment: An easy drinking, smooth, fruity cocktail with grassy hints courtesy of bison vodka.

AUTUMN PUNCH

Glass: Sling
Garnish: Physalis (Cape gooseberry) on rim
Method: Cut passion fruit in half and scoop out flesh into shaker. Add vodka, passion fruit sugar syrup, pear and lemon juice, SHAKE with ice and strain into ice-filled glass. TOP with champagne.

1	fresh	Passion fruit
2	shot(s)	Zubrówka bison vodka
¼	shot(s)	Passion fruit sugar syrup
1	shot(s)	Freshly extracted pear juice
½	shot(s)	Freshly squeezed lemon juice
Top up with		Brut champagne

Origin: Created in 2001 by Max Warner at Baltic Bar, London, England.
Comment: Autumnal in colour with a wonderful meld of complementary flavours.

AVALANCHE

Glass: Collins
Garnish: Banana slice on rim
Method: BLEND ingredients with 12oz scoop of crushed ice. Pour into glass and serve with straws.

2	shot(s)	Giffard crème de banane du Brésil
1	shot(s)	Bols White crème de cacao
½	shot(s)	Luxardo Amaretto di Saschira
1	shot(s)	Double (heavy) cream
1	shot(s)	Milk
½	fresh	Peeled banana

Origin: Created in 1979 at Maudes Bar, New York City, USA.
Comment: Creamy, rich and smooth. Fluffy but lovely.

AVALANCHE SHOT

Glass: Shot
Method: Refrigerate ingredients then LAYER in chilled glass by carefully pouring in the following order.

½	shot(s)	Kahlúa coffee liqueur
½	shot(s)	Giffard White crème de cacao
½	shot(s)	Southern Comfort

Comment: Rich, smooth and sticky – peculiarly, this has an almost nutty taste.

AVENUE

Glass: Martini
Garnish: Orange zest twist
Method: Cut passion fruit in half and scoop flesh into shaker. Add other ingredients, SHAKE with ice and fine strain into chilled glass.

1	fresh	Passion fruit
1	shot(s)	Bourbon whiskey
1	shot(s)	Boulard Grand Solage Calvados
¼	shot(s)	Pomegranate (grenadine) syrup
⅛	shot(s)	Orange flower water
¾	shot(s)	Chilled mineral water (omit if wet ice)

Origin: A modern adaptation of a classic.
Comment: Fruity and floral.

B
C
D
E
F
G
H
I
J
K
L
M
N
O
P
Q
R
S
T
U
V
W
X
Y
Z

A

●●●●◐

AVIATION #1 (SIMPLE FORMULA) UPDATED

Glass: Martini
Garnish: Lemon zest twist
Method: SHAKE all ingredients with ice and fine strain into chilled glass.

2	shot(s)	Plymouth gin
1/2	shot(s)	Luxardo maraschino liqueur
1/2	shot(s)	Freshly squeezed lemon juice
1/2	shot(s)	Chilled mineral water (omit if wet ice)

Variant: Bee's Knees, Blue Moon
Origin: A classic cocktail thought to have originated in 1916.
Comment: This is a fantastic, tangy cocktail and dangerously easy to drink – too many of these and you really will be flying.

●●●●◐

AVIATION #2 (CLASSIC FORMULA) NEW

Glass: Martini
Garnish: Lemon zest twist
Method: SHAKE all ingredients with ice and fine strain into chilled glass.

2	shot(s)	Plymouth gin
1/2	shot(s)	Benoit Serres violet liqueur
1/4	shot(s)	Luxardo maraschino liqueur
1/2	shot(s)	Freshly squeezed lemon juice
1/2	shot(s)	Chilled mineral water (omit if wet ice)

Variant: Blue Moon
Origin: The original 1916 Aviation recipe used crème de violette (violet liqueur), which is sadly almost always omitted in modern day bars.
Comment: This floral Aviation still retains its dry sourness and punch.

●●●●○

AVIATOR UPDATED

Glass: Martini
Garnish: Lemon zest twist
Method: STIR all ingredients with ice and strain into chilled glass.

1	shot(s)	Plymouth gin
1	shot(s)	Dry vermouth
1	shot(s)	Sweet vermouth
1	shot(s)	Dubonnet Red

Origin: A classic cocktail of unknown origins.
Comment: On the bitter side of bittersweet.

FOR MORE INFORMATION SEE OUR

INGREDIENTS
APPENDIX
ON PAGE 272

●●●●○

AWOL

Glass: Shot
Method: LAYER in chilled glass by carefully pouring ingredients in the following order. Then FLAME drink and allow to burn for no more than ten seconds before extinguishing flame and consuming. Take extreme care and beware of hot glass.

1/2	shot(s)	Midori melon liqueur
1/2	shot(s)	Pressed pineapple juice
1/2	shot(s)	Ketel One vodka
1/2	shot(s)	Wray & Nephew overproof rum

Origin: Created in 1993 by Lane Zellman at Louis XVI Restaurant, St. Louis Hotel, New Orleans, USA.
Comment: A strong but surprisingly palatable shot.

●●●●○

AZURE MARTINI

Glass: Martini
Garnish: Apple slice on rim
Method: SHAKE all ingredients with ice and fine strain into chilled glass.

2	shot(s)	Cachaça
1/4	shot(s)	Goldschläger cinnamon schnapps
1	shot(s)	Pressed apple juice
1/2	shot(s)	Freshly squeezed lime juice
1/4	shot(s)	Sugar syrup (2 sugar to 1 water)

Origin: Created in 1998 by Ben Reed at the Met Bar, London, England, and originally made with muddled fresh apple.
Comment: A tangy cocktail – reminiscent of a cinnamon laced apple pie. Shame it's not blue.

●●●●○○

B2C2

Glass: Martini
Garnish: Orange zest twist
Method: SHAKE first three ingredients with ice and strain into ice-filled glass. TOP with champagne.

1	shot(s)	Rémy Martin cognac
1	shot(s)	Bénédictine D.O.M. liqueur
1	shot(s)	Cointreau triple sec
Top up with		Brut champagne

Origin: Named after the four ingredients and created in France during World War II by American soldiers using ingredients liberated from retreating Germans.
Comment: Strong and sweet. This wartime drink can still be deadly if not handled with care.

●●●○○

B5200

Glass: Shot
Method: Refrigerate ingredients then LAYER in chilled glass by carefully pouring in the following order.

1/2	shot(s)	Kahlúa coffee liqueur
1/2	shot(s)	Baileys Irish cream liqueur
1/2	shot(s)	Wood's 100 rum

Origin: Discovered in 2003 at Circus Bar, London, England.
Origin: Layering this drink is as easy as inflating a lifejacket – drink a few and you'll need one.

B-52 SHOT

●●●○○

Glass: Shot
Method: Refrigerate ingredients then **LAYER** in chilled glass by carefully pouring in the following order.

½	shot(s)	**Kahlúa coffee liqueur**
½	shot(s)	**Baileys Irish cream liqueur**
½	shot(s)	**Grand Marnier**

Origin: Named after B-52 bombers in Vietnam.
Comment: Probably the best-known and most popular shot.

B-53 SHOT

●●●○○

Glass: Shot
Method: Refrigerate ingredients then **LAYER** in chilled glass by carefully pouring in the following order.

½	shot(s)	**Kahlúa coffee liqueur**
½	shot(s)	**Baileys Irish cream liqueur**
½	shot(s)	**Ketel One vodka**

Comment: Why settle for a 52 when you can have a 53?

B-54 SHOT

●●●○○

Glass: Shot
Method: Refrigerate ingredients then **LAYER** in chilled glass by carefully pouring in the following order.

½	shot(s)	**Luxardo Amaretto di Saschira**
½	shot(s)	**Kahlúa coffee liqueur**
½	shot(s)	**Baileys Irish cream liqueur**

Comment: Layered and sticky – but nice.

B-55 SHOT

●●●○○

Glass: Shot
Method: Refrigerate ingredients then **LAYER** in chilled glass by carefully pouring in the following order.

½	shot(s)	**Kahlúa coffee liqueur**
½	shot(s)	**Baileys Irish cream liqueur**
½	shot(s)	**La Fée Parisian (68%) absinthe**

Comment: The latest and scariest of the B-something range of layered shots.

B-52 FROZEN

●●●○○

Glass: Old-fashioned
Garnish: Crumbled Cadbury's Flake bar
Method: **BLEND** ingredients with 6oz scoop of crushed ice. Pour into glass and serve with straws.

1	shot(s)	**Baileys Irish cream liqueur**
1	shot(s)	**Grand Marnier**
1	shot(s)	**Kahlúa coffee liqueur**

Comment: The classic shot blended with ice.

B & B

●●●●○

Glass: Old-fashioned
Garnish: Lemon zest twist
Method: **STIR** ingredients with ice and strain into ice-filled glass.

2	shot(s)	**Bénédictine D.O.M. liqueur**
2	shot(s)	**Rémy Martin cognac**

Origin: Created in 1937 by a bartender at New York's famous 21 Club.
Comment: Honeyed and spiced cognac.

B. J. SHOT

●●●○○

Glass: Shot
Garnish: Thin layer of single cream
Method: Refrigerate ingredients then **LAYER** in chilled glass by carefully pouring in the following order.

½	shot(s)	**Grand Marnier**
½	shot(s)	**Baileys Irish cream liqueur**

Comment: You know what the letters stand for – tastes better!

BABY BLUE MARTINI

●●●●○

Glass: Martini
Garnish: Orange zest twist
Method: **SHAKE** all ingredients with ice and fine strain into chilled glass.

2	shot(s)	**Plymouth gin**
¾	shot(s)	**Bols Blue curaçao liqueur**
¾	shot(s)	**Squeezed pink grapefruit juice**
¾	shot(s)	**Pressed pineapple juice**

Comment: Turquoise blue, easy drinking, fruity gin.

BABY GUINNESS

●●●●○

Glass: Shot
Method: Refrigerate ingredients then **LAYER** in chilled glass by carefully pouring in the following order.

1	shot(s)	**Kahlúa coffee liqueur**
½	shot(s)	**Baileys Irish cream liqueur**

Comment: Looks like a miniature pint of Guinness stout.

BABY WOO WOO

●●●○○

Glass: Shot
Garnish: Lime wedge
Method: **SHAKE** all ingredients with ice and fine strain into chilled glass.

½	shot(s)	**Ketel One vodka**
½	shot(s)	**Peach schnapps liqueur**
½	shot(s)	**Cranberry juice**

Comment: Pink, sweet and all too easy to shoot.

●●●●●○

BACARDI COCKTAIL UPDATED

Glass: Martini
Garnish: Maraschino cherry
Method: SHAKE all ingredients with ice and fine strain into chilled glass.

2¹/₂	shot(s)	Bacardi light rum
1	shot(s)	Freshly squeezed lime juice
¹/₂	shot(s)	Pomegranate (grenadine) syrup
¹/₄	shot(s)	Chilled mineral water (omit if wet ice)

Origin: In 1936, a bar in New York was found to be selling the Bacardi Cocktail – without including Bacardi rum. To protect their brand, Bacardi sued. A premise of their case was that Bacardi was a unique rum: although the president of the company refused to reveal any details of production, the court found that it was indeed unique and ruled that a Bacardi Cocktail must be made with Bacardi.
Comment: This classic pinky drink is a perfectly balanced combination of the flavour of rum, the sourness of lime juice and the sweetness of pomegranate syrup.

●●●●●○

BAHAMA MAMA

Glass: Collins
Garnish: Pineapple wedge & cherry
Method: SHAKE all ingredients with ice and strain into ice-filled glass.

³/₄	shot(s)	Pusser's navy rum
³/₄	shot(s)	Aged rum
1	shot(s)	Malibu coconut rum liqueur
1³/₄	shot(s)	Freshly squeezed orange juice
2¹/₂	shot(s)	Pressed pineapple juice
3	dashes	Angostura aromatic bitters

Comment: A tropical, fruity number laced with flavoursome rum.

●●●●●○

BAHAMAS DAIQUIRI

Glass: Martini
Garnish: Pineapple wedge on rim
Method: SHAKE all ingredients with ice and fine strain into chilled glass.

1¹/₂	shot(s)	Myers's Planter's Punch rum
³/₄	shot(s)	Malibu coconut rum liqueur
¹/₄	shot(s)	Kahlúa coffee liqueur
1¹/₂	shot(s)	Freshly extracted pineapple juice
¹/₂	shot(s)	Freshly squeezed lime juice

Origin: Adapted from the Bahamas Martini created in 2002 by Yannick Miseriaux at the Fifth Floor Bar, London, England.
Comment: Totally tropical with a sweet tangy edge.

●●●●○○

BAHIA NEW

Glass: Collins
Garnish: Mint sprig, pineapple wedge & cherry
Method: BLEND all ingredients with 12oz scoop crushed ice and serve with straws.

2¹/₂	shot(s)	Light white rum
3	shot(s)	Pressed pineapple juice
¹/₂	shot(s)	Coco López cream of coconut

Origin: Bahia is one of the 26 states of Brazil. It is also a pre-Prohibition drink containing dry vermouth, sherry, absinthe and bitters. This more recent Piña Colada style offering has more mass market appeal.
Comment: If you like Piña Coladas but are too embarrassed to order one then this drink is for you.

●●●●○

BAJAN DAIQUIRI NEW

Glass: Martini
Garnish: Lime wedge
Method: SHAKE all ingredients with ice and fine strain into chilled glass.

2	shot(s)	Mount Gay golden rum
¹/₂	shot(s)	Velvet Falernum liqueur
³/₄	shot(s)	Freshly squeezed lime juice
¹/₂	shot(s)	Chilled mineral water (omit if wet ice)

Origin: Created in 2006 by yours truly.
Comment: A full-flavoured Daiquiri with clove spice.

●●●●○○

BAJAN MOJITO UPDATED

Glass: Collins
Garnish: Passion fruit slice / mint sprig
Method: Cut passion fruit in half and scoop flesh into glass. Add mint and gently MUDDLE (just to bruise mint). Add Gold Rum, lime juice and crushed ice. Churn drink in glass to mix. DRIZZLE passion fruit liqueur.

1	fresh	Passion fruit
8	fresh	Mint leaves
2	shot(s)	Mount Gay Eclipse golden rum
¹/₂	shot(s)	Freshly squeezed lime juice
¹/₂	shot(s)	Sugar syrup (2 sugar to 1 water)

Origin: Adapted from a recipe by Wayne Collins, London, England
Comment: A laid-back fruity Mojito.

●●●●●

BAJAN PASSION

Glass: Martini
Garnish: Float passion fruit slice
Method: Cut passion fruit in half and scoop flesh into shaker. Add other ingredients, SHAKE with ice and fine strain into chilled glass.

1	fresh	Passion fruit
1¹/₂	shot(s)	Mount Gay Eclipse golden rum
¹/₂	shot(s)	Giffard apricot brandy du Roussillon
1	shot(s)	Freshly squeezed lime juice
¹/₄	shot(s)	Sugar syrup (2 sugar to 1 water)
¹/₄	shot(s)	Vanilla sugar syrup

Origin: Created in 2004 by Wayne Collins for Maxxium UK.
Comment: A Daiquiri laced with fruit and spice.

BAJITO

Glass: Collins
Garnish: Mint sprig
Method: Lightly **MUDDLE** mint and basil in glass just enough to bruise. Add rum, sugar and lime juice. Half fill glass with crushed ice and **CHURN** (stir) with bar spoon. Add more crushed ice and churn some more. Continue adding crushed ice and churning until glass is full.

6	fresh	**Basil leaves**
6	fresh	**Mint leaves**
2	shot(s)	**Light white rum**
1	shot(s)	**Freshly squeezed lime juice**
1/4	shot(s)	**Sugar syrup (2 sugar to 1 water)**

Origin: Discovered in 2004 at Excelsior Bar, Boston, USA.
Comment: Basically a Mojito with basil as well as mint.

BALALAIKA 🗝

Glass: Martini
Garnish: Orange zest twist
Method: SHAKE all ingredients with ice and fine strain into chilled glass.

1¼	shot(s)	**Ketel One vodka**
1¼	shot(s)	**Cointreau triple sec**
1¼	shot(s)	**Freshly squeezed lemon juice**

Comment: Richly flavoured with orange and lemon.

BALD EAGLE SHOT

Glass: Shot
Method: Refrigerate ingredients then **LAYER** in chilled glass by carefully pouring in the following order.

1/2	shot(s)	**Giffard white crème de Menthe Pastille**
3/4	shot(s)	**Partida tequila**

Comment: Minty tequila – fresh breath tastic.

BALD EAGLE UPDATED 🗝

Glass: Martini
Garnish: Salt rim
Method: SHAKE all ingredients with ice and fine strain into chilled glass.

2	shot(s)	**Partida tequila**
3/4	shot(s)	**Freshly squeezed pink grapefruit juice**
1/2	shot(s)	**Cranberry juice**
1/4	shot(s)	**Freshly squeezed lime juice**
1/4	shot(s)	**Freshly squeezed lemon juice**
1/4	shot(s)	**Sugar syrup (2 sugar to 1 water)**

Origin: Created for me in 2001 by Salvatore Calabrese at The Lanesborough Library Bar, London, England.
Comment: If you like Tequila and you like your drinks on the sour side, this is for you.

BALI TRADER

Glass: Martini
Garnish: Banana chunk on rim
Method: SHAKE all ingredients with ice and fine strain into chilled glass.

2	shot(s)	**Ketel One vodka**
1	shot(s)	**Pisang Ambon green banana liqueur**
1	shot(s)	**Pressed pineapple juice**

Comment: A tasty Caribbean combination of banana and pineapple.

BALLET RUSSE 🗝

Glass: Martini
Garnish: Lime wedge on rim
Method: SHAKE all ingredients with ice and fine strain into chilled glass.

2	shot(s)	**Ketel One vodka**
3/4	shot(s)	**Giffard Cassis Noir de Bourgogne**
1	shot(s)	**Freshly squeezed lime juice**
1/4	shot(s)	**Sugar syrup (2 sugar to 1 water)**

Comment: Intense sweet blackcurrant balanced by lime sourness.

BALTIC SPRING PUNCH

Glass: Collins
Garnish: Mint sprig
Method: MUDDLE peach in base of shaker. Add other ingredients, SHAKE with ice and fine strain into ice-filled glass.

1	ripe	**Peach skinned and diced**
1½	shot(s)	**Rose petal liqueur**
1/2	shot(s)	**Freshly squeezed lemon juice**
1/4	shot(s)	**Sugar syrup (2 sugar to 1 water)**
Top up with		**Brut champagne**

Variant: If using peach purée omit the sugar.
Origin: Created in 2002 at Baltic, London, England.
Comment: Just peachy, baby.

BALTIMORE EGG NOG

Glass: Collins
Garnish: Dust with freshly grated nutmeg
Method: SHAKE all ingredients with ice and fine strain into ice-filled glass.

1½	shot(s)	**Rémy Martin cognac**
1½	shot(s)	**Madeira**
1	shot(s)	**Pusser's Navy rum**
1	shot(s)	**Double (heavy) cream**
1	shot(s)	**Milk**
1	shot(s)	**Sugar syrup (2 sugar to 1 water)**
1	fresh	**Beaten egg**

Comment: A flavoursome liquid meal.

A
B
C
D
E
F
G
H
I
J
K
L
M
N
O
P
Q
R
S
T
U
V
W
X
Y
Z

●●●●◐

BAMBOO UPDATED

Glass: Martini
Garnish: Orange zest twist
Method: STIR all ingredients with ice and strain
into chilled glass.

2	shot(s)	Tio Pepe fino sherry
2	shot(s)	Dry vermouth
1/4	shot(s)	Cointreau triple sec
3	dashes	Fee Brothers orange bitters

Variants: Add two dashes of Angostura aromatic
bitters in place of triple sec. Also see East Indian.
Origin: A classic and all but forgotten cocktail
from the 1940s.
Comment: Dry, refined and subtle - for sophisticated palates only.

●●●●◐○

BANANA BATIDA

Glass: Collins
Garnish: Banana chunk on rim
Method: BLEND ingredients with 12oz scoop
of crushed ice. Pour into glass and serve
with straws.

2½	shot(s)	Cachaça
1	shot(s)	Giffard crème de banane du Brésil
3/4	shot(s)	Freshly squeezed lemon juice
1	fresh	Peeled banana

Origin: The Batida is a traditional Brazilian drink.
Comment: A wonderfully tangy drink for a
summer's afternoon.

●●●●○

BANANA BLISS UPDATED

Glass: Martini
Garnish: Orange zest twist
Method: STIR all ingredients with ice and strain
into chilled glass.

2	shot(s)	Rémy Martin cognac
1	shot(s)	Giffard crème de banane du Brésil
1/2	shot(s)	Chilled mineral water (omit if wet ice)
2	dashes	Fee Brothers orange bitters

AKA: Golden Brown
Comment: Crème de bananes and cognac go
shockingly well together.

●●●●○

BANANA BOOMER

Glass: Martini
Garnish: Banana chunk on rim
Method: SHAKE all ingredients with ice and strain
into chilled glass.

1	shot(s)	Ketel One vodka
1	shot(s)	Giffard crème de banane du Brésil
1/2	shot(s)	Giffard apricot brandy du Roussillon
1/2	shot(s)	Cherry (brandy) liqueur
3/4	shot(s)	Freshly squeezed orange juice
3/4	shot(s)	Pressed pineapple juice

Comment: Fortified bubble gum for the young
at heart.

●●●●○

BANANA COLADA

Glass: Hurricane
Garnish: Banana chunk on rim
Method: BLEND ingredients with 12oz scoop of
crushed ice. Pour into glass and serve with straws.

2	shot(s)	Mount Gay Eclipse golden rum
1/2	shot(s)	Giffard crème de banane du Brésil
4	shot(s)	Pressed pineapple juice
1	fresh	Peeled banana
1	shot(s)	Coco López cream of coconut

Comment: Don't skimp, use a whole banana per
drink for real flavour.

●●●○○

BANANA COW NEW

Glass: Collins
Garnish: Banana chunk on rim
Method: BLEND all ingredients with 12oz scoop
crushed ice and serve with straws.

1	shot(s)	Light white rum
3	shot(s)	Fresh milk
1	dash	Vanilla extract
1/4	shot(s)	Sugar syrup (2 sugar to 1 water)
1	fresh	Peeled banana
1	dash	Angostura aromatic bitters

Origin: Created by Victor J. Bergeron. This recipe
is adapted from his 'Trader Vic's Bartender's
Guide' (1972 revised edition).
Comment: The Trader writes of his drink, "The
world's finest, greatest, oh-so good peachy
hangover special. This'll do it when nothing else
will." I think Vic is somewhat overselling this
malty banana meal of a drink.

●●●●◐○

BANANA DAIQUIRI UPDATED

Glass: Hurricane
Garnish: Banana chunk on rim
Method: BLEND all ingredients with 12oz scoop of
crushed ice. Pour into glass and serve with
straws.

2	shot(s)	Havana Club light rum
1	shot(s)	Giffard crème de banane du Brésil
1/2	shot(s)	Freshly squeezed lime juice
1	fresh	Peeled banana

Variant: Add a dash of maraschino liqueur.
Comment: A tangy banana disco drink that's not
too sweet.

●●●●● ◖

BANANA SMOOTHIE (MOCKTAIL)

Glass: Hurricane
Garnish: Banana chunk on rim
Method: BLEND ingredients with 12oz scoop of crushed ice. Pour into glass and serve immediately with straws.

3	shot(s)	Pressed apple juice
7	spoons	Natural yoghurt
3	spoons	Runny honey
1	fresh	Banana

Origin: Created in 2005 by Lisa Ball, London, England.
Comment: Serve with breakfast cereal and you'll be set up for the day. The high fresh banana content means this drink will quickly turn brown if left. This can be countered by adding fresh lemon juice and balancing with more honey but this detracts from the fresh banana flavour.

●●●●● ○

BANANAS & CREAM

Glass: Collins
Garnish: Banana chunk on rim
Method: BLEND ingredients with 12oz scoop of crushed ice. Pour into glass and serve with straws.

2	shot(s)	Giffard crème de banane du Brésil
1	shot(s)	Luxardo Amaretto di Saschira
1	shot(s)	Baileys Irish cream liqueur
1	shot(s)	Double (heavy) cream
2	shot(s)	Milk

Comment: Banana and cream frappé with hints of almond – one for a summer afternoon.

●●●●● ○

BANOFFEE MARTINI

Glass: Martini
Garnish: Dust with cocoa powder
Method: MUDDLE banana in base of shaker. Add other ingredients, SHAKE with ice and fine strain into chilled glass.

1/4	fresh	Banana
1 1/2	shot(s)	Vanilla flavoured vodka
3/4	shot(s)	Butterscotch schnapps liqueur
3/4	shot(s)	Giffard crème de banane du Brésil
1	spoon	Maple syrup
1/2	shot(s)	Double (heavy) cream
1/2	shot(s)	Milk

Origin: Adapted from a recipe created in 2002 by Barry Wilson, Zinc Bar & Grill, Edinburgh, Scotland.
Comment: Thick and rich, one for after the cheese course.

●●●○○

BANSHEE

Glass: Shot
Method: SHAKE all ingredients with ice and fine strain into chilled glass.

1/2	shot(s)	Giffard crème de banane du Brésil
1/2	shot(s)	Giffard White crème de cacao
1/2	shot(s)	Double (heavy) cream

Comment: Creamy chocolate banana.

●●●●○○

BARBARA

Glass: Martini
Garnish: Dust with freshly grated nutmeg
Method: SHAKE all ingredients with ice and fine strain into chilled glass.

1 1/2	shot(s)	Ketel One vodka
3/4	shot(s)	Giffard White crème de cacao
3/4	shot(s)	Double (heavy) cream
3/4	shot(s)	Milk

Comment: Quite neutral and subtle – the nutmeg garnish is as important to the flavour as cacao.

●●●●◖○

BARBARA WEST

Glass: Martini
Garnish: Lemon twist
Method: SHAKE all ingredients with ice and fine strain into chilled glass.

2	shot(s)	Plymouth gin
1	shot(s)	Amontillado sherry
1/2	shot(s)	Freshly squeezed lemon juice
1/4	shot(s)	Sugar syrup (2 sugar to 1 water)
2	dashes	Angostura aromatic bitters

Origin: A classic from the 1930s.
Comment: Well balanced but for serious gin and sherry drinkers only.

●●●●◖○

BARBARY COAST HIGHBALL

Glass: Collins
Method: SHAKE all but soda with ice and strain into ice-filled glass. TOP with soda and stir.

1	shot(s)	Bourbon whiskey
1	shot(s)	Plymouth gin
1	shot(s)	Giffard brown crème de cacao
1/2	shot(s)	Double (heavy) cream
1/2	shot(s)	Milk
Top up with		Soda water (club soda)

Variant: Omit soda and serve straight-up in a Martini glass.
Comment: Looks like a glass of frothy weak tea - bourbon and chocolate predominate.

●●●●○

BARBARY COAST UPDATED

Glass: Martini
Garnish: Dust with cinnamon powder
Method: SHAKE all ingredients with ice and fine strain into chilled glass.

1	shot(s)	Scotch whisky
1	shot(s)	Plymouth gin
1	shot(s)	Giffard white crème de cacao
1	shot(s)	Double (heavy) cream

Origin: Adapted from Victor Bergeron's 'Trader Vic's Bartender's Guide' (1972 revised edition).
Comment: It may be creamy, but this is a serious drink.

A
B
C
D
E
F
G
H
I
J
K
L
M
N
O
P
Q
R
S
T
U
V
W
X
Y
Z

A

B

C

D

E

F

G

H

I

J

K

L

M

N

O

P

Q

R

S

T

U

V

W

X

Y

Z

●●●○○

BARNACLE BILL UPDATED

Glass: Old-fashioned
Garnish: Mint sprig
Method: SHAKE all ingredients with ice and strain into glass filled with crushed ice.

1/2	shot(s)	Yellow Chartreuse
1/2	shot(s)	Parfait Amour liqueur
1/2	shot(s)	Pernod anis
1/2	shot(s)	Chilled mineral water (omit if wet ice)

Origin: Adapted from Victor Bergeron's 'Trader Vic's Bartender's Guide' (1972 revised edition).
Comment: This sweetie is great after a meal on a warm night.

●●●○○

BARNAMINT

Glass: Hurricane
Garnish: Oreo cookie
Method: BLEND ingredients with 12oz scoop of crushed ice. Pour into glass and serve with straws.

2	shot(s)	Baileys Irish cream liqueur
1 1/2	shot(s)	Giffard green crème de menthe
1	shot(s)	Double (heavy) cream
1	shot(s)	Milk
2	scoops	Vanilla ice cream
3	whole	Oreo cookies

Origin: This original TGI Friday's cocktail is named after the Barnum & Bailey Circus, which also inspired the red and white awnings outside Friday's restaurants.
Comment: If you're after a drinkable dessert, then this TGI classic may be the cocktail for you.

●●●●○

BARNUM (WAS RIGHT) UPDATED 🗝

Glass: Martini
Garnish: Lemon zest twist
Method: SHAKE all ingredients with ice and fine strain into chilled glass.

2	shot(s)	Plymouth gin
1	shot(s)	Giffard apricot brandy du Roussillon
1/2	shot(s)	Freshly squeezed lemon juice
2	dashes	Angostura aromatic bitters
1/2	shot(s)	Chilled mineral water (omit if wet ice)

Origin: 1930s classic resurrected by Ted Haigh in his 2004 book 'Vintage Spirits & Forgotten Cocktails'.
Comment: A classic cocktail flavour combination that still pleases.

●●●○○

BARRANQUILLA GREEN JADE NEW

Glass: Martini
Garnish: Green cherry & mint sprig
Method: SHAKE all ingredients with ice and fine strain into chilled glass.

2	shot(s)	Plymouth gin
1	shot(s)	Giffard green crème de menthe
1/2	shot(s)	Double (heavy) cream
1/2	shot(s)	Milk
1/4	fresh	Egg white

Comment: Lime green in colour, a tad minty and creamy smooth.

●●●●○

BARTENDER'S MARTINI

Glass: Martini
Garnish: Orange zest twist
Method: SHAKE all ingredients with ice and fine strain into chilled glass.

1	shot(s)	Plymouth gin
1	shot(s)	Tio Pepe fino sherry
1	shot(s)	Dubonnet Red
1	shot(s)	Dry vermouth
1/2	shot(s)	Grand Marnier

Comment: This classic cocktail resembles an aromatic Martini. Hints of sherry and orange are followed by a dry finish.

●●●●○

BARTENDER'S ROOT BEER

Glass: Collins
Garnish: Lime wedge on rim
Method: POUR first three ingredients into ice-filled glass and top up with cola.

1	shot(s)	Galliano liqueur
1	shot(s)	Kahlúa coffee liqueur
1/4	shot(s)	Freshly squeezed lime juice
Top up with		Cola

Comment: Not quite the root of all evil, but tasty all the same.

●●●●●

BASIL & HONEY DAIQUIRI UPDATED

Glass: Martini
Garnish: Float basil leaf
Method: STIR honey and rum in base of shaker until honey dissolves. Add other ingredients, SHAKE with ice and fine strain into chilled glass.

2	spoons	Runny honey
2 1/2	shot(s)	Havana Club light rum
3	torn	Fresh basil leaves
1/2	shot(s)	Freshly squeezed lime juice

Origin: Formula by yours truly in 2005.
Comment: Basil adds dry vegetable notes to this outstanding classic drink.

●●●●◖

BASIL GIMLET NEW

Glass: Martini
Garnish: Lime wedge or cherry
Method: SHAKE all ingredients with ice and fine strain into chilled glass.

2 1/2	shot(s)	Plymouth gin
1/4	shot(s)	Freshly squeezed lime juice
1 1/2	shot(s)	Rose's lime cordial
3	torn	fresh basil leaves

Origin: Adapted from a drink discovered in 2006 at Stella, Boston, USA.
Comment: Tangy, citrus fresh and balanced.

BASIL BEAUTY UPDATED

Glass: Martini
Garnish: Pineapple wedge on rim
Method: Cut passion fruit in half and scoop flesh into shaker. Add other ingredients, **SHAKE** with ice and fine strain into chilled glass.

1	whole	Passion fruit
3	torn	Basil leaves
2	shot(s)	Ketel One Citroen vodka
2	shot(s)	Pressed pineapple juice
¼	shot(s)	Freshly squeezed lime juice
½	shot(s)	Coconut syrup (or sugar syrup)

Origin: Created in 1999 by Wayne Collins, London, England.
Comment: Pineapple and passion fruit laced with citrus vodka and infused with hints of lime, basil and coconut.

BASIL BRAMBLE SLING

Glass: Sling
Garnish: Mint sprig
Method: **MUDDLE** basil in base of shaker. Add rest of ingredients, **SHAKE** with ice and strain into ice-filled glass. Serve with straws.

7	fresh	Basil leaves
2	shot(s)	Plymouth gin
1½	shot(s)	Freshly squeezed lemon juice
½	shot(s)	Sugar syrup (2 sugar to 1 water)
½	shot(s)	Giffard mûre (blackberry)

Origin: Created in 2003 by Alexandra Fiot at Lonsdale House, London, UK.
Comment: Wonderfully refreshing and balanced.

BASIL GRANDE

Glass: Martini
Garnish: Strawberry and dust with black pepper.
Method: **MUDDLE** strawberries and basil in base of shaker. Add other ingredients, **SHAKE** with ice and fine strain into glass.

4	fresh	Hulled strawberries
5	fresh	Basil leaves
¾	shot(s)	Ketel One vodka
¾	shot(s)	Chambord black raspberry liqueur
¾	shot(s)	Grand Marnier
2	shot(s)	Cranberry juice

Origin: Created in 2001 by Jamie Wilkinson at Living Room, Manchester, England.
Comment: Fruity, with interest courtesy of the basil and grind of pepper.

BASIL MARY UPDATED

Glass: Collins
Garnish: Basil leaf
Method: **SHAKE** all ingredients with ice and fine strain into ice-filled glass.

7	fresh	Torn basil leaves
2	shot(s)	Pepper-infused Ketel One vodka
4	shot(s)	Pressed tomato juice
½	shot(s)	Freshly squeezed lemon juice
8	drops	Tabasco pepper sauce
4	dashes	Lea & Perrins Worcestershire sauce
½	spoon	Horseradish sauce
½	shot(s)	Tawny port
2	pinch	Celery salt
2	pinch	Black pepper

Origin: Discovered in 2004 at Indigo Yard, Edinburgh, Scotland.
Comment: A Mary with a herbal twist.

BASILIAN NEW

Glass: Collins
Garnish: Lime slice & basil leaf
Method: **MUDDLE** cucumber and basil in base of shaker. Add next four ingredients, **SHAKE** with ice and fine strain into ice-filled glass. **TOP** with ginger ale.

1	inch	Fresh cucumber peeled and chopped
5	fresh	Basil leaves
2	shot(s)	Cachaça
¾	shot(s)	Grand Marnier liqueur
½	shot(s)	Freshly squeezed lime juice
¼	shot(s)	Sugar syrup (2 sugar to 1 water)
Top up with		Ginger ale

Origin: Created in 2005 by Duncan McRae at Dragonfly, Edinburgh, Scotland.
Comment: Vegetable notes with hints of orange and ginger. Healthy tasting!

BASILICO

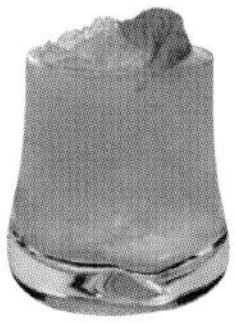

Glass: Old-fashioned
Garnish: Basil leaf
Method: **MUDDLE** basil in base of shaker. Add other ingredients, **SHAKE** with ice and strain into glass filled with crushed ice.

7	fresh	Basil leaves
2	shot(s)	Ketel One vodka
½	shot(s)	Luxardo limoncello
½	shot(s)	Freshly squeezed lemon juice
½	shot(s)	Sugar syrup (2 sugar to 1 water)

Origin: Discovered in 2004 at Atlantic Bar & Grill, London, England.
Comment: A lemon Caipirovska with basil.

HOW TO MAKE SUGAR SYRUP

To make your own sugar syrup, gradually pour TWO cups of granulated sugar into a saucepan containing ONE cup of hot water. Stir as you pour and carry on stirring and simmering until the sugar is dissolved. Do not let the water even come close to boiling and only simmer for as long as it takes to dissolve the sugar. Allow syrup to cool and pour into an empty bottle. Ideally, you should finely strain your syrup into the bottle to remove any undissolved crystals which could otherwise encourage crystallisation. If kept in a refrigerator this mixture will last for a couple of months.

A
B
C
D
E
F
G
H
I
J
K
L
M
N
O
P
Q
R
S
T
U
V
W
X
Y
Z

● ● ● ● ○

BATANGA NEW

Glass: Collins
Garnish: Salt rim
Method: POUR ingredients into ice-filled glass, stir and serve with straws.

2	shot(s)	Partida tequila
¹/₂	shot(s)	Freshly squeezed lime juice
Top up with		Cola

Origin: The signature drink of the now legendary Don Javier Delgado Corona, the owner/bartender of La Capilla (The Chapel) in Tequila, Mexico. Still mixing, even in his eighties, Corona is noted for ritualistically stirring this drink with a huge knife.
Comment: Basically a Cuba Libre made with tequila in place of rum – an improvement.

● ● ● ○ ○

BATIDA DE COCO

Glass: Collins
Method: BLEND ingredients with 12oz scoop of crushed ice. POUR into glass and serve with straws.

2¹/₂	shot(s)	Cachaça
1¹/₂	shot(s)	Coco López cream of coconut
1	shot(s)	Coconut milk

Origin: Traditional Brazilian drink.
Comment: Sweet, almost creamy coconut with a hint of cachaça.

● ● ● ● ○

BAY BREEZE UPDATED

Glass: Collins
Garnish: Pineapple wedge on rim
Method: SHAKE all ingredients with ice and strain into ice-filled glass.

2	shot(s)	Ketel One vodka
1¹/₂	shot(s)	Cranberry juice
2¹/₂	shot(s)	Pressed pineapple juice

Comment: Pink, fluffy, sweet and easy to drink.

● ● ○ ○ ○

BAZOOKA

Glass: Shot
Method: SHAKE all ingredients with ice and fine strain into chilled glass.

³/₄	shot(s)	Southern Comfort
¹/₂	shot(s)	Giffard crème de banane du Brésil
¹/₈	shot(s)	Pomegranate (grenadine) syrup
¹/₄	shot(s)	Double (heavy) cream

Comment: A sticky, pink shot.

● ● ● ○ ○

BAZOOKA JOE

Glass: Shot
Method: Refrigerate ingredients then LAYER in chilled glass by carefully pouring in the following order.

¹/₂	shot(s)	Bols Blue curaçao liqueur
¹/₂	shot(s)	Giffard crème de banane du Brésil
¹/₂	shot(s)	Baileys Irish cream liqueur

Comment: Banana and orange topped with whiskey cream.

● ● ● ● ○

BBC

Glass: Martini
Garnish: Dust with freshly grated nutmeg
Method: SHAKE all ingredients with ice and fine strain into chilled glass.

1¹/₄	shot(s)	Rémy Martin cognac
1	shot(s)	Bénédictine D.O.M. liqueur
³/₄	shot(s)	Double (heavy) cream
³/₄	shot(s)	Milk

Origin: Thought to have originated in the UK in the late 1970s and named, not after the British Broadcasting Company, but brandy, Bénédictine and cream.
Comment: Brandy and Bénédictine (a classic combo) smoothed with cream. Drier than you might expect.

● ● ● ● ○

BE-TON

Glass: Collins
Garnish: Squeezed lime wedge in glass
Method: POUR Becherovka into ice-filled glass, then top up with tonic water and stir.

2	shot(s)	Becherovka (Carlsbad Becher)
Top up with		Tonic water

Origin: Becherovka (or Carlsbad Becher as it's sometimes known) is the Czech national liqueur. Matured in oak, it contains cinnamon, cloves, nutmeg and other herbs.
Comment: This spicy drink is the Czech Republic's answer to the Gin 'n' Tonic.

● ● ● ● ○

BEACH BLONDE

Glass: Collins
Garnish: Banana slice on rim
Method: BLEND ingredients with 12oz scoop of crushed ice. Pour into glass and serve with straws.

¹/₂	fresh	Peeled banana
1	shot(s)	Wray & Nephew overproof white rum
3	shot(s)	Advocaat liqueur
3	shot(s)	Freshly squeezed orange juice

Origin: Created in 2002 by Alex Kammerling, London, England.
Comment: Fruity, creamy holiday drinking.

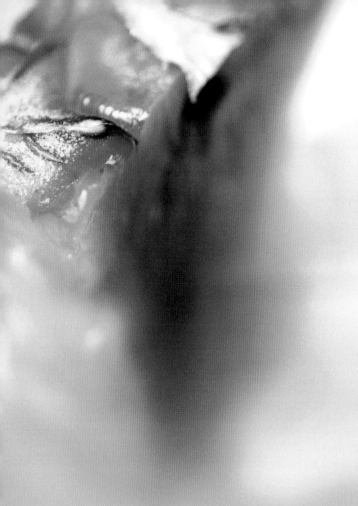

BATIDA

The Batida is a traditional Brazilian drink based on cachaça mixed with fresh fruit, sugar and/or sweetened condensed milk (leite condensado). They are usually blended with crushed ice or shaken and served over crushed ice.

In Brazil the most popular Batidas are made with passion fruit (batida de maracujá) and coconut milk (batida de coco). Unfortunately, this excellent drink has not transferred as quickly from its homeland as the Caipirinha.

Batida variations include
Abaci (pineapple) Batida
Banana Batida
Batida de Coco (with coconut milk)
Carneval (mango) Batida
Goiaba (guava) Batida
Mango Batida
Maracujá (passion fruit) Batida
Milho Verde (sweetcorn) Batida
Morango (strawberry) Batida

A
B
C
D
E
F
G
H
I
J
K
L
M
N
O
P
Q
R
S
T
U
V
W
X
Y
Z

BEACH ICED TEA ⚷ ●●●●○

Glass: Sling
Garnish: Lemon slice
Method: SHAKE all ingredients with ice and strain into ice-filled glass.

¹/₂	shot(s)	Light white rum
¹/₂	shot(s)	Plymouth gin
¹/₂	shot(s)	Ketel One vodka
¹/₂	shot(s)	Partida tequila
¹/₂	shot(s)	Cointreau triple sec
1	shot(s)	Freshly squeezed lemon juice
¹/₂	shot(s)	Sugar syrup (2 sugar to 1 water)
3	shot(s)	Cranberry juice

Comment: A Long Island Iced Tea with cranberry juice instead of cola.

BEACHCOMBER ●●●●○

Glass: Martini
Garnish: Lime wedge on rim
Method: SHAKE all ingredients with ice and fine strain into chilled glass.

2	shot(s)	Light white rum
¹/₂	shot(s)	Cointreau triple sec
³/₄	shot(s)	Freshly squeezed lime juice
¹/₄	shot(s)	Luxardo maraschino liqueur
¹/₂	shot(s)	Chilled mineral water (omit if wet ice)

Comment: A Daiquiri with the addition of a dash of triple sec and maraschino.

BEAM-ME-UP SCOTTY SHOT NEW ●●○○○

Glass: Shot
Method: Refrigerate ingredients then LAYER in chilled glass by carefully pouring in the following order.

¹/₂	shot(s)	Kahlúa coffee liqueur
¹/₂	shot(s)	Giffard crème de banane du Brésil
¹/₂	shot(s)	Baileys Irish cream liqueur

Comment: Coffee, banana and creamy whiskey. Very sweet but not too offensive and easy to layer.

BEBBO UPDATED ⚷ ●●●●◐

Glass: Martini
Garnish: Lemon zest twist
Method: STIR honey with gin in base of shaker until honey dissolves. Add other ingredients, SHAKE with ice and fine strain into chilled glass.

2	spoons	Runny honey
1¹/₂	shot(s)	Plymouth gin
1	shot(s)	Freshly squeezed lemon juice
¹/₂	shot(s)	Freshly squeezed orange juice
¹/₄	shot(s)	Chilled mineral water (omit if wet ice)

Origin: A long lost relation of the Bee's Knees below. This recipe is based on one from Ted Haigh's 2004 book 'Vintage Spirits & Forgotten Cocktails'.
Comment: Fresh, clean and citrusy with honeyed notes. Choose your honey wisely.

BEE STING ●●●●○

Glass: Collins
Garnish: Apple slice
Method: STIR honey with whiskey in base of shaker until honey dissolves. Add tequila and apple juice, SHAKE with ice and strain into ice-filled glass. TOP with a splash of ginger ale.

1	spoon	Runny honey
1	shot(s)	Jack Daniel's Tennessee whiskey
1	shot(s)	Partida tequila
2	shot(s)	Pressed apple juice
Top up with		Ginger ale

Origin: Discovered in 2005 at The Royal Exchange Grand Café & Bar, London, England.
Comment: A delicately spiced, long, refreshing drink.

BEE'S KNEES #1 ●●●●○

Glass: Martini
Garnish: Orange zest twist
Method: STIR honey with rum until honey dissolves. Add other ingredients, SHAKE with ice and fine strain into chilled glass.

1¹/₄	shot(s)	Light white rum
1¹/₄	shot(s)	Pusser's navy rum
2	spoons	Runny honey
1	shot(s)	Freshly squeezed orange juice
¹/₂	shot(s)	Double (heavy) cream
¹/₂	shot(s)	Milk

Comment: Smooth and orangey to start, with a rum and honey finish.

BEE'S KNEES #2 UPDATED ⚷ ●●●●◐

Glass: Martini
Garnish: Orange zest twist
Method: In base of shaker STIR honey with gin until honey dissolves. Add lemon and orange juice, SHAKE with ice and fine strain into chilled glass.

2	shot(s)	Plymouth gin
3	spoons	Runny honey
1	shot(s)	Freshly squeezed lemon juice
1	shot(s)	Freshly squeezed orange juice

Variant: Made with light rum in place of gin this drink becomes a Honeysuckle Martini.
Origin: Adapted from David A. Embury's 1948 'The Fine Art of Mixing Drinks'.
Comment: This concoction really is the bee's knees.

BEE'S KNEES #3 NEW ⚷ ●●●●◐

Glass: Martini
Garnish: Lemon zest twist
Method: In base of shaker STIR honey with gin until honey dissolves. Add lemon juice, SHAKE with ice and fine strain into chilled glass.

2	shot(s)	Plymouth gin
3	spoons	Runny honey
³/₄	shot(s)	Freshly squeezed lemon juice

Comment: The combination of honey and lemon suggests flu relief but don't wait for an ailment before trying this soothing concoction.

BELLINI

It has long been traditional in Italy to marinade fresh peaches in wine and the Bellini draws on this tradition, combining prosecco wine with puréed white peaches (with added sugar and lemon juice).

Giuseppe Cipriani created this drink at Harry's Bar, Venice, in 1945, fourteen years after he opened his tiny place on the edge of the Grand Canal, not far from St. Mark's Square. Cipriani named his cocktail after the 15th-century Venetian painter Giovanni Bellini due to the drink's pink hue and the painter's penchant for using rich pinks on his canvases.

Like many other legendary bars around the world, Harry's owes some of its notoriety to being patronised by probably the world's greatest drinker, Ernest Hemingway. It was also the haunt of Sinclair Lewis, Orson Welles, F. Scott Fitzgerald and Dorothy Parker, and continues to attract celebrities to this day. But you don't have to be a celebrity to go to Harry's Bar. Cocktail aficionados from around the world make pilgrimages to the birthplace of the Bellini to sample the original recipe.

Prosecco is a sparkling wine which must come from a specific region in Northern Italy. White peaches are in season in Italy from May to September, so in Venice the best bars only sell the drink between May and October. Bars which serve the drink year round use frozen purée.

Bellini variations include
Bellini (original)
Bellini (Difford's formula)
Bellini-Tini
Kiwi Bellini
Puccini (tangerine/mandarin) Bellini
Raspberry Bellini
Rhubarb & Honey Bellini
Rossini (strawberry)
Tintoretto (pomegranate) Bellini
Tiziano (Fragola grape) Bellini

●●●●○

BEETLE JEUSE

Glass: Collins
Garnish: Mint sprig
Method: Lightly **MUDDLE** mint in base of shaker just enough to bruise. Add other ingredients, **SHAKE** with ice and strain into ice-filled glass.

7	fresh	Mint leaves
1	shot(s)	Green Chartreuse
1	shot(s)	Zubrówka bison vodka
3¹/₂	shot(s)	Pressed apple juice
¹/₄	shot(s)	Passion fruit sugar syrup

Origin: Created in 2003 by Milo Rodriguez at Raoul's Bar, Oxford, and named after Beetlejuice, the Tim Burton black comedy about a young couple whose premature death leads them to a series of bizarre afterlife exploits.
Comment: Long and refreshing with a flavour reminiscent of caramelised apple.

●●●●○

BEHEMOTH

Glass: Martini
Garnish: Lemon zest twist
Method: SHAKE all ingredients with ice and fine strain into chilled glass.

1¹/₂	shot(s)	Bourbon whiskey
1	shot(s)	Sweet vermouth
³/₄	shot(s)	Giffard White crème de cacao
³/₄	shot(s)	Freshly squeezed lemon juice
¹/₂	shot(s)	Sugar syrup (2 sugar to 1 water)
¹/₂	fresh	Egg white (optional)
2	dashes	Peychaud's aromatic bitters (optional)

Origin: This monstrous beast was created in 2004 by yours truly.
Comment: Tangy, citrus bourbon with a hint of chocolate.

●●●●○

BEJA FLOR

Glass: Martini
Garnish: Banana chunk on rim
Method: SHAKE all ingredients with ice and fine strain into chilled glass.

2	shot(s)	Cachaça
1	shot(s)	Cointreau triple sec
1	shot(s)	Giffard crème de banane du Brésil
¹/₂	shot(s)	Freshly squeezed lemon juice

Comment: Sharp and quite dry but with a sweet banana twang.

FOR MORE INFORMATION SEE OUR
INGREDIENTS APPENDIX ON PAGE 272

●●●●○

BELLA DONNA DAIQUIRI

Glass: Martini
Garnish: Wipe rim with lemon & dust with cinnamon powder
Method: SHAKE all ingredients with ice and fine strain into chilled glass.

1¹/₂	shot(s)	Gosling's Black Seal rum
1¹/₂	shot(s)	Luxardo Amaretto di Saschira
¹/₂	shot(s)	Freshly squeezed lemon juice
¹/₄	shot(s)	Sugar syrup (2 sugar to 1 water)
¹/₂	shot(s)	Chilled mineral water (omit if wet ice)

Origin: Adapted from a drink discovered in 2003 at Bellagio, Las Vegas, USA.
Comment: This was the hit cocktail for diffords-guide staff at the Bellagio, Las Vegas, after working at the Nightclub & Bar Beverage Convention. Try one and see why.

●●●●○

BELLINI #1 (ORIGINAL) UPDATED

Glass: Flute
Garnish: Peach slice on rim
Method: STIR all ingredients with ice and strain into chilled glass.

1	shot(s)	Puréed white peaches (10% added sugar)
¹/₈	shot(s)	Freshly squeezed lemon juice
2	shot(s)	Prosecco sparkling wine (chilled)

Origin: Created in 1934 by Giuseppe Cipriani at Harry's Bar, Venice, Italy.
Comment: It's hard not to like this blend of peaches and sparkling wine.

●●●●○

BELLINI #2 (DIFFORD'S FORMULA) UPDATED

Glass: Flute
Garnish: Peach slice on rim
Method: SHAKE first four ingredients with ice and fine strain into chilled glass.
Add Prosecco and gently stir. (Alternatively, refrigerate all ingredients, blend briefly without ice and serve in chilled glass.)

2	shot(s)	Puréed white peaches (10% added sugar)
¹/₄	shot(s)	Peach schnapps liqueur
¹/₄	shot(s)	Peach eau de vie (de pêche)
¹/₈	shot(s)	Freshly squeezed lemon juice
Top up with		Prosecco sparkling wine

Origin: Created in 2003 by yours truly.
Comment: My version is more alcoholic and drier than the classic Bellini.

●●●●○

BELLINI-TINI

Glass: Martini
Garnish: Peach wedge
Method: SHAKE all ingredients with ice and fine strain into chilled glass.

2	shot(s)	Ketel One vodka
¹/₂	shot(s)	Peach schnapps liqueur
2	shot(s)	Fresh white peach purée
3	dashes	Peach bitters (optional)

Comment: Peachy, peachy, peachy! Based on the Bellini, funnily enough.

●●●●○○

BELLISSIMO

Glass: Old-fashioned
Garnish: Orange slice
Method: SHAKE all ingredients with ice and fine strain into ice-filled glass.

1	shot(s)	Hazelnut (crème de noisette) liqueur
1	shot(s)	Campari
1	shot(s)	Luxardo limoncello liqueur
¹/₂	shot(s)	Freshly squeezed lemon juice

Origin: Adapted from a drink created in 2003 by Ben Davidson at Posh Lounge, Sydney, Australia.
Comment: An unusual meld of flavours, but Campari lovers should give this a try.

●●●●○

BENSONHURST NEW

Glass: Martini
Garnish: Maraschino cherry
Method: STIR all ingredients with ice and strain into chilled glass.

2	shot(s)	Bourbon whiskey
1	shot(s)	Dry vermouth
¹/₂	shot(s)	Luxardo maraschino liqueur
¹/₄	shot(s)	Cynar artichoke liqueur

Origin: Adapted from a drink created in 2006 by Chad Solomon and named after a neighbourhood close to his home in Brooklyn, New York City, USA
Comment: A refined and balanced Manhattan-style drink.

●●●●○○

BENTLEY UPDATED

Glass: Old-fashioned
Garnish: Orange zest twist
Method: STIR all ingredients with ice and strain into ice-filled glass.

1¹/₂	shot(s)	Boulard Grand Solage Calvados
1¹/₂	shot(s)	Dubonnet Red
2	dashes	Peychaud's aromatic bitters (optional)

Variant: Served straight-up.
Origin: Adapted from Harry Craddock's 1930 'The Savoy Cocktail Book'.
Comment: Dry, spiced wine impregnated with apple – pretty damn good.

●●●●○○

BERMUDA COCKTAIL NEW

Glass: Martini
Garnish: Orange zest twist
Method: SHAKE all ingredients with ice and fine strain into chilled glass.

2	shot(s)	Plymouth gin
¹/₂	shot(s)	Peach schnapps liqueur
¹/₂	shot(s)	Freshly squeezed orange juice
¹/₄	shot(s)	Pomegranate (grenadine) syrup

Origin: Adapted from Victor Bergeron's 'Trader Vic's Bartender's Guide' (1972 revised edition).
Comment: Gin with a sweetening touch of peach, orange and pomegranate.

●●●●○

BERMUDA ROSE COCKTAIL NEW

Glass: Martini
Garnish: Apricot slice (dried or fresh) on rim
Method: SHAKE all ingredients with ice and fine strain into chilled glass.

2	shot(s)	Plymouth gin
¹/₂	shot(s)	Giffard apricot brandy du Roussillon
¹/₄	shot(s)	Pomegranate (grenadine) syrup
¹/₂	shot(s)	Chilled mineral water (omit if wet ice)

Origin: Adapted from Victor Bergeron's 'Trader Vic's Bartender's Guide' (1972 revised edition).
Comment: Delicate, floral and aromatic. A hint of sweetness but not so as to offend.

●●●●○○

BERMUDA RUM SWIZZLE NEW

Glass: Collins
Garnish: Orange & cherry on stick (sail)
Method: POUR all ingredients into glass, add crushed ice and SWIZZLE. Serve with straws.

2	shot(s)	Goslings Black Seal dark rum
1	shot(s)	Freshly squeezed lime juice
1	shot(s)	Pressed pineapple juice
1	shot(s)	Freshly squeezed orange juice
¹/₄	shot(s)	Velvet Falernum liqueur

Origin: Recipe adapted from drinkboy.com.
Comment: Tangy fruit for the poolside.

●●●●○

BERRY CAIPIRINHA

Glass: Old-fashioned
Method: MUDDLE lime and berries in base of glass. Add other ingredients and fill glass with crushed ice. CHURN drink with bar spoon and serve with short straws.

³/₄	fresh	Lime cut into wedges
3	fresh	Raspberries
3	fresh	Blackberries
2	shot(s)	Cachaça
³/₄	shot(s)	Sugar syrup (2 sugar to 1 water)

Variant: Black 'N' Blue Caipirovska
Comment: A fruity version of the popular Brazilian drink.

●●●●○○

BERRY NICE UPDATED

Glass: Collins
Garnish: Blackberries
Method: MUDDLE blackberries in base of shaker. Add next three ingredients, SHAKE with ice and strain into ice-filled glass. TOP with ginger beer and serve with straws.

9	fresh	Blackberries
2	shot(s)	Ketel One vodka
¹/₄	shot(s)	Chambord black raspberry liqueur
¹/₂	shot(s)	Freshly squeezed lemon juice
Top up with		Jamaican ginger beer

Origin: Adapted from a drink created in 2001 in the UK's The Living Room chain of bars.
Comment: Rich blackberry flavour with a ginger finish.

A
B
C
D
E
F
G
H
I
J
K
L
M
N
O
P
Q
R
S
T
U
V
W
X
Y
Z

A

B

BESSIE & JESSIE

Glass: Collins
Garnish: Orange slice
Method: SHAKE all ingredients with ice and strain into ice-filled glass.

2	shot(s)	Scotch whisky
2	shot(s)	Advocaat liqueur
3¹/₂	shot(s)	Milk

Comment: Malty, creamy and eggy, but tasty.

BETWEEN DECKS NEW

Glass: Collins
Garnish: Pineapple wedge, mint & cherry
Method: SHAKE all ingredients with ice and strain into ice-filled glass.

2¹/₂	shot(s)	Plymouth gin
1	shot(s)	Freshly squeezed orange juice
1	shot(s)	Cranberry juice
¹/₂	shot(s)	Freshly squeezed lime juice
¹/₄	shot(s)	Sugar syrup
¹/₂	shot(s)	Chilled mineral water (omit if wet ice)

Origin: Adapted from Victor Bergeron's 'Trader Vic's Bartender's Guide' (1972 revised edition).
Comment: I've upped the ante on this drink with more gin and less fruit than the original - so beware.

BETWEEN THE SHEETS #1 NEW
(CLASSIC FORMULA)

Glass: Martini
Garnish: Lemon zest twist
Method: SHAKE all ingredients with ice and fine strain into chilled glass.

1	shot(s)	Light White rum
1	shot(s)	Rémy Martin cognac
1	shot(s)	Cointreau triple sec
¹/₄	shot(s)	Freshly squeezed lemon juice

Origin: Created in the 1930s by Harry MacElhone, of Harry's New York Bar in Paris, and derived from the Sidecar.
Comment: Three shots of 40% alcohol and a splash of lemon juice make for a tart drink which should not be undertaken lightly.

BETWEEN THE SHEETS #2 UPDATED
(DIFFORD'S FORMULA)

Glass: Martini
Garnish: Lemon zest twist
Method: SHAKE all ingredients with ice and fine strain into chilled glass.

³/₄	shot(s)	Light White rum
³/₄	shot(s)	Rémy Martin cognac
³/₄	shot(s)	Cointreau triple sec
¹/₄	shot(s)	Freshly squeezed lemon juice
¹/₂	shot(s)	Chilled mineral water (omit if wet ice)

Comment: Maintains the essential flavour and ingredients of the classic formula but is a little more approachable.

BEVERLY HILLS ICED TEA

Glass: Sling
Garnish: Lime zest spiral
Method: SHAKE first five ingredients with ice and strain into ice-filled glass. TOP with champagne and gently stir.

³/₄	shot(s)	Plymouth gin
³/₄	shot(s)	Ketel One vodka
1	shot(s)	Cointreau triple sec
¹/₂	shot(s)	Freshly squeezed lime juice
¹/₂	shot(s)	Sugar syrup (2 sugar to 1 water)
Top up with		Brut champagne

Comment: Very strong and refreshing.

BIARRITZ

Glass: Old-fashioned
Garnish: Orange slice & cherry (orange sail)
Method: SHAKE all ingredients with ice and strain into ice-filled glass.

2	shot(s)	Rémy Martin cognac
1	shot(s)	Grand Marnier
³/₄	shot(s)	Freshly squeezed lemon juice
¹/₂	fresh	Egg white
3	dashes	Angostura aromatic bitters

Comment: Basically a brandy sour with a little something extra from the orange liqueur.

BIG APPLE MARTINI

Glass: Martini
Garnish: Apple wedge on rim
Method: SHAKE all ingredients with ice and fine strain into chilled glass.

2¹/₂	shot(s)	Ketel One vodka
1	shot(s)	Sour apple liqueur
1	shot(s)	Apple schnapps liqueur

AKA: Apple Martini, Sour Apple Martini
Comment: There's no apple juice in this Martini, but it has an appealing light minty green hue.

THE BIG EASY

Glass: Collins
Garnish: Half orange slice
Method: SHAKE first three ingredients with ice and strain into ice-filled glass. TOP with ginger ale.

1³/₄	shot(s)	Southern Comfort
³/₄	shot(s)	Cointreau triple sec
2	shot(s)	Freshly squeezed orange juice
Top up with		Ginger ale

Comment: Fruity and refreshing with a hint of spice.

BIJOU NEW

●●●●◐

Glass: Martini
Garnish: Cherry & discarded lemon zest twist
Method: SHAKE all ingredients with ice and fine strain into chilled glass.

1¹/₂	shot(s)	Plymouth gin
¹/₂	shot(s)	Green Chartreuse
¹/₂	shot(s)	Sweet vermouth
2	dashes	Fee Brothers orange bitters
¹/₂	shot(s)	Chilled mineral water (omit if wet ice)

AKA: Amber Dream, Golden Glow
Origin: A forgotten Classic
Comment: Serious and packed with bold flavours. Fellow Chartreuse fans will approve.

BIKINI MARTINI UPDATED

●●●●○

Glass: Martini
Garnish: Orange zest twist
Method: SHAKE all ingredients with ice and fine strain into chilled glass.

2	shot(s)	Plymouth gin
³/₄	shot(s)	Bols Blue curaçao liqueur
¹/₄	shot(s)	Peach schnapps liqueur
¹/₄	shot(s)	Freshly squeezed lemon juice
¹/₂	shot(s)	Chilled mineral water (omit if wet ice)

Origin: Adapted from a cocktail created in 1999 by Dick Bradsell for an Agent Provocateur swimwear launch. The bikini swimsuit was named after Bikini Atoll, where A-bombs were tested after World War II, on the basis that such a revealing garment would cause as much shock as a thermonuclear device.
Comment: A vivid blue combination of lemon, orange and peach laced with gin.

BINGO 🔑

●●●○○

Glass: Collins
Garnish: Lemon wheel
Method: SHAKE first four ingredients with ice and strain into ice filledglass. Top with soda water.

1	shot(s)	Ketel One vodka
1	shot(s)	Grand Marnier
1	shot(s)	Giffard apricot brandy du Roussillon
¹/₂	shot(s)	Freshly squeezed lemon juice
Top up with		Soda water (club soda)

Comment: Refreshing, fruity long drink.

BIRD OF PARADISE

●●●◐○

Glass: Martini
Garnish: Dust with freshly grated nutmeg
Method: SHAKE all ingredients with ice and fine strain into chilled glass.

1¹/₄	shot(s)	Partida tequila
³/₄	shot(s)	Giffard White crème de cacao
¹/₂	shot(s)	Luxardo Amaretto di Saschira
1	shot(s)	Double (heavy) cream
³/₄	shot(s)	Milk

Comment: If you like tequila and creamy drinks, the two don't mix much better than this.

BISHOP UPDATED

●●●●○

Glass: Toddy
Garnish: Dust with freshly grated nutmeg
Method: MUDDLE cloves in the base of shaker. Add boiling water and STIR in honey and other ingredients. Fine strain into glass and MICROWAVE for twenty seconds to boost temperature. STIR, garnish and serve.

7	whole	Cloves
3	shot(s)	Boiling water
2	spoons	Runny honey
2¹/₂	shot(s)	Tawny port
1	shot(s)	Freshly squeezed orange juice

Origin: My quick 'n' easy take on this variation of the 18th century Negus - reputedly a favourite of the writer Dr. Johnson. The traditional recipe begins with studding an orange with cloves and roasting it in the oven.
Comment: A flavoursome and warming variation on mulled wine.

THE BISTRO SIDECAR NEW

●●●●○

Glass: Martini
Garnish: Lemon zest twist
Method: SHAKE all ingredients with ice and fine strain into chilled glass.

1¹/₂	shot(s)	Rémy Martin cognac
¹/₂	shot(s)	Tuaca liqueur
¹/₂	shot(s)	Frangelico liqueur
¹/₄	shot(s)	Freshly squeezed lemon juice
¹/₄	shot(s)	Freshly squeezed orange juice

Origin: Adapted from a recipe by chef Kathy Casey of Kathy Casey Food Studios, Seattle, USA. Kathy's original recipe called for a sugar rim and tangerine juice.
Comment: Although significantly twisted from the classic, this is still recognisably a Sidecar in style.

BIT-O-HONEY

●●●○○

Glass: Shot
Method: Refrigerate ingredients then LAYER in chilled glass by carefully pouring in the following order.

³/₄	shot(s)	Butterscotch schnapps liqueur
³/₄	shot(s)	Baileys Irish cream liqueur

Variant: Layered with butterscotch, then honey liqueur and an Irish cream float.
Comment: A sweet but pleasant tasting shot.

A
B
C
D
E
F
G
H
I
J
K
L
M
N
O
P
Q
R
S
T
U
V
W
X
Y
Z

● ● ● ● ○ ○

BITTER ELDER UPDATED

Glass: Collins
Garnish: Lemon wedge
Method: SHAKE all ingredients with ice and strain into ice-filled glass.

2	shot(s)	Plymouth gin
1	shot(s)	St Germain elderflower liqueur
2	shot(s)	Pressed apple juice
3/4	shot(s)	Freshly squeezed lemon juice
3	dashes	Angostura aromatic bitters

Origin: Adapted from a short drink created in 2005 by Tonin Kacaj at Maze, London, England.
Comment: The eponymous elderflower is well balanced with the other ingredients to make a dry refreshing long drink.

● ● ● ● ○ ○

BITTER SWEET SYMPHONY ⌐

Glass: Martini
Garnish: Apricot slice
Method: SHAKE all ingredients with ice and fine strain into chilled glass.

1/2	shot(s)	Ketel One vodka
1	shot(s)	Cointreau triple sec
1	shot(s)	Giffard apricot brandy du Roussillon
1/2	shot(s)	Freshly squeezed lime juice
1 1/2	shot(s)	Freshly squeezed grapefruit juice

Origin: Adapted from a drink created in 2003 by Wayne Collins for Maxxium UK.
Comment: This roller coaster ride of bitter and sweet mainly features apricot and grapefruit.

● ● ● ● ○ ○

BITTEREST PILL

Glass: Shot
Method: Refrigerate ingredients then LAYER in chilled glass by carefully pouring in the following order.

1/2	shot(s)	Passion fruit sugar syrup
1/2	shot(s)	Campari
1/2	shot(s)	Ketel One vodka

Created by: Alex Kammerling, London, England
Comment: The bitterness of Campari, toned down by passion fruit sugar syrup.

● ● ● ○ ○

BLACK & TAN

Glass: Boston
Method: POUR lager into chilled glass then float Guinness on top.

1/2	pint	Lager
1/2	pint	Guinness stout

Comment: Lager downstairs, Guinness upstairs.

● ● ● ● ○ ○

BLACK & VELVET NEW

Glass: Boston
Method: POUR cider into chilled glass then float Guinness on top.

1/2	pint	Cider
1/2	pint	Guinness stout

Comment: Cider downstairs, Guinness upstairs.

● ● ● ● ●

BLACK & WHITE DAIQUIRI

Glass: Martini
Garnish: Blackberry in drink
Method: MUDDLE berries in base of shaker. Add other ingredients, SHAKE with ice and fine strain into chilled glass.

12	fresh	Blackberries
2	shot(s)	Malibu coconut rum liqueur
1	shot(s)	Light white rum
3/4	shot(s)	Giffard mûre (blackberry)
1/2	shot(s)	Freshly squeezed lime juice
1/2	shot(s)	Chilled mineral water (omit if wet ice)

Origin: I named this drink after the black berries and the white Malibu bottle.
Comment: Blackberries and coconut add depth to the classic Daiquiri.

● ● ● ○ ○

BLACK BEARD

Glass: Boston
Method: POUR ingredients into glass and serve.

2	shot(s)	Spiced rum
1/2	pint	Guinness (chilled)
Top up with		Cola (chilled)

Origin: Thought to have originated in Stirling, Scotland, during the late 1990s.
Comment: Something of a student drink, this tastes better than it sounds.

● ● ● ● ●

BLACK BISON MARTINI

Glass: Martini
Garnish: Apple wedge
Method: SHAKE all ingredients with ice and fine strain into chilled glass.

2	shot(s)	Plymouth gin
1/2	shot(s)	Apple schnapps liqueur
1 1/2	shot(s)	Pressed apple juice
1/4	shot(s)	Dry vermouth

Origin: Adapted from a drink discovered in 2001 at Oxo Tower Bar, London, England.
Comment: A fragrant cocktail with a dry finish. As the name suggests, also works well with Zubrówka bison vodka in place of gin.

BLACK BISON MARTINI #2

●●●●○

Glass: Martini
Garnish: Apple wedge
Method: SHAKE all ingredients with ice and fine strain into chilled glass.

1¹/₂	shot(s)	Plymouth gin
¹/₂	shot(s)	Apple schnapps liqueur
2	shot(s)	Pressed apple juice
¹/₄	shot(s)	Dry vermouth

Origin: Adapted from a drink discovered in 2001 at Oxo Tower Bar, London, England.
Comment: A dry, fragrant cocktail, which, as the name suggests, also works well with Zubrówka bison vodka in place of gin.

BLACK FOREST GATEAU MARTINI

●●●●○

Glass: Martini
Garnish: Dust with cocoa powder
Method: SHAKE first four ingredients with ice and strain into chilled glass. FLOAT cream on drink.

2	shot(s)	Ketel One vodka
³/₄	shot(s)	Chambord black raspberry liqueur
³/₄	shot(s)	Giffard crème de fraise de bois
¹/₄	shot(s)	Giffard Cassis Noir de Bourgogne
1	shot(s)	Double (heavy) cream

Origin: Created in 2002 at Hush, London, England.
Comment: Dessert by name and dessert by nature. Wonderfully moreish, naughty but very nice.

BLACK CHERRY MARTINI NEW ⌐

●●●●○

Glass: Martini
Garnish: Fresh or maraschino cherry
Method: SHAKE all ingredients with ice and fine strain into chilled glass.

2¹/₂	shot(s)	Ketel One vodka
1	shot(s)	Chambord liqueur

Comment: Subtle berry fruit tames vodka's sting.

BLACK IRISH

●●●○○

Glass: Hurricane
Garnish: Dust with cocoa powder
Method: BLEND ingredients with 12oz scoop of crushed ice. Pour into glass and serve with straws.

1	shot(s)	Ketel One vodka
1	shot(s)	Baileys Irish cream liqueur
1	shot(s)	Kahlúa coffee liqueur
2	scoops	Vanilla ice cream

AKA: Frozen Black Irish
Comment: Like a very sweet, alcoholic, frozen caffè latte.

BLACK DREAM

●●●○○

Glass: Shot
Method: Refrigerate ingredients then LAYER in chilled glass by carefully pouring in the following order.

¹/₂	shot(s)	Opal Nera black sambuca
¹/₂	shot(s)	Baileys Irish cream liqueur

Comment: Slippery Nipple with black sambuca.

BLACK JACK SHOT

●●●○○

Glass: Shot
Method: Refrigerate ingredients then LAYER in chilled glass by carefully pouring in the following order.

³/₄	shot(s)	Opal Nera black sambuca
³/₄	shot(s)	Jack Daniel's Tennessee whiskey

Comment: Whiskey sweetened with sambuca.

BLACK FEATHER NEW ⌐

●●●●○

Glass: Martini
Garnish: Lemon zest twist
Method: STIR all ingredients with ice and strain into chilled glass.

2	shot(s)	Rémy Martin cognac
1	shot(s)	Dry vermouth
¹/₂	shot(s)	Cointreau triple sec
1	dash	Angostura aromatic bitters

Origin: Adapted from a drink created in 2000 by Robert Hess and published on drinkboy.com.
Comment: Rounded cognac notes with a hint of orange. For dry, adult palates.

BLACK JACK COCKTAIL NEW

●●●●○

Glass: Martini
Garnish: Lemon peel twist
Method: STIR all ingredients with ice and strain into chilled glass.

1¹/₂	shot(s)	Plymouth gin
¹/₂	shot(s)	Kirschwasser eau de vie
¹/₂	shot(s)	Giffard Cassis Noir de Bourgogne
³/₄	shot(s)	Chilled mineral water (reduce if wet ice)

Origin: The name Black Jack traditionally refers to a water bottle made from air dried leather. When the leather was dried it tended to turn black.
Comment: More burgundy than black but dark fruits of the forest dominate this medium dry cocktail.

A
B
C
D
E
F
G
H
I
J
K
L
M
N
O
P
Q
R
S
T
U
V
W
X
Y
Z

BLACK JAPAN NEW

● ● ◐ ○ ○

Glass: Collins
Method: POUR melon liqueur into chilled glass then float Guinness on top.

1½ shot(s)	Midori green melon liqueur
Float & Top	Guinness Original stout

Origin: Black Japan' is the name of a protective lacquer applied to metal.
Comment: This student-style drink will appeal to those with youthful exuberance and a sweet tooth.

BLACK 'N' BLUE CAIPIROVSKA

● ● ● ● ○

Glass: Old-fashioned
Method: MUDDLE berries in base of glass. Add other ingredients. Fill glass with crushed ice, CHURN (stir) with bar spoon and serve with straws.

6	fresh	Blackberries
10	fresh	Blueberries
2	shot(s)	Ketel One vodka
½	shot(s)	Freshly squeezed lime juice
¾	shot(s)	Sugar syrup (2 sugar to 1 water)

Comment: A great fruity twist on the regular Caipirovska.

BLACK MAGIC UPDATED

● ● ● ● ○

Glass: Flute
Garnish: Black grape on rim
Method: MUDDLE grapes in base of shaker. Add liqueur, SHAKE with ice and fine strain into chilled glass. TOP with champagne.

12	fresh	Red grapes
½	shot(s)	Grand Marnier liqueur
Top up with		Brut champagne

Comment: More peachy in colour than black but balanced and tasty. Not sweet.

BLACK NUTS

● ● ◐ ○ ○

Glass: Shot
Method: LAYER in chilled glass by carefully pouring ingredients in the following order.

¾	shot(s)	Opal Nera black sambuca
¾	shot(s)	Hazelnut (crème de noisette) liqueur

Comment: It's something of a challenge to get the Hazelnut liqueur to float on the black sambuca. If you store the Opal Nera in a freezer and the hazelnut liqueur at room temperature, this helps.

BLACK MARTINI

● ● ● ● ●

Glass: Martini
Garnish: Float grated white chocolate
Method: SHAKE all ingredients with ice and fine strain into chilled glass.

1½	shot(s)	Light white rum
1½	shot(s)	Giffard brown crème de cacao
1½	shot(s)	Espresso coffee (cold)

Origin: Created in March 2004 by yours truly.
Comment: This flavoursome mix of coffee and chocolate is further enhanced if vanilla-infused rum is used.

BLACK RUSSIAN ⚷

● ● ● ○ ○

Glass: Old-fashioned
Garnish: Lemon slice & cherry (sail)
Method: STIR all ingredients with ice and strain into ice-filled glass.

2	shot(s)	Ketel One vodka
½	shot(s)	Kahlúa coffee liqueur

Variants: 1/ Served straight-up in a Martini glass. 2/ Topped with cola and served over ice in a Collins glass. 3/ Made into a White Russian.
Comment: Most popularly served with cola. With or without, this drink is not that interesting.

BLACK MUSSEL

● ● ● ◐ ○

Glass: Flute
Garnish: Orange zest twist discarded
Method: POUR first two ingredients into glass and top up with champagne.

½	shot(s)	Blue curaçao liqueur
¼	shot(s)	Giffard Cassis Noir de Bourgogne
Top up with		Brut champagne

Comment: Blue curaçao adds a hint of orange to a Kir Royale.

BLACK VELVET

● ● ● ● ○

Glass: Flute
Garnish: Shamrock or mint leaf
Method: POUR ingredients into chilled glass.

2½ shot(s)	Guinness stout
Top up with	Brut champagne

Origin: Thought to have originated in 1861 at Brook's Club, London, after the death of Prince Albert. Some credit it to the Shelbourne Hotel, Dublin, Ireland.
Comment: A fitting tipple for Saint Patrick's Day in honour of Ireland's patron saint, who's credited with banishing snakes from the island back in 441 AD.

BLACK WIDOW

Glass: Martini
Garnish: Liquorice
Method: SHAKE all ingredients with ice and fine strain into chilled glass.

1	shot(s)	Opal Nera black sambuca
1	shot(s)	Giffard crème de fraise de bois
1	shot(s)	Malibu coconut rum liqueur
1/2	shot(s)	Double (heavy) cream
1/2	shot(s)	Milk

Comment: This sticky, fruity, liquorice cocktail tastes a little like an Allsort sweet.

BLACKTHORN COCKTAIL NEW

Glass: Martini
Garnish: Lemon zest twist
Method: STIR all ingredients with ice and strain into chilled glass.

1 1/2	shot(s)	Plymouth gin
3/4	shot(s)	Dubonnet Red
3/4	shot(s)	Kirschwasser eau de vie

Comment: This drink benefits from a long, chilling and diluting stir. The result is Martini-style, fruity but dry.

BLACKTHORN ENGLISH

Glass: Martini
Garnish: Flamed orange zest twist
Method: SHAKE all ingredients with ice and fine strain into chilled glass.

1 1/2	shot(s)	Plymouth sloe gin liqueur
3/4	shot(s)	Plymouth gin
3/4	shot(s)	Sweet vermouth
3	dashes	Fee Brothers orange bitters
1/2	shot(s)	Chilled mineral water (omit if wet ice)

Origin: A classic cocktail whose origins are unknown.
Comment: A dry, subtle rust-coloured Martini.

BLACKTHORN IRISH

Glass: Martini
Garnish: Flamed lemon zest twist
Method: SHAKE all ingredients with ice and fine strain into chilled glass.

1 1/2	shot(s)	Irish whiskey
1	shot(s)	Dry vermouth
1/4	shot(s)	Pernod anis
4	dashes	Angostura aromatic bitters
1/2	shot(s)	Chilled mineral water (omit if wet ice)

Origin: A classic cocktail whose origins are unknown.
Comment: A dry and aromatic Martini with hints of anis. Some may prefer to add a dash of sugar syrup.

BLADE RUNNER NEW

Glass: Collins
Garnish: Pineapple wedge & cherry
Method: SHAKE all ingredients with ice and strain into ice-filled glass.

2	shot(s)	Light white rum
1/2	shot(s)	Myers's dark rum
2 1/2	shot(s)	Pressed pineapple juice
1/4	shot(s)	Sugar syrup (2 sugar to 1 water)
2	shot(s)	Angostura aromatic bitters
1/2	shot(s)	Freshly squeezed lime juice

Origin: Discovered in 2005 at Zoulou Bar, Berlin, Germany.
Comment: Tangy and fruity but not too sweet.

BLIMEY UPDATED

Glass: Old-fashioned
Garnish: Lime wedge
Method: MUDDLE blackberries in base of shaker. Add other ingredients, SHAKE with ice and fine strain into glass filled with crushed ice. Serve with straws.

7	fresh	Blackberries
2	shot(s)	Ketel One vodka
3/4	shot(s)	Giffard Cassis Noir de Bourgogne
1	shot(s)	Freshly squeezed lime juice
1/8	shot(s)	Sugar syrup (2 sugar to 1 water)

Origin: Created in 2002 by yours truly.
Comment: This blackberry and lime blend is both fruity and aptly named.

BLING! BLING!

Glass: Shot
Method: MUDDLE raspberries in base of shaker. Add vodka, lime and sugar, SHAKE with ice and fine strain into glass. TOP with champagne.

8	fresh	Raspberries
1/2	shot(s)	Ketel One vodka
1/2	shot(s)	Freshly squeezed lime juice
1/2	shot(s)	Sugar syrup (2 sugar to 1 water)
Top up with		Brut champagne

Origin: Created in 2001 by Phillip Jeffrey at the GE Club, London, England.
Comment: An ostentatious little number.

BLINKER UPDATED

Glass: Martini
Garnish: Lemon twist
Method: SHAKE all ingredients with ice and fine strain into chilled glass.

2	shot(s)	Bourbon whiskey
1	shot(s)	Freshly squeezed pink grapefruit juice
1/4	shot(s)	Pomegranate (grenadine) syrup

Origin: A 1930s classic revisited.
Comment: Back in the 1930s David Embury wrote of this drink, "One of a few cocktails using grapefruit juice. Not particularly good but not too bad." How times have changed!

BLOODY MARY

The Bloody Mary was originally created in 1920 by Fernand Petiot, at that time a young bartender at Harry's New York Bar in Paris. Contrary to popular belief the drink was not named after Queen Mary the First, whose nickname was 'Bloody Mary' for her persecution of Protestants in the 17th century, or even after the silent-movie actress Mary Pickford. The drink was actually named by one of Petiot's customers, entertainer Roy Barton, as a homage to the Bucket of Blood nightclub in Chicago, where he once performed. The first version contained just vodka and tomato juice.

Petiot left Paris for the US in 1933 and was hired as a bartender at the King Cole Bar in Manhattan's Hotel Saint Regis. Here he mixed his drink for Serge Obolansky, the hotel's President, who pronounced it "too flat". Petiot mixed him another with added salt, pepper, lemon juice and Worcestershire sauce and so gave birth to this classic drink.

Vincent Astor, who owned the hotel, found the name Bloody Mary a little crude for his clientele and so the drink was officially renamed the Red Snapper – although customers continued to order Bloody Marys. (Nowadays a Red Snapper is a Bloody Mary made with gin.)

Petiot's rich and famous clientele helped spread the popularity of the Bloody Mary which quickly gained a reputation as a restorative to be consumed the morning after.

The celery stick garnish dates back to 1960 when a bartender at the Ambassador Hotel in Chicago noticed a lady stirring her drink with a celery stick.

Bloody Mary recipes are as personal as Martinis. Purists will only use Tabasco, Worcestershire sauce, salt and lemon to spice up tomato and vodka but everything from oysters to V8 can be added.

The Bloody Mary's many variations include
Asian Mary (with wasabi, ginger & soy sauce)
Bloody Bull (with beef consommé)
Bloody Caesar (with clam juice)
Bloody Joseph (with Scotch whisky)
Bloody Maria (with tequila)
Bloody Maru (with sake)
Bloody Mary (original)
Bloody Mary (modern)
Bloody Shame (mocktail)
Bullshot (with beef bouillon)
Cubanita (with rum)
Peppered Mary (with pepper vodka)
Red Snapper (with gin)

●●●●○

BLOOD & SAND #1 (CLASSIC FORMULA) UPDATED

Glass: Martini
Garnish: Orange zest twist
Method: SHAKE all ingredients with ice and fine strain into chilled glass.

³/₄	shot(s)	Scotch whisky
³/₄	shot(s)	Cherry brandy liqueur
³/₄	shot(s)	Sweet vermouth
³/₄	shot(s)	Freshly squeezed orange juice

Origin: Created for the premiere of the 1922 Rudolph Valentino movie, Blood and Sand. This equal parts formula comes from the 1930 edition of 'The Savoy Cocktail Book'.
Comment: One of the best classic Scotch cocktails but a little sweet.

●●●●◖

BLOOD & SAND #2 (DIFFORD'S FORMULA) NEW

Glass: Martini
Garnish: Orange zest twist
Method: SHAKE all ingredients with ice and fine strain into chilled glass.

1¹/₂	shot(s)	Scotch whisky
³/₄	shot(s)	Cherry brandy liqueur
³/₄	shot(s)	Sweet vermouth
³/₄	shot(s)	Freshly squeezed orange juice

Origin: Formula by yours truly in 2006.
Comment: A dry, more spirited Blood & Sand for those who like Scotch.

●●●○○

BLOODHOUND

Glass: Collins
Garnish: Lime wedge
Method: SHAKE all ingredients with ice and strain into ice-filled glass.

2	shot(s)	Campari
1	shot(s)	Ketel One vodka
3¹/₂	shot(s)	Freshly squeezed grapefruit juice

Comment: A dry, tart, refreshing long drink.

●●●●○

BLOOD ORANGE UPDATED

Glass: Collins
Garnish: Raspberries
Method: MUDDLE raspberries in base of shaker. Add other ingredients, SHAKE with ice and fine strain into ice-filled glass.

7	fresh	Raspberries
2	shot(s)	Orange zest infused Ketel One vodka
¹/₂	shot(s)	Raspberry (framboise) liqueur
1¹/₂	shot(s)	Freshly squeezed orange juice
1¹/₄	shot(s)	Cranberry juice
¹/₂	shot(s)	Freshly squeezed lime juice

Origin: Adapted from a drink created in 2005 by Mark Pratt at Maze, London, England.
Comment: Long, refreshing and very fruity. Appropriately named given its colour and taste.

BLOODY CAESAR NEW

●●●●○

Glass: Collins
Garnish: Pickled bean
Method: SHAKE all ingredients with ice and strain into ice-filled glass.

2	shot(s)	Ketel One vodka
4	shot(s)	Mott's Clamato juice
1/2	shot(s)	Freshly squeezed lime juice
7	drops	Tabasco pepper sauce
3	dashes	Lea & Perrins Worcestershire sauce
2	pinch	Celery salt
2	pinch	Black pepper

Origin: Created by Walter Chell in 1969 to celebrate the opening of Marco's Italian restaurant at the Calgary Inn, Canada. Walter was inspired by the flavours of Spaghetti Vongole (spaghetti with clams) and named the drink after the Roman emperor.
Comment: A peculiarly Canadian fishy twist on the classic Bloody Mary.

BLOODY JOSEPH

●●●●○○

Glass: Collins
Garnish: Stick of celery
Method: SHAKE all ingredients with ice and strain into ice-filled glass.

2	shot(s)	Scotch whisky
4	shot(s)	Pressed tomato juice
1/2	shot(s)	Freshly squeezed lemon juice
8	drops	Tabasco pepper sauce
4	dashes	Lea & Perrins Worcestershire sauce
1/2	spoon	Horseradish sauce
1/2	shot(s)	Tawny port
2	pinch	Celery salt
2	pinch	Black pepper

Comment: A Bloody Mary with whisky.

BLOODY MARIA

●●●●○

Glass: Collins
Garnish: Salt & pepper rim plus celery stick
Method: SHAKE all ingredients with ice and strain into ice-filled glass.

2	shot(s)	Partida tequila
4	shot(s)	Pressed tomato juice
1/2	shot(s)	Freshly squeezed lemon juice
8	drops	Tabasco pepper sauce
4	dashes	Lea & Perrins Worcestershire sauce
1/2	spoon	Horseradish sauce
1/2	shot(s)	Tawny port
2	pinch	Celery salt
2	pinch	Black pepper

Comment: Tequila adds a very interesting kick to the classic Bloody Mary.

BLOODY MARU

●●●●○○

Glass: Collins
Garnish: Lemongrass stick
Method: SHAKE all ingredients with ice and strain into ice-filled glass.

3	shot(s)	Sake
3	shot(s)	Pressed tomato juice
1/2	shot(s)	Freshly squeezed lemon juice
8	drops	Tabasco pepper sauce
4	dashes	Lea & Perrins Worcestershire sauce
2	pinch	Celery salt
2	pinch	Black pepper

Origin: A Bloody Mary based on sake.

BLOODY MARY (1930S RECIPE)

●●○○○

Glass: Old-fashioned
Garnish: Salt & pepper rim
Method: SHAKE all ingredients with ice and strain into empty glass.

2	shot(s)	100-proof (50% alc./vol.) vodka
2	shot(s)	Thick pressed tomato juice
1/4	shot(s)	Freshly squeezed lemon juice
5	dashes	Lea & Perrins Worcestershire sauce
4	pinch	Salt
2	pinch	Black pepper
2	pinch	Cayenne pepper

Variant: Red Snapper
Origin: A 1933 version of the classic created in 1920 by Fernand Petiot at Harry's New York Bar, Paris, France.
Comment: Fiery stuff. The modern version is more user friendly.

BLOODY MARY (MODERN RECIPE)

●●●●○

Glass: Collins
Garnish: Salt & pepper rim plus celery stick
Method: SHAKE all ingredients with ice and strain into ice-filled glass.

2	shot(s)	Ketel One vodka
4	shot(s)	Pressed tomato juice
1/2	shot(s)	Freshly squeezed lemon juice
8	drops	Tabasco pepper sauce
4	dashes	Lea & Perrins Worcestershire sauce
1/2	spoon	Horseradish sauce
1/2	shot(s)	Tawny port
2	pinch	Celery salt
2	pinch	Black pepper

Comment: A fiery Mary with the heat fuelled by horseradish. If you like to fight a hangover with spice, this is for you.

HOW TO MAKE SUGAR SYRUP

To make your own sugar syrup, gradually pour **TWO** cups of granulated sugar into a saucepan containing **ONE** cup of hot water. Stir as you pour and carry on stirring and simmering until the sugar is dissolved. Do not let the water even come close to boiling and only simmer for as long as it takes to dissolve the sugar. Allow syrup to cool and pour into an empty bottle. Ideally, you should finely strain your syrup into the bottle to remove any undissolved crystals which could otherwise encourage crystallisation. If kept in a refrigerator this mixture will last for a couple of months.

A B C D E F G H I J K L M N O P Q R S T U V W X Y Z

BLOODY SHAME (MOCKTAIL)

●●●○○

Glass: Collins
Garnish: Celery stick
Method: SHAKE all ingredients with ice and strain into ice-filled glass.

5	shot(s)	Pressed tomato juice
1/2	shot(s)	Freshly squeezed lemon juice
8	drops	Tabasco pepper sauce
4	dashes	Lea & Perrins Worcestershire sauce
1/2	spoon	Horseradish sauce
2	pinch	Celery salt
2	pinch	Black pepper

AKA: Virgin Mary
Comment: Somehow missing something.

BLOOMSBURY MARTINI NEW

●●●●○

Glass: Martini
Garnish: Lemon zest twist
Method: STIR all ingredients with ice and strain into chilled glass.

2	shot(s)	Plymouth gin
1/2	shot(s)	Cuarenta Y Tres (Licor 43) liqueur
1/2	shot(s)	Dry vermouth
2	dashes	Peychaud's aromatic bitters

Origin: Adapted from a drink created in 2003 by Robert Hess and published on drinkboy.com.
Comment: This pinky/rusty drink benefits from a good long stir but the result is an aromatic, medium dry, spicy vanilla Martini.

BLOW JOB

●●●●○

Glass: Shot
Garnish: Drop cherry into glass then float cream
Method: SHAKE all ingredients with ice and fine strain into chilled glass.

1/2	shot(s)	Grand Marnier
1/2	shot(s)	Giffard crème de banane du Brésil
1/2	shot(s)	Kahlúa coffee liqueur

Comment: A juvenile but pleasant tasting sweet shot.

BLUE ANGEL

●●○○○

Glass: Martini
Garnish: Orange zest twist
Method: SHAKE all ingredients with ice and fine strain into chilled glass.

3/4	shot(s)	Bols Blue curaçao liqueur
3/4	shot(s)	Parfait Amour liqueur
3/4	shot(s)	Rémy Martin cognac
3/4	shot(s)	Freshly squeezed lemon juice
3/4	shot(s)	Double (heavy) cream

Comment: This baby blue cocktail is sweet, creamy and floral.

BLUE BIRD

●●●○○

Glass: Martini
Garnish: Orange zest twist
Method: SHAKE all ingredients with ice and fine strain into chilled glass.

2	shot(s)	Plymouth gin
1	shot(s)	Bols Blue curaçao liqueur
3/4	shot(s)	Freshly squeezed lemon juice
1/4	shot(s)	Almond (orgeat) syrup

Origin: Thought to have been created in the late 1950s in Montmartre, Paris, France.
Comment: A blue rinsed, orange washed, gin based 'tini' that benefits from being sweetened with almond rather than plain syrup.

BLUE BLAZER

●●●○○

Glass: Two old-fashioned glasses
Method: STIR honey with boiling water until honey dissolves. Add Scotch and peel. FLAME the mixture and stir with a long handled bar spoon. If still alight, extinguish flame and strain into second glass.

2	spoons	Runny honey
3/4	shot(s)	Boiling water
3	shot(s)	Scotch whisky
6	twists	Lemon peel

Variant: This drink was originally mixed by pouring the ingredients from one metal mug to another while ignited.
Origin: Created by 'Professor' Jerry Thomas, inventor of many famous cocktails in the 19th century. Thomas toured the world like a travelling showman, displaying this and other drinks.
Comment: Only attempt to make this the original way if you're very experienced or very stupid.

BLUE CHAMPAGNE

●●●○○

Glass: Flute
Method: SHAKE first four ingredients with ice and strain into glass. TOP with champagne.

3/4	shot(s)	Ketel One vodka
1/8	shot(s)	Cointreau triple sec
1/4	shot(s)	Blue curaçao liqueur
1/4	shot(s)	Freshly squeezed lemon juice
Top up with		Brut champagne

Variant: With gin in place of vodka.
Comment: Fortified, citrussy champagne.

DRINKS ARE GRADED AS FOLLOWS:

● DISGUSTING ●○ PRETTY AWFUL ●● BEST AVOIDED
●●○ DISAPPOINTING ●●● ACCEPTABLE ●●●○ GOOD
●●●● RECOMMENDED ●●●●○ HIGHLY RECOMMENDED
●●●●● OUTSTANDING / EXCEPTIONAL

BLUE COSMO

● ● ● ● ○ ○

Glass: Martini
Garnish: Orange zest twist
Method: SHAKE all ingredients with ice and fine strain into chilled glass.

2	shot(s)	Ketel One Citroen vodka
³⁄₄	shot(s)	Bols Blue curaçao liqueur
1¹⁄₂	shot(s)	White cranberry & grape drink
¹⁄₄	shot(s)	Freshly squeezed lime juice

Variant: Purple Cosmo
Comment: This blue rinsed drink may have sales appeal but sadly is not quite as good as a traditional red Cosmo.

BLUE FIN

● ● ● ● ○ ○

Glass: Martini
Garnish: Gummy fish
Method: SHAKE all ingredients with ice and fine strain into chilled glass.

2	shot(s)	Ketel One Citroen vodka
1	shot(s)	Hpnotiq tropical liqueur
1¹⁄₂	shot(s)	White cranberry & grape juice

Origin: Created in 2003 at The Blue Fin, W Hotel, Times Square, New York, USA.
Comment: Citrussy, reminiscent of a blue Cosmo.

BLUE HAWAIIAN

● ● ● ○ ○

Glass: Hurricane
Garnish: Pineapple wedge & cherry on rim
Method: BLEND ingredients with 12oz scoop of crushed ice. Pour into glass and serve with straws.

2	shot(s)	Light white rum
1	shot(s)	Bols Blue curaçao liqueur
1¹⁄₂	shot(s)	Coco López cream of coconut
3	shot(s)	Pressed pineapple juice
¹⁄₄	shot(s)	Freshly squeezed lemon juice

Origin: Probably created by Don the Beachcomber in Los Angeles, USA.
Comment: A blue rinsed Piña Colada.

BLUE HEAVEN

● ● ● ○ ○ ○

Glass: Collins
Garnish: Pineapple wedge & cherry sail
Method: SHAKE all ingredients with ice and strain into ice-filled glass.

2	shot(s)	Light white rum
1	shot(s)	Bols Blue curaçao liqueur
¹⁄₂	shot(s)	Luxardo Amaretto di Saschira
¹⁄₂	shot(s)	Rose's lime cordial
4	shot(s)	Pressed pineapple juice

Comment: Actually more aqua than blue, this sweet concoction includes orange, almond, lime cordial and pineapple.

BLUE KAMIKAZE

● ● ● ● ○ ○

Glass: Shot
Method: SHAKE all ingredients with ice and fine strain into chilled glass.

¹⁄₂	shot(s)	Ketel One vodka
¹⁄₂	shot(s)	Bols Blue curaçao liqueur
¹⁄₂	shot(s)	Freshly squeezed lime juice

Comment: Tangy orange - but it's blue.

BLUE LADY

● ● ● ○ ○

Glass: Martini
Garnish: Orange zest twist
Method: SHAKE all ingredients with ice and fine strain into chilled glass.

1	shot(s)	Plymouth gin
2	shot(s)	Bols Blue curaçao liqueur
1	shot(s)	Freshly squeezed lemon juice
¹⁄₂	fresh	Egg white

Comment: Quite sweet with an orange, citrus finish.

BLUE LAGOON

● ● ● ○ ○

Glass: Collins
Garnish: Orange slice
Method: BLEND ingredients with 18oz scoop of crushed ice. Pour into glass and serve with straws.

1	shot(s)	Plymouth gin
1	shot(s)	Ketel One vodka
1	shot(s)	Bols Blue curaçao liqueur
1	shot(s)	Freshly squeezed lime juice
1	shot(s)	Sugar syrup (2 sugar to 1 water)

Variant: Vodka, blue curaçao and lemonade on the rocks.
Origin: Created in 1972 by Andy MacElhone (son of Harry) at Harry's New York Bar, Paris, France.
Comment: Better than the film – not hard!

BLUE MARGARITA UPDATED

● ● ● ● ○ ○

Glass: Coupette
Garnish: Lime slice on rim
Method: BLEND all ingredients with one 12oz scoop crushed ice. Serve with straws.

2	shot(s)	Partida tequila
1	shot(s)	Bols blue curaçao liqueur
1	shot(s)	Freshly squeezed lime juice
¹⁄₂	shot(s)	Sugar syrup

Comment: As the name suggests, a Margarita, only blue. This 'Disco Drink' looks scary but tastes pretty good.

A
B
C
D
E
F
G
H
I
J
K
L
M
N
O
P
Q
R
S
T
U
V
W
X
Y
Z

B

BLUE MONDAY UPDATED

●●●◐○

Glass: Old-fashioned
Garnish: Orange zest twist
Method: SHAKE all ingredients with ice and fine strain into ice filled glass.

1½	shot(s)	Ketel One Citroen vodka
¾	shot(s)	Bols blue curaçao liqueur
½	shot(s)	Cointreau triple sec
½	shot(s)	Dry vermouth
2	dashes	Fee Brothers orange bitters

Origin: Created in 2003 by yours truly.
Comment: Disco blue but medium dry with a bittersweet orange taste.

BLUE MOON UPDATED

●●●●○

Glass: Martini
Garnish: Orange zest twist
Method: SHAKE all ingredients with ice and fine strain into chilled glass.

2	shot(s)	Plymouth gin
¾	shot(s)	Benoit Serres violet liqueur (or Parfait Amour)
½	shot(s)	Freshly squeezed lemon juice
½	fresh	Egg white

AKA: Blue Devil
Variant: Aviation
Origin: Adapted from David A. Embury's 1948 'The Fine Art of Mixing Drinks'. This long lost drink was originally made with the now extinct Crème Yvette liqueur. 'Blue Moon' is an astronomical term for the second of two full moons to occur in the same calendar month.
Comment: More dirty grey than blue but a must for Aviation lovers, whatever the colour.

BLUE PASSION

●●●●○

Glass: Old-fashioned
Garnish: Orange zest twist
Method: SHAKE all ingredients with ice and strain into glass filled with crushed ice.

1	shot(s)	Light white rum
1	shot(s)	Bols Blue curaçao liqueur
1¾	shot(s)	Freshly squeezed lime juice
1	shot(s)	Sugar syrup (2 sugar to 1 water)

Comment: This sweet and sour tangy drink is surprisingly good.

FOR MORE INFORMATION SEE OUR

INGREDIENTS APPENDIX ON PAGE 272

BLUE RIBAND

●●●○○

Glass: Martini
Garnish: Cherry dropped into glass
Method: STIR all ingredients with ice and strain into chilled glass.

2	shot(s)	Plymouth gin
1	shot(s)	Cointreau triple sec
1	shot(s)	Bols Blue curaçao liqueur

Origin: The 'Blue Riband' was awarded to the liner that made the fastest Atlantic crossing. This cocktail is thought to have been created on one of these ships.
Comment: A sweetened, blue rinsed, orange and gin Martini.

BLUE STAR

●●●○○

Glass: Martini
Garnish: Orange zest twist
Method: SHAKE all ingredients with ice and fine strain into chilled glass.

1½	shot(s)	Plymouth gin
¾	shot(s)	Dry vermouth
¾	shot(s)	Freshly squeezed orange juice
¾	shot(s)	Bols Blue curaçao liqueur

Comment: Gin, orange and a kick.

BLUE VELVET MARGARITA

●●●●○

Glass: Coupette
Garnish: Lime wedge on rim
Method: SHAKE all ingredients with ice and fine strain into chilled glass.

2	shot(s)	Partida tequila
½	shot(s)	Cointreau triple sec
½	shot(s)	Bols Blue curaçao liqueur
1	shot(s)	Freshly squeezed lime juice

Origin: Discovered in 2005 at Velvet Margarita Cantina, Los Angeles, USA.
Comment: May look lurid but is a surprisingly tasty Margarita.

BLUE WAVE

●●●○○

Glass: Hurricane
Garnish: Pineapple wedge on rim
Method: SHAKE ingredients with ice and strain into ice-filled glass.

1	shot(s)	Plymouth gin
1	shot(s)	Light white rum
½	shot(s)	Bols Blue curaçao liqueur
3	shot(s)	Pressed pineapple juice
1¾	shot(s)	Freshly squeezed lime juice
¾	shot(s)	Sugar syrup (2 sugar to 1 water)

Comment: A fruity holiday drink.

●●●●◐○

BLUEBERRY DAIQUIRI UPDATED

Glass: Martini
Garnish: Blueberries on stick
Method: MUDDLE blueberries in base of shaker. Add other ingredients, SHAKE with ice and fine strain into chilled glass.

20	fresh	Blueberries
2	shot(s)	Havana Club light rum
1/2	shot(s)	Giffard Blueberry liqueur (crème de myrtille)
1/2	shot(s)	Freshly squeezed lime juice

Origin: Created in December 2002 by yours truly.
Comment: Blueberry juice and liqueur lengthens and sweetens an otherwise classic Daiquiri.

●●●●◐○

BLUEBERRY MARTINI #1 UPDATED

Glass: Martini
Garnish: Lemon zest twist (discarded) & blueberries on stick
Method: MUDDLE blueberries in base of shaker. Add other ingredients, SHAKE with ice and fine strain into chilled glass.

20	fresh	Blueberries
2	shot(s)	Ketel One vodka
1/4	shot(s)	Giffard Blueberry liqueur (crème de myrtilles)
1/8	shot(s)	Sugar syrup (2 sugar to 1 water)

Comment: Rich blueberry fruit fortified with grainy vodka. Not too sweet.

●●●●●○

BLUEBERRY MARTINI #2

Glass: Martini
Garnish: Blueberries on stick.
Method: MUDDLE blueberries in base of shaker. Add other ingredients, SHAKE with ice and fine strain into chilled glass.

30	fresh	Blueberries
2	shot(s)	Ketel One vodka
1/4	shot(s)	Sugar syrup (2 sugar to 1 water)
3/4	shot(s)	Sauvignon Blanc wine

Comment: Rich blueberry fruit fortified with vodka – much more interesting with the additional splash of wine.

●●●●●○

BLUEBERRY TEA

Glass: Toddy
Garnish: Lemon slice & cinnamon stick
Method: POUR first two ingredients into glass, top up with tea and stir.

3/4	shot(s)	Luxardo Amaretto di Saschira
3/4	shot(s)	Grand Marnier
	Top up with	Black breakfast tea (hot)

Comment: This does indeed taste just as described on the tin.

●●●●◐○

BLUSH MARTINI

Glass: Martini
Garnish: Dust with cinnamon powder
Method: SHAKE all ingredients with ice and fine strain into chilled glass.

1	shot(s)	Ketel One vodka
3/4	shot(s)	Vanilla schnapps liqueur
1/2	shot(s)	Luxardo Amaretto di Saschira
3/4	shot(s)	Milk
3/4	shot(s)	Double (heavy) cream
1/4	shot(s)	Cranberry juice

Origin: Created by Colin William Crowden, Mashed Bar, Leicester, England.
Comment: Drier than it looks, but still one to follow the dessert trolley.

●●●●●○

BLUSHIN' RUSSIAN

Glass: Martini
Garnish: Float three coffee beans
Method: SHAKE all ingredients with ice and fine strain into chilled glass.

1	shot(s)	Ketel One vodka
1	shot(s)	Kahlúa coffee liqueur
1/2	shot(s)	Luxardo Amaretto di Saschira
3/4	shot(s)	Double (heavy) cream
3/4	shot(s)	Milk

Comment: White Russian with a hint of almond.

●●●●●○

BOBBY BURNS

Glass: Martini
Garnish: Maraschino cherry in drink
Method: SHAKE all ingredients with ice and fine strain into chilled glass.

1 1/2	shot(s)	Scotch whisky
1 1/2	shot(s)	Sweet vermouth
1/4	shot(s)	Bénédictine D.O.M. liqueur

Comment: Strictly speaking this drink should be stirred, but I prefer mine shaken so that's how it appears here.

●●●●●●

BOHEMIAN ICED TEA

Glass: Old-fashioned
Garnish: Lemon zest twist
Method: STIR all ingredients with ice and strain into ice-filled glass.

1 1/2	shot(s)	Becherovka liqueur
1/2	shot(s)	Ketel One Citroen vodka
1/2	shot(s)	Krupnik honey liqueur
1/2	shot(s)	Peach schnapps liqueur
2 1/2	shot(s)	Chilled Earl Grey lemon tea

Origin: Created by Alex Kammerling at Detroit, London, England. Originally stirred in a tea pot and served in tea cups.
Comment: A fruity and refreshing drink with surprising flavours.

A
B
C
D
E
F
G
H
I
J
K
L
M
N
O
P
Q
R
S
T
U
V
W
X
Y
Z

B

BOILERMAKER UPDATED

●●○○○

Glass: Boston & shot
Method: POUR whiskey to brim of shot glass and then manoeuvre shot glass so it is held tight up against the inside base of an upturned Boston glass. Then quickly flip the Boston glass over so that the bourbon is trapped in the now upside-down shot glass. Now pour beer into Boston glass over the whiskey filled shot glass.

| 1 | shot(s) | Bourbon Whiskey |
| 1 | pint | Beer (well chilled) |

Origin: Unknown but in his book The Joy of Mixology Gary Regan credits steelworkers in western Pennsylvania.
Comment: When you get to the end of the beer the shot glass lifts and the whiskey is released as a chaser.

BOLERO

●●●○○

Glass: Martini
Garnish: Float apple slice
Method: STIR all ingredients with ice and strain into chilled glass.

1½	shot(s)	Light white rum
¾	shot(s)	Boulard Grand Solage Calvados
¼	shot(s)	Sweet vermouth

Origin: A classic of unknown origins.
Comment: A dry, challenging drink for modern palates. Be sure to stir well as dilution is key.

BOLERO SOUR UPDATED

●●●●●

Glass: Old-fashioned
Garnish: Orange & lime zest twists (discarded)
Method: SHAKE all ingredients with ice and strain into ice-filled glass.

1	shot(s)	Aged rum
1	shot(s)	Rémy Martin cognac
½	shot(s)	Freshly squeezed orange juice
1	shot(s)	Freshly squeezed lime juice
½	shot(s)	Sugar syrup (2 sugar to 1 water)
½	fresh	Egg white

Origin: Adapted from David A. Embury's 1948 'The Fine Art of Mixing Drinks'.
Comment: A beautifully balanced, flavoursome medley of sweet and sour.

BOLSHOI PUNCH

●●●●○

Glass: Old-fashioned
Method: SHAKE all ingredients with ice and strain into glass filled with crushed ice.

1½	shot(s)	Wray & Nephew white overproof rum
1	shot(s)	Giffard Cassis Noir de Bourgogne
¾	shot(s)	Freshly squeezed lime juice
½	shot(s)	Sugar syrup (2 sugar to 1 water)

Comment: Innocuous-seeming pink classic – richly flavoured and easy to drink.

BOMBAY NO. 2 UPDATED

●●●●◐

Glass: Martini
Garnish: Orange zest twist
Method: SHAKE all ingredients with ice and fine strain into chilled glass.

1½	shot(s)	Rémy Martin cognac
¾	shot(s)	Dry vermouth
¾	shot(s)	Sweet vermouth
¼	shot(s)	Cointreau triple sec
⅛	shot(s)	La Fée Parisian (68%) absinthe

Origin: My 2006 adaptation of a recipe from Harry Craddock's 1930 'The Savoy Cocktail Book'.
Comment: A smooth, complex, Sazerac-style Martini.

BOMBER

●●●●○

Glass: Collins
Garnish: Lime squeeze
Method: SHAKE first three ingredients with ice and strain into ice-filled glass. **TOP** with ginger beer, stir and serve with straws.

1	shot(s)	Light white rum
1	shot(s)	Spiced rum
1	shot(s)	Freshly squeezed lime juice
Top up with		Ginger beer

Origin: Created in 1998 by the B. Bar crew at The Reading Festival, England.
Comment: Cross between a Moscow Mule and a Cuba Libre.

BON BON UPDATED

●●●○○

Glass: Martini
Garnish: Lemon zest twist (or a Bon Bon)
Method: SHAKE all ingredients with ice and fine strain into chilled glass.

1	shot(s)	Vanilla-infused Ketel One vodka
½	shot(s)	Butterscotch schnapps liqueur
¾	shot(s)	Luxardo limoncello liqueur
¾	shot(s)	Freshly squeezed lemon juice
¼	shot(s)	Sugar syrup (2 sugar to 1 water)
½	shot(s)	Chilled mineral water (omit if wet ice)

Origin: Adapted from a drink discovered in 2001 at Lab Bar, London, England.
Comment: Relive your youth and the taste of those big round sweets in this bitter-sweet, lemony cocktail.

FOR MORE INFORMATION SEE OUR
INGREDIENTS APPENDIX ON PAGE 272

BONNIE PRINCE CHARLES NEW

● ● ● ● ○

Glass: Martini
Garnish: Lime wedge on rim
Method: SHAKE all ingredients with ice and fine strain into chilled glass.

2¼	shot(s)	Rémy Martin cognac
¾	shot(s)	Drambuie liqueur
¾	shot(s)	Freshly squeezed lime juice

Origin: Recipe to proportions found in Victor Bergeron's 'Trader Vic's Bartender's Guide' (1972 revised edition).
Comment: Honeyed, spiced cognac with a touch of citrus. But is it fit for a Prince?

BOSOM CARESSER

● ● ● ● ○

Glass: Martini
Garnish: Orange peel twist (discarded)
Method: SHAKE all ingredients with ice and fine strain into chilled glass.

2	shot(s)	Rémy Martin cognac
½	shot(s)	Grand Marnier
½	shot(s)	Malmsey Madeira
¼	shot(s)	Pomegranate (grenadine) syrup
1	fresh	Egg yolk

Comment: No bosoms to hand? Then caress your throat.

BOOMERANG UPDATED

● ● ● ● ○

Glass: Martini
Garnish: Maraschino cherry
Method: SHAKE all ingredients with ice and fine strain into chilled glass.

1½	shot(s)	Bourbon Whiskey
¾	shot(s)	Dry vermouth
¾	shot(s)	Sweet vermouth
¼	shot(s)	Luxardo maraschino liqueur
½	shot(s)	Freshly squeezed lemon juice
½	shot(s)	Sugar syrup (2 sugar to 1 water)
2	dashes	Angostura aromatic bitters

Comment: A very Sweet Manhattan with lemon juice.

BOSSA NOVA #1 UPDATED

● ● ● ● ○

Glass: Collins
Garnish: Lime wheel
Method: SHAKE all ingredients with ice and strain into ice-filled glass.

2	shot(s)	Mount Gay Eclipse golden rum
¾	shot(s)	Galliano liqueur
¾	shot(s)	Giffard apricot brandy du Roussillon
2	shot(s)	Pressed apple juice
¾	shot(s)	Freshly squeezed lime juice

Origin: Named after the Brazilian dance which in turn comes from the Portuguese 'bossa', meaning 'tendency', and 'nova', meaning 'new'.
Comment: Apple with the added zing of rum, Galliano, apricot and lime juice.

BORA BORA BREW MOCKTAIL 🗝

● ● ● ○ ○

Glass: Collins
Garnish: Pineapple wedge
Method: SHAKE first two ingredients with ice and strain into ice-filled glass.

3	shot(s)	Pressed pineapple juice
⅛	shot(s)	Pomegranate (grenadine) syrup
Top up with		Ginger ale

Comment: Fruity and frothy ginger beer.

BOSSA NOVA #2 UPDATED

● ● ● ● ◐

Glass: Collins
Garnish: Pineapple wedge
Method: SHAKE all ingredients with ice and strain into ice-filled glass.

2	shot(s)	Mount Gay Eclipse golden rum
½	shot(s)	Galliano liqueur
½	shot(s)	Giffard apricot brandy du Roussillon
2	shot(s)	Pressed pineapple juice
½	shot(s)	Freshly squeezed lemon juice

Comment: Long and frothy with fruity rum and subtle anis notes. Not too sweet.

BORDERLINE

● ● ● ● ◐

Glass: Martini
Garnish: Orange twist
Method: SHAKE all ingredients with ice and fine strain into chilled glass.

2	shot(s)	Bourbon whiskey
½	shot(s)	Maple syrup
½	shot(s)	Freshly squeezed lemon juice
¾	shot(s)	Punt E Mes

Origin: Created in 2004 by James Mellor at Mint Leaf, London, England.
Comment: Bourbon sweetened with maple syrup, soured by lemon and made more complex by vermouth.

BOSTON 🗝

● ● ● ● ◐

Glass: Martini
Garnish: Apricot slice on rim
Method: SHAKE all ingredients with ice and fine strain into chilled glass.

1¾	shot(s)	Plymouth gin
1	shot(s)	Giffard apricot brandy du Roussillon
1	shot(s)	Freshly squeezed lemon juice
¼	shot(s)	Sugar syrup (2 sugar to 1 water)
⅛	shot(s)	Pomegranate (grenadine) syrup

Comment: Gin laced tangy fruit.

A
B
C
D
E
F
G
H
I
J
K
L
M
N
O
P
Q
R
S
T
U
V
W
X
Y
Z

BOSTON FLIP

●●●●○

Glass: Wine goblet
Garnish: Dust with freshly grated nutmeg
Method: SHAKE all ingredients with ice and fine strain into chilled glass.

2	shot(s)	Bourbon whiskey
2	shot(s)	Blandy's Alvada Madeira
1	fresh	Egg
¼	shot(s)	Sugar syrup (2 sugar to 1 water)

Comment: A good dusting of freshly grated nutmeg makes this old school drink.

BOSTON TEA PARTY

●●●○○

Glass: Collins
Garnish: Orange slice
Method: SHAKE first ten ingredients with ice and strain into ice-filled glass. TOP with cola and serve with straws.

½	shot(s)	Ketel One vodka
½	shot(s)	Scotch whisky
½	shot(s)	Dry vermouth
½	shot(s)	Cointreau triple sec
½	shot(s)	Pusser's navy rum
½	shot(s)	Plymouth gin
½	shot(s)	Partida tequila
½	shot(s)	Freshly squeezed orange juice
1	shot(s)	Freshly squeezed lime juice
½	shot(s)	Sugar syrup (2 sugar to 1 water)
Top up with		Cola

Origin: Named after the revolt by early US settlers against the imposition of tax by the British Crown, which became the War of Independence.
Comment: Just about every spirit from the speedrail plus a splash of orange, lime and coke.

BOULEVARD NEW ⚷

●●●●○

Glass: Martini
Garnish: Twist of orange (discarded) & two maraschino cherries
Method: STIR all ingredients with ice and strain into chilled glass.

2½	shot(s)	Bourbon whiskey
1	shot(s)	Dry vermouth
½	shot(s)	Grand Marnier liqueur
2	dashes	Fee Brothers orange bitters

Origin: A classic of unknown origins.
Comment: A Manhattan-style cocktail which takes no prisoners.

DRINKS ARE GRADED AS FOLLOWS:

● DISGUSTING ●◐ PRETTY AWFUL ●● BEST AVOIDED
●●◐ DISAPPOINTING ●●● ACCEPTABLE ●●●◐ GOOD
●●●● RECOMMENDED ●●●●◐ HIGHLY RECOMMENDED
●●●●● OUTSTANDING / EXCEPTIONAL

BOURBON BLUSH

●●●●◐

Glass: Martini
Garnish: Strawberry on rim
Method: MUDDLE strawberries in base of shaker. Add other ingredients, SHAKE with ice and fine strain into chilled glass.

3	fresh	Strawberries
2	shot(s)	Bourbon whiskey
¾	shot(s)	Giffard crème de framboise
¼	shot(s)	Maple syrup

Origin: Created in 2003 by Simon King at MJU @ Millennium Hotel, London, England.
Comment: Strawberry and maple syrup combine brilliantly with bourbon in this drink.

BOURBON COOKIE

●●●●○

Glass: Old-fashioned
Garnish: Dust with cinnamon powder
Method: SHAKE all ingredients with ice and strain into ice-filled glass.

2	shot(s)	Bourbon whiskey
½	shot(s)	Double (heavy) cream
½	shot(s)	Milk
½	shot(s)	Mango or passion fruit sugar syrup
½	shot(s)	Butterscotch schnapps liqueur

Origin: Created in 2002 by Andres Masso, London, England.
Comment: Looks tame but packs a flavoursome punch.

BOURBON CRUSTA NEW

●●●●◐

Glass: Small wine goblet or flute
Garnish: See 'Crusta' for instructions
Method: SHAKE all ingredients with ice and fine strain into pre-prepared glass.

2	shot(s)	Bourbon whiskey
¼	shot(s)	Cointreau triple sec
⅛	shot(s)	Luxardo maraschino liqueur
½	shot(s)	Freshly squeezed lemon juice
¼	shot(s)	Sugar syrup (2 sugar to 1 water)
2	dashes	Fee Brothers orange bitters
½	shot(s)	Chilled mineral water (omit if wet ice)

Variant: Brandy Crusta
Comment: Beautifully balanced bourbon and fresh lemon.

BOURBON MILK PUNCH

●●●◐○

Glass: Martini
Garnish: Dust with freshly grated nutmeg
Method: SHAKE all ingredients with ice and fine strain into chilled glass.

1½	shot(s)	Bourbon whiskey
½	shot(s)	Galliano liqueur
1	shot(s)	Double (heavy) cream
1	shot(s)	Milk
¼	shot(s)	Sugar syrup (2 sugar to 1 water)

Comment: The character of bourbon shines through in this creamy number.

BOURBON SMASH 🗝

Glass: Collins
Garnish: Lime wheel
Method: MUDDLE raspberries in base of shaker. Add other ingredients, SHAKE with ice and fine strain into ice-filled glass.

12	fresh	Raspberries
4	fresh	Torn mint leaves
2¹/₂	shot(s)	Bourbon whiskey
3	shot(s)	Cranberry juice
1	shot(s)	Freshly squeezed lime juice
¹/₂	shot(s)	Sugar syrup (2 sugar to 1 water)
2	dashes	Angostura aromatic bitters

Comment: This refreshing long drink has a sharp edge that adds to its appeal.

BOURBONELLA

Glass: Martini
Garnish: Stemmed cherry on rim
Method: STIR all ingredients with ice and fine strain into chilled glass.

1³/₄	shot(s)	Bourbon whiskey
³/₄	shot(s)	Dry vermouth
³/₄	shot(s)	Cointreau triple sec
¹/₄	shot(s)	Pomegranate (grenadine) syrup
3	dashes	Peychaud's aromatic bitters

Comment: If you like bourbon, you'll love this fruity Manhattan.

BRADFORD 🗝

Glass: Martini
Garnish: Olive on stick or lemon zest twist
Method: SHAKE all ingredients with ice and fine strain into chilled glass.

2¹/₂	shot(s)	Plymouth gin
¹/₂	shot(s)	Dry vermouth
3	dashes	Fee Brothers orange bitters (optional)

Origin: A Bradford is a Martini which is shaken rather than stirred. Like the Martini itself, the origin of the Bradford is lost in time.
Comment: More approachable than a stirred Traditional Dry Martini and downright soft compared to a Naked Martini.

BRAINSTORM

Glass: Martini
Garnish: Orange zest twist
Method: STIR all ingredients with ice and strain into chilled glass.

1¹/₂	shot(s)	Bourbon whiskey
1	shot(s)	Dry vermouth
³/₄	shot(s)	Bénédictine D.O.M. liqueur
¹/₂	shot(s)	Chilled mineral water (omit if wet ice)

Origin: Another long lost classic.
Comment: Spiced and slightly sweetened bourbon.

BRAKE TAG NEW

Glass: Old-fashioned
Garnish: Orange zest twist
Method: SHAKE all ingredients with ice and strain into ice-filled glass.

1¹/₂	shot(s)	Southern Comfort
¹/₂	shot(s)	Luxardo Amaretto di Saschira
1	shot(s)	Freshly squeezed orange juice
1	shot(s)	Cranberry juice
3	dashes	Peychaud's aromatic bitters

Origin: Discovered in 2005 at Café Adelaide's Swizzle Stick Bar, New Orleans, USA.

BRAMBLE

Glass: Old-fashioned
Garnish: Blackberry & lemon slice
Method: SHAKE first three ingredients with ice and strain into glass filled with crushed ice. DRIZZLE liqueur over drink to create a 'bleeding' effect in the glass. Serve with short straws.

2	shot(s)	Plymouth gin
1¹/₂	shot(s)	Freshly squeezed lemon juice
¹/₂	shot(s)	Sugar syrup (2 sugar to 1 water)
¹/₂	shot(s)	Giffard mûre (blackberry)

Origin: Created in the mid-80s by Dick Bradsell at Fred's Club, Soho, London, England.
Comment: One of the best and most popular drinks created in the 1980s.

BRAMBLETTE

Glass: Martini
Garnish: Orange zest twist
Method: SHAKE all ingredients with ice and fine strain into chilled glass.

2	shot(s)	Plymouth gin
1	shot(s)	Serres liqueur de violette
³/₄	shot(s)	Freshly squeezed lemon juice
¹/₄	shot(s)	Sugar syrup (2 sugar to 1 water)

Comment: A martini style drink with a floral, gin laced palate.

BRANDY ALEXANDER

Glass: Martini
Garnish: Dust with freshly grated nutmeg
Method: SHAKE all ingredients with ice and fine strain into chilled glass.

2	shot(s)	Rémy Martin cognac
¹/₂	shot(s)	Giffard brown crème de cacao
¹/₂	shot(s)	Giffard White crème de cacao
¹/₂	shot(s)	Double (heavy) cream
¹/₂	shot(s)	Milk

AKA: The Panama
Origin: Created prior to 1930, this classic blend of brandy and chocolate smoothed with cream is based on the original Alexander which calls for gin as its base.
Comment: This after dinner classic is rich, creamy and spicy.

BRANDY BLAZER ●●●○○

Glass: Snifter & old-fashioned
Garnish: Lemon & orange zest twists
Method: POUR cognac into a warmed glass and rest the bowl of the glass on an old-fashioned glass so it lies on its side supported by the rim. FLAME the cognac and carefully move the glass back to an upright position sitting normally on your work surface. POUR in hot water (this will extinguish any remaining flame) and sugar. Stir, garnish and serve.

2	shot(s)	Rémy Martin cognac
2	shot(s)	Hot water
1/4	shot(s)	Sugar syrup (2 sugar to 1 water)

Origin: A variation on 'Professor' Jerry Thomas' Blue Blazer which involved theatrically pouring ignited brandy between two mugs. Please don't try this at home, kids.
Comment: One way to warm your winter nights.

BRANDY BUCK ⌐ ●●●○○

Glass: Collins
Garnish: Lemon wedge
Method: SHAKE first three ingredients with ice and strain into ice-filled glass. TOP with ginger ale and serve with straws.

2 1/2	shot(s)	Rémy Martin cognac
1/4	shot(s)	Grand Marnier
1/4	shot(s)	Freshly squeezed lemon juice
Top up with		Ginger ale

Comment: Lemon juice adds balance to the sweet ginger ale. Cognac provides the backbone.

BRANDY CRUSTA UPDATED ●●●●◐

Glass: Small wine goblet or flute
Garnish: See 'Crusta' for instructions
Method: SHAKE all ingredients with ice and fine strain into pre-prepared glass.

2	shot(s)	Rémy Martin cognac
1/4	shot(s)	Cointreau triple sec
1/8	shot(s)	Luxardo maraschino liqueur
1/2	shot(s)	Freshly squeezed lemon juice
1/4	shot(s)	Sugar syrup (2 sugar to 1 water)
2	dashes	Angostura aromatic bitters
3/4	shot(s)	Chilled mineral water (reduce if wet ice)

Variant: Bourbon Crusta
Origin: Created in the 1840s-50s by Joseph Santina at Jewel of the South, Gravier Street, New Orleans, USA. The name refers to the crust of sugar around the rim. This recipe is adapted from David A. Embury's 1948 'The Fine Art of Mixing Drinks'.
Comment: This old classic zings with fresh lemon and is beautifully balanced by the cognac base.

BRANDY FIX ●●●●◐

Glass: Old-fashioned
Garnish: Lemon zest twist
Method: SHAKE all ingredients with ice and strain into ice-filled glass.

2	shot(s)	Rémy Martin cognac
1/2	shot(s)	Pressed pineapple juice
1/2	shot(s)	Freshly squeezed lemon juice
1/4	shot(s)	Sugar syrup (2 sugar to 1 water)
1/8	shot(s)	Yellow Chartreuse

Comment: This wonderful classic is on the tart side of well balanced.

BRANDY FIZZ UPDATED ⌐ ●●●●○

Glass: Collins (8oz max)
Garnish: Lemon wheel
Method: SHAKE first three ingredients with ice and fine strain into chilled glass (without ice). TOP with soda.

2	shot(s)	Rémy Martin cognac
1/2	shot(s)	Freshly squeezed lemon juice
1/4	shot(s)	Sugar syrup (2 sugar to 1 water)
Top up with		Soda water (from siphon)

Comment: A refreshing and tasty dry drink: cognac and lemon balanced with a little sugar and lengthened with soda.

BRANDY FLIP UPDATED ⌐ ●●●●◐

Glass: Wine goblet or Martini
Garnish: Dust with freshly ground nutmeg
Method: SHAKE all ingredients with ice and fine strain into chilled glass.

1 1/2	shot(s)	Rémy Martin cognac
1/4	shot(s)	Sugar syrup (2 sugar to 1 water)
1/4	shot(s)	Double (heavy) cream
1	fresh	Egg

Origin: A forgotten classic.
Comment: A serious alternative to advocaat for those without raw egg inhibitions.

BRANDY MILK PUNCH ●●●●○

Glass: Collins
Garnish: Dust with freshly grated nutmeg
Method: SHAKE all ingredients with ice and strain into glass filled with crushed ice.

2	shot(s)	Rémy Martin cognac
3	shot(s)	Milk
1	shot(s)	Double (heavy) cream
1/4	shot(s)	Sugar syrup (2 sugar to 1 water)
1/8	shot(s)	Vanilla extract

Origin: A New Orleans variant of the drink that enjoyed nationwide popularity during Prohibition.
Comment: This traditional New Orleans hangover cure beats your bog-standard vanilla milkshake.

BRANDY SMASH

Glass: Old-fashioned
Garnish: Mint sprig
Method: Lightly **MUDDLE** mint in base of shaker just enough to bruise. Add other ingredients, **SHAKE** with ice and fine strain into ice-filled glass.

7	fresh	Mint leaves
2	shot(s)	Rémy Martin cognac
¼	shot(s)	Sugar syrup (2 sugar to 1 water)

Origin: A classic from the 1850s.
Comment: Sweetened cognac flavoured with mint. Simple but beautiful.

BRANDY SOUR

Glass: Old-fashioned
Garnish: Lemon slice & cherry (sail)
Method: SHAKE all ingredients with ice and strain into ice-filled glass.

2	shot(s)	Rémy Martin cognac
1	shot(s)	Freshly squeezed lemon juice
½	shot(s)	Sugar syrup (2 sugar to 1 water)
½	fresh	Egg white
3	dashes	Angostura aromatic bitters

Comment: After the Whiskey Sour, this is the most requested sour. Try it and you'll see why – but don't omit the egg white.

BRASS MONKEY NEW

Glass: Collins
Garnish: Lemon slice
Method: SHAKE all ingredients with ice and strain into ice-filled glass.

1	shot(s)	Light white rum
1	shot(s)	Ketel One Citroen vodka
2½	shot(s)	Freshly squeezed lemon juice
1	shot(s)	Sugar syrup (2 sugar to 1 water)

Comment: Tangy, alcoholic, almost sherbety lemonade. Packed with Vitamin C.

BRASS RAIL NEW

Glass: Martini
Garnish: Cape gooseberry
Method: SHAKE all ingredients with ice and fine strain into chilled glass.

1½	shot(s)	Aged rum
½	shot(s)	Bénédictine D.O.M. liqueur
½	shot(s)	Freshly squeezed lemon juice
½	shot(s)	Sugar syrup (2 sugar to 1 water)
½	fresh	Egg white
2	dashes	Fee Brothers orange bitters
½	shot(s)	Chilled mineral water (omit if wet ice)

Origin: Adapted from a recipe by Tony Abou Ganim. He was apparently inspired by his cousin Helen's penchant for a nightcap after a special occasion; her favourite was Bénédictine.
Comment: Rather like a Daiquiri, yet subtly sweetened and spiced.

BRAZEN MARTINI

Glass: Martini
Garnish: Frozen blueberries
Method: STIR all ingredients with ice and strain into chilled glass.

| 2½ | shot(s) | Zubrówka bison vodka |
| ¼ | shot(s) | Parfait Amour |

Comment: Not for the faint hearted – a great combination of strawy bison vodka with violet Parfait Amour.

BRAZILIAN BERRY

Glass: Old-fashioned
Garnish: Mint sprig
Method: MUDDLE fruit in base of shaker. Add other ingredients, SHAKE with ice and fine strain into glass filled with crushed ice. Serve with straws.

4	fresh	Blackcurrants
3	fresh	Raspberries
1½	shot(s)	Sauvignon Blanc wine
1	shot(s)	Cachaça
1	shot(s)	Giffard Cassis Noir de Bourgogne

Origin: Created in 2002 by Dan Spink at Browns, St Martin's Lane, London, England.
Comment: This drink combines wine, cachaça and rich berry fruits.

BRAZILIAN COFFEE

Glass: Toddy
Garnish: Float 3 coffee beans
Method: BLEND ingredients with 6oz scoop of crushed ice. Pour into glass and serve with straws.

1	shot(s)	Cachaça
1	shot(s)	Double (heavy) cream
¾	shot(s)	Sugar syrup (2 sugar to 1 water)
2	shot(s)	Espresso coffee (cold)

Comment: Strong coffee and plenty of sugar are essential in this Brazilian number.

BRAZILIAN COSMOPOLITAN NEW

Glass: Martini
Garnish: Orange zest twist
Method: SHAKE all ingredients with ice and fine strain into chilled glass.

1	shot(s)	Cachaça
1	shot(s)	Cointreau triple sec
1½	shot(s)	Cranberry juice
½	shot(s)	Freshly squeezed lime juice

Comment: The distinctive character of cachaça bursts through the fruit in this twist on the contemporary classic.

BRAZILIAN MONK

Glass: Hurricane
Garnish: Cadbury's Flake in drink
Method: BLEND ingredients with two 12oz scoops of crushed ice. Pour into glass and serve with straws.

1	shot(s)	Hazelnut (crème de noisette) liqueur
1	shot(s)	Kahlúa coffee liqueur
1	shot(s)	Giffard brown crème de cacao
3	scoops	Vanilla ice cream

Comment: Nutty and rich dessert in a glass.

BREAKFAST AT TERRELL'S

Glass: Flute
Garnish: Kumquat half
Method: SHAKE first four ingredients with ice and strain into chilled glass. TOP with champagne.

³/₄	shot(s)	Mandarine Napoléon liqueur
³/₄	shot(s)	Freshly squeezed orange juice
³/₄	shot(s)	Double (heavy) cream
¹/₈	shot(s)	Sugar syrup (2 sugar to 1 water)
Top up with		Brut champagne

Origin: Created by Jamie Terrell for Philip Holzberg at Vinexpo, Bordeaux, France, 1999.
Comment: This creamy orange champagne cocktail is almost as smooth as a Sgroppino.

BREAKFAST MARTINI UPDATED

Glass: Martini
Garnish: Orange zest twist, slice of toast on rim
Method: STIR marmalade with gin in base of shaker until it dissolves. Add other ingredients, SHAKE with ice and fine strain into chilled glass.

1	spoon	Orange marmalade
2	shot(s)	Plymouth gin
³/₄	shot(s)	Cointreau triple sec
³/₄	shot(s)	Freshly squeezed lemon juice

Origin: Created in the late 1990s by Salvatore Calabrese at the Library Bar, London, England. It is very similar to the 'Marmalade Cocktail' created in the 1920s by Harry Craddock and published in his 1930 'The Savoy Cocktail Book'.
Comment: The success or failure of this tangy drink is partly reliant on the quality of marmalade used. Basically a White Lady with Marmalade.

DRINKS ARE GRADED AS FOLLOWS:

● DISGUSTING ●○ PRETTY AWFUL ●● BEST AVOIDED
●●○ DISAPPOINTING ●●● ACCEPTABLE ●●● GOOD
●●●○ RECOMMENDED ●●●●○ HIGHLY RECOMMENDED
●●●●● OUTSTANDING / EXCEPTIONAL

BRIGHTON PUNCH

Glass: Collins
Garnish: Pineapple wedge
Method: SHAKE all ingredients with ice and strain into ice-filled glass.

1¹/₂	shot(s)	Rémy Martin cognac
1¹/₂	shot(s)	Bourbon whiskey
1¹/₂	shot(s)	Bénédictine D.O.M. liqueur
2¹/₂	shot(s)	Pressed pineapple juice
2	shot(s)	Freshly squeezed lemon juice

Variant: With orange juice in place of pineapple juice.
Origin: Popular in the bars of Berlin, Germany.
Comment: Don't bother trying the version with orange juice but do try halving the quantities and serving up. Served long or short this is beautifully balanced.

THE BROADMOOR UPDATED

Glass: Martini
Garnish: Flamed orange zest twist
Method: SHAKE all ingredients with ice and fine strain into chilled glass.

2	shot(s)	Scotch whisky
¹/₂	shot(s)	Green Chartreuse liqueur
¹/₂	shot(s)	Sugar syrup (2 sugar to 1 water)
4	dashes	Fee Brothers orange bitters

Origin: Created in 2001 by Swedish bartender Andreas Norén at The Player, London, and popularised at Milk & Honey, London, England. Named after the infamous British mental institution.
Comment: Beautifully simple and seriously complex.

BRONX UPDATED

Glass: Martini
Garnish: Maraschino cherry
Method: SHAKE all ingredients with ice and fine strain into chilled glass.

1¹/₂	shot(s)	Plymouth gin
³/₄	shot(s)	Dry vermouth
³/₄	shot(s)	Sweet vermouth
1	shot(s)	Freshly squeezed orange juice

Variants: 1/ Bloody Bronx – made with the juice of a blood orange. 2/ Golden Bronx – with the addition of an egg yolk. 3/ Silver Bronx - with the addition of egg white. 4/ Income Tax Cocktail – with two dashes Angostura bitters. Also see the Abbey Martini.
Origin: Created in 1906 by Johnny Solon, a bartender at New York's Waldorf-Astoria Hotel (the Empire State Building occupies the site today), and named after the newly opened Bronx Zoo. Reputedly the first cocktail to use fruit juice.
Comment: A serious, dry, complex cocktail – less bitter than many of its era, but still quite challenging to modern palates.

BROOKLYN #1

Glass: Martini
Garnish: Maraschino cherry
Method: STIR all ingredients with ice and strain into chilled glass.

2¹/₂	shot(s)	**Bourbon whiskey**
¹/₂	shot(s)	**Dry vermouth**
¹/₂	shot(s)	**Sweet vermouth**
¹/₄	shot(s)	**Luxardo maraschino liqueur**
3	dashes	**Angostura aromatic bitters**

Origin: Though to have originated at the St George Hotel, Brooklyn, New York City, USA.
Comment: A Perfect Manhattan with maraschino liqueur.

BROOKLYN #2

Glass: Martini
Garnish: Maraschino cherry
Method: STIR all ingredients with ice and strain into chilled glass.

2	shot(s)	**Bourbon whiskey**
³/₄	shot(s)	**Dry vermouth**
¹/₂	shot(s)	**Luxardo Amaretto di Saschira**

Comment: A simple, very approachable Manhattan.

BRUBAKER OLD-FASHIONED

Glass: Old-fashioned
Garnish: Two lemon zest twists
Method: STIR malt extract in glass with Scotch until malt extract dissolves. Add ice and one shot of Scotch and stir. Add remaining Scotch, sugar and Angostura and stir some more. Add more ice and keep stirring so that ice dilutes the drink.

2	spoons	**Malt Extract** (available in health-food shops)
2	shot(s)	**Scotch whisky**
¹/₄	shot(s)	**Sugar syrup (2 sugar to 1 water)**
3	dashes	**Angostura aromatic bitters**

Origin: Created in 2003 by Shelim Islam at the GE Club, London, England. Shelim named this drink after a horse in the sports section of a paper (also a film made in the seventies starring Robert Redford).
Comment: If you like Scotch you should try this extra malty dram. After all that stirring you'll deserve one.

BUBBLEGUM SHOT

Glass: Shot
Method: SHAKE all ingredients with ice and fine strain into chilled glass.

¹/₂	shot(s)	**Midori melon liqueur**
¹/₂	shot(s)	**Luxardo Amaretto di Saschira**
¹/₄	shot(s)	**Double (heavy) cream**

Comment: As the name suggests, this tastes a little like bubble gum.

THE BUCK

The Buck originated during the Prohibition era in the form of the Gin Buck. Like the Ricky, the Collins and the Fizz it is a tall drink served with citrus juice and a carbonate. (A Highball is also tall but never contains citrus juice.)

Originally a Buck was made by cutting a large lemon into quarters and squeezing the juice of one quarter into the drink using a hand squeezer. The squeezed shell was also dropped into the glass with the juice. Unlike the other drinks above, no sugar is added – sufficient sweetness to balance the lemon is provided by the sweet carbonate.

THE BUCK

Glass: Collins
Garnish: Lemon wedge
Method: POUR first two ingredients into ice-filled glass and top up with ginger ale. Stir and serve with straws.

2¹/₂	shot(s)	Plymouth gin (or other spirit)
¹/₂	shot(s)	Freshly squeezed lemon juice
Top up with		Ginger ale

Variant: The recipe above is for a Gin Buck, but this drink can also be based on brandy, calvados, rum, whiskey, vodka etc.
Comment: The Buck can be improved by adding a dash of liqueur appropriate to the spirit base. E.g. add a dash of Grand Marnier to a Brandy Buck.

BUCK'S FIZZ

Glass: Flute
Method: POUR ingredients into chilled glass and gently stir.

2	shot(s)	Freshly squeezed orange juice
Top up with		Brut champagne

AKA: Mimosa
Origin: Created in 1921 by Mr McGarry, first bartender at the Buck's Club, London.
Comment: Not really a cocktail and not that challenging, but great for brunch.

BUENA VIDA

Glass: Old-fashioned
Garnish: Pineapple wedge on rim
Method: SHAKE all ingredients with ice and strain into glass filled with crushed ice.

2	shot(s)	Partida tequila
1³/₄	shot(s)	Squeezed pink grapefruit juice
³/₄	shot(s)	Pressed pineapple juice
¹/₂	shot(s)	Vanilla sugar syrup
3	dashes	Angostura aromatic bitters

Comment: The fruits combine brilliantly with the tequila and spice comes courtesy of Angostura.

BULLDOG

Glass: Collins
Method: SHAKE first four ingredients with ice and strain into ice-filled glass. TOP with cola, stir and serve with straws.

1	shot(s)	Light white rum
1	shot(s)	Kahlúa coffee liqueur
1¹/₂	shot(s)	Double (heavy) cream
1¹/₂	shot(s)	Milk
Top up with		Cola

Comment: Surprisingly nice – cola cuts through the cream.

BULLFROG

Glass: Old-fashioned
Garnish: Maraschino cherry
Method: SHAKE all ingredients with ice and strain into glass filled with crushed ice.

1¹/₂	shot(s)	Ketel One vodka
³/₄	shot(s)	Giffard white crème de Menthe Pastille
1	shot(s)	Double (heavy) cream
1	shot(s)	Milk

Comment: Mint ice cream.

BULL'S BLOOD

Glass: Martini
Garnish: Orange zest twist
Method: SHAKE all ingredients with ice and fine strain into chilled glass.

¹/₂	shot(s)	Light white rum
1	shot(s)	Rémy Martin cognac
1	shot(s)	Grand Marnier
1¹/₂	shot(s)	Freshly squeezed orange juice

Comment: This beautifully balanced fruity cocktail has a dry finish.

BULL'S MILK

Glass: Collins
Method: SHAKE all ingredients with ice and strain into ice-filled glass.

1	shot(s)	Gosling's Black Seal rum
1¹/₂	shot(s)	Rémy Martin cognac
4	shot(s)	Milk
¹/₂	shot(s)	Maple syrup

Comment: Dark spirits tamed by thick maple syrup and milk.

BUMBLE BEE

Glass: Shot
Method: Refrigerate ingredients then LAYER in chilled glass by carefully pouring in the following order.

¹/₂	shot(s)	Kahlúa coffee liqueur
¹/₂	shot(s)	Luxardo Sambuca dei Cesari
¹/₂	shot(s)	Baileys Irish cream liqueur

Comment: A B-52 with a liquorice kick.

BUONA SERA SHOT

Glass: Shot
Method: SHAKE all ingredients with ice and fine strain into chilled glass.

¹/₂	shot(s)	Kahlúa coffee liqueur
¹/₂	shot(s)	Luxardo Amaretto di Saschira
¹/₂	shot(s)	Vanilla-infused light white rum

Comment: As sweet shots go this is one of my favourites.

BURNING BUSH SHOT

●●○○○

Glass: Shot
Method: POUR ingredients into chilled glass.

| 1 | shot(s) | Partida tequila |
| 6 | drops | Tabasco pepper sauce |

AKA: Prairie Dog, Prairie Fire
Comment: Hold onto your bowels!

BURNT TOASTED ALMOND

●●●○○

Glass: Martini
Garnish: Dust with freshly grated nutmeg
Method: SHAKE all ingredients with ice and fine strain into chilled glass.

1	shot(s)	Ketel One vodka
1/2	shot(s)	Baileys Irish cream liqueur
1/2	shot(s)	Kahlúa coffee liqueur
1	shot(s)	Luxardo Amaretto di Saschira
1	shot(s)	Double (heavy) cream
1	shot(s)	Milk

Variant: Toasted Almond
Comment: There's more than just almond to this sweety.

BUTTERFLY'S KISS

●●●○○

Glass: Martini
Garnish: Cinnamon stick
Method: STIR all ingredients with ice and strain into chilled glass.

2	shot(s)	Vanilla-infused Ketel One vodka
1	shot(s)	Hazelnut (crème de noisette) liqueur
1/2	shot(s)	Goldschläger cinnamon schnapps
1/2	shot(s)	Sugar syrup (2 sugar to 1 water)
1/2	shot(s)	Chilled mineral water (omit if wet ice)

Origin: Adapted from a drink I discovered in 2003 at Bar Marmont, Los Angeles, USA.
Comment: Golden coloured Martini style drink complete with the odd gold flake and a hazelnut cinnamon twang.

BUTTERSCOTCH DAIQUIRI

●●●○○

Glass: Martini
Garnish: Butterscotch sweet in drink
Method: SHAKE all ingredients with ice and fine strain into chilled glass.

2	shot(s)	Light white rum
1	shot(s)	Butterscotch schnapps liqueur
1/2	shot(s)	Freshly squeezed lime juice
1/2	shot(s)	Chilled mineral water (omit if wet ice)

Comment: A candified Daiquiri.

BUTTERSCOTCH DELIGHT

●●●●○

Glass: Shot
Method: Refrigerate ingredients then LAYER in chilled glass by carefully pouring in the following order.

| 3/4 | shot(s) | Butterscotch schnapps liqueur |
| 3/4 | shot(s) | Baileys Irish cream liqueur |

Origin: The origin of this drink is unknown but it is very popular in the bars in and around Seattle, USA.
Comment: Sweet connotations!

BUTTERSCOTCH MARTINI

●●●●○

Glass: Martini
Garnish: Butterscotch sweet
Method: SHAKE all ingredients with ice and fine strain into chilled glass.

2	shot(s)	Mount Gay Eclipse golden rum
3/4	shot(s)	Butterscotch schnapps liqueur
3/4	shot(s)	Giffard White crème de cacao
1/8	shot(s)	Sugar syrup (2 sugar to 1 water)
1/2	shot(s)	Chilled mineral water (omit if wet ice)

Comment: Sweet and suckable.

BUZZARD'S BREATH

●●●○○

Glass: Hurricane
Garnish: Pineapple wedge on rim
Method: BLEND ingredients with 12oz scoop of crushed ice. Pour into glass and serve with straws.

2 1/2	shot(s)	Cachaça
1	shot(s)	Coco López cream of coconut
2	shot(s)	Pressed pineapple juice
1/4	shot(s)	Double (heavy) cream

Comment: A Piña Colada made with cachaça.

BYZANTINE

●●●●○

Glass: Collins
Garnish: Basil leaf
Method: MUDDLE basil in base of shaker. Add other ingredients apart from tonic water, SHAKE with ice and strain into ice-filled glass. TOP with tonic water.

6	fresh	Basil leaves
1 1/2	shot(s)	Plymouth gin
1/2	shot(s)	Passion fruit sugar syrup
2	shot(s)	Pressed pineapple juice
1/2	shot(s)	Lime & lemongrass cordial
Top up with		Tonic water

Origin: Created in 2001 by Douglas Ankrah for Akbar, Soho, London, England.
Comment: This fruity, herbal drink is even better made the way Douglas originally intended, with basil infused gin instead of muddled leaves.

C C KAZI

Glass: Martini
Garnish: Lime wedge on rim
Method: SHAKE all ingredients with ice and fine strain into chilled glass.

1³/₄	shot(s)	Partida tequila
1³/₄	shot(s)	Cranberry juice
¹/₂	shot(s)	Freshly squeezed lime juice
¹/₄	shot(s)	Sugar syrup (2 sugar to 1 water)

Comment: A Rude Cosmo without the liqueur.

CABLE CAR UPDATED

Glass: Martini
Garnish: Half cinnamon & sugar rim
Method: SHAKE all ingredients with ice and fine strain into chilled glass.

2	shot(s)	Spiced rum
1	shot(s)	Cointreau triple sec
¹/₂	shot(s)	Freshly squeezed lemon juice
¹/₄	shot(s)	Sugar syrup (2 sugar to 1 water)
¹/₂	fresh	Egg white

Origin: Created in 1996 by Cory Reistad at the Starlight Room, atop San Francisco's Sir Francis Drake Hotel. The Nob Hill cable cars pass by the bar, hence its catchphrase 'Between the stars and the cable cars'.
Comment: Vanilla and spice from the rum interact with the orange liqueur in this balanced, Daiquiri style drink.

CACHAÇA DAIQUIRI

Glass: Martini
Garnish: Lime wedge on rim
Method: SHAKE all ingredients with ice and fine strain into chilled glass.

2	shot(s)	Cachaça
¹/₂	shot(s)	Freshly squeezed lime juice
¹/₄	shot(s)	Sugar syrup (2 sugar to 1 water)
¹/₂	shot(s)	Chilled mineral water

Comment: Might be in a Martini glass but it tastes like a Caipirinha.

CACTUS BANGER

Glass: Martini
Garnish: Lime wedge on rim
Method: SHAKE all ingredients with ice and fine strain into chilled glass.

1	shot(s)	Partida tequila
1	shot(s)	Grand Marnier
2	shot(s)	Freshly squeezed orange juice
¹/₂	shot(s)	Freshly squeezed lime juice

Comment: A golden, sunny looking and sunny tasting drink.

CACTUS JACK

Glass: Martini
Garnish: Pineapple leaf
Method: SHAKE all ingredients with ice and fine strain into chilled glass.

1	shot(s)	Partida tequila
³/₄	shot(s)	Bols Blue curaçao liqueur
1¹/₄	shot(s)	Freshly squeezed orange juice
1	shot(s)	Pressed pineapple juice
¹/₂	shot(s)	Freshly squeezed lemon juice

Comment: Vivid in colour, this orange led, tequila based drink has a balanced sweet and sourness.

CAFÉ GATES

Glass: Toddy
Garnish: Three coffee beans
Method: Place bar spoon in glass, **POUR** first three ingredients and top up with coffee, then **FLOAT** cream by pouring over the back of a spoon.

³/₄	shot(s)	Grand Marnier
³/₄	shot(s)	Kahlúa coffee liqueur
³/₄	shot(s)	Giffard brown crème de cacao
Top up with		Filter coffee (hot)
³/₄	shot(s)	Double (heavy) cream

Comment: Chocolate orange with coffee and cream.

CAIPIGINGER NEW

Glass: Old-fashioned
Garnish: Lime zest twist (discarded) & lime wedge
Method: MUDDLE ginger in base of shaker. Add other ingredients, **SHAKE** with ice and strain into glass filled with crushed ice. Serve with straws.

2	slices	Fresh root ginger (thumbnail sized)
2	shot(s)	Cachaça
1	shot(s)	Freshly squeezed lime juice
³/₄	shot(s)	Sugar syrup (2 sugar to 1 water)

Comment: A ginger spiced take on the Caipirinha.

CAIPIRINHA (CLASSIC SERVE) UPDATED

Glass: Old-fashioned
Method: MUDDLE lime in base of glass to release the juices and oils in its skin. Pour cachaça and sugar into glass, add crushed ice and CHURN (stir) with bar spoon. Serve with straws.

³/₄	fresh	Lime cut into wedges
2	shot(s)	Cachaça
³/₄	shot(s)	Sugar syrup (2 sugar to 1 water)

Origin: A traditional Brazilian drink
Comment: Those who enjoy chewing on undissolved sugar should use granulated sugar in place of syrup.

CAIPIRINHA (DIFFORD'S SERVE) NEW

Glass: Old-fashioned
Garnish: Lime zest twist (squeezed & discarded) & lime wedge
Method: SHAKE all ingredients with ice and strain into ice-filled glass. Serve with straws.

2	shot(s)	Cachaça
1	shot(s)	Freshly squeezed lime juice
1/2	shot(s)	Sugar syrup (2 sugar to 1 water)

Origin: My adaptation of the traditional Brazilian drink.
Variant: Strained over crushed ice, with a quarter shot more sugar syrup.
Comment: Using measures of freshly squeezed lime juice and sugar syrup ensures a perfect balance of sweet and sour. I'm not a fan of crushed ice, hence this is served on the rocks.

CAIPIRISSIMA

Glass: Old-fashioned
Method: MUDDLE lime in base of glass. Add other ingredients and fill glass with crushed ice. CHURN (stir) drink with bar spoon and serve with straws.

3/4	fresh	Lime cut into wedges
2	shot(s)	Light white rum
3/4	shot(s)	Sugar syrup (2 sugar to 1 water)

Comment: A Daiquiri style drink made like a Caipirinha to give that rustic edge.

CAIPIROVSKA

Glass: Old-fashioned
Method: MUDDLE lime in base of glass. Add other ingredients and fill glass with crushed ice. CHURN (stir) drink with bar spoon and serve with straws.

3/4	fresh	Lime cut into wedges
2	shot(s)	Ketel One vodka
3/4	shot(s)	Sugar syrup (2 sugar to 1 water)

Comment: Lacks the character of a cachaça-based Caipirinha.

CAIPIRUVA

Glass: Old-fashioned
Method: MUDDLE grapes in base of shaker. Add other ingredients, SHAKE with ice and fine strain into glass filled with crushed ice.

10	fresh	Seedless grapes
2	shot(s)	Cachaça
3/4	shot(s)	Freshly squeezed lime juice
3/4	shot(s)	Sugar syrup (2 sugar to 1 water)

Comment: A grape juice laced twist on the Caipirinha.

CAIPIRINHA

Pronounced 'Kie-Pur-Reen-Yah', the name of this traditional Brazilian cocktail means 'little countryside drink'. It is made by muddling green lemons known as 'limon subtil', which are native to Brazil (limes are the best substitute when these are not available), and mixing with sugar and cachaça. Be sure to muddle in a sturdy, non-breakable glass.

There is much debate among bartenders as to whether granulated sugar or syrup should be used to make this drink. Those who favour granulated sugar argue that muddling with the abrasive crystals helps extract the oils from the lime's skin. Personally, I hate the crunch of sugar as inevitably not all the granulated sugar dissolves. Whether you should use brown or white sugar to make your syrup is another question! Either way, this is a refreshing drink.

Cachaça, a spirit distilled from fermented sugar cane juice, is the national spirit of Brazil - and Brazilians consume an astonishing 2,000,000,000 litres of it a year.

Caipirinhas and variations on the theme are staples in cachaçerias, Brazilian bars which specialise in cachaça.

Caipirinha variations include
Berry Caipirinha
Black 'N' Blue Caipirovska
Caipirissima
Caipirovska
Caipiruva
Citrus Caipirovska
Grapefruit & Ginger Caipirinha
Passionate Caipirinha
Pineapple & Basil Caipirinha

●●●○○

CAJUN MARTINI UPDATED

Glass: Martini
Garnish: Chilli pepper
Method: STIR vermouth with ice. Strain, discarding vermouth to leave only a coating on the ice. Pour pepper vodka into mixing glass, stir with coated ice and strain into chilled glass.

¹/₂	shot(s)	Dry vermouth
2¹/₂	shot(s)	Ketel One pepper infused vodka

Comment: A very hot vodka Martini. I dare you!

●●●●○

CALIFORNIAN MARTINI NEW

Glass: Martini
Garnish: Orange zest twist
Method: STIR all ingredients with ice and strain into chilled glass.

2	shot(s)	Ketel One vodka
1	shot(s)	Grand Marnier liqueur
¹/₂	shot(s)	Dry vermouth
2	dashes	Fee Brothers orange bitters (optional)

Comment: A medium dry, fragrant orange Martini.

●●●●○○

CALIFORNIA ROOT BEER

Glass: Sling
Garnish: Lime wedge
Method: SHAKE first three ingredients with ice and strain into ice-filled glass. **TOP** with soda.

1	shot(s)	Ketel One vodka
¹/₂	shot(s)	Kahlúa coffee liqueur
³/₄	shot(s)	Galliano liqueur
Top up with		Soda water (club soda)

Variant: Bartender's Root Beer
Comment: Does indeed taste like root beer.

●●●●●○

CALL ME OLD-FASHIONED

Glass: Old-fashioned
Garnish: Orange peel twist
Method: STIR sugar syrup and bitters with two ice cubes in a glass. Add one shot of cognac and two more ice cubes. Stir some more and add another two ice cubes and another shot of cognac. Stir lots more and add more ice.

2	shot(s)	Rémy Martin cognac
¹/₄	shot(s)	Sugar syrup (2 sugar to 1 water)
2	dashes	Angostura aromatic bitters

Origin: Created in 2001 by yours truly.
Comment: An Old-Fashioned made with cognac instead of whiskey – works well.

●●●●●

CALVADOS COCKTAIL UPDATED

Glass: Martini
Garnish: Orange zest twist
Method: SHAKE all ingredients with ice and fine strain into chilled glass.

1¹/₂	shot(s)	Boulard Grand Solage Calvados
³/₄	shot(s)	Cointreau triple sec
1¹/₂	shot(s)	Freshly squeezed orange juice
2	dashes	Fee Brothers orange bitters

Origin: Adapted from Harry Craddock's 1930 'The Savoy Cocktail Book'.
Comment: Tangy orange with an alcoholic apple bite.

●●●●○

CAMERON'S KICK UPDATED

Glass: Martini
Garnish: Lemon zest twist
Method: SHAKE all ingredients with ice and fine strain into chilled glass.

1¹/₂	shot(s)	Scotch whisky
1¹/₂	shot(s)	Irish whiskey
³/₄	shot(s)	Freshly squeezed lemon juice
¹/₂	shot(s)	Almond (orgeat) syrup

Origin: Adapted from Harry Craddock's 1930 'The Savoy Cocktail Book'.
Comment: Peaty, honeyed whiskey with a cleansing hint of lemon rounded by almond.

●●●●○

CAMOMILE & BLACKFRUIT BREEZE UPDATED

Glass: Collins
Garnish: Lemon slice
Method: SHAKE all ingredients with ice and strain into ice-filled glass.

2	shot(s)	Ketel One Citroen vodka
1	shot(s)	Chambord black raspberry liqueur
3	shot(s)	Cold camomile tea

Origin: Created in 2002 by yours truly.
Comment: Adult, clean and subtle in flavour with a twang of fruit.

●●●●○

CANADIAN APPLE (MOCKTAIL) NEW

Glass: Collins
Garnish: Apple slice
Method: SHAKE all ingredients with ice and fine strain into ice-filled glass.

3¹/₂	shot(s)	Pressed apple juice
1¹/₂	shot(s)	Freshly squeezed lemon juice
³/₄	shot(s)	Maple syrup

Origin: Adapted from a drink discovered in 2005 at the Four Seasons Hotel, Prague, Czech Republic.
Comment: Refreshing and balanced with just the right amount of citrus acidity.

A B C D E F G H I J K L M N O P Q R S T U V W X Y Z

CANARIE

Glass: Collins (10oz/290ml max)
Method: POUR pastis and lemon syrup into glass. Serve iced water separately in a small jug (known in France as a 'broc') so the customer can dilute to their own taste (I recommend five shots). Lastly, add ice to fill glass.

1	shot(s)	Ricard pastis
1/2	shot(s)	Lemon (citron) sugar syrup
Top up with		Chilled mineral water

Origin: Very popular throughout France, this drink is fittingly named after the bird, which is typically bred for its bright yellow plumage.
Comment: The traditional French café drink with a twist of lemon sweetness.

CANARIES

Glass: Hurricane
Garnish: Pineapple wedge on rim
Method: SHAKE ingredients with ice and strain into ice-filled glass.

3/4	shot(s)	Light white rum
3/4	shot(s)	Cointreau triple sec
3/4	shot(s)	Giffard crème de banane du Brésil
3/4	shot(s)	Cherry (brandy) liqueur
2	shot(s)	Pressed pineapple juice
2	shot(s)	Freshly squeezed orange juice

Comment: A long, fruity sweet drink that's only fit for consumption on a tropical beach.

CANARY FLIP

Glass: Martini
Garnish: Lemon zest twist
Method: SHAKE all ingredients with ice and fine strain into chilled glass.

2	shot(s)	Advocaat liqueur
2	shot(s)	Sauvignon Blanc wine
3/4	shot(s)	Freshly squeezed lemon juice

Origin: Created in 2002 by Alex Kammerling, London, England.
Comment: A delightful balance of egg, brandy and wine.

CANCHANCHARA NEW ⚷

Glass: Old-fashioned
Garnish: Lemon slice
Method: STIR honey with rum in the glass drink is to be served in. ADD lemon juice and ice. STIR and serve.

3	spoons	Runny honey
2	shot(s)	Light white rum
1 1/2	shot(s)	Freshly squeezed lemon juice

Origin: The Cuban forerunner of the Daiquiri, as drunk by Cuban revolutionaries fighting off the Spanish at the end of the nineteenth century. To be really authentic omit the ice. Origin and this recipe from Christine Sismondo's 2005 'Mondo Cocktail'.
Comment: Achieve the perfect balance between sweet honey and sour lemon and this is a great drink.

CANTEEN MARTINI

Glass: Martini
Garnish: Cherry in drink
Method: SHAKE all ingredients with ice and fine strain into chilled glass.

1 1/2	shot(s)	Light white rum
1 1/2	shot(s)	Southern Comfort
1/2	shot(s)	Luxardo Amaretto di Saschira
1/2	shot(s)	Freshly squeezed lime juice

Origin: Originally created by Joey Guerra at Canteen, New York City, and adapted by author and columnist Gary Regan.
Comment: Tangy, sweet and sour – Southern Comfort drinkers will love this.

CAPE CODDER ⚷

Glass: Old-fashioned
Garnish: Lime wedge
Method: SHAKE all ingredients with ice and strain into ice-filled glass.

2	shot(s)	Ketel One vodka
3	shot(s)	Cranberry juice
1/4	shot(s)	Freshly squeezed lime juice

Variant: Without lime juice this is a Cape Cod. Lengthened with soda becomes the Cape Cod Cooler.
Origin: Named after the resort on the Massachusetts coast. This fish shaped piece of land is where some of the first Europeans settled in the US. Here they found cranberries, the indigenous North American berry on which this drink is based.
Comment: Dry and refreshing but not particularly interesting.

CAPPERCAILLE ⚷

Glass: Martini
Garnish: Pineapple wedge on rim
Method: STIR honey with whisky until honey dissolves. Add other ingredients, SHAKE with ice and fine strain into chilled glass.

2	spoons	Runny honey
2	shot(s)	Scotch whisky
1/2	shot(s)	Cointreau triple sec
1/2	shot(s)	Giffard apricot brandy du Roussillon
1	shot(s)	Pressed pineapple juice
1/2	shot(s)	Freshly squeezed lemon juice

Origin: Created by Wayne Collins for Maxxium UK.
Comment: Wonderfully tangy, fruity Scotch.

CAPRICE NEW

Glass: Martini
Garnish: Orange zest twist
Method: STIR all ingredients with ice and strain into chilled glass.

1 1/2	shot(s)	Plymouth gin
1/2	shot(s)	Dry vermouth
1/2	shot(s)	Bénédictine D.O.M. liqueur
1	dash	Fee Brothers orange bitters

Comment: A long stir delivers the dilution necessary for this aromatic, spiced Wet Martini.

●●●●○○

CAPTAIN COLLINS

Glass: Collins
Garnish: Orange slice & cherry on stick (sail)
Method: SHAKE first three ingredients with ice and strain into ice-filled glass. **TOP** with soda, stir and serve with straws.

2	shot(s)	Canadian whiskey
1	shot(s)	Freshly squeezed lemon juice
1/2	shot(s)	Sugar syrup (2 sugar to 1 water)
Top up with		Soda water (club soda)

Origin: Classic Collins variation.
Comment: Sweetened, soured and diluted whiskey.

●●●●●

CARAMEL MANHATTAN

Glass: Martini
Garnish: Lemon twist (discarded) & pineapple wedge on rim
Method: SHAKE all ingredients with ice and fine strain into chilled glass.

1½	shot(s)	Bourbon whiskey
¾	shot(s)	Cartron Caramel liqueur
½	shot(s)	Sweet vermouth
1	shot(s)	Pressed pineapple juice
2	dashes	Peychaud's aromatic bitters

Origin: Adapted from a drink created in 2002 by Nick Strangeway, London, England.
Comment: Flavours combine harmoniously with the character of the bourbon still evident.

●●●○○

CARAVAN

Glass: Collins
Garnish: Cherries
Method: POUR ingredients into ice-filled glass. Stir and serve with straws.

3	shot(s)	Red wine
½	shot(s)	Grand Marnier
Top up with		Cola

Origin: Popular in the French Alpine ski resorts.
Comment: A punch-like long drink.

●●●●○○

CARDINAL PUNCH

Glass: Old-fashioned
Method: POUR cassis into ice-filled glass and top up with wine. Stir and serve with straws.

1	shot(s)	Giffard Cassis Noir de Bourgogne
Top up with		Red wine

Comment: A particularly fruity red.

●●●●○

CARDINALE NEW

Glass: Old-fashioned
Garnish: Orange slice
Method: SHAKE all ingredients with ice and fine strain into chilled glass.

2	shot(s)	Plymouth gin
1½	shot(s)	Campari
1	shot(s)	Dry vermouth

Origin: A varaition on the classic equal parts Negroni.
Comment: An extra dry Negroni for hardcore fans. I have to admit to being one.

●●●●●

CARIBBEAN BREEZE

Glass: Collins
Garnish: Pineapple wedge on rim
Method: SHAKE all ingredients with ice and strain into ice-filled glass.

1¼	shot(s)	Pusser's navy rum
½	shot(s)	Giffard crème de banane du Brésil
2½	shot(s)	Pressed pineapple juice
2	shot(s)	Cranberry juice
½	shot(s)	Rose's lime cordial

Comment: A long drink with bags of tangy fruit flavours.

●●●●○○

CARIBBEAN CRUISE

Glass: Collins
Garnish: Pineapple wedge on rim
Method: SHAKE all ingredients with ice and strain into ice-filled glass.

1½	shot(s)	Light white rum
1½	shot(s)	Malibu coconut rum liqueur
4	shot(s)	Pressed pineapple juice
1	spoon	Pomegranate (grenadine) syrup

Comment: Long, frothy and fruity - one for the beach bar.

●●●●○○

CARIBBEAN PIÑA COLADA

Glass: Hurricane
Garnish: Pineapple wedge with cherry on stick.
Method: BLEND ingredients with 12oz scoop of crushed ice. Pour into glass and serve with straws.

2	shot(s)	Light white rum
3	shot(s)	Pressed pineapple juice
½	shot(s)	Coco López cream of coconut
4	dashes	Angostura aromatic bitters
1	pinch	Salt

Comment: Angostura and salt make this a less sticky Colada.

CARIBBEAN PUNCH

Glass: Collins
Method: SHAKE all ingredients with ice and strain into glass filled with crushed ice.

2 1/4	shot(s)	Wray & Nephew overproof rum
1/2	shot(s)	Luxardo Amaretto di Saschira
1/2	shot(s)	Malibu coconut rum liqueur
1/4	shot(s)	Galliano liqueur
1/4	shot(s)	Pomegranate (grenadine) syrup
3/4	shot(s)	Freshly squeezed lemon juice
3	shot(s)	Pressed pineapple juice

Comment: Red in colour and innocent looking, this flavoursome drink sure packs a punch.

CARIBE DAIQUIRI NEW

Glass: Martini
Garnish: Lemon zest wedge
Method: SHAKE all ingredients with ice and fine strain into chilled glass.

2	shot(s)	Light white rum
1	shot(s)	Pressed pineapple juice
1/2	shot(s)	Freshly squeezed lemon juice
1/4	shot(s)	Velvet Falernum liqueur

Comment: A dry, fruity spicy Daiquiri.

CARNEVAL BATIDA

Glass: Collins
Garnish: Mango slice on rim
Method: SHAKE all ingredients with ice and strain into glass filled with crushed ice.

2 1/2	shot(s)	Cachaça
1 1/2	shot(s)	Mango purée
1 1/2	shot(s)	Freshly squeezed orange juice
1/2	shot(s)	Freshly squeezed lime juice
1/2	shot(s)	Sugar syrup (2 sugar to 1 water)

Origin: The Batida is a traditional Brazilian drink.
Comment: Long, rich, refreshing and strangely filling.

CAROL CHANNING

Glass: Flute
Garnish: Raspberries
Method: SHAKE first three ingredients with ice and strain into chilled glass. **TOP** with champagne.

1/4	shot(s)	Giffard Crème de framboise
1/4	shot(s)	Framboise eau de vie
1/8	shot(s)	Sugar syrup (2 sugar to 1 water)
Top up with		Brut champagne

Origin: Created by Dick Bradsell in 1984 with the milliner Stephen Jones. Named after the famously large mouthed American comedienne Carol Channing because of her appearance in the film 'Thoroughly Modern Milly', where, for some unknown reason, she spends much of the time running around shouting 'raspberries'.
Comment: Fortified raspberry and champagne.

CARROL COCKTAIL NEW

Glass: Martini
Garnish: Pickled walnut or onion
Method: STIR all ingredients with ice and strain into chilled glass.

2	shot(s)	Rémy Martin cognac
1	shot(s)	Sweet vermouth

Origin: Adapted from Victor Bergeron's 'Trader Vic's Bartender's Guide' (1972 revised edition).
Comment: Aromatic wine and cognac – dry yet easy.

CARROT CAKE

Glass: Martini
Garnish: Dust with cinnamon powder
Method: SHAKE all ingredients with ice and fine strain into chilled glass.

2	shot(s)	Baileys Irish cream liqueur
3/4	shot(s)	Goldschläger cinnamon schnapps
1 1/2	shot(s)	Kahlúa coffee liqueur

Comment: Tastes nothing like carrot cake - surely that's a good thing.

CARUSO MARTINI NEW

Glass: Martini
Garnish: Mint leaf
Method: SHAKE all ingredients with ice and fine strain into chilled glass.

1	shot(s)	Plymouth gin
1	shot(s)	Dry vermouth
1	shot(s)	Giffard green crème de menthe

Origin: The recipe is adapted from Harry Craddock's 1930 'The Savoy Cocktail Book'. The drink was created at The Savoy for the tenor Enrico Caruso in the early 20th century.
Comment: Emerald green with full-on mint. Good as a digestif after a tenor-sized meal.

CASABLANCA #1 NEW

Glass: Martini
Garnish: Orange zest twist
Method: SHAKE all ingredients with ice and fine strain into chilled glass.

2	shot(s)	Light white rum
3/4	shot(s)	Cointreau triple sec
3/4	shot(s)	Freshly squeezed lime juice
1/2	shot(s)	Luxardo maraschino liqueur
1/2	fresh	Egg white

Origin: Named after Michael Curtiz's 1942 classic starring Bogie and Ingrid Bergman.
Comment: A rum based variation on the White Lady, with zingy citrus and sweet maraschino.

CASABLANCA #2 UPDATED

●●●○○

Glass: Martini
Garnish: Dust with freshly grated nutmeg
Method: SHAKE all ingredients with ice and fine strain into chilled glass.

1	shot(s)	Ketel One vodka
¼	shot(s)	Galliano liqueur
1	shot(s)	Advocaat liqueur
¼	shot(s)	Freshly squeezed lemon juice
1	shot(s)	Freshly squeezed orange juice
½	shot(s)	Double (heavy) cream

Comment: Creamy, fruity, alcoholic custard. Different!

CASANOVA

●●●●○

Glass: Martini
Garnish: Crumble Cadbury's Flake bar over drink
Method: SHAKE all ingredients with ice and fine strain into chilled glass.

1½	shot(s)	Bourbon whiskey
¾	shot(s)	Blandy's Alvada madeira
¾	shot(s)	Kahlúa coffee liqueur
¾	shot(s)	Double (heavy) cream
¾	shot(s)	Milk
⅛	shot(s)	Sugar syrup (2 sugar to 1 water)

Comment: Rich, medium-sweet and creamy with a mocha coffee finish.

CASCADE MARTINI UPDATED

●●●◐○

Glass: Martini
Garnish: Raspberries on stick
Method: SHAKE all ingredients with ice and fine strain into chilled glass.

8	fresh	Raspberries
2	shot(s)	Ketel One vodka
1	shot(s)	Cranberry juice
¾	shot(s)	Freshly squeezed lemon juice
¼	shot(s)	Chambord black raspberry liqueur
¼	shot(s)	Vanilla sugar syrup

Comment: Rich raspberry with hints of citrus and vanilla.

CASINO

●●●●○

Glass: Martini
Garnish: Maraschino cherry
Method: SHAKE all ingredients with ice and fine strain into chilled glass.

2½	shot(s)	Plymouth gin
½	shot(s)	Luxardo maraschino liqueur
½	shot(s)	Freshly squeezed lemon juice
½	shot(s)	Chilled mineral water (omit if wet ice)
3	dashes	Fee Brothers orange bitters

Variant: Bee's Knees, Blue Moon
Comment: Basically an Aviation dried with orange bitters.

CASSINI UPDATED 🔑

●●●●○

Glass: Martini
Garnish: Three blackberries
Method: SHAKE all ingredients with ice and fine strain into chilled glass.

2	shot(s)	Ketel One vodka
1½	shot(s)	Cranberry juice
¼	shot(s)	Giffard Cassis (or Chambord)

Origin: Created in 1998 by yours truly.
Comment: A simple but pleasant berry drink.

CASTRO

●●●●◐○

Glass: Martini
Garnish: Lime wedge on rim
Method: SHAKE all ingredients with ice and fine strain into chilled glass.

1½	shot(s)	Aged rum
¾	shot(s)	Boulard Grand Solage Calvados
¼	shot(s)	Freshly squeezed orange juice
½	shot(s)	Freshly squeezed lime juice
¼	shot(s)	Rose's lime cordial
¼	shot(s)	Sugar syrup (2 sugar to 1 water)

Origin: Named after the Cuban.
Comment: Tangy and fruity.

CAUSEWAY

●●●●◐○

Glass: Collins
Method: SHAKE first five ingredients with ice and strain into ice-filled glass, **TOP** with ginger ale.

2	shot(s)	Black Bush Irish whiskey
1	shot(s)	Drambuie liqueur
4	dashes	Angostura aromatic bitters
2	dashes	Fee Brothers orange bitters
¼	shot(s)	Freshly squeezed lemon juice
Top up with		Ginger ale

Origin: Created by David Myers at Titanic, London, England.
Comment: Dry aromatic long whiskey drink.

CELERY MARTINI

●●●●○

Glass: Martini
Garnish: Salt rim & celery
Method: SHAKE all ingredients with ice and fine strain into chilled glass.

1¾	shot(s)	Freshly extracted celery juice
2	shot(s)	Ketel One vodka
¼	shot(s)	Sugar syrup (2 sugar to 1 water)

Origin: Created by Andreas Tsanos at Momos, London, England in 2001.
Comment: I only usually like celery when loaded with blue cheese - but I love this Martini.

CHAMPAGNE COCKTAILS

In most bars cocktails and champagne are the two most expensive things available by the glass so a champagne cocktail makes a very bling bar call. Yet put all thoughts of Donald Trump aside - champagne cocktails don't have to be a crying waste of decent bubbly and can even be superb.

Champagne cocktails have been around for as long as the cocktail: one of the earliest references appears in Mark Twain's 1869 novel, Innocents Abroad. One of the earliest champagne cocktails is also by far the best known: 'The Champagne Cocktail', which is referenced in Jerry Thomas's 1862 book 'How To Mix Drinks'. Sadly this is a very overrated drink.

Be aware that sugar makes champagne fizz profusely. Try sprinkling a few grains over a glass of champagne and watch the effect. Champagne cocktails often include a sweet liqueur or even sugar, so when adding the champagne pour even more slowly and carefully than you would normally. Also consider pouring down the handle of a barspoon.

For a complete list of champagne cocktails, please see 'Champagne' in the ingredients index.

A
B
C
D
E
F
G
H
I
J
K
L
M
N
O
P
Q
R
S
T
U
V
W
X
Y
Z

CELTIC MARGARITA ●●●●○

Glass: Coupette
Garnish: Salt rim & lemon wedge
Method: SHAKE all ingredients with ice and fine strain into chilled glass.

2	shot(s)	Scotch whisky
1	shot(s)	Cointreau triple sec
1	shot(s)	Freshly squeezed lemon juice

Origin: Discovered in 2004 at Milk & Honey, London, England.
Comment: A Scotch Margarita – try it, it works.

CHAM 69 #1 ●●●●○

Glass: Sling
Garnish: Berries
Method: SHAKE first four ingredients with ice and strain into ice-filled glass. TOP with 7-Up, stir and serve with straws.

2	shot(s)	Ketel One vodka
3/4	shot(s)	Chambord black raspberry liqueur
3/4	shot(s)	Luxardo Amaretto di Saschira
3/4	shot(s)	Freshly squeezed lime juice
Top up with		7-Up (or lemonade)

Origin: I created this drink back in 1998 and I've noticed it on cocktail menus across Europe. I was something of a beginner with a sweet tooth at the time but this new formulation is better balanced.
Comment: Medium sweet, long and fruity.

CHAM 69 #2 ●●●●○

Glass: Sling
Garnish: Berries
Method: SHAKE first four ingredients with ice and strain into ice-filled glass. TOP with champagne, stir and serve with straws.

1	shot(s)	Ketel One vodka
1/2	shot(s)	Chambord black raspberry liqueur
1/2	shot(s)	Luxardo Amaretto di Saschira
1/4	shot(s)	Freshly squeezed lime juice
Top up with		Brut champagne

Origin: While re-examining my old creation in 2005 I decided champagne would be more appropriate considering the name.
Comment: Long, fruity and refreshing.

CHAM CHAM ●●●●○

Glass: Flute
Garnish: Berries
Method: POUR liqueur into chilled glass and top with champagne.

1/2	shot(s)	Chambord black raspberry liqueur
Top up with		Brut champagne

Comment: A pleasing blend of fruit and champagne to rival the Kir Royale.

CHAMPAGNE COCKTAIL ●●●○○

Glass: Flute
Garnish: Lemon peel twist
Method: Rub sugar cube with lemon peel, coat with bitters and drop into glass. Cover soaked cube with cognac, then POUR champagne.

1	cube	Brown sugar
3	dashes	Angostura aromatic bitters
1	shot(s)	Rémy Martin cognac
Top up with		Brut champagne

Origin: First recorded in Jerry Thomas's 1862 book 'How To Mix Drinks', or 'The Bon Vivant's Companion', where he almost certainly mistakenly specifies this as a shaken drink. That would be explosive. It's thought the drink found popularity after a bartender named John Dougherty won an 1899 New York cocktail competition with a similar drink named Business Brace.
Comment: An over hyped classic cocktail that gets sweeter as you reach the dissolving cube at the bottom.

CHAMPAGNE CUP ●●●●○

Glass: Flute
Garnish: Maraschino cherry
Method: STIR first three ingredients with ice and strain into chilled glass. TOP with champagne and gently stir.

3/4	shot(s)	Rémy Martin cognac
1/2	shot(s)	Grand Marnier
1/4	shot(s)	Maraschino syrup (from cherry jar)
Top up with		Brut champagne

Comment: Sweet maraschino helps balance this dry drink.

CHAMPAGNE DAISY ●●●○○

Glass: Flute
Garnish: Pomegranate wedge
Method: SHAKE first three ingredients with ice and fine strain into chilled glass, TOP with champagne.

1	shot(s)	Yellow Chartreuse
1/8	shot(s)	Pomegranate (grenadine) syrup
1	shot(s)	Freshly squeezed lemon juice
Top up with		Brut champagne

Comment: You'll need to like Chartreuse and citrus champagne to appreciate this drink.

DRINKS ARE GRADED AS FOLLOWS:

● DISGUSTING ●○ PRETTY AWFUL ●● BEST AVOIDED
●●○ DISAPPOINTING ●●● ACCEPTABLE ●●●○ GOOD
●●●● RECOMMENDED ●●●●○ HIGHLY RECOMMENDED
●●●●● OUTSTANDING / EXCEPTIONAL

●●●●◐

CHAMPS-ELYSÉES

Glass: Martini
Garnish: Lemon zest twist
Method: SHAKE all ingredients with ice and fine strain into chilled glass.

1 3/4	shot(s)	**Rémy Martin cognac**
1/4	shot(s)	**Green Chartreuse**
1/2	shot(s)	**Freshly squeezed lemon juice**
1/2	shot(s)	**Sugar syrup (2 sugar to 1 water)**
3	dashes	**Angostura aromatic bitters**
3/4	shot(s)	**Chilled mineral water (omit if wet ice)**
1/2	fresh	**Egg white (optional)**

Origin: Named after the touristy Parisian boulevard where (coincidentally) Rémy Cointreau have their offices.
Comment: A great after dinner drink for lovers of cognac and Chartreuse.

●●●●◐

CHANCELLOR NEW

Glass: Martini
Garnish: Orange zest twist
Method: SHAKE all ingredients with ice and fine strain into chilled glass.

2	shot(s)	**Scotch whisky**
1	shot(s)	**Tawny port**
1/2	shot(s)	**Dry vermouth**
1/4	shot(s)	**Sugar syrup (2 sugar to 1 water)**
2	dashes	**Fee Brothers orange bitters**

Origin: A classic of unknown origins.
Comment: Complex and sophisticated Scotch with fruity notes.

●●●●○

CHARENTE COLLINS NEW

Glass: Collins
Garnish: Mint sprig & orange zest twist
Method: Lightly MUDDLE mint in base of shaker (just to bruise). Add other ingredients, SHAKE with ice and strain into glass filled with crushed ice. Serve with straws.

5	fresh	**Mint leaves**
2	shot(s)	**Grand Marnier liqueur**
1	shot(s)	**Freshly squeezed lemon juice**
1	shot(s)	**St Germain elderflower liqueur**

Origin: Created in 2005 by Kieran Bailey, The Light Bar, London, England.
Comment: Refreshing orange and lemon with a hint of elderflower.

DRINKS ARE GRADED AS FOLLOWS:

● DISGUSTING ●◐ PRETTY AWFUL ●● BEST AVOIDED
●●◐ DISAPPOINTING ●●● ACCEPTABLE ●●●◐ GOOD
●●●● RECOMMENDED ●●●●◐ HIGHLY RECOMMENDED
●●●●● OUTSTANDING / EXCEPTIONAL

●●●●◐

CHARLES DAIQUIRI

Glass: Martini
Garnish: Lime wedge on rim
Method: SHAKE all ingredients with ice and fine strain into chilled glass.

1	shot(s)	**Light white rum**
1	shot(s)	**Pusser's navy rum**
1/2	shot(s)	**Cointreau triple sec**
1/2	shot(s)	**Freshly squeezed lime juice**
1/8	shot(s)	**Sugar syrup (2 sugar to 1 water)**
1/2	shot(s)	**Chilled mineral water (omit if wet ice)**

Comment: Navy rum and triple sec add special interest to this Daiquiri.

●●●◐○

CHARLIE CHAPLIN

Glass: Old-fashioned
Garnish: Lemon zest twist
Method: SHAKE all ingredients with ice and strain into ice-filled glass.

1 1/2	shot(s)	**Plymouth sloe gin liqueur**
1 1/2	shot(s)	**Giffard apricot brandy du Roussillon**
1	shot(s)	**Freshly squeezed lemon juice**

Comment: This fruity number was originally served 'up' but is better over ice.

●●●●○

CHARLIE LYCHEE'TINI

Glass: Martini
Garnish: Whole lychee from tin in drink
Method: STIR all ingredients with ice and strain into chilled glass.

1	shot(s)	**Tio Pepe fino sherry**
1	shot(s)	**Pisco**
1	shot(s)	**Sake**
1	shot(s)	**Lychee syrup from tinned fruit**
1/8	shot(s)	**Elderflower cordial**

Origin: I created this drink in 2002 and named it for Charlie Rouse, who loves sherry.
Comment: Subtle with an interesting salty edge, this tastes almost like a wine.

●●●●○

CHAS

Glass: Martini
Garnish: Orange zest twist
Method: SHAKE all ingredients with ice and fine strain into chilled glass.

1 3/4	shot(s)	**Bourbon whiskey**
1/2	shot(s)	**Bénédictine D.O.M. liqueur**
1/2	shot(s)	**Luxardo Amaretto di Saschira**
1/2	shot(s)	**Cointreau triple sec**
1/2	shot(s)	**Grand Marnier**

Origin: Created in 2003 by Murray Stenson at Zig Zag Café, Seattle, USA.
Comment: A wonderfully tangy cocktail with great bourbon personality and hints of almond and orange.

CHATHAM HOTEL SPECIAL NEW

Glass: Martini
Garnish: Nutmeg dust
Method: SHAKE all ingredients with ice and fine strain into chilled glass.

2	shot(s)	Rémy Martin cognac
3/4	shot(s)	Tawny port
1/2	shot(s)	Giffard brown crème de cacao
1/4	shot(s)	Double (heavy) cream
1/4	shot(s)	Milk

Origin: This mid-1900s classic from New York's Chatham Hotel was resurrected by Ted Haigh in his 2004 book 'Vintage Spirits & Forgotten Cocktails'.
Comment: I've slightly changed the proportions and replaced the original lemon zest garnish with a little extra spice.

CHEEKY MONKEY UPDATED

Glass: Martini
Garnish: Orange zest twist
Method: SHAKE all ingredients with ice and fine strain into chilled glass.

1	shot(s)	Ketel One Citroen vodka
1	shot(s)	Yellow Chartreuse
1 1/2	shot(s)	Freshly squeezed orange juice
1/4	shot(s)	Sugar syrup (2 sugar to 1 water)
3	dashes	Fee Brothers orange bitters

Origin: Adapted from a recipe created by Tony Conigliaro in 2001 at Isola, Knightsbridge, London, England.
Comment: Fire yellow in colour, this drink features the distinctive flavour of Chartreuse with a citrus supporting cast.

CHELSEA SIDECAR

Glass: Martini
Garnish: Lemon zest twist
Method: SHAKE all ingredients with ice and fine strain into chilled glass.

1 1/2	shot(s)	Plymouth gin
1	shot(s)	Cointreau triple sec
1	shot(s)	Freshly squeezed lemon juice
1/4	shot(s)	Sugar syrup (2 sugar to 1 water)

Comment: Gin replaces cognac in this variation on the classic Sidecar.

CHERRUTE

Glass: Martini
Garnish: Maraschino cherry in drink
Method: SHAKE all ingredients with ice and fine strain into chilled glass.

2	shot(s)	Ketel One vodka
3/4	shot(s)	Cherry (brandy) liqueur
1 1/2	shot(s)	Freshly squeezed golden grapefruit juice

Comment: Sweet cherry brandy balanced by the fruity acidity of grapefruit, laced with vodka.

CHERRY ALEXANDER

Glass: Martini
Garnish: Maraschino cherry
Method: SHAKE all ingredients with ice and fine strain into chilled glass.

1	shot(s)	Vanilla flavoured vodka
1/2	shot(s)	Cherry (brandy) liqueur
1/2	shot(s)	Giffard White crème de cacao
1	shot(s)	Double (heavy) cream
1	shot(s)	Milk

Origin: Created by Wayne Collins for Maxxium UK.
Comment: A fruity twist on the creamy classic.

CHERRY & HAZELNUT DAIQUIRI

Glass: Martini
Garnish: Cherry on rim
Method: SHAKE all ingredients with ice and fine strain into chilled glass.

2	shot(s)	Light white rum
3/4	shot(s)	Luxardo maraschino liqueur
1 1/2	shot(s)	Hazelnut (crème de noisette) liqueur
1/2	shot(s)	Freshly squeezed lime juice
1/2	shot(s)	Chilled mineral water

Origin: Adam Wyartt and I created this in 2003.
Comment: Nutty and surprisingly tangy.

CHERRY BLOSSOM

Glass: Martini
Garnish: Maraschino cherry in drink
Method: SHAKE all ingredients with ice and fine strain into chilled glass.

3/4	shot(s)	Cherry (brandy) liqueur
3/4	shot(s)	Kirsch eau de vie
1/2	shot(s)	Cointreau triple sec
1 1/4	shot(s)	Freshly squeezed lemon juice
1/4	shot(s)	Maraschino syrup (from cherry jar)

Comment: Bundles of flavour – tangy and moreish.

CHERRY DAIQUIRI

Glass: Martini
Garnish: Cherry on rim
Method: MUDDLE cherries in base of shaker. Add other ingredients, SHAKE with ice and fine strain into chilled glass.

8	fresh	Stoned cherries
2	shot(s)	Vanilla-infused rum
1	shot(s)	Cherry (brandy) liqueur
1/8	shot(s)	Maraschino syrup (from cherry jar)
1/2	shot(s)	Freshly squeezed lime juice
1/2	shot(s)	Chilled mineral water

Origin: Created in 2003 by yours truly.
Comment: Cherry sweetness paired with Daiquiri sharpness.

●●●●○

CHERRY MARTINI UPDATED

Glass: Martini
Garnish: Lemon zest twist
Method: SHAKE all ingredients with ice and fine strain into chilled glass.

2	shot(s)	Ketel One Citroen vodka
3/4	shot(s)	Cherry brandy liqueur
1/2	shot(s)	Dry vermouth
1/2	shot(s)	Chilled mineral water (omit if wet ice)

Origin: Created in 2005 by yours truly.
Comment: A hint of cherry is balanced by citrus freshness, and dried and deepened by vermouth.

●●●●○

CHERRY MASH SOUR

Glass: Old-fashioned
Garnish: Lemon twist & cherry
Method: SHAKE all ingredients with ice and strain into ice-filled glass.

2	shot(s)	Jack Daniel's Tennessee whiskey
1/2	shot(s)	Cherry (brandy) liqueur
3/4	shot(s)	Freshly squeezed lemon juice
1/2	shot(s)	Sugar syrup (2 sugar to 1 water)

Origin: Created by Dale DeGroff when Beverage Manager at the Rainbow Room Promenade Bar, New York City, USA.
Comment: The rich flavour of Tennessee whiskey soured with lemon and sweetened with cherry liqueur.

●●●●●

CHE'S REVOLUTION

Glass: Martini
Garnish: Pineapple wedge on rim
Method: MUDDLE mint with rum in base of shaker. Add other ingredients, SHAKE with ice and fine strain into chilled glass.

4	fresh	Mint leaves
2	shot(s)	Light white rum
1/4	shot(s)	Maple syrup
2	shot(s)	Pressed pineapple juice

Origin: Created in 2003 by Ben Reed for the launch party of MJU Bar @ Millennium Hotel, London, England.
Comment: Complex and smooth with hints of maple syrup and mint amongst the pineapple and rum.

●●●●○○

CHICLET DAIQUIRI

Glass: Martini
Garnish: Banana slice on rim
Method: BLEND ingredients with a 12oz scoop of crushed ice and serve in large chilled glass.

2 1/2	shot(s)	Light white rum
1/2	shot(s)	Giffard crème de banane du Brésil
1/8	shot(s)	Giffard white crème de Menthe Pastille
1/2	shot(s)	Freshly squeezed lime juice
1/4	shot(s)	Sugar syrup (2 sugar to 1 water)

Origin: Often found on Cuban bar menus, this was created at La Floridita, Havana.
Comment: A wonderfully refreshing drink on a summer's day with surprisingly subtle flavours.

●●●●○○

CHIHUAHUA MAGARITA

Glass: Martini
Method: SHAKE all ingredients with ice and fine strain into chilled glass.

2	shot(s)	Partida tequila
2	shot(s)	Freshly squeezed golden grapefruit juice
1/8	shot(s)	Agave syrup (from health food shop)
3	dashes	Angostura aromatic bitters

Comment: Tequila and grapefruit juice pepped up with Angostura.

●●●○○

CHILL-OUT MARTINI

Glass: Martini
Garnish: Pineapple wedge on rim
Method: SHAKE all ingredients with ice and fine strain into chilled glass.

1	shot(s)	Orange flavoured vodka
1	shot(s)	Malibu coconut rum
1	shot(s)	Baileys Irish cream liqueur
1	shot(s)	Freshly squeezed orange juice

Comment: Smooth, creamy sweet orange and surprisingly strong.

●●●●○

CHIMAYO UPDATED

Glass: Martini
Garnish: Float apple slice
Method: SHAKE all ingredients with ice and fine strain into chilled glass.

2	shot(s)	Partida tequila
1/2	shot(s)	Giffard Cassis (or Chambord)
3/4	shot(s)	Pressed apple juice
1/4	shot(s)	Freshly squeezed lemon juice

Origin: Named after El Potrero de Chimayó in northern New Mexico, USA.
Comment: Apple juice and cassis take the sting off tequila.

A
B
C
D
E
F
G
H
I
J
K
L
M
N
O
P
Q
R
S
T
U
V
W
X
Y
Z

CHIN CHIN UPDATED ⊶

Glass: Flute
Method: STIR honey with Scotch in base of shaker. Add apple juice, **SHAKE** with ice and strain into chilled glass**TOP** with champagne.

1	spoon	Runny honey
2	shot(s)	Scotch whisky
1	shot(s)	Pressed apple juice
Top up with		Brut champagne

Origin: Created by Tony Conigliaro at Isola, Knightsbridge, London, England.
Comment: Golden honey in colour and also in flavour. An unusual and great tasting Champagne cocktail.

CHINA BEACH

Glass: Martini
Garnish: Ginger slice on rim
Method: SHAKE all ingredients with ice and fine strain into chilled glass.

1	shot(s)	Ketel One vodka
1	shot(s)	Giffard Ginger of the Indies
2	shot(s)	Cranberry juice

Comment: Dry and lightly spiced.

CHINA BLUE

Glass: Collins
Garnish: Orange slice in drink
Method: SHAKE all ingredients with ice and strain into ice-filled glass.

1	shot(s)	Blue curaçao liqueur
1	shot(s)	Soho lychee liqueur
4	shot(s)	Freshly squeezed grapefruit juice

Origin: Emerged in Japan in the late 1990s and still popular along the Pacific Rim.
Comment: Looks sweet, but due to a generous splash of grapefruit is actually balanced and refreshing.

CHINA BLUE MARTINI

Glass: Martini
Garnish: Peeled lychee in drink
Method: SHAKE all ingredients with ice and fine strain into chilled glass.

1	shot(s)	Blue curaçao liqueur
1	shot(s)	Soho lychee liqueur
2	shot(s)	Freshly squeezed grapefruit juice
1/4	shot(s)	Freshly squeezed lemon juice

Origin: An almost inevitable short adaptation of the original long drink above.
Comment: This simple cocktail with its turquoise colour tastes more adult and interesting than its colour might suggest.

CHINA MARTINI

Glass: Martini
Garnish: Orange zest twist & lychee in glass
Method: STIR all ingredients with ice and fine strain into chilled glass.

1½	shot(s)	Plymouth gin
1/2	shot(s)	Soho lychee liqueur
1/4	shot(s)	Cointreau triple sec
1/2	shot(s)	Dry vermouth

Origin: Created in 2004 by Wayne Collins for Maxxium UK.
Comment: A complex, not too sweet lychee Martini.

CHINESE COSMOPOLITAN

Glass: Martini
Garnish: Flamed orange zest twist
Method: SHAKE all ingredients with ice and fine strain into chilled glass.

2	shot(s)	Krupnik honey liqueur
3/4	shot(s)	Soho lychee liqueur
1/2	shot(s)	Freshly squeezed lime juice
1	shot(s)	Cranberry juice

Origin: Discovered in 2003 at Raoul's Bar, Oxford, England.
Comment: Oriental in name and style – perhaps a tad sweeter than your standard Cosmo.

CHINESE WHISPER MARTINI

Glass: Martini
Garnish: Lemon zest twist
Method: MUDDLE ginger in base of shaker. Add other ingredients, **SHAKE** with ice and fine strain into chilled glass.

2	slices	Fresh root ginger (thumbnail sized)
2	shot(s)	Ketel One Citroen vodka
1	shot(s)	Soho lychee liqueur
1/2	shot(s)	Freshly squeezed lime juice
1/4	shot(s)	Ginger syrup

Origin: Adapted from a recipe discovered in 2003 at Oxo Tower Bar, London, England.
Comment: There's more than a whisper of ginger in this spicy Martini.

CHOC & NUT MARTINI

Glass: Martini
Garnish: Wipe rim with orange and dust with cocoa powder.
Method: SHAKE all ingredients with ice and fine strain into chilled glass.

2	shot(s)	Ketel One vodka
1	shot(s)	Hazelnut (crème de noisette) liqueur
1	shot(s)	Giffard White crème de cacao
1/4	shot(s)	Chilled mineral water

Comment: Surprise, surprise - it's sweet chocolate and hazelnut.

CHOCOLARITA NEW

●●●●●○

Glass: Coupette
Garnish: Chocolate rim
Method: SHAKE all ingredients with ice and fine strain into chilled glass.

2	shot(s)	Partida tequila
1/4	shot(s)	Giffard brown crème de cacao
1/4	shot(s)	Kahlúa liqueur
1	shot(s)	Freshly squeezed lime juice
1/4	shot(s)	Sugar syrup (2 sugar to 1 water)

Origin: Adapted from a recipe discovered in 2005 at Agave, Hong Kong, China.
Comment: As the name suggests – a Margarita with chocolate and coffee.

CHOCOLATE & CRANBERRY MARTINI

●●●●○○

UDATED #6.1

Glass: Martini
Garnish: Wipe rim with cacao liqueur & dust with cocoa powder
Method: SHAKE all ingredients with ice and fine strain into chilled, rimmed glass.

2	shot(s)	Ketel One vanilla infused vodka
1/2	shot(s)	Giffard white crème de cacao
1/2	shot(s)	Dry vermouth
1	shot(s)	Cranberry juice

Origin: Created in 2003 by yours truly.
Comment: The chocolate rim sounds naff but makes this drink. Surprisingly dry.

CHOCOLATE BISCUIT

●●●●○○

Glass: Martini
Garnish: Bourbon cream biscuit on rim
Method: SHAKE all ingredients with ice and fine strain into chilled glass.

2	shot(s)	Rémy Martin cognac
1	shot(s)	Kahlúa coffee liqueur
1	shot(s)	Giffard brown crème de cacao

Origin: Created in 1999 by Gillian Stanfield at The Atlantic Bar & Grill, London, England.
Comment: Sweet and rich, with coffee and chocolate – one to chase dessert.

CHOCOLATE MARTINI

●●●●○

Glass: Martini
Garnish: Wipe rim with cacao liqueur & dust with cocoa powder
Method: SHAKE all ingredients with ice and fine strain into chilled glass.

2	shot(s)	Ketel One vodka
1	shot(s)	Giffard White crème de cacao
1	shot(s)	Dry vermouth

Comment: Vodka and chocolate made more interesting with a hint of vermouth.

CHOCOLATE MINT MARTINI

●●●●○

Glass: Martini
Garnish: Wipe rim with cacao liqueur & dust with cocoa powder
Method: STIR all ingredients with ice and strain into chilled glass.

2	shot(s)	Ketel One vodka
1/2	shot(s)	Giffard white crème de Menthe Pastille
1/2	shot(s)	Giffard White crème de cacao
1/2	shot(s)	Dry vermouth

Comment: An after dinner sweety that tastes of chocolate mints.

CHOCOLATE PUFF

●●●●○

Glass: Old-fashioned
Garnish: Crumbled Cadbury's Flake bar
Method: SHAKE all ingredients with ice and fine strain into chilled glass.

1	shot(s)	Mount Gay Eclipse golden rum
1	shot(s)	Giffard brown crème de cacao
6	spoons	Natural yoghurt
2	zests	Fresh orange
1/4	shot(s)	Sugar syrup (2 sugar to 1 water)

Origin: Created by Wayne Collins for Maxxium UK.
Comment: Smooth as you like. The orange is surprisingly evident.

CHOCOLATE SAZERAC

●●●●○

Glass: Old-fashioned
Garnish: Lemon twist (discarded) & apple wedge
Method: Fill glass with ice, POUR in absinthe, top up with water and leave the mixture to stand in the glass. Separately SHAKE bourbon, cacao, sugar and bitters with ice. Finally discard contents of glass (absinthe, water and ice) and strain contents of shaker into empty absinthe-coated glass.

1/2	shot(s)	La Fée Parisian (68%) absinthe
2	shot(s)	Bourbon whiskey
1/2	shot(s)	Giffard White crème de cacao
1/4	shot(s)	Sugar syrup (2 sugar to 1 water)
2	dashes	Peychaud's aromatic bitters

Origin: Created in 2005 by Tonin Kacaj at Maze, London, England.
Comment: This twist on the classic Sazerac pairs absinthe, bourbon and chocolate to great effect.

CHOCOLATE SIDECAR

●●●●○

Glass: Martini
Garnish: Wipe rim with cacao liqueur & dust with cocoa powder
Method: SHAKE all ingredients with ice and fine strain into chilled glass.

1	shot(s)	Rémy Martin cognac
1	shot(s)	Giffard brown crème de cacao
1	shot(s)	Ruby port
1	shot(s)	Freshly squeezed lime juice
1/2	shot(s)	Sugar syrup (2 sugar to 1 water)

Origin: Created in 2005 by Wayne Collins for Maxxium UK.

CICADA COCKTAIL

●●●●○○

Glass: Martini
Garnish: Dust with freshly grated nutmeg
Method: SHAKE all ingredients with ice and fine strain into chilled glass.

2	shot(s)	Jack Daniel's Tennessee whiskey
1	shot(s)	Luxardo Amaretto di Saschira
1/2	shot(s)	Double (heavy) cream
3/4	shot(s)	Sugar syrup (2 sugar to 1 water)

Origin: Those familiar with the Grasshopper cocktail (named for its green colour) will understand why this one is called the Cicada (they're a bit browner).
Comment: Smoothed whisky with more than a hint of almond.

CINNAMON DAIQUIRI

●●●●○○

Glass: Martini
Garnish: Dust with cinnamon powder
Method: SHAKE all ingredients with ice and fine strain into chilled glass.

2	shot(s)	Light white rum
1/2	shot(s)	Goldschläger cinnamon schnapps
1/2	shot(s)	Freshly squeezed lime juice

Origin: Created in 1999 by Porik at Che, London, England.
Comment: A subtle spicy cinnamon taste with tangy length.

CIDER APPLE COOLER

●●●●○

Glass: Collins
Method: SHAKE all ingredients with ice and strain into ice-filled glass.

2	shot(s)	Boulard Grand Solage Calvados
1	shot(s)	Apple schnapps liqueur
4 1/2	shot(s)	Pressed apple juice

Comment: Not unlike the taste of strong dry cider.

CITRUS CAIPIROVSKA

●●●●●○

Glass: Old-fashioned
Method: MUDDLE lemon in base of glass. Add other ingredients and fill glass with crushed ice. CHURN drink with bar spoon and serve with short straws.

3/4	fresh	Lemon cut into wedges
2	shot(s)	Ketel One Citroen vodka
3/4	shot(s)	Sugar syrup (2 sugar to 1 water)

Comment: Superbly refreshing balance of sweet and citrus sourness.

CIDER APPLE MARTINI

●●●●○

Glass: Martini
Garnish: Apple wedge
Method: SHAKE all ingredients with ice and fine strain into chilled glass.

1 1/2	shot(s)	Boulard Grand Solage Calvados
3/4	shot(s)	Apple schnapps liqueur
3/4	shot(s)	Freshly squeezed lemon juice
1	shot(s)	Pressed apple juice
1/4	shot(s)	Sugar syrup (2 sugar to 1 water)

Origin: Created in 1998 by Jamie Terrell at Lab, London, England.
Comment: As the name suggests, rich cider flavours with a sharp finish.

CITRUS MARTINI

●●●●○

Glass: Martini
Garnish: Orange zest twist
Method: SHAKE all ingredients with ice and fine strain into chilled glass.

1 1/2	shot(s)	Ketel One Citroen vodka
1	shot(s)	Freshly squeezed lemon juice
1/4	shot(s)	Sugar syrup (2 sugar to 1 water)
1/4	shot(s)	Cointreau triple sec
3	dashes	Fee Brothers orange bitters

AKA: Lemon Martini
Origin: Created by Dick Bradsell at Fred's, London, England, in the late 80s.
Comment: Orange undertones add citrus depth to the lemon explosion.

CINDERELLA 🔑

●●○○○

Glass: Collins
Garnish: Lemon wheel
Method: SHAKE first five ingredients with ice and strain into ice-filled glass. TOP with soda water.

2	shot(s)	Freshly squeezed orange juice
1 1/2	shot(s)	Pressed pineapple juice
3/4	shot(s)	Freshly squeezed lemon juice
1/8	shot(s)	Pomegranate (grenadine) syrup
3	dashes	Angostura aromatic bitters
Top up with		Soda water (club soda)

Comment: Long, fresh and fruity.

CLARET COBBLER

●●●●○

Glass: Goblet
Garnish: Mint sprig
Method: SHAKE all ingredients with ice and fine strain into glass filled with crushed ice. Serve with straws.

1 1/2	shot(s)	Rémy Martin cognac
1	shot(s)	Grand Marnier
2 1/2	shot(s)	Red wine

Origin: My version of an old classic.
Comment: Fortified and slightly sweetened wine cooled and lengthened by ice.

CLARIDGE COCKTAIL UPDATED 🔑

●●●●○

Glass: Martini
Garnish: Lemon zest twist
Method: SHAKE all ingredients with ice and fine strain into chilled glass.

1¹/₂	shot(s)	Plymouth gin
1¹/₂	shot(s)	Dry vermouth
¹/₂	shot(s)	Cointreau triple sec
¹/₂	shot(s)	Giffard apricot brandy du Roussillon

Origin: Adapted from Harry Craddock's 1930 'The Savoy Cocktail Book'.
Comment: Gin for strength, vermouth for dryness and liqueur to sweeten – an interesting combination.

CLASSIC COCKTAIL UPDATED

●●●●●

Glass: Martini
Garnish: Lemon zest twist (optional sugar rim)
Method: SHAKE all ingredients with ice and fine strain into chilled glass.

2	shot(s)	Rémy Martin cognac
¹/₂	shot(s)	Freshly squeezed lemon juice
¹/₂	shot(s)	Grand Marnier liqueur
¹/₂	shot(s)	Luxardo maraschino liqueur
¹/₂	shot(s)	Chilled mineral water (omit if wet ice)

Origin: Adapted from Harry Craddock's 1930 'The Savoy Cocktail Book'.
Comment: Reminiscent of a Sidecar with maraschino.

CLEMENTINE

●●●●○○

Glass: Shot
Garnish: Sugar coated orange wedge
Method: Refrigerate ingredients then LAYER in chilled glass by carefully pouring in the following order. Instruct drinker to down in one and bite into the wedge.

¹/₂	shot(s)	Luxardo limoncello liqueur
¹/₂	shot(s)	Mandarine Napoléon liqueur

Comment: Short, sweet and very fruity.

CLIPPER COCKTAIL 🔑

●●●○○

Glass: Martini
Garnish: Lemon peel knot
Method: SHAKE all ingredients and fine strain into glass filled with crushed ice.

2	shot(s)	Light white rum
2	shot(s)	Dry vermouth
¹/₂	shot(s)	Pomegranate (grenadine) syrup

Origin: Peggy Guggenheim's biography mentions that this cocktail was served during the 1940s on the Boeing flying boats known as Clippers.
Comment: Light, easy drinking and very refreshing.

CLOCKWORK ORANGE UPDATED 🔑

●●●○○

Glass: Collins
Garnish: Orange wheel in glass
Method: SHAKE all ingredients with ice and strain into ice-filled glass.

1¹/₂	shot(s)	Rémy Martin cognac
1¹/₂	shot(s)	Grand Marnier liqueur
3	shot(s)	Freshly squeezed orange juice

Comment: Neither as memorable nor as controversial as the film but a pleasant orange drink all the same.

CLOVER LEAF COCKTAIL #1 NEW 🔑
(CLASSIC FORMULA)

●●●●○

Glass: Martini
Garnish: Float mint leaf
Method: SHAKE all ingredients with ice and fine strain into chilled glass.

2	shot(s)	Plymouth gin
³/₄	shot(s)	Freshly squeezed lemon juice
³/₄	shot(s)	Pomegranate (grenadine) syrup
¹/₂	fresh	Egg white

Variant: With raspberry syrup in place of pomegranate syrup.
AKA: Without the mint garnish this drink called a 'Clover Club'.
Origin: This classic cocktail is thought to have been created at the Bellevue-Stratford Hotel in Philadelphia.
Comment: Smooth, aromatic, fruity and medium sweet.

HOW TO MAKE SUGAR SYRUP

To make your own sugar syrup, gradually pour **TWO** cups of granulated sugar into a saucepan containing **ONE** cup of hot water. Stir as you pour and carry on stirring and simmering until the sugar is dissolved. Do not let the water even come close to boiling and only simmer for as long as it takes to dissolve the sugar. Allow syrup to cool and pour into an empty bottle. Ideally, you should finely strain your syrup into the bottle to remove any undissolved crystals which could otherwise encourage crystallisation. If kept in a refrigerator this mixture will last for a couple of months.

A B C D E F G H I J K L M N O P Q R S T U V W X Y Z

●●●○○

CLOVER LEAF COCKTAIL #2 UPDATED 🔑
(MODERN FORMULA)

Glass: Martini
Garnish: Clover/mint leaf
Method: MUDDLE raspberries in base of shaker. Add other ingredients, SHAKE with ice and fine strain into chilled glass.

7	fresh	Raspberries
3	fresh	Mint leaves (torn)
2	shot(s)	Plymouth gin
3/4	shot(s)	Freshly squeezed lemon juice
1/2	shot(s)	Pomegranate (grenadine) syrup
1/2	fresh	Egg white

Comment: Carpet scaring red, this fruity adaptation perhaps has a wider appeal than the original Clover Leaf.

●●●●○

CLUB COCKTAIL #1 NEW

Glass: Martini
Garnish: Orange zest twist
Method: STIR all ingredients with ice and strain into chilled glass.

1 1/2	shot(s)	Fino sherry
1 1/2	shot(s)	Tawny port
1	dash	Fee Brothers orange bitters

Origin: In his 1948 'The Fine Art of Mixing Drinks', David A. Embury writes, "Perhaps it would not be too much of an exaggeration to say there are as many Club Cocktails as there are clubs." This example is adapted from the same book.
Comment: Dry and incredibly aromatic. A perfect aperitif.

●●●●○

CLUB COCKTAIL #2 NEW

Glass: Martini
Garnish: Stuffed olive
Method: SHAKE all ingredients with ice and strain into chilled glass.

2	shot(s)	Plymouth gin
1	shot(s)	Sweet vermouth
1/8	shot(s)	Yellow Chartreuse

Origin: Adapted from Harry Craddock's 1930 'The Savoy Cocktail Book'.
Comment: A sweet Martini with a hint of Chartreuse.

FOR MORE INFORMATION SEE OUR

INGREDIENTS
APPENDIX
ON PAGE 272

●●●●○

CLUB COCKTAIL #3 UPDATED

Glass: Martini
Garnish: Maraschino cherry in drink
Method: STIR all ingredients with ice and fine strain into chilled glass.

2	shot(s)	Mount Gay Eclipse golden rum
1/2	shot(s)	Sweet vermouth
1/2	shot(s)	Dry vermouth
1/2	shot(s)	Maraschino syrup (from cherry jar)
3	dashes	Angostura aromatic bitters
3/4	shot(s)	Chilled mineral water (reduce if wet ice)

Origin: Adapted from a drink created in 2002 by Michael Butt at Milk & Honey, London, England.
Comment: An aromatic, spirited, classical cocktail.

●●●●○

COBBLED RASPBERRY MARTINI UPDATED

Glass: Martini
Garnish: Mint leaf/raspberries on stick
Method: MUDDLE raspberries in base of shaker. Add other ingredients, SHAKE with ice and fine strain into chilled glass.

12	fresh	Raspberries
2	shot(s)	Ketel One vodka
1	shot(s)	Red wine
1/4	shot(s)	Sugar syrup (2 sugar to 1 water)

Origin: Created by yours truly in 2004.
Comment: The addition of a splash of wine to a simple Raspberry Martini adds another level of complexity.

●●●●○

COCO CABANA

Glass: Martini
Garnish: Pineapple wedge on rim
Method: SHAKE all ingredients with ice and fine strain into chilled glass.

1 1/2	shot(s)	Malibu coconut rum liqueur
1/2	shot(s)	Midori melon liqueur
2	shot(s)	Pressed pineapple juice
3/4	shot(s)	Double (heavy) cream
3/4	shot(s)	Milk

Comment: A sweet, creamy tropical number for Barry Manilow fans.

●●○○○

COCO NAUT

Glass: Hurricane
Garnish: Pineapple wedge & cherry on rim
Method: BLEND ingredients with 12oz scoop of crushed ice. Pour into glass and serve with straws.

2	shot(s)	Wray & Nephew overproof rum
1 1/2	shot(s)	Coco López cream of coconut
1	shot(s)	Freshly squeezed lime juice

Comment: This snow-white drink is hardly innocent with a double shot of overproof rum masked by the sweet coconut.

COCONUT DAIQUIRI

Glass: Martini
Garnish: Lime wedge
Method: SHAKE all ingredients with ice and fine strain into chilled glass.

2	shot(s)	Light white rum
1	shot(s)	Malibu coconut rum liqueur
1/2	shot(s)	Freshly squeezed lime juice
1/2	shot(s)	Coconut syrup
3/4	shot(s)	Chilled mineral water (omit if wet ice)

Variant: Blend with a 12oz scoop of crushed ice and a tad more coconut syrup.
Comment: That special Daiquiri flavour with a pleasing tropical touch.

COCONUT WATER

Glass: Martini
Method: STIR all ingredients with ice and fine strain into chilled glass.

2 1/4	shot(s)	Malibu coconut rum liqueur
1	shot(s)	Ketel One vodka
1/8	shot(s)	Coconut syrup
1 1/4	shot(s)	Chilled mineral water (reduce if wet ice)

Origin: Created in 2003 by yours truly.
Comment: Have you ever drunk from a fresh coconut in the Caribbean? Well, this is the alcoholic equivalent.

COFFEE BATIDA NEW

Glass: Old-fashioned
Garnish: Float three coffee beans
Method: BLEND all ingredients with crushed ice and serve with straws.

2	shot(s)	Cachaça
1	shot(s)	Espresso coffee
1	shot(s)	Coffee liqueur
1/2	shot(s)	Sugar syrup (2 sugar to 1 water)

Comment: Looks like frozen mud with a frothy head but fortunately this caffeine and cachaça laced cocktail tastes a good deal better than it looks.

COFFEE & VANILLA DAIQUIRI ⚷

Glass: Martini
Garnish: Float three coffee beans
Method: SHAKE all ingredients with ice and fine strain into chilled glass.

2	shot(s)	Vanilla-infused Havana Club rum
1	shot(s)	Kahlúa coffee liqueur
1/2	shot(s)	Freshly squeezed lime juice
1/8	shot(s)	Sugar syrup (2 sugar to 1 water)
3/4	shot(s)	Chilled mineral water (omit if wet ice)

Origin: Created in 2002 by yours truly.
Comment: Coffee, vanilla, sweetness and sourness all in harmony.

COBBLERS

Cobblers emerged in the mid 1800s and circa 1880 the bartender Harry Johnson said of the Sherry Cobbler, "This drink is without doubt the most popular beverage in this country, with ladies as well as with gentlemen. It is a very refreshing drink for old and young."

Cobblers are served with straws in a goblet filled with crushed ice and decorated with fruit and a sprig or two of mint. They are based on spirits and/or wine sweetened with sugar syrup or sweet liqueur. Classically Cobblers contain little or no citrus but modern variations often call for citrus and other fruits to be muddled. Personally I believe it's the lack of citrus that sets Cobblers apart. The best examples of these use the tannin and acidity in the wine to bitter and so balance.

Cobblers are also classically built in the glass. I prefer to shake mine to properly cool and mix them before straining over fresh crushed ice and stirring (see my recipe for the Claret Cobbler). I've also recently taken to calling neo-Martinis which use wine in place of citrus 'Cobbled Martinis' (see Cobbled Raspberry Martini).

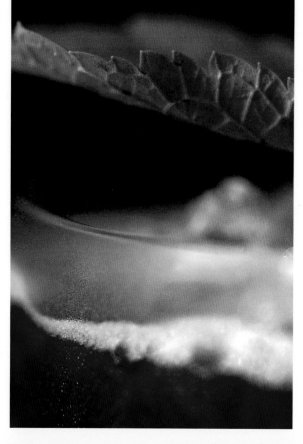

COLLINS

The Collins is thought to have been created by John Collins, a bartender at Limmer's Hotel, Conduit Street, London, circa 1800. However, others claim that the drink was invented around the same time in New Jersey, USA, by a different Mr Collins, an Irish immigrant who named it after his brother. There is also debate as to whether Old Tom gin, London Dry gin or Dutch jenever was the original spirit base. Other spirits have since spawned an entire family of variants.

Collins variations include
Captain Collins (with Canadian whiskey)
Colonel Collins (with bourbon)
Jack Collins (with applejack)
Joe Collins (with vodka)
John Collins (with London Dry gin or jenever)
José or Pepito Collins (with tequila)
Mike Collins (with Irish whiskey)
Pedro Collins (with rum)
Pierre Collins (with cognac/brandy)
Raspberry Collins
Sandy or Jock Collins (with Scotch whisky)
Tom Collins (with Old Tom gin)
Vodka Collins (AKA Joe Collins)

COLA DE MONO

Glass: Martini
Garnish: Dust with cinnamon powder
Method: MUDDLE cinnamon stick and pisco in base of shaker. Add other ingredients, **SHAKE** with ice and fine strain into a chilled glass.

1	inch	Cinnamon stick
2	shot(s)	Pisco
1	shot(s)	Espresso coffee (cold)
1	shot(s)	Kahlúa coffee liqueur

Origin: I based this on a Chilean drink traditionally consumed at Christmas, the name of which literally translates as 'Tail of Monkey'. The original uses milk and sugar instead of coffee liqueur.
Comment: Coffee and cinnamon – a drink to be savoured.

COLD COMFORT

Glass: Old-fashioned
Method: SHAKE all ingredients with ice and strain into ice-filled glass.

2	shot(s)	Wray & Nephew overproof rum
6	spoons	Runny honey
1	shot(s)	Freshly squeezed lime juice

Origin: I discovered this while in Jamaica in 2001.
Comment: Take at the first sign of a cold, and then retreat under your bedcovers. Repeat dose regularly while symptoms persist. Warning – do not consume with other forms of medication.

THE COLD WINTER WARMER SOUR NEW

Glass: Old-fashioned
Garnish: Orange slice & cherry on stick (sail)
Method: STIR honey with vodka in base of shaker until honey dissolves. Add other ingredients, **SHAKE** with ice and strain into ice-filled glass.

1	spoon	Runny honey
1	shot(s)	Ketel One Citroen vodka
1/2	shot(s)	Bénédictine D.O.M. liqueur
1	shot(s)	Freshly squeezed lemon juice
1/2	fresh	Egg white

Origin: Created in 2006 by yours truly.
Comment: Flavours reminiscent of a hot toddy but served in a cold sour.

COLLAR & CUFF UPDATED

Glass: Toddy
Garnish: Orange slice
Method: PLACE bar spoon in glass, add ingredients and STIR.

2	spoons	Runny honey
1	shot(s)	Scotch whisky
1	shot(s)	Giffard Ginger of the Indies
1	shot(s)	Freshly squeezed lemon juice
Top up with		Boiling water

Origin: Created in 2003 by yours truly.
Comment: This blonde drink is warmed with ginger. But do they match?

COLLECTION MARTINI

Glass: Martini
Garnish: Lime wedge
Method: SHAKE all ingredients with ice and fine strain into chilled glass.

3/4	shot(s)	Ketel One vodka
3/4	shot(s)	Ketel One Citroen vodka
3/4	shot(s)	Bénédictine D.O.M liqueur
3/4	shot(s)	Giffard mûre (blackberry)
1/2	shot(s)	Freshly squeezed lime juice

Origin: Originally created by Matthew Randall whilst at The Collection, London, England.
Comment: Honey, spice and vodka enhanced by blackberries, with a very alcoholic edge.

COLLINS

Glass: Collins
Garnish: Orange slice & cherry on stick (sail)
Method: SHAKE first three ingredients with ice and strain into ice-filled glass. **TOP** with soda, stir and serve with straws.

2	shot(s)	Jonge jenever
1	shot(s)	Freshly squeezed lemon juice
1/2	shot(s)	Sugar syrup (2 sugar to 1 water)
Top up with		Soda water (club soda)

Comment: A refreshing combination of spirit, lemon and sugar.

COLONEL COLLINS ⌐

Glass: Collins
Garnish: Orange slice & cherry on stick (sail)
Method: SHAKE first three ingredients with ice and strain into ice-filled glass. **TOP** with soda, stir and serve with straws.

2	shot(s)	Bourbon whiskey
1	shot(s)	Freshly squeezed lemon juice
1/2	shot(s)	Sugar syrup (2 sugar to 1 water)
Top up with		Soda water (club soda)

Origin: Classic Collins variation.
Comment: Sweetened, soured and diluted bourbon.

COLONEL T ⌐

Glass: Sling
Garnish: Pineapple wedge
Method: SHAKE all ingredients with ice and strain into ice-filled glass.

2	shot(s)	Bourbon whiskey
1	shot(s)	Giffard apricot brandy du Roussillon
2 1/2	shot(s)	Pressed pineapple juice

Comment: Mellow and long with pineapple, apricot and bourbon.

COLONEL'S BIG OPU NEW 🗝 ●●●○○

Glass: Collins
Garnish: Orange slice & cherry (sail)
Method: SHAKE first three ingredients with ice and strain into ice-filled glass. **TOP** with champagne and serve with straws.

1	shot(s)	Plymouth gin
1	shot(s)	Cointreau triple sec
1/2	shot(s)	Freshly squeezed lime juice
Top up with		Brut Champagne
1	dash	Fee Brothers orange bitters (optional)

Origin: Adapted from a recipe created by Victor J. Bergeron and taken from his 'Trader Vic's Bartender's Guide' (1972 revised edition), where he writes "This is one of our old drinks. The colonel's big opu: the colonel's big belly."
Comment: A long, fruity yet dry drink charged with champagne.

COLONIAL ROT ●●●○○

Glass: Collins
Garnish: Mint sprig
Method: Lightly MUDDLE mint in base of shaker just enough to bruise. Add next four ingredients, SHAKE with ice and fine strain into ice-filled glass. **TOP** up with half soda and half lemonade.

7	fresh	Mint leaves
1/2	shot(s)	La Fée Parisian (68%) absinthe
1	shot(s)	Ketel One Citroen vodka
1/2	shot(s)	Sugar syrup (2 sugar to 1 water)
1/2	shot(s)	Freshly squeezed lime juice
Top up with		Half soda and half lemonade

Comment: Long and green with more than a touch of the green fairy.

COLORADO BULLDOG 🗝 ●●○○○

Glass: Collins
Method: SHAKE first four ingredients with ice and strain into ice-filled glass. **TOP** with cola.

1 1/2	shot(s)	Ketel One vodka
1	shot(s)	Kahlúa coffee liqueur
1	shot(s)	Double (heavy) cream
1	shot(s)	Milk
Top up with		Cola

Variant: Colorado Mother (with tequila in place of vodka).
Comment: This dog's bite is hidden by cream.

COLUMBUS DAIQUIRI NEW ●●●○○

Glass: Martini
Garnish: Lime wedge on rim
Method: SHAKE all ingredients with ice and fine strain into chilled glass.

1	shot(s)	Mount Gay golden rum
1	shot(s)	Giffard Apricot brandy
1	shot(s)	Freshly squeezed lime juice
1/2	shot(s)	Chilled mineral water (omit if wet ice)

Comment: A tangy, apricot flavoured Daiquiri.

THE COMET NEW ●●●●◐

Glass: Martini
Garnish: Lemon zest twist
Method: MUDDLE grapes in base of shaker. Add other ingredients, SHAKE with ice and fine strain into chilled glass.

7	fresh	White grapes
2	shot(s)	Rémy Martin cognac
3/4	shot(s)	Grand Marnier liqueur
1	dash	Angostura aromatic bitters

Origin: Created by Eddie Clark at the Albany Club, Albermarle Street, London, to celebrate the launch of the Comet jetliner in 1952.
Comment: Cognac with freshly extracted grape juice and a splash of orange liqueur.

COMMODORE #1 NEW ●●●●○

Glass: Martini
Garnish: Maraschino cherry
Method: SHAKE all ingredients with ice and fine strain into chilled glass.

2	shot(s)	Mount Gay golden rum
1/2	shot(s)	Freshly squeezed lemon juice
1/4	shot(s)	Sugar syrup (2 sugar to 1 water)
1/8	shot(s)	Pomegranate (grenadine) syrup
1/2	fresh	Egg white

Origin: Adapted from David A. Embury's 1948 'The Fine Art of Mixing Drinks', where he writes, "Another version of the Commodore calls for whisky instead of rum, omits the egg white, and uses orange bitters in place of the grenadine. Obviously, the two Commodores command two different fleets."
Comment: A smooth, sweet Daiquiri with flavoursome rum.

COMMODORE #2 NEW ●●●○○

Glass: Martini
Garnish: Maraschino cherry
Method: SHAKE all ingredients with ice and fine strain into chilled glass.

2	shot(s)	Bourbon whiskey
3/4	shot(s)	Giffard white crème de cacao
1/2	shot(s)	Freshly squeezed lemon juice
1/4	shot(s)	Pomegranate (grenadine) syrup
2	dashes	Fee Brothers orange bitters (optional)

Comment: Fruity, tangy Bourbon - surprisingly dry.

●●●○○

CONCEALED WEAPON NEW

Glass: Old-fashioned
Garnish: Lemon zest twist
Method: SHAKE all ingredients with ice and strain into ice-filled glass.

1	shot(s)	La Feé Parisian (68%) absinthe
1	shot(s)	Chambord black raspberry liqueur
³/₄	shot(s)	Freshly squeezed lemon juice
¹/₂	shot(s)	Sugar syrup (2 sugar to 1 water)
1	dash	Peychaud's aromatic bitters
1	dash	Angostura aromatic bitters
¹/₂	fresh	Egg white

Origin: Created in 2000 by Danny Smith at Che, London, England.
Comment: Absinthe is the 'weapon' that's 'concealed' in this full-on short berry drink.

●●●●○

COOL ORCHARD

Glass: Old-fashioned
Garnish: Pineapple wedge & cherry
Method: MUDDLE ginger in base of shaker. Add other ingredients, SHAKE with ice and fine strain into ice-filled glass.

2	slices	Fresh root ginger (thumbnail sized)
1¹/₂	shot(s)	Aged rum
¹/₂	shot(s)	Ginger sugar syrup
¹/₄	shot(s)	Almond (orgeat) sugar syrup
1	shot(s)	Pressed pineapple juice
¹/₂	shot(s)	Vanilla schnapps liqueur
¹/₄	shot(s)	Freshly squeezed lime juice

Origin: Created in 2001 by Douglas Ankrah for Akbar, Soho, London, England.
Comment: An unusual line up of cocktail ingredients combine to make a great drink.

●●●●○

CONGO BLUE

Glass: Martini
Garnish: Lemon zest twist
Method: SHAKE all ingredients with ice and fine strain into chilled glass.

1¹/₄	shot(s)	Zubrówka bison vodka
¹/₂	shot(s)	Midori melon liqueur
1	shot(s)	Pressed apple juice
¹/₂	shot(s)	Giffard mûre (blackberry)
¹/₄	shot(s)	Freshly squeezed lemon juice

Origin: Created in 1999 by Marc Dietrich at Atlantic Bar & Grill, London and apparently named after the beauty of the Congo sunset.
Comment: Flavoursome and sweet.

●●●●○

COOLMAN MARTINI

Glass: Martini
Garnish: Orange zest twist
Method: SHAKE all ingredients with ice and fine strain into chilled glass.

1³/₄	shot(s)	Zubrówka bison vodka
¹/₂	shot(s)	Cointreau triple sec
2	shot(s)	Pressed apple juice
¹/₄	shot(s)	Freshly squeezed lemon juice

Origin: Created in 2001 by Jack Coleman at The Library Bar, Lanesborough Hotel, London, England.
Comment: Fragrant and complex. Integrated hints of apple and orange are laced with grassy vodka.

●●●●○

COPPER ILLUSION

Glass: Old-fashioned
Garnish: Orange zest twist
Method: STIR all ingredients with ice and strain into ice-filled glass.

1¹/₂	shot(s)	Plymouth gin
³/₄	shot(s)	Campari
³/₄	shot(s)	Cointreau triple sec

Variant: Negroni
Origin: Unknown but brought to my attention in 2005 courtesy of Angus Winchester and www.alconomics.com.
Comment: Basically a Negroni with liqueur replacing sweet vermouth. Like the Italian classic this is both bitter and sweet.

●●●●○

COOL MARTINI

Glass: Martini
Garnish: Apple slice chevron
Method: SHAKE all ingredients with ice and fine strain into chilled glass.

1¹/₂	shot(s)	Midori melon liqueur
1	shot(s)	Partida tequila
1¹/₂	shot(s)	Cranberry juice

Comment: Tastes nothing like the ingredients - which include melon, tequila and cranberry juice. Try it and see if you taste toffee.

●●●●○

COQUETAIL AU VANILLA NEW

Glass: Old-fashioned
Garnish: Maraschino cherry
Method: SHAKE all ingredients with ice and strain into glass filled with crushed ice. Serve with straws.

2	shot(s)	Vanilla infused light white rum
¹/₄	shot(s)	Velvet Falernum liqueur

Origin: My adaptation of a classic.
Comment: This drink may look fluffy and sweet but it's dry and lightly spiced. Perfect for a sunny afternoon.

CORDLESS SCREWDRIVER UPDATED ●●●○○

Glass: Shot
Garnish: Sugar coated half orange slice
Method: POUR vodka and champagne into chilled glass and serve. Instruct drinker to down in one and then bite into the orange wedge.

| 1 | shot(s) | Ketel One orange infused vodka |
| Top up with | | Brut champagne |

Comment: A slammer style drink for those looking for a fruity alternative to tequila.

CORONATION ●●●○○

Glass: Collins
Garnish: Maraschino cherry
Method: STIR first five ingredients with ice and strain into ice-filled glass. TOP with soda, stir and serve with straws.

1	shot(s)	Tio Pepe fino sherry
1	shot(s)	Dry vermouth
2	shot(s)	Sauvignon Blanc / unoaked Chardonnay wine
1/4	shot(s)	Luxardo maraschino liqueur
2	dashes	Angostura aromatic bitters
Top up with		Soda water (club soda)

Comment: Light and aromatic.

CORONATION COCKTAIL NO. 1 UPDATED ●●●●◐

Glass: Martini
Garnish: Orange zest twist
Method: STIR all ingredients with ice and strain into chilled glass.

1½	shot(s)	Tio Pepe fino sherry
1½	shot(s)	Dry vermouth
1/4	shot(s)	Luxardo maraschino liqueur
2	dashes	Fee Brothers orange bitters

Origin: Adapted from Harry Craddock's 1930 'The Savoy Cocktail Book'.
Comment: Medium dry and wonderfully aromatic.

CORPSE REVIVER NO. 1 #1 UPDATED ●●●◐○

Glass: Martini
Garnish: Orange zest twist
Method: STIR ingredients with ice and strain into chilled glass.

1½	shot(s)	Rémy Martin cognac
3/4	shot(s)	Boulard Grand Solage Calvados
3/4	shot(s)	Sweet vermouth
1/2	shot(s)	Chilled mineral water (omit if wet ice)

Origin: Created by Frank Meier, Ritz Bar, Paris, France. This recipe is adapted from Harry Craddock's 1930 'The Savoy Cocktail Book', where he writes, "To be taken before 11am, or whenever steam and energy are needed."
Comment: Dry and potent. A 'pick-me-up' hangover cure – or possibly put-you-right-back-down-again!

CORPSE REVIVER #2 NEW ●●●●○

Glass: Martini
Garnish: Lemon zest twist
Method: SHAKE all ingredients with ice and fine strain into chilled glass.

3/4	shot(s)	Plymouth gin
3/4	shot(s)	Carlshamns Flaggpunsch Torr Swedish punch
3/4	shot(s)	Cointreau triple sec
1/8	shot(s)	La Feé Parisian (68%) absinthe
3/4	shot(s)	Freshly squeezed lemon juice

Origin: Adapted from Victor Bergeron's 'Trader Vic's Bartender's Guide' (1972 revised edition).
Comment: Perhaps a tad sweet but the kill or cure alcohol is well masked. Steady!

COSMOPOLITAN #1 (SIMPLE VERSION) UPDATED ●●●●◐

Glass: Martini
Garnish: Flamed orange zest twist
Method: SHAKE all ingredients with ice and fine strain into chilled glass.

1	shot(s)	Ketel One Citroen vodka
1	shot(s)	Cointreau triple sec
1½	shot(s)	Cranberry juice
1/2	shot(s)	Freshly squeezed lime juice

Origin: Formula by yours truly in 2005.
Comment: When a quality juice with at least 24% cranberry is used, the balance of citrus, berry fruit and sweetness is perfect.

COSMOPOLITAN #2 (COMPLEX) ●●●●●

Glass: Martini
Garnish: Flamed orange zest twist
Method: SHAKE all ingredients with ice and fine strain into chilled glass.

1	shot(s)	Ketel One Citroen vodka
1	shot(s)	Cointreau triple sec
1½	shot(s)	Cranberry juice
1/2	shot(s)	Freshly squeezed lime juice
1/4	shot(s)	Rose's lime cordial
4	dashes	Fee Brothers orange bitters

Origin: Formula by yours truly in 2005.
Comment: For those who are not content with simplicity..

COSMOPOLITAN #3 (POPULAR VERSION) NEW ●●●●◐

Glass: Martini
Garnish: Orange zest twist
Method: SHAKE all ingredients with ice and fine strain into chilled glass.

1½	shot(s)	Ketel One Citroen vodka
1/2	shot(s)	Cointreau triple sec
1	shot(s)	Cranberry juice
1/4	shot(s)	Freshly squeezed lime juice

Origin: The most widely used Cosmopolitan recipe.
Comment: Every bar has a different Cosmo recipe but this seems to be the most popular.

COSMOPOLITAN

The Cosmopolitan was thought to have derived from a drink called the Harpoon, promoted by Ocean Spray during the 1960s. This consisted of vodka, cranberry juice and a squeeze of fresh lime.

Then one Cheryl Cook emerged with claims that she invented the drink in the latter half of the 1980s while head bartender at The Strand on Washington Avenue, South Beach, Miami. She apparently based her drink on the newly available Absolut Citron vodka and added a splash of triple sec, a dash of Rose's lime and, in her own words, "just enough cranberry to make it oh so pretty in pink".

The drink is believed to have travelled by way of San Francisco to Manhattan where Toby Cecchini is credited with first using fresh lime juice in place of Rose's at his Passerby bar. Whatever the origin, however, it was Sex And The City's Carrie Bradshaw who popularised the drink when she swapped Martinis for Cosmos.

In 2006 the following recipe for a Cosmopolitan was discovered in a 1934 book of gin recipes: 'Pioneers of Mixing Gin at Elite Bars'.

Cosmopolitan
Jigger Gordons Gin
2 dashes Cointreau
Juice of one Lemon
Teaspoon Raspberry
Glass No. 4 Shake and strain

This bears an uncanny resemblance to the modern day, vodka based Cosmopolitan so casting yet more questions over the drink's origin.

Cosmopolitan variations include
Apricot Cosmo
Blue Cosmo
Blue Fin
Chinese Cosmopolitan
Cosmopolitan #1 (simple version)
Cosmopolitan # 2 (complex version)
Cosmopolitan #3 (popular version)
Cosmopolitan #4 (1934 version)
Creole Cosmo
Detropolitan
Ginger Cosmo
Grand Cosmopolitan
Hawaiian Cosmopolitan
Limey Cosmo
Metropolitan
Raspberry Cosmo
Royal Cosmopolitan
Rude Cosmopolitan
Rude Ginger Cosmopolitan
Sake'politan
Strawberry Cosmo
Watermelon Cosmo
White Cosmo
The Windsor Rose

●●●●○

COSMOPOLITAN #4 (1934 RECIPE) NEW 🔑

Glass: Martini
Garnish: Orange zest twist
Method: SHAKE all ingredients with ice and fine strain into chilled glass.

2	shot(s)	Plymouth gin
¹/₂	shot(s)	Cointreau triple sec
³/₄	shot(s)	Freshly squeezed lemon juice
¹/₄	shot(s)	Raspberry syrup (or Pomegranate syrup)

Origin: Recipe adapted from 1934 'Pioneers of Mixing Gin at Elite Bars'.
Comment: Reminiscent of a Sidecar and, dependent on your syrup, well balanced. Thanks to drinkboy.com forum for first bringing this drink to my attention.

●●●●○

COSMOPOLITAN DELIGHT

Glass: Martini
Garnish: Flamed orange zest twist
Method: SHAKE all ingredients with ice and fine strain into chilled glass.

1¹/₂	shot(s)	Rémy Martin cognac
¹/₂	shot(s)	Grand Marnier
1¹/₄	shot(s)	Shiraz red wine
³/₄	shot(s)	Freshly squeezed lemon juice
¹/₄	shot(s)	Almond (orgeat) syrup
¹/₄	shot(s)	Sugar syrup (2 sugar to 1 water)

Origin: Adapted from Dale DeGroff's book, 'The Craft of the Cocktail'. He credits the original recipe to a 1902 book by Charlie Paul.
Comment: No relation to the modern Cosmopolitan, this is a mellow, balanced blend of citrus, brandy and red wine.

●●●●○

COUNTRY BREEZE 🔑

Glass: Collins
Garnish: Berries
Method: SHAKE all ingredients with ice and strain into ice-filled glass.

2	shot(s)	Plymouth gin
¹/₂	shot(s)	Giffard Cassis Noir de Bourgogne
3¹/₂	shot(s)	Pressed apple juice

Comment: Not too sweet. The gin character shines through the fruit.

●●●○○

COVADONGA NEW

Glass: Martini
Garnish: Orange slice
Method: SHAKE all ingredients with ice and fine strain into chilled glass.

1¹/₂	shot(s)	Campari
1	shot(s)	Sweet vermouth
1	shot(s)	Freshly squeezed orange juice
¹/₂	shot(s)	Pomegranate (grenadine) syrup
5	dashes	Angostura aromatic bitters

Origin: Adapted from Victor Bergeron's 'Trader Vic's Bartender's Guide' (1972 revised edition).
Comment: Sweet, tart and fruity. My kinda girl!

●●●●○○

COWBOY MARTINI 🔑

Glass: Martini
Garnish: Orange zest twist
Method: Lightly MUDDLE mint in base of shaker just enough to bruise. Add other ingredients, SHAKE with ice and fine strain into chilled glass.

7	fresh	Mint leaves
3	shot(s)	Plymouth gin
¹/₂	shot(s)	Sugar syrup (2 sugar to 1 water)
3	dashes	Fee Brothers orange bitters (optional)

AKA: The Cooperstown Cocktail
Origin: Created in the early 90s by Dick Bradsell at Detroit, London, England.
Comment: Sweetened gin shaken with fresh mint.

●●●●●

COX'S DAIQUIRI

Glass: Martini
Garnish: Cox's apple ring (in memory of Jennings Cox)
Method: SHAKE all ingredients with ice and fine strain into chilled glass.

2¹/₂	shot(s)	Vanilla-infused Havana Club rum
¹/₂	shot(s)	Freshly squeezed lime juice
¹/₄	shot(s)	Vanilla sugar syrup
1	shot(s)	Freshly pressed pineapple juice

Origin: One of two cocktails with which I won 'The Best Daiquiri in London Competition' in 2002. It is named after Jennings Cox, the American mining engineer credited with first creating the Daiquiri.
Comment: Vanilla and pineapple bring out the sweetness of the rum against a citrus background.

●●●●○

CRANAPPLE BREEZE

Glass: Collins
Garnish: Lime wheel on rim
Method: SHAKE first five ingredients with ice and strain into ice-filled glass. TOP with ginger ale and stir.

1	shot(s)	Ketel One Citroen vodka
1	shot(s)	Cointreau triple sec
1	shot(s)	Cranberry juice
1	shot(s)	Pressed apple juice
¹/₂	shot(s)	Freshly squeezed lime juice
Top up with		Ginger ale

Origin: Created in 2002 by Wayne Collins.
Comment: A refreshing cooler for a hot day by the pool.

●●●○○

CRANBERRY COOLER

Glass: Collins
Garnish: Orange slice
Method: SHAKE all ingredients with ice and strain into ice-filled glass.

2	shot(s)	Luxardo Amaretto di Saschira
2	shot(s)	Cranberry juice
2	shot(s)	Freshly squeezed orange juice

Comment: Easy drinking for those with a sweet tooth.

A B C D E F G H I J K L M N O P Q R S T U V W X Y Z

CRANBERRY DELICIOUS (MOCKTAIL) NEW

Glass: Collins
Garnish: Mint sprig
Method: MUDDLE mint in base of shaker. Add other ingredients, SHAKE with ice and strain into ice-filled glass.

12	fresh	Mint leaves
1	shot(s)	Freshly squeezed lime juice
1/2	shot(s)	Sugar syrup (2 sugar to 1 water)
4	shot(s)	Cranberry juice
3	dashes	Angostura aromatic bitters

Origin: Adapted from a drink created in 2006 by Damian Windsor at Bin 8945 Wine Bar & Bistro, West Hollywood, USA.
Comment: Cranberry juice given more interest with mint, lime and bitters. This drink contains trace amounts of alcohol but remains an effective driver's option.

CRANBERRY & MINT MARTINI UPDATED

Glass: Martini
Garnish: Dried cranberries in base of glass & float mint leaf.
Method: Lightly MUDDLE mint in base of shaker, just enough to bruise. Add other ingredients, SHAKE with ice and fine strain into chilled glass.

9	fresh	Mint leaves
2	shot(s)	Ketel One vodka
1 1/2	shot(s)	Cranberry juice
1/4	shot(s)	Pomegranate (grenadine) syrup

Origin: Created in 2003 by yours truly.
Comment: This little red number combines the dryness of cranberry, the sweetness of grenadine and the fragrance of mint.

CRANBERRY SAUCE UPDATED

Glass: Martini
Garnish: Lime wedge
Method: SHAKE all ingredients with ice and fine strain into chilled glass.

2	shot(s)	Ketel One vodka
3/4	shot(s)	Lapponia cranberry liqueur
2 1/2	shot(s)	Cranberry juice
1/4	shot(s)	Freshly squeezed lime juice

Origin: Created in 2003 by yours truly.
Comment: Rich and fruity with that customary dry cranberry finish.

CREAMSICLE UPDATED

Glass: Martini
Garnish: Orange zest twist
Method: SHAKE all ingredients with ice and fine strain into chilled glass.

1 1/2	shot(s)	Ketel One orange infused vodka
1	shot(s)	Grand Marnier liqueur
1/2	shot(s)	Double cream
1/2	shot(s)	Milk
1/8	shot(s)	Sugar syrup (2 sugar to 1 water)

Comment: A milky orange number with a surprisingly pleasant taste.

CREAMY BEE

Glass: Martini
Garnish: Cinnamon rim & raspberry
Method: SHAKE all ingredients with ice and fine strain into chilled glass.

1 1/2	shot(s)	Krupnik honey liqueur
1/2	shot(s)	Baileys Irish cream liqueur
1/2	shot(s)	Chambord black raspberry liqueur
1/2	shot(s)	Hazelnut (crème de noisette) liqueur
1/4	shot(s)	Goldschläger cinnamon schnapps

Origin: Created in 2002 at Hush, London, England and originally made with cinnamon syrup in place of Goldschläger.
Comment: Creamy cinnamon with hints of honey, nuts and berries.

CREAMY CREAMSICLE UPDATED

Glass: Martini
Method: SHAKE all ingredients with ice and fine strain into chilled glass.

1/2	shot(s)	Ketel One orange infused vodka
1 1/4	shot(s)	Disaronno Originale amaretto
1	shot(s)	Freshly squeezed orange juice
3/4	shot(s)	Double (heavy) cream
3/4	shot(s)	Milk

Comment: Ultra smooth and creamy. Dessert, anyone?

CREAM CAKE

Glass: Martini
Garnish: Crumbled Cadbury's Flake bar
Method: SHAKE all ingredients with ice and fine strain into chilled glass.

1 1/4	shot(s)	Baileys Irish cream liqueur
1 1/4	shot(s)	Peach schnapps liqueur
1 1/4	shot(s)	Luxardo Amaretto di Saschira
1	shot(s)	Double (heavy) cream

Comment: Creamy pleasure for the sweet of tooth.

CRUSTAS

The invention of the Crusta is credited to a Joseph Santina at the Jewel of the South or a Joseph Santini at the City Exchange in New Orleans sometime during the 1840s or 1850s. It first appeared in print as 'The Brandy Crusta' in Jerry Thomas' 1862 bartender's guide.

Crustas always contain a spirit, lemon juice and sugar – sometimes in the form of a liqueur or liqueurs. They are so named due to their sugar rim, which should be applied hours before the drink is made so that it is dried hard, or indeed crusty, when the drink is served. Crustas are also distinguished by being garnished with a band of orange or lemon zest, and are drunk from the rim of the fruit, rather than the rim of the glass.

As David A. Embury writes in his 1948 'The Fine Art of Mixing Drinks', "The distinguishing feature of the Crusta is that the entire inside of the glass is lined with lemon or orange peel. The drink may be served in either a wineglass or an Old-Fashioned glass, although it is much harder to make the peel fit in the Old-Fashioned glass. Take a large lemon or a small orange of a size approximating that of the glass to be used. Cut off both ends and peel the remainder in spiral fashion so as to keep the peel all in one place. Line the inside of the glass with this peel, wet the edge of the glass, and dip in powdered sugar to frost the edge of both peel and glass."

The trick is to find a fruit. I favour lemon, which fits into a small wineglass tightly enough to act as a watertight extension to the glass. The fact that wineglasses tend to curve in on themselves helps retain the fruit. You have little or no chance of successfully making a Crusta using a classically shaped old-fashioned glass.

Embury goes on to say, "While the 'Brandy Crusta' is the most common form of this drink, it is, after all, merely a Sour-type drink served in fancy style. Substitution of a different liquor as a base will give a Gin Crusta, a Rum Crusta, an Applejack Crusta, A Whisky Crusta, and so on." Please see my Bourbon Crusta and Brandy Crusta recipe in this guide and Jerry Thomas' below.

Some cocktail historians, Ted Haigh included, consider the Crusta the forerunner of the Sidecar and in turn the Margarita. It's a very logical argument.

THE BRANDY CRUSTA (JERRY THOMAS' RECIPE)

Sadly, I don't have a copy of Jerry Thomas' 1862 bartender's guide so I've taken this recipe from Ted Haigh's 'Vintage Spirits & Forgotten Cocktails'. "Cut a lemon in half. Pare the full peel off half, and squeeze the juice from the lemon. Moisten glass rim with lemon juice, and dip it in bar or table sugar. Insert a lemon peel into the glass. Mix in a cocktail shaker of crushed ice:"

2	ounces Cognac
1	teaspoon Orange curaçao
½	teaspoon Freshly squeezed lemon juice
1	dash Broker's bitters (substitute Angostura)

CRÈME ANGLAISE MARTINI

●●●●○

Glass: Martini
Garnish: Dust with cocoa powder
Method: SHAKE all ingredients with ice and fine strain into chilled glass.

1	shot(s)	Vanilla-infused Ketel One vodka
2	shot(s)	Advocaat liqueur
1	shot(s)	Milk

Origin: Created in 2004 by yours truly.
Comment: Very reminiscent of alcoholic crème anglaise.

CRIMEA NEW

●●●○○

Glass: Martini
Garnish: Float coriander leaf
Method: MUDDLE coriander in base of shaker. Add other ingredients, SHAKE with ice and fine strain into chilled glass.

5	fresh	Coriander leaves (not stems)
2	shot(s)	Plymouth gin
1	shot(s)	Pressed apple juice
1/4	shot(s)	Freshly squeezed lemon juice
1/8	shot(s)	Sugar syrup (2 sugar to 1 water)
1/2	shot(s)	Chilled mineral water (omit if wet ice)

Origin: Adapted from a drink discovered in 2006 at the Ballroom, London, England.
Comment: Fragrant, herbal gin with a hint of citrus.

CRÈME BRÛLÉE MARTINI UPDATED

●●●◖○

Glass: Martini
Garnish: Dust with cinnamon powder
Method: SHAKE all ingredients with ice and fine strain into chilled glass.

2	shot(s)	Vanilla infused Ketel One vodka
1/2	shot(s)	Cartron caramel liqueur
3/4	shot(s)	Licor 43 (Cuarenta Y Tres) liqueur
1	shot(s)	Double (heavy) cream
1/2	fresh	Egg yolk

Origin: Adapted from a drink created in 2002 by Yannick Miseriaux at the Fifth Floor Bar, London, England.
Comment: OK, so there's no crust, but this does contain egg yolk, caramel, vanilla, sugar and cream. Due to the cinnamon, it even has a brown top.

CRIMSON BLUSH

●●●●○

Glass: Martini
Garnish: Berries
Method: SHAKE all ingredients with ice and fine strain into chilled glass.

2	shot(s)	Ketel One Citroen vodka
1/2	shot(s)	Chambord black raspberry liqueur
2	shot(s)	Squeezed golden grapefruit juice
1/4	shot(s)	Sugar syrup (2 sugar to 1 water)

Origin: Created in 2004 by Jonathan Lamm at The Admirable Crichton, London, England.
Comment: Well balanced, fruity sweet and sour.

CRÈME DE CAFÉ

●●●◖○

Glass: Old-fashioned
Method: SHAKE ingredients with ice and strain into ice-filled glass.

1	shot(s)	Kahlúa coffee liqueur
3/4	shot(s)	Mount Gay Eclipse golden rum
3/4	shot(s)	Luxardo Sambuca dei Cesari
1	shot(s)	Double (heavy) cream
1	shot(s)	Milk

Comment: Coffee predominates over the creaminess with hints of aniseed and rum.

CROSSBOW NEW

●●●○○

Glass: Martini
Garnish: Orange zest twist
Method: SHAKE all ingredients with ice and fine strain into chilled glass.

2	shot(s)	Plymouth gin
1/2	shot(s)	Cointreau triple sec
1/4	shot(s)	Giffard white crème de cacao
1/2	shot(s)	Chilled mineral water (omit if wet ice)

Origin: Adapted from a drink discovered in 2005 at Bar Opiume, Singapore.
Comment: Surprisingly dry orange and chocolate laced with gin.

CREOLE COSMO NEW

●●●●◖

Glass: Martini
Garnish: Lime zest twist
Method: SHAKE all ingredients with ice and fine strain into chilled glass.

1	shot(s)	Martinique agricole white rum (50% abv)
1	shot(s)	Clément Creole Shrubb
1	shot(s)	Cranberry juice
1/2	shot(s)	Freshly squeezed lime juice

Comment: Dry, tangy and more sophisticated than your bog-standard Cosmo.

CROUCHING TIGER

●●●○○

Glass: Shot
Method: SHAKE all ingredients with ice and fine strain into chilled glass.

| 3/4 | shot(s) | Partida tequila |
| 1/2 | shot(s) | Soho lychee liqueur |

Comment: Tequila and lychee combine harmoniously in this semi –sweet shot.

A
B
C
D
E
F
G
H
I
J
K
L
M
N
O
P
Q
R
S
T
U
V
W
X
Y
Z

●●●○○

THE CROW COCKTAIL NEW ⌐

Glass: Martini
Garnish: Lemon zest twist
Method: SHAKE all ingredients with ice and fine strain into chilled glass.

2	shot(s)	Scotch whisky
1	shot(s)	Freshly squeezed lemon juice
½	shot(s)	Pomegranate (grenadine) syrup

Origin: Adapted from Harry Craddock's 1930 'The Savoy Cocktail Book'.
Comment: If you use great syrup and have a penchant for Scotch then you could be pleasantly surprised by this drink.

●●●●○

CROWN STAG

Glass: Old-fashioned
Garnish: Slice of lemon
Method: SHAKE ingredients with ice and strain into ice-filled glass.

1½	shot(s)	Ketel One vodka
1½	shot(s)	Jägermeister liqueur
1	shot(s)	Chambord black raspberry liqueur

Comment: A surprisingly workable combination.

●●●●○

CRUEL INTENTION NEW

Glass: Martini
Garnish: Lime slice on rim
Method: SHAKE all ingredients with ice and fine strain into chilled glass.

2	shot(s)	Bourbon whiskey
¼	shot(s)	Giffard apricot brandy du Roussillon
¼	shot(s)	Luxardo Amaretto
1	shot(s)	Pressed pineapple juice
½	shot(s)	Freshly squeezed lime juice

Origin: Discovered in 2005 at The Mansion, Amsterdam, The Netherlands.
Comment: Bourbon with a hint of apricot, almond, pineapple and lime. Hardly cruel!

●●●●○

CRUX NEW

Glass: Martini
Garnish: Orange zest twist
Method: SHAKE all ingredients with ice and fine strain into chilled glass.

1	shot(s)	Rémy Martin cognac
1	shot(s)	Dubonnet Red
1	shot(s)	Cointreau triple sec
1	shot(s)	Freshly squeezed lemon juice

Comment: The 'crux' of the matter is rarely as tasty as this fruity and none too sweet cognac.

●●●●○○

CUBA LIBRE UPDATED ⌐

Glass: Collins
Garnish: Lime wedge
Method: POUR ingredients into ice-filled glass, stir and serve with straws.

2	shot(s)	Light rum
½	shot(s)	Freshly squeezed lime juice
Top up with		Cola

Variants: Cuba Pintada & Cuba Campechana
Origin: Said to have been created in Cuba by American soldiers fighting the Spanish-American War of 1898.
Comment: Basically a rum and cola with a squeeze of lime – Cuba Libre sounds better though!

●●●●○○

CUBA PINTADA NEW ⌐

Glass: Collins
Garnish: Lime wedge
Method: POUR ingredients into ice-filled glass, stir and serve with straws.

2	shot(s)	Havana Club light rum
1	shot(s)	Cola
Top up with		Soda water

Variant: Cuba Campechana – rum with half soda and half cola; Cuba Libre – rum, cola and a dash of lime juice.
Origin: The name of this popular Cuban drink literally means 'stained Cuba' and there is just enough cola in this rum and soda to stain the drink brown.

●●●●○○

CUBAN COCKTAIL NO. 2 #1 NEW

Glass: Martini
Garnish: Lemon peel twist
Method: SHAKE all ingredients with ice and fine strain into chilled glass.

1½	shot(s)	Light white rum
⅛	shot(s)	Luxardo maraschino liqueur
⅛	shot(s)	Pomegranate (grenadine) syrup
¼	shot(s)	Freshly squeezed lemon juice
1	dash	Fee Brothers orange bitters
½	shot(s)	Chilled mineral water (omit if wet ice)

Origin: Adapted from Victor Bergeron's 'Trader Vic's Bartender's Guide' (1972 revised edition).
Comment: Perfumed yet not sweetened rum.

CUBA LIBRE

The Cuba Libre (Spanish for 'Free Cuba') was allegedly so named in August 1900 when some off-duty members of Teddy Roosevelt's Rough Rider soldiers were celebrating a victory during the Spanish-American war to free Cuba. They gathered in a bar in Havana when John Doe, a captain in the U.S. Signal Corp, entered the bar and ordered a rum and Coca Cola. The Captain raised his glass and sang out the battle cry that had inspired Cuba's victorious soldiers at war, 'Cuba Libre'.

This touching story, however, is unlikely to be true. The Spanish-American war was in 1898; Coca-Cola was bottled in America for the first time in 1899 and did not begin international exports for a decade or more; and John Doe is US slang for an unknown individual.

The Cuba Libre peaked in popularity during the 1940s, partly aided by the Andrews Sisters who in 1945 had a hit with 'Rum and Coca-Cola', named after the drink's ingredients. During the war, all spirits production went over to industrial alcohol - in the absence of whiskey and gin, Americans turned to imported rum.

CUBAN COCKTAIL NO. 3 #2 NEW ●●●◐○○

Glass: Martini
Garnish: Lemon peel twist
Method: SHAKE all ingredients with ice and fine strain into chilled glass.

1¹/₂	shot(s)	Mount Gay golden rum
¹/₄	shot(s)	Rémy Martin cognac
¹/₂	shot(s)	Giffard apricot brandy du Roussillon
¹/₂	shot(s)	Freshly squeezed lime juice
1	dash	Fee Brothers orange bitters
¹/₂	shot(s)	Chilled mineral water (omit if wet ice)

Origin: Adapted from Victor Bergeron's 'Trader Vic's Bartender's Guide' (1972 revised edition).
Comment: Like much of the Caribbean, this drink has French influences. Thank goodness for Admiral Rodney.

CUBAN ISLAND NEW ●●●◐○○

Glass: Martini
Garnish: Orange zest twist
Method: SHAKE all ingredients with ice and fine strain into chilled glass.

2	shot(s)	Light white rum
¹/₂	shot(s)	Dry vermouth
¹/₂	shot(s)	Freshly squeezed lemon juice
¹/₄	shot(s)	Sugar syrup (2 sugar to 1 water)

Origin: Adapted from a drink discovered in 2005 at DiVino's, Hong Kong, China.
Comment: The Daiquiri meets the Wet Martini. Interesting!

CUBAN MASTER ●●●○○

Glass: Collins
Garnish: Pineapple wedge
Method: SHAKE all ingredients with ice and strain into ice-filled glass.

1¹/₂	shot(s)	Light white rum
1	shot(s)	Rémy Martin cognac
1¹/₂	shot(s)	Freshly squeezed orange juice
1¹/₂	shot(s)	Pressed pineapple juice
¹/₂	shot(s)	Freshly squeezed lemon juice
¹/₄	shot(s)	Sugar syrup (2 sugar to 1 water)

Origin: A classic cocktail I discovered in 1999 during a trip to Cuba.
Comment: Well balanced, wonderfully fruity.

DRINKS ARE GRADED AS FOLLOWS:

● DISGUSTING	●○ PRETTY AWFUL	●● BEST AVOIDED
●●○ DISAPPOINTING	●●● ACCEPTABLE	●●●○ GOOD
●●●● RECOMMENDED	●●●●○ HIGHLY RECOMMENDED	
	●●●●● OUTSTANDING / EXCEPTIONAL	

CUBAN SPECIAL ●●●○○

Glass: Old-fashioned
Garnish: Orange zest twist
Method: SHAKE ingredients with ice and strain into ice-filled glass.

1¹/₂	shot(s)	Light white rum
³/₄	shot(s)	Cointreau triple sec
2	shot(s)	Pressed pineapple juice
¹/₄	shot(s)	Freshly squeezed lime juice

Comment: Not that special, but certainly OK.

CUBANITA ●●●●○

Glass: Collins
Garnish: Lime wedge
Method: SHAKE all ingredients with ice and strain into ice-filled glass.

2	shot(s)	Light white rum
4	shot(s)	Pressed tomato juice
¹/₂	shot(s)	Freshly squeezed lemon juice
8	drops	Tabasco pepper sauce
4	dashes	Lea & Perrins Worcestershire sauce
¹/₂	spoon	Horseradish sauce
2	pinch	Celery salt
2	pinch	Black pepper

Comment: The Bloody Mary returns - this time with rum.

CUCUMBER MARTINI ●●●●◐

Glass: Martini
Garnish: Strip of cucumber
Method: MUDDLE cucumber in base of shaker. Add other ingredients, SHAKE with ice and strain into glass.

2	inches	Peeled chopped cucumber
1	shot(s)	Zubrówka bison vodka
1	shot(s)	Ketel One vodka
¹/₂	shot(s)	Sugar syrup (2 sugar to 1 water)

Origin: There are many different Cucumber Martini recipes; this is mine.
Comment: Cucumber has never tasted so good.

CUCUMBER & MINT MARTINI ●●●●◐

Glass: Martini
Garnish: Cucumber wheel
Method: MUDDLE cucumber and mint in base of shaker. Add other ingredients, SHAKE with ice and fine strain into chilled glass.

2	inches	Peeled diced cucumber
7	fresh	Mint leaves
2	shot(s)	Ketel One vodka
1	shot(s)	Pressed apple juice
¹/₄	shot(s)	Sugar syrup (2 sugar to 1 water)

Origin: Created in 2004 by David Ramos in the Netherlands.
Comment: A well balanced fortified salad in a glass – almost healthy.

CUCUMBER SAKE-TINI

●●●●○

Glass: Martini
Garnish: Three cucumber slices
Method: MUDDLE cucumber in base of shaker. Add other ingredients, **SHAKE** with ice and fine strain into chilled glass.

1 1/2	inch	Peeled diced cucumber
1 1/2	shot(s)	Ketel One vodka
1 1/2	shot(s)	Sake
1/4	shot(s)	Sugar syrup (2 sugar to 1 water)

Origin: Created in 2004 by Lisa Ball, London, England.
Comment: Subtle and dry. Cucumber and sake are made for each other.

CUMBERSOME

●●●●○

Glass: Martini
Garnish: Physalis (Cape gooseberry) on rim
Method: MUDDLE cucumber in base of shaker. Add other ingredients, **SHAKE** with ice and strain into a chilled Martini glass.

4	inch	Fresh chopped peeled cucumber
2	shot(s)	Plymouth gin
1/2	shot(s)	Campari
1	shot(s)	Freshly squeezed orange juice
1/2	shot(s)	Sugar syrup (2 sugar to 1 water)

Origin: Created in 2002 by Shelim Islam at the GE Club, London, England.
Comment: Interesting and fresh as you like with a pleasant bitterness.

CUPPA JOE

●●●●○

Glass: Martini
Garnish: Lemon zest twist
Method: SHAKE all ingredients with ice and fine strain into chilled glass.

1 1/2	shot(s)	Ketel One vodka
1 1/2	shot(s)	Hazelnut (crème de noisette) liqueur
1 1/2	shot(s)	Espresso coffee (cold)

Origin: Created in 2003 at Cellar Bar, New York City, USA.
Comment: Nutty coffee fortified with vodka – well balanced.

CURDISH MARTINI UPDATED

●●●●○

Glass: Martini
Garnish: Lemon zest twist
Method: STIR lemon curd with gin in base of shaker until curd dissolves. Add other ingredients, **SHAKE** with ice and fine strain into chilled glass.

2	spoons	Lemon curd
2	shot(s)	Plymouth gin
1/2	shot(s)	Sourz Sour apple liqueur
1/2	shot(s)	Freshly squeezed lemon juice

Origin: Created in 2001 by Tadgh Ryan at West Street, London, England.
Comment: Beautifully balanced with the tang of lemon curd.

THE CURRIER NEW

●●●●○

Glass: Martini
Garnish: Float mint leaf
Method: SHAKE all ingredients with ice and fine strain into chilled glass.

1 1/2	shot(s)	Bourbon whiskey
1/2	shot(s)	Kümmel liqueur
1/4	shot(s)	Freshly squeezed lime juice
1/4	shot(s)	Rose's lime cordial

Origin: Recipe submitted in July 2006 by Murray Stenson at ZigZag Café, Seattle, USA.
Comment: A wonderfully cleansing after dinner cocktail with bourbon and lime plus hints of caraway and fennel courtesy of the Kümmel.

CUSTARD TART

●●●●○

Glass: Shot
Garnish: Physalis (Cape gooseberry) on rim
Method: MUDDLE physalis fruits in base of shaker can. Add other ingredients, **SHAKE** with ice and strain.

3	fresh	Physalis fruits
3/4	shot(s)	Light white rum
1/2	shot(s)	Peach schnapps liqueur
1/4	shot(s)	Freshly squeezed lime juice
1/2	shot(s)	Advocaat liqueur

Origin: Created by Alex Kammerling in 2001.
Comment: Custardy, strangely enough.

CVO FIREVAULT NEW

●●●●○

Glass: Martini
Garnish: Orange zest twist
Method: SHAKE all ingredients with ice and fine strain into chilled glass.

1 1/2	shot(s)	Ketel One orange infused vodka
3/4	shot(s)	Campari
3/4	shot(s)	Freshly squeezed orange juice
3/4	shot(s)	Pressed pineapple juice

Origin: Discovered in 2005 at CVO Firevault, London, England.
Comment: Fruity yet slightly bitter. Orange predominates with strong bursts of Campari.

CYDER PRESS NEW

●●●●○

Glass: Martini
Garnish: Float wafer thin apple slice
Method: SHAKE all ingredients with ice and fine strain into chilled glass.

2	shot(s)	Boulard Grand Solage Calvados
1/2	shot(s)	St Germain elderflower liqueur
1	shot(s)	Apple cider
3/4	shot(s)	Pressed apple juice

Origin: Created in 2006 by yours truly.
Comment: Fresh, fermented and distilled apple juice with a hint of elderflower.

INGREDIENTS
APPENDIX

ABSINTHE

There are two basic styles of absinthe commonly available – French and Czech. French styles, which are mostly still banned in their country of origin, have a full-bodied aniseed flavour and a deep green colour. When served with water the colour should change and eventually go cloudy. This process of precipitation is known as the louche.

Czech absinth (spelt without the 'e') usually has a bluer tinge to its green colour. The aniseed flavour is more subtle than in its French counterpart and it is not usual for it to turn cloudy with the addition of water.

Absinthe Cocktail #1 ●●●○○
Absinthe Cocktail #2 ●●●○○
Absinthe Drip Cocktail #1 ●●●○○
Absinthe Drip Cocktail #2 ●●●○○
Absinthe Frappé ●●●●○
Absinthe Italiano Cocktail ●●●○○
Absinthe Sour ●●●○○
Absinthe Special Cocktail ●●●○○
Absinthe Suisesse ●●●○○
Absinthe Without Leave ●●○○○
Applesinth ●●●●○
The Atty Cocktail ●●●●○
B-55 Shot ●●●○○
Chocolate Sazerac ●●●●○
Colonial Rot ●●●○○
Concealed Weapon ●●●○○
Corpse Reviver #2 ●●●●○

ADVOCAAT LIQUEUR

This Dutch liqueur is derived from an alcoholic drink that colonists in South Africa made from the yellowish pulp of the abacate fruit. In Holland, egg yolks took the place of abacate and the name, already evolved into 'avocado' by Portuguese colonists, became Advocaat in Dutch.

Advocaat is made from brandy, egg yolks, sugar and vanilla. It has a thick, indulgent, luscious custardy consistency. The palate features subtle, creamy vanilla, cocoa powder and a hint of cooked egg yolk.

Ambrosia'tini ●●●○○
Apple & Custard Martini ●●●○○
Beach Blonde ●●●●○
Bessie & Jessie ●●●○○
Canary Flip ●●●●○
Casablanca ●●●○○
Crème Anglaise Martini ●●●●○
Custard Tart ●●●●○

AMARETTO LIQUEUR

See 'Luxardo Amaretto di Saschira Liqueur'

AMONTILLADO

See 'Sherry – Amontillado'

ANGOSTURA AROMATIC BITTERS

44.7% alc./vol. (89.4°proof)

www.angostura.com

Producer: Angostura Ltd, Laventille, Port of Spain, Trinidad, West Indies.

These famous bitters were first made in 1824 by the German Surgeon-General of a military hospital in the town of Angostura, Venezuela, to help treat stomach disorders and indigestion. In 1875, due to unrest in Venezuela, production was moved to Trinidad. It was here that the laid-back Caribbean attitude affected Angostura's packaging. One day a new batch of labels was ordered and a simple mistake led to them being too big for the bottles. The error was spotted in time but everyone thought somebody else would deal with the problem. No one did, so they simply stuck the labels on the bottles, intending to fix the next batch. No one quite got round to it and the oversized label became a trademark of the brand.

One of the smallest bottles on any bar, Angostura is packed with flavour: Turkish coffee, jasmine, dried mint, fruit poached with cloves and cinnamon, cherry, orange and lemon zest. A dash adds that indefinable something which brings cocktails to life.

Abbey Martini ●●●○○
Absinthe Cocktail #2 ●●●●○
Absinthe Special Cocktail ●●●○○
Adam & Eve ●●●●○

Affinity ●●●○○
The Alamagoozlum Cocktail ●●●●○
Alfonso ●●●●○
Alfonso Martini ●●●●○
Amaretto Sour ●●●○○
Americana ●●●●○
Ante ●●●●○
Apple Brandy Sour ●●●●●
Apple Virgin Mojito ●●●●○
Apricot Martini ●●●○○
Aunt Agatha ●●●○○
Bahama Mama ●●●●○
Banana Cow ●●●●○
Barbara West ●●●○○
Barnum ●●●○○
Biarritz ●●●○○
Bitter Elder ●●●○○
Black Feather ●●●●○
Blackthorn Irish ●●●○○
Blade Runner ●●●●○
Boomerang ●●●●○
Bourbon Smash ●●●○○
Brandy Crusta ●●●●○
Brandy Sour ●●●●●
Bronx ●●●○○
Brooklyn #1 ●●●●○
Brubaker Old-Fashioned ●●●●○
Buena Vida ●●●●○
Call Me Old-Fashioned ●●●●○
Caribbean Piña Colada ●●●○○
Causeway ●●●●○
Champagne Cocktail ●●●○○
Champs-Elysées ●●●●○
Chihuahua Magarita ●●●●○
Cinderella ●●●○○
Club Cocktail ●●●●○
The Comet ●●●●○
Concealed Weapon ●●●○○
Coronation ●●●○○
Covadonga ●●●○○
Cranberry Delicious ●●●○○

ANIS

See 'Pernod Anis'

ANISETTE LIQUEUR

This sweet, aniseed-flavoured liqueur with coriander and various other herbs is popular throughout the Mediterranean – in France, Spain and North Africa.

Absinthe Cocktail #2 ●●●○○
Absinthe Frappé ●●●●○
Absinthe Italiano Cocktail ●●●○○
Absinthe Special Cocktail ●●●○○

APPLEJACK BRANDY

See 'Calvados Boulard Grand Solage'

APPLE JUICE

Apples are a good source of dietary fibre, vitamin C and vitamin B5, plus minerals such as copper, iron and potassium. Choose a flavoursome variety like Bramley over more bland types like Washington Red or Golden Delicious.

The best way to use apples in cocktails is as a juice. You can make your own in a standard electric juice extractor. There is no need to peel or core apples, as the skin and core contain over half the fruit's nutrients. Simply remove the stalks and chop the fruit into small enough chunks to fit through the feeder.

Unchecked, the juice will quickly oxidise and discolour but a splash of lime juice helps prevent this without too much effect on the flavour. You'll find that crisper apples yield clearer juice.

Most supermarkets carry at least one quality pressed apple juice and the best of these cloudy juices make DIY juicing unnecessary. Avoid the packaged 'pure', clear apple juices as these tend to be overly sweet and artificial tasting.

Achilles Heel ●●●●○
Alan's Apple Breeze ●●●●○
Almond Martini #1 ●●●●○
Amber ●●●●●
American Pie Martini ●●●●○
Aphrodisiac ●●●●○
Apple & Blackberry Pie ●●●○○
Apple & Elderflower Collins ●●●●○
Apple & Elderflower Martini (Fresh Fruit) ●●●●○
Apple Breeze ●●●●○
Apple Buck ●●●●○
Apple Crumble Martini #1 ●●●○○
Apple Crumble Martini #2 ●●●●○
Apple Daiquiri ●●●●○
Apple Mac ●●●●○
Apple Of My Eire ●●●●○
Apple Pie Martini ●●●●○
Appleissimo ●●●●○
Apple Strudel Martini ●●●○○
Apple Strudel Martini #2 ●●●●●
Apple Virgin Mojito (mocktail) ●●●●○
Applesinth ●●●●○
Apple 'N' Pears ●●●●●
Applily Married ●●●●●
Apricot Sour ●●●●○
Artlantic ●●●○○
Auntie's Hot Xmas Punch ●●●●○
Autumn Martini ●●●●○
Azure Martini ●●●●○
Banana Smoothie (mocktail) ●●●●●
Bee Sting ●●●●○
Beetle Jeuse ●●●●○
Bitter Elder ●●●○○
Black Bison Martini ●●●●●
Black Bison Martini #2 ●●●●○
Bossa Nova # 1 ●●●●○
Canadian Apple (Mocktail) ●●●●○
Caramelised Apple Martini ●●●●○
Chimayo ●●●○○

Chin Chin ●●●●○
Cider Apple Cooler ●●●●○
Congo Blue
Coolman Martini ●●●●○
Country Breeze ●●●○○
Cranapple Breeze ●●●○○
Crimea ●●●○○
Cucumber & Mint Martini ●●●●○
Cyder Press ●●●●○

Avalanche ●●●○○
Banana Batida ●●●○○
Banana Colada ●●●●○
Banana Cow ●●●○○
Banana Daiquiri ●●●○○
Banana Smoothie (mocktail) ●●●●●
Banoffee Martini ●●●●○
Beach Blonde ●●●●○

B2C2 ●●●○○
B & B ●●●●○
BBC ●●●○○
Bobby Burns ●●●●○
Brainstorm ●●●●○
Brass Rail ●●●●○
Brighton Punch ●●●●○
Caprice ●●●●○
Chas ●●●●○
The Cold Winter Warmer Sour ●●●●○
Collection Martini ●●●○○

These soft berries are best muddled in the base of your shaker or glass. Recipes in this guide specify the number required for each drink. Alternatively, you can make a purée. Just stick them in the blender and add a touch of sugar syrup. Fresh blueberries should not be stored in the refrigerator.

Black & Blue Caipirovska ●●●●○
Blueberry Daiquiri ●●●●○
Blueberry Martini #1 ●●●●○
Blueberry Martini #2 (simple) ●●●●○

APPLE SCHNAPPS LIQUEUR

The term schnapps traditionally suggests a clear strong spirit. However, in recent years the term has come to refer to sweet liqueurs of only 20-24% alc./vol., bearing no resemblance to the strong dry schnapps from which they take their name. I call such drinks 'schnapps liqueurs' to avoid confusion.

Amber ●●●●●
American Beauty ●●●●○
Apple & Cranberry Pie ●●●●○
Apple & Custard Martini ●●●●○
Apple Manhattan #1 ●●●●○
Apple Manhattan #2 ●●●●○
Apple Mojito ●●●●○
Apple Pie Shot ●●●●○
Appleissimo ●●●●○
Apple Spritz ●●●●○
Apple Strudel Martini ●●●○○
Apple Strudel Martini #2 ●●●●●
Big Apple Martini ●●●●○
Black Bison Martini ●●●●●
Cider Apple Cooler ●●●●○

APRICOT BRANDY LIQUEUR

See 'Giffard Apricot Brandy du Roussillon'

BANANA

A rich source of potassium and vitamin B6, bananas also contain malic acid, which makes them refreshing when eaten raw.

Bananas are transported green and ripened prior to sale in dedicated ripening warehouses. They should not be stored in refrigerators as exposure to low temperatures turns the fruit black.

BASIL LEAVES

This aromatic herb has a strong lemon and jasmine flavour.

Bajito ●●●●●
Basil & Honey Daiquiri ●●●●●
Basil & Lime Gimlet ●●●●●
Basil Beauty ●●●●○
Basil Bramble Sling ●●●●○
Basil Grande ●●●●○
Basil Mary ●●●●○
Basilian ●●●○○
Basilico ●●●○○
Byzantine ●●●●○

BECHEROVKA (CARLSBAD BECHER)

The Czech national liqueur.

Be-ton ●●●●○
Bohemian Iced Tea ●●●●●

BEER

Although beer is one of the widely consumed alcoholic beverages, sadly it does not greatly feature in the world of cocktails. At least, not yet! Suggestions to simon@diffordsguide.com please.

Black & Tan ●●●○○
Boiler Maker ●●●●●

BÉNÉDICTINE D.O.M. LIQUEUR

April Shower ●●●●○

BLACKBERRIES

See 'Raspberries & Blackberries'

BLACKBERRY (CRÈME DE MÛRE) LIQUEUR

See 'Giffard Crème de Mûre Liqueur'

BLACKCURRANTS

The fruit of a native northern European shrub that is now widely cultivated in France, Germany, The Netherlands and Belgium. Cultivation began in the French Côte d'Or where blackcurrants are heavily used in the production of cassis liqueur.

Brazilian Berry ●●●●○

BLUEBERRIES

Blueberry pie is as much an American icon as the Stars and Stripes. This bushy shrub, which is related to the bilberry, is native to the States and many different types grow there – not all of them blue. The lowbush blueberry, which is called the 'bleuet' in Quebec, tends to be smaller and sweeter than other varieties and is often marketed as 'wild blueberry'. The larger, highbush blueberry is the variety most cultivated in the US.

BLUEBERRY LIQUEUR

See 'Giffard Crème de Myrtille' Liqueur

BOLS BLUE CURAÇAO LIQUEUR

21% alc./vol. (42°proof)

www.Bols.com

Producer: Bols Royal Distilleries, Zoetermeer, The Netherlands.

This vivid blue curaçao liqueur is probably the best known of the Bols range. Part of Rémy Cointreau, Bols Royal Distilleries originated from a firm started in 1575 by a Dutchman called Lucas Bols. Prevented from distilling within the city walls due to the fire risk, Lucas distilled from a wooden shed outside Amsterdam. Today Bols is one of the largest liqueur producers in the world.

Bols Blue is distilled from a blend of predominantly natural products from around the world – herbs, sweet red oranges, the characteristically flavourful bitter Curaçao oranges and the rare Kinnow oranges. This gives Bols Blue a fresh, yet complex orange scent and taste.

Bols Blue is frequently used by bartenders due to its distinctive deep blue colour and refreshing taste, which feature orange zest with a hint of spice.

Alexander's Big Brother ●●●○○
Artlantic ●●●○○
Baby Blue Martini ●●●●○
Bazooka Joe ●●○○○
Bikini Martini ●●●●○
Black Mussel ●●●●○
Blue Angel ●●●○○
Blue Bird ●●●○○
Blue Champagne ●●●○○
Blue Cosmo ●●●●○
Blue Hawaiian ●●●○○
Blue Heaven ●●○○○
Blue Kamikaze ●●●●○
Blue Lady ●●●○○
Blue Lagoon ●●●○○
Blue Margarita ●●●●○
Blue Monday ●●●●○
Blue Passion ●●●●○
Blue Riband ●●●○○
Blue Star ●●●○○
Blue Velvet Margarita ●●●●○
Blue Wave ●●●○○
Cactus Jack ●●●●○
China Blue ●●●○○

BOURBON

See 'Whiskey – Bourbon'

BUTTERSCOTCH SCHNAPPS LIQUEUR

Butterscotch is one of those indulgent flavours that take us back to our youth, a world of cookies, ice-cream toppings and candies. Sweet and creamy, it also has a wonderfully tangy bite.

The name has nothing to do with Scotch whisky, or anything Scottish at all. It comes from the term 'scotch', meaning to cut or score a surface, and 'butter' for the butter in the candy. When butterscotch candy is poured out to cool, it is scotched to make it easier to break into pieces later.

Butterscotch liqueur captures the heart of butterscotch so you can easily add that wonderful burnt, buttery, sugary flavour to cocktails.

Apple Cart ●●●●○
Banoffee Martini ●●●●○
Bit-O-Honey ●●●○○
Bon Bon Martini ●●●●○
Bourbon Cookie ●●●●○
Butterscotch Daiquiri ●●●●○
Butterscotch Delight ●●●●○
Butterscotch Martini ●●●●○

CACAO DARK (CRÈME DE) LIQUEUR

See 'Giffard Brown Crème de Cacao Liqueur'

CACAO WHITE (CRÈME DE) LIQUEUR

See 'Giffard White Crème de Cacao Liqueur'

CACHAÇA

Pronounced 'Ka-Shah-Sa', cachaça is the spirit of Brazil. As it is based on sugar cane, it is very similar to a rum. However, maize meal is traditionally used to start the fermentation, so many brands of cachaça are not strictly rums. Further, most rums are produced from molasses, a by-product of sugar refining, but the best cachaça is distilled from fermented sugar cane juice. (Many bigger brands, however, use molasses, which ferments more quickly as the sugars break down faster after they have been burnt. And a lot of smaller distillers use sugar cane syrup.)

Cachaça is distilled to a maximum of 75% alcoholic strength, unlike most light rums which are usually distilled to 96% strength. This lower distillation strength means cachaça retains more of the aroma and flavour of the sugar cane and is less refined than most rums.

Abaci Batida ●●●●○
Azure Martini ●●●●○
Banana Batida ●●●●○
Basilian ●●●○○
Batida De Coco ●●●○○
Beja Flor ●●●●○
Berry Caipirinha ●●●●○
Brazilian Berry ●●●●○
Brazilian Coffee ●●●●○
Brazilian Cosmopolitan ●●●○○
Buzzard's Breath ●●●●○
Cachaca Daiquiri ●●●●○
Caipiginger ●●●○○
Caipirinha ●●●●●
Caipirinha (Difford's serve) ●●●●●
Caipiruva ●●●●○
Carneval Batida ●●●●○
Coffee Batida ●●●○○

CALVADOS BOULARD GRAND SOLAGE

40% alc./vol. (80°proof)

www.calvados-boulard.com

Producer: Calvados Boulard S.A., Fécamp, France.

Calvados is a French brandy made from apples. The name is an appellation contrôlée, meaning that Calvados can only be produced in defined areas of north-west France.

Pays d'Auge, the area around the villages of Orne and Eure, produces the best Calvados and by law all AOC Pays d'Auge Calvados must be double-distilled in pot stills.

Boulard, founded in 1825 and still family-owned, blend Grand Solage from cider brandies aged between three and five years. The intense fruit and light smoothness of this Pays D'auge makes it perfect for cocktails.

A.J. ●●●●○
Ambrosia ●●●●○
Angel Face ●●●●●
Ante ●●●●○
Apple Blossom Cocktail ●●●●●
Apple & Custard Martini ●●●○○
Apple & Spice ●●●○○
Apple Brandy Sour ●●●●○
Apple Buck ●●●●○
Apple Cart ●●●●○
Apple Sunrise ●●●○○
Apples 'N' Pears ●●●●●
Aunt Emily ●●●●○
Avenue ●●●○○
Bentley ●●●●○
Bolero ●●●○○
Calvados Cocktail ●●●●○
Castro ●●●●○
Cider Apple Cooler ●●●●○
Corpse Reviver ●●●●○
Cyder Press ●●●●○

CHAMBORD LIQUEUR

Achilles Heel ●●●●○
Basil Grande ●●●●○
Black Cherry Martini ●●●●○
Black Forest Gateau Martini ●●●●●
Cascade Martini ●●●●○
Cham 69 #1 ●●●●○
Cham 69 #2 ●●●○○

Cham Cham ●●●●○
Concealed Weapon ●●●○○
Creamy Bee ●●●●○
Crimson Blush ●●●●○
Crown Stag ●●●●○

CAMPARI

Americano ●●●●○
Bellissimo ●●●○○
Bitterest Pill ●●●●○
Bloodhound ●●●●○
Cardinale ●●●●○
Copper Illusion ●●●●○
Covadonga ●●●○○
Cumbersome ●●●●○
CVO Firevault ●●●●○

CARAMEL LIQUEUR

Derived from the Latin 'cannamella' for sugar cane, caramel means melted sugar that has been browned by heating. Tiny amounts of caramel have long been used to colour spirits and liqueurs but caramel flavoured liqueurs are a relatively recent phenomenon.

Caramel Manhattan ●●●●●
Crème Brûlée Martini ●●●●○

CHAMPAGNE

The vineyards of the Champagne region are the most northerly in France, lying north-east of Paris, on either side of the River Marne. Most of the champagne houses are based in one of two towns: Epernay and Reims.

Champagne, surprisingly, is made predominantly from black grapes. The three grape varieties used are Pinot Noir (the red grape of Burgundy), Pinot Meunier (a fruitier relative of Pinot Noir) and Chardonnay. Pinot Meunier is the most commonly used of these three varieties with Chardonnay, the only white grape, accounting for less than 30% of vines in the Champagne region. Pinot Meunier buds late and ripens early so can be relied upon to ripen throughout the Champagne region, which probably explains its domination.

Absolutely Fabulous ●●●●○
Air Mail ●●●●○
Alfonso ●●●○○
Ambrosia ●●●●○
Americana ●●●●○
Anita's Attitude Adjuster ●●●●○

Apple Spritz ●●●●○
Atomic Cocktail ●●●○○
Autumn Punch ●●●●○
B2C2 ●●●○○
Baltic Spring Punch ●●●●○
Beverly Hills Iced Tea ●●●●○
Black Magic
Black Mussel ●●●○○
Black Velvet ●●●○○
Bling! Bling! ●●●●○
Blue Champagne ●●●○○
Breakfast At Terrell's ●●●●○
Buck's Fizz ●●●○○
Carol Channing ●●●○○
Cham 69 #2 ●●●●○
Cham Cham ●●●●○
Champagne Cocktail ●●●○○
Champagne Cup ●●●●○
Champagne Daisy ●●●○○
Chin Chin ●●●●○
Colonel's Big Opu ●●●●○
Cordless Screwdriver ●●●○○

CHARTREUSE GREEN

Angel's Share #2 ●●●●●
Beetle Jeuse ●●●●○
Bijou ●●●●○
The Broadmoor ●●●●●
Champs-Elysées ●●●●●

CHARTREUSE YELLOW

The Alamagoozlum Cocktail ●●●●●
Alaska Martini ●●●●○
Alaskan Martini ●●●●○
Ambrosia'tini ●●●○○
Apache ●●●○○
Barnacle Bill ●●●○○
Brandy Fix ●●●●○
Champagne Daisy ●●●○○
Cheeky Monkey ●●●●○
Club Cocktail #2 ●●●●○

CHERRY (BRANDY) LIQUEUR

This richly flavoured liqueur is made from the juice of ripe, dark red cherries. Crushing the kernels while pressing the cherries enhances almond notes in the cherry juice and is often evident in the finished liqueur.

Extracts of herbs and spices such as cinnamon and cloves produce a well-balanced liqueur. With its luscious cherry flavour and hints of almond and spice, this traditional liqueur is a versatile mixer.

Aquarius ●●●●○
Banana Boomer ●●●●○
Blood & Sand #1 ●●●●●
Blood & Sand #2 (Difford's formula) ●●●●●
Canaries ●●●○○
Cherrute ●●●●○
Cherry Alexander ●●●●○
Cherry Blossom ●●●●○
Cherry Daiquiri ●●●●○
Cherry Martini ●●●●○
Cherry Mash Sour ●●●●○

CINNAMON SCHNAPPS LIQUEUR

Cinnamon is obtained from the bark of several tropical trees. Sri Lanka and China are the largest producers. Cinnamon liqueurs have a warm, sweet, spicy flavour.

Apple Pie Martini ●●●●○
Apple Strudel Martini ●●●○○
Azure Martini ●●●●○
Butterfly's Kiss ●●●●○
Carrot Cake ●●●●○
Cinnamon Daiquiri ●●●○○
Creamy Bee ●●●●○

COCONUT RUM LIQUEUR

Coconut rums are mostly made in the Caribbean but are also common in France and Spain. They are made by blending rectified white rum with coconut extracts and tend to be presented in opaque white bottles.

Alien Secretion ●●●●○
Atomic Dog ●●●○○
Bahama Mama ●●●●○
Bahamas Daiquiri ●●●●○
Black & White Daiquiri ●●●●●
Black Widow ●●●○○
Caribbean Cruise ●●●●○
Caribbean Punch ●●●●○
Chill-Out Martini ●●●○○
Coco Cabana ●●●●○
Coconut Daiquiri ●●●●○
Coconut Water ●●●●○

COFFEE (ESPRESSO)

Coffee beans are the dried and roasted seed of a cherry which grows on a bush in the tropics. There are two main species of coffee plant: Coffea Arabica and Coffea Canephora. These are commonly known as Arabica and Robusta. Arabica is relatively low in caffeine, more delicate and requires more intensive cultivation. Robusta is higher in caffeine, more tolerant of climate and parasites, and can be grown fairly cheaply. Robusta beans tend to be woody and bitter while Arabica beans have well-rounded, subtle flavours.

Most of the recipes in this guide which use coffee call for espresso and, as with other ingredients, the quality of this will greatly affect the finished drink. I strongly recommend using an Arabica coffee brewed in an espresso machine or a moka pot.

Black Martini ●●●●●
Brazilian Coffee ●●●●○
Café Gates (filter coffee) ●●●●○
Coffee Batida ●●●○○
Cola De Mono ●●●●●
Cuppa Joe ●●●●○

COFFEE LIQUEUR

Coffee flavoured liqueurs are made by infusing coffee beans in alcohol or by infusing beans in hot water and then blending with alcohol. Look for brands made using Arabica coffee beans.

Adios ●●●○○
After Six Shot ●●●○○
Afterburner ●●●●○
Aggravation ●●●●○
Alexander The Great ●●●●○
Alexandra ●●●●○
Alice From Dallas ●●●●○
All Fall Down ●●●●○
Apache ●●●○○
Attitude Adjuster ●●●○○
Avalanche Shot ●●●○○
B5200 ●●●○○
B-52 Shot ●●●●○
B-53 Shot ●●●○○
B-54 Shot ●●●○○
B-55 Shot ●●●●○
B-52 Frozen ●●●●○
Baby Guinness ●●●●○
Bahamas Daiquiri ●●●●●
Bartender's Root Beer ●●●●○
Beam-Me-Up Scotty ●●●○○
Beam-Me-Up Scotty Shot ●●●○○
Black Irish ●●●○○
Black Russian ●●●○○
Blow Job ●●●○○
Blushin' Russian ●●●●○
Brazilian Monk ●●●●○
Bulldog ●●●●○
Bumble Bee ●●●●○
Buona Sera Shot ●●●●○
Burnt Toasted Almond ●●●○○
Café Gates ●●●●○
California Root Beer ●●●●○
Carrot Cake ●●●●○
Casanova ●●●●○

Chocolarita ●●●●○
Chocolate Biscuit ●●●●○
Coffee & Vanilla Daiquiri ●●●●○
Coffee Batida ●●●○○
Cola De Mono ●●●●○
Colorado Bulldog ●●●○○
Crème De Café ●●●○○

COGNAC

Cognac is a fine French brandy from the region around the little town of Cognac in south-west France, recognised with its own appellation contrôlée. With its rolling countryside, groves of trees and the Charente River, the area is picturesque. It is divided into six sub-regions, reflecting variations in climate and soil. As a general rule, the best soil is the chalkiest. The most regarded (and most central) region, Grande Champagne, has only a very thin layer of top soil over solid chalk. The biggest houses only use grapes from the best four sub-regions to produce their cognacs.

A.B.C. ●●●●○
Adios Amigos Cocktail ●●●●○
Ambrosia ●●●●○
Ambrosia'tini ●●●●○
American Beauty #1 ●●●●●
American Beauty #2 ●●●●○
Angel's Share #1 ●●●●●
Angel's Share #2 ●●●●●
April Shower ●●●●○
Atomic Cocktail ●●●○○
Auntie's Hot Xmas Punch ●●●●○
B2C2 ●●●●○
B & B ●●●●○
Baltimore Egg Nog ●●●○○
Banana Bliss ●●●○○
BBC ●●●○○
Between the Sheets #1 (Classic Formula) ●●●○○
Between The Sheets #2 ●●●●●
Biarritz ●●●●○
The Bistro Sidecar ●●●●○
Black Feather ●●●●○
Blue Angel ●●●○○
Bolero Sour ●●●●●
Bombay ●●●●●
Bonnie Prince Charles ●●●●○
Bosom Caresser ●●●●○
Brandy Alexander ●●●●○
Brandy Blazer ●●●●○
Brandy Buck ●●●●○
Brandy Crusta ●●●●○
Brandy Fix ●●●●○
Brandy Fizz ●●●●○
Brandy Flip ●●●●●
Brandy Milk Punch ●●●●○
Brandy Smash ●●●●○
Brandy Sour ●●●●○
Brighton Punch ●●●●●
Bull's Blood ●●●●○
Bull's Milk ●●●●○
Call Me Old-Fashioned ●●●●●
Carrol Cocktail ●●●●○
Champagne Cocktail ●●●○○
Champagne Cup ●●●●○
Champs-Elysées ●●●●●
Chatham Hotel Special ●●●●○

Chocolate Biscuit ●●●○○
Chocolate Sidecar ●●●●○
Claret Cobbler ●●●●○
Classic ●●●●●
Clockwork Orange ●●●○○
The Comet ●●●●○
Corpse Reviver ●●●●○
Cosmopolitan Delight ●●●●●
Crux ●●●●○
Cuban Cocktail No. 3 #2 ●●●●○
Cuban Master ●●○○○

COINTREAU LIQUEUR

**40% alc./vol.
(80°proof)**

www.cointreau.com

**Producer: Rémy
Cointreau, Angers,
France**

The distilling firm of
Cointreau was
started in 1849 by
two brothers, Adolphe and
Edouard-Jean Cointreau, who
were confectioners in Angers.
The liqueur we know today was
created by Edouard Cointreau,
the son of Edouard-Jean, and first
marketed in the 1870s.

Cointreau is a triple sec - a
confusing term that means 'triple
dry', although triple secs are
sweet.

Where cocktail recipes call for
the use of triple sec, we
recommend Cointreau, which is
made from the fragrant peels of
bitter and sweet oranges,
carefully grown and meticulously
selected for their quality. A
versatile cocktail ingredient,
Cointreau can also be served
straight over ice, or mixed with
fruit juices, tonic or lemonade.

The mainstay of many classic
recipes, Cointreau has a luscious,
ripe taste featuring bitter orange,
zesty, citrus hints, a splash of
orange juice and a hint of spice.

Acapulco Daiquiri ●●●●○
Agent Orange ●●●●○
Alexander's Big Brother ●●●○○
Algeria ●●●●●
Allegrottini ●●●○○
Ambrosia ●●●●○
Amsterdam Cocktail ●●●●○
Anita's Attitude Adjuster ●●●●○
Ante ●●●●○
Apple Cart ●●●●○
Apple Manhattan #2 ●●●●○
Attitude Adjuster ●●○○○
B2C2 ●●●○○
Balalaika ●●●●○
Bamboo ●●●●●
Beach Iced Tea ●●●●○

Beachcomber ●●●●○
Beja Flor ●●●●○
Between the Sheets #1 (Classic
Formula) ●●●●○
Between The Sheets #2 ●●●●●
Beverly Hills Iced Tea ●●●○○
The Big Easy ●●●●○
Bitter Sweet Symphony ●●●○○
Black Feather ●●●●○
Blue Champagne ●●●○○
Blue Monday ●●●○○
Blue Riband ●●●●○
Blue Velvet Margarita ●●●●○
Boston Tea Party ●●●○○
Bourbon Crusta ●●●●●
Bourbonella ●●●●○
Brandy Crusta ●●●●○
Brazilian Cosmopolitan ●●●○○
Breakfast Martini ●●●●●
Cable Car ●●●●○
Call Me Old-Fashioned ●●●●●
Canaries ●●●○○
Cappercaille ●●●●○
Casablanca #1 ●●●●○
Celtic Margarita ●●●●●
Charles Daiquiri ●●●●○
Chas ●●●●○
Chelsea Sidecar ●●●●○
Cherry Blossom ●●●○○
China Martini ●●●○○
Citrus Martini ●●●●○
Claridge ●●●●○
Colonel's Big Opu ●●●●○
Coolman Martini ●●●●●
Copper Illusion ●●●●○
Corpse Reviver #2 ●●●●○
Cosmopolitan #1 (simple version)
●●●●●
Cosmopolitan #2 (complex version)
●●●●●
Cosmopolitan #3 (Popular version)
●●●●●
Cosmopolitan #4 (1934 recipe) ●●●●○
Cranapple Breeze ●●●●○
Crossbow ●●●○○
Crux ●●●●○
Cuban Special ●●●○○

CRANBERRY JUICE - RED

Cranberries are native to
America and are grown in
large, flooded fields, known
as cranberry bogs. Experts
say you can tell when a
cranberry is ready to eat
because it bounces.
Cranberries are high in
vitamin C and pectin, and a
popular natural remedy for
cystitis.

Cranberry is the exception
which proves the 'fresh is
best' rule. Don't even
contemplate muddling fresh
berries: pure cranberry juice
is extremely sour and is
normally sweetened and
blended to make it more
palatable.

Pick up a carton of cranberry
juice from the refrigerated
display of your local
supermarket. As with other
juices, avoid the non-refriger-
ated products and read the
small print carefully – some
products end up with barely
any cranberry and taste far
too sweet. Look for products
containing at least 20%
cranberry juice.

Absolutely Fabulous ●●●●○
Alan's Apple Breeze ●●●●○
American Pie Martini ●●●●○
Apple & Cranberry Pie ●●●●○
Apple Breeze ●●●●○
Apple Of My Eire ●●●●○
Apple Pie Martini ●●●●○
Appleissimo ●●●●○
Apricot Cosmo ●●●●●
Aquarius ●●●○○
Arizona Breeze ●●●●○
Baby Woo Woo ●●●○○
Basil Grande ●●●●○
Bay Breeze ●●●○○
Beach Iced Tea ●●●●○
Between Decks ●●●●○
Blood Orange ●●●○○
Blush Martini ●●●●○
Bourbon Smash ●●●●○
Brake Tag ●●●○○
Brazilian Cosmopolitan ●●●●○
C C Kazi ●●●●○
Cape Codder ●●●●○
Caribbean Breeze ●●●●○
Cascade Martini ●●●●○
Cassini ●●●●○
China Beach ●●●●○
Chinese Cosmopolitan ●●●●○
Chocolate & Cranberry Martini ●●●●○
Cool Martini ●●●●○
Cosmopolitan #1 (simple version)
●●●●●
Cosmopolitan #2 (complex version)
●●●●●
Cosmopolitan #3 (Popular version)
●●●●●
Cranberry & Mint Martini ●●●●○
Cranapple Breeze ●●●●○
Cranberry Cooler ●●●○○
Cranberry Delicious (Mocktail) ●●●○○
Cranberry Sauce ●●○○○
Creole Cosmo ●●●●●

CRANBERRY (WHITE) & GRAPE DRINK

White cranberry juice drinks are
made with white cranberries,
harvested before they develop
their familiar red colour. They
tend to be less tart than red
cranberry drinks.

Blue Cosmo ●●●●○
Blue Fin ●●●○○

CUCUMBER

The fruit of a climbing plant
originating from the foothills of
the Himalayas, cucumbers
should be used as fresh as
possible, so look for firm,
unwrinkled fruit. The skin can be
quite bitter so cucumber is best
peeled before use in cocktails.
Either muddle in the base of your
shaker or juice using an
extractor.

Basilian ●●●○○
Cucumber Martini ●●●●●
Cucumber & Mint Martini ●●●●○
Cucumber Sake-Tini ●●●●○
Cumbersome ●●●●○

DOUBLE (HEAVY) CREAM

I've specified 'double' or 'heavy
cream' in preference to lighter
creams. In many recipes this is
diluted with an equal measure of
milk – a combination known in the
trade as 'half & half'.

Absinthe Suisesse ●●●○○
Ace ●●●●○
Aggravation ●●●●○
Alessandro ●●●○○
Alexander ●●●●○
Alexander's Big Brother ●●●○○
Alexander's Sister ●●●●○
Alexander The Great ●●●●○
Alexandra ●●●●○
Apple & Cranberry Pie ●●●●○
Apple & Spice ●●●●○
Apple Pie Shot ●●●●○
Apple Strudel Martini ●●●○○
Atholl Brose ●●●●○
Avalanche ●●●●○
Baltimore Egg Nog ●●●○○
Bananas & Cream ●●●●○
Banoffee Martini ●●●●○
Banshee ●●○○○
Barbara ●●●○○
Barbary Coast Highball ●●●●○
Barnamint ●●●○○
Barranquilla Green Jade ●●●○○
Bazooka ●●●○○
BBC ●●●●○
Bee's Knees #1 ●●●●○
Bird Of Paradise ●●●●●
Black Forest Gateau Martini ●●●●●
Black Widow ●●●●○
Blue Angel ●●●○○
Blush Martini ●●●●○
Blushin' Russian ●●●●○
Bourbon Cookie ●●●●○
Bourbon Milk Punch ●●●●○
Brandy Alexander ●●●●○
Brandy Milk Punch ●●●●○
Brazilian Coffee ●●●●○
Breakfast At Terrell's ●●●●○
Bubblegum Shot ●●●○○
Bulldog ●●●○○

Bullfrog ●●○○○
Burnt Toasted Almond ●●●○○
Buzzard's Breath ●●●●○
Café Gates ●●●●○
Casanova ●●●●○
Chatham Hotel Special ●●●●○
Cherry Alexander ●●●●○
Coco Cabana ●●●○○
Colorado Bulldog ●●●○○
Cream Cake ●●●○○
Creamsicle ●●●●○
Creamy Creamsicle ●●●●○
Crème Brûlée Martini ●●●●○
Créme De Cafè ●●●○○

CREAM OF COCONUT

This is a non-alcoholic, sticky blend of coconut juice, sugar, emulsifier, cellulose, thickeners, citric acid and salt. Fortunately it tastes better than it sounds and is an essential ingredient of a good Piña Colada. One 15oz/425ml can will make approximately 25 drinks. Once opened the contents should be transferred to a suitable container and stored in a refrigerator. This may thicken the product, so gentle warming may be required prior to use. Coconut milk is very different and cannot be substituted.

Bahia ●●●○○
Banana Colada ●●●●○
Batida de Coco ●●●○○
Blue Hawaiian ●●●●○
Buzzard's Breath ●●●●○
Coco Naut ●●○○○

CRÈME DE BANANE LIQUEUR

See 'Giffard Crème de Banane du Brésil liqueur'

CRÈME DE CACAO LIQUEUR

See 'Giffard Brown Crème de Cacao liqueur' and 'Giffard White Crème de Cacao liqueur'

CRÈME DE CASSIS LIQUEUR

See 'Giffard Crème de Cassis Noir de Bourgogne'

CRÈME DE FRAISE LIQUEUR

See 'Giffard Crème de Fraise de Bois'

CRÈME DE FRAMBOISE LIQUEUR

See 'Giffard Crème de Framboise Liqueur'

CRÈME DE MENTHE GREEN LIQUEUR

See 'Giffard Green Crème de Menthe'

CRÈME DE MENTHE WHITE LIQUEUR

See 'Giffard White Crème de Menthe Pastille'

CRÈME DE MYRTILLE LIQUEUR

See 'Giffard Crème de Myrtille' Liqueur

CRÈME DE MÛRE LIQUEUR

See 'Giffard Crème de Mûres Liqueur'

DRAMBUIE LIQUEUR

Apple of My Eire ●●●●○
Atholl Brose ●●●●○
Bonnie Prince Charles ●●●●○
Causeway ●●●●○

DUBONNET RED

Alfonso ●●●●○
Ante ●●●●○
Aviator ●●●●○
Bartender's Martini ●●●●○
Bentley ●●●●○
Blackthorn Cocktail ●●●●○
Crux ●●●●○

EGGS

Raw eggs can be hazardous to health so you may decide it is safer to use commercially produced pasteurised egg white, particularly if you are infirm or pregnant (but then you probably shouldn't be drinking cocktails anyway).

Many cocktails only taste their best when made with fresh eggs. I'm sure I've suffered more upset stomachs from drinking too much alcohol than I have as a result of bad eggs. That said, it's worth taking steps to reduce the risk of Salmonella poisoning and therefore I recommend you store small, free range eggs in a refrigerator and use them well before the sell-by-date. Don't consume eggs if:

1. You are uncertain about their freshness.
2. There is a crack or flaw in the shell.
3. They don't wobble when rolled across a flat surface.
4. The egg white is watery instead of gel-like.

5. The egg yolk is not convex and firm.
6. The egg yolk bursts easily.
7. They smell foul.

Absinthe Sour ●●●●○
Absinthe Suisesse ●●●○○
Acapulco Daiquiri ●●●●○
Ace ●●●○○
The Alamagoozlum Cocktail ●●●●●
Amaretto Sour ●●●●○
Apple Brandy Sour ●●●●●
Apricot Lady Sour ●●●○○
Autumn Martini ●●●●○
Barranquilla Green Jade ●●●○○
Biarritz ●●●●○
Blue Lady ●●●○○
Bolero Sour ●●●●●
Brandy Sour ●●●●●
Brass Rail ●●●●○
Cable Car ●●●●○
Casablanca #1 ●●●●○
Champs-Elysées ●●●●●
Clover Leaf Cocktail #1 ●●●●○
Clover Leaf Martini ●●●●●
The Cold Winter Warmer Sour ●●●●○
Commodore #1 ●●●●○
Concealed Weapon ●●●○○

ELDERFLOWER LIQUEUR

See 'St. Germain'

FINO

See under 'Sherry – Fino'

GIFFARD APRICOT BRANDY DU ROUSSILLON

25% alc./vol. (50°proof)

www.giffard.com

Producer: Giffard & Cie, Angers, France

Apricot Brandy is sometimes also known as 'apry'. It is a liqueur produced by infusing apricots in selected cognacs and flavouring the infusion with various herbs to bring out the best flavour and aroma of the apricots. This amber coloured liqueur is one of Giffard's most popular liqueurs.

With a aroma of juicy apricots, this distinctively flavoured liqueur is suited to use in a variety of different cocktails. The light clean taste features apricot with a hint of brandy and almond.

Alan's Apple Breeze ●●●○○
Algeria ●●●●●
Angel Face ●●●●●
Apricot Fizz ●●●○○
Apricot Lady Sour ●●●●○
Apricot Mango Martini ●●●●○
Apricot Martini ●●●○○
Apricot Sour ●●●●●
Atlantic Breeze ●●●○○
Aunt Emily ●●●●○
Bajan Passion ●●●●○
Banana Boomer ●●●●○
Barnum ●●●○○
Bermuda Rose Cocktail ●●●●○
Bingo ●●●○○
Bitter Sweet Symphony ●●●○○
Bossa Nova #1 ●●●●○
Bossa Nova #2 ●●●○○
Boston ●●●○○
Cappercaille ●●●●○
Charlie Chaplin ●●●○○
Claridge ●●●●○
Colonel T ●●●●○
Columbus Daiquiri ●●●○○
Cruel Intention ●●●●○
Cuban Cocktail NO. 3 #2 ●●●●○

GIFFARD BROWN CRÈME DE CACAO LIQUEUR

25% alc./vol. (50°proof)

www.giffard.com

Producer: Giffard & Cie, Angers, France

The finest roasted cacao beans are used to prepare Giffard brown crème de cacao. The cacao seeds are first broken open and then percolated. Various herbs are added to give the liqueur its own distinctive flavour. Please note that 'brown crème de cacao' liqueurs are sometimes alternatively named 'dark crème de cacao'.

Giffard brown crème de cacao is perfect for adding a rich chocolate flavour to any cocktail. Choose between the lighter, more delicately flavoured white or this rich, dark version.

Apple Strudel Martini ●●●○○

Brandy Alexander ●●●●○
Brazilian Monk ●●●●○
Café Gates ●●●○○
Chatham Hotel Special ●●●●○
Chocolarita ●●●●○
Chocolate Biscuit ●●●○○
Chocolate Puff ●●●●○
Chocolate Sidecar ●●●●○

GIFFARD CRÈME DE FRAMBOISE LIQUEUR

18% alc./vol. (36°proof)

www.giffard.com

Producer: Giffard & Cie, Angers, France

The French refer to raspberry liqueurs as 'crème de framboise'. This comes from the French word for raspberry – 'framboise'– and 'crème', as in the French phrase 'crème de la crème', meaning 'best of the best'.

Giffard crème de framboise is made by macerating fesh raspberries in neutral alcohol which gives this liqueur an intense, rich, raspberry flavour.

Blood Orange ●●●○○
Carol Channing ●●●○○

GIFFARD CRÈME DE MÛRE LIQUEUR

16% alc./vol. (32°proof)

www.giffard.com

Producer: Giffard & Cie, Angers, France

The French refer to blackberry liqueurs as 'crème de mûre'. This comes from the French word for blackberry - 'mûre' - and 'crème', as in the French phrase 'crème de la crème', meaning 'best of the best'.

Giffard crème de mûre is made by macerating fresh blackberries in neutral alcohol which gives this

liqueur an intense, rich, blackberry flavour.

Basil Bramble Sling ●●●●○
Black & White Daiquiri ●●●●○
Bramble ●●●●●
Collection Martini ●●●○○
Congo Blue ●●●○○

GIFFARD CRÈME DE MYRTILLE LIQUEUR

The French refer to blueberry liqueurs as 'crème de myrtille'. This comes from the French word for blueberry 'myrtille' and 'crème' as in the French phrase 'crème de la crème', means 'best of the best'.

Giffard Crème de Myrtille is made by macerating fresh blueberries in neutral alcohol which gives this liqueur an intense, rich, blueberry flavour.

Blueberry Daiquiri ●●●○○
Blueberry Martini #1 ●●●●○

GIFFARD CRÈME DE BANANE DU BRÉSIL LIQUEUR

25% alc./vol. (50°proof)

www.giffard.com

Producer: Giffard & Cie, Angers, France

The French term 'crème de' indicates that one particular flavour predominates in the liqueur - it does not imply that the liqueur contains cream. Many fruit liqueurs are described as 'crème de' followed by the name of a fruit. This refers to the liqueur's quality, as in the phrase 'crème de la crème'. Therefore crème de banane is a banana flavoured liqueur made by infusion and maceration of the fruit in neutral spirit.

Giffard Banane du Brésil liqueur is made by slow maceration of best bananas from Brazil. Essence of banana adds an intense aroma, strengthened by a touch of Cognac.

Avalanche ●●●○○
Banana Batida ●●●●○
Banana Bliss ●●●○○
Banana Boomer ●●●●○
Banana Colada ●●●●○
Banana Daiquiri ●●●○○
Bananas & Cream ●●●●○
Banoffee Martini ●●●●○
Banshee ●●●○○
Bazooka ●●●○○
Bazooka Joe ●●●○○
Beam-Me-Up Scotty ●●●○○
Beam-Me-Up Scotty Shot ●●○○○
Beja Flor ●●●●○
Blow Job ●●●○○
Canaries ●●●○○
Caribbean Breeze ●●●●○
Chiclet Daiquiri ●●●○○

GIFFARD CRÈME DE CASSIS NOIR DE BOURGOGNE

20% alc./vol. (40°proof)

www.giffard.com

Producer: Giffard & Cie, Angers, France

As with other 'crème de' liqueurs, this term does not mean the liqueur contains any cream. Crème de cassis is a blackcurrant liqueur which originated in France and can be made by infusion and/or maceration. The original recipe for a crème de cassis is thought to have been formulated by Denis Lagoute in 1841 in the French Dijon region.

EEC law states that crème de cassis must have a minimum of 400g of sugar per litre and a minimum alcoholic strength of 15%. Unfortunately no minimum is set for the fruit content although the best brands will contain as much as 600g of blackcurrants per litre. Giffard has a high fruit content so a more fruity taste and a deeper colour than lesser brands.

Apple Sunrise ●●●○○
Arnaud Martini ●●●●○
Ballet Russe ●●●○○
Black Jack Cocktail ●●●●○
Black Forest Gateau Martini ●●●●●
Black Mussel ●●●○○
Blimey ●●●○○
Bolshoi Punch ●●●●○
Brazilian Berry ●●●●○
Cardinal Punch ●●●○○
Cassini ●●●●○
Chimayo ●●●○○
Country Breeze ●●●●○

GIFFARD CRÈME DE FRAISE DE BOIS

18% alc./vol.
(36°proof)

www.giffard.com

Producer: Giffard & Cie, Angers, France

'Fraise' is French for strawberry and Giffard crème de fraise is a strawberry liqueur made by infusion and maceration. The term 'bois' indicates that this liqueur is produced from wild strawberries.

This liqueur has a rich ripe strawberry flavour with light hints of citrus fruit. It is great served chilled, in a cocktail, over strawberries or in a fruit salad.

Black Forest Gateau Martini ●●●●●
Black Widow ●●●○○
Bourbon Blush ●●●●●

GIFFARD GREEN CRÈME DE MENTHE LIQUEUR

21% alc./vol.
(48°proof)

www.giffard.com

Producer: Giffard & Cie, Angers, France

Giffard Green Crème de Menthe is a green coloured liqueur flavoured with peppermint - the flavour is extracted from fresh mint leaves. Mint oils are distilled, creating a high quality and a very refreshing mint flavour. Crème de menthe has been long favoured as a digestive liqueur.

After Eight ●●●○○
Alexander's Sister ●●●○○
Barnamint ●●●○○
Barranquilla Green Jade ●●●○○
Bullfrog ●●○○○
Caruso Martini ●●●○○

GIFFARD WHITE CRÈME DE CACAO LIQUEUR

25% alc./vol.
(50°proof)

www.giffard.com

Producer: Giffard & Cie, Angers, France

A number of recipes require the chocolate flavour of crème de cacao but without the dark brown colour. In order to preserve the taste but eliminate the colour, Giffard extract the flavour of the finest roasted cacao beans by means of distillation instead of percolation. This process also gives Giffard white crème de cacao a lighter flavour than Giffard brown crème de cacao.

Giffard crème de cacao is perfect for adding a rich chocolate flavour to any cocktail. Choose between this lighter, more delicately flavoured white or the rich, dark version.

Ace of Clubs Daiquiri ●●●●●
After Eight ●●●○○
Alexander ●●●○○
Alexander the Great ●●●○○
All White Frappé ●●●○○
Apple Strudel Martini ●●●○○
Autumn Punch ●●●●○
Avalanche Shot ●●○○○
Banshee ●●●○○
Barbara ●●●○○
Barbary Coast Highball ●●●○○
Barbary Coast Martini ●●●●○
Behemoth ●●●○○
Bird of Paradise ●●●●●
Black Martini ●●●●●
Brandy Alexander ●●●●○
Butterscotch Martini ●●●●○
Cherry Alexander ●●●●○
Choc & Nut Martini ●●●○○
Chocolate & Cranberry Martini ●●●●○
Chocolate Martini ●●●●○
Chocolate Mint Martini ●●●●○
Chocolate Sazerac ●●●●○
Commodore #2 ●●●○○
Crossbow ●●●○○

GIFFARD WHITE CRÈME DE MENTHE PASTILLE

24% alc./vol.
(48°proof)

www.giffard.com

Producer: Giffard & Cie, Angers, France

More than a century ago, Emile Giffard was a dispensing chemist in Angers. Whilst working late one night a patron from the hotel next door arrived on his doorstep complaining of indigestion. She asked if Emile could concoct a drink from mint tablets. He ground the tablets into a fine powder, to which he added some spirit. The mixture cured her indigestion and left Emile with a great idea.

He imported peppermint leaves from England, which he used to distil a clear liqueur he called 'Menthe Pastille'. He began to market the liqueur, which proved an instant success, leading him to establish his own distillery. Menthe Pastille is still made to the original recipe at a distillery run by Emile's great grandson.

This aromatic liqueur is great served over crushed ice as a digestif or blended in a range of cocktails.

After Six Shot ●●○○○
Afterburner ●●●○○
All White Frappé ●●●○○
American Beauty #1 ●●●●●
American Beauty #2 ●●●●○
Bald Eagle Shot ●●○○○
Chiclet Daiquiri ●●●○○
Chocolate Mint Martini ●●●●○

GALLIANO LIQUEUR

30% alc./vol.
(60°proof)

www.galliano.com

Producer: Rémy Cointreau, Angers, France.

Galliano is a vibrant, golden, vanilla flavoured liqueur from Italy, easily recognised by its distinctive, tall fluted bottle, inspired by Roman columns. Invented in 1896, Galliano is made from over 30 ingredients including star anise, lavender, ginger and vanilla. A noted cocktail ingredient, Galliano's signature drink is the Harvey Wallbanger. Apparently, Harvey was a surfer at Manhattan Beach, California, and his favourite drink was a Screwdriver with added Galliano. One day in the late 60s, while celebrating winning a surfing competition, he staggered from bar to bar banging his surfboard on the walls and so the cocktail was born.

The versatility of Galliano ensures that it can be enjoyed in cocktails and as a long drink. It also works particularly well as a hot shot with coffee and cream. The lovely smell of Galliano is reminiscent of a pack of Tic-Tac sweets, while its smooth vanilla taste is complimented by peppermint and spiced with cinnamon, ginger, nutmeg and citrus.

Adam & Eve ●●●●○
Atlantic Breeze ●●●○○
Bartender's Root Beer ●●●●○
Bossa Nova #1 ●●●●○
Bossa Nova #2 ●●●●○
Bourbon Milk Punch ●●●●○
California Root Beer ●●●●○
Caribbean Punch ●●●●○
Casablanca ●●●○○

GIN

See 'Plymouth Gin'

GINGER ALE

A non-alcoholic drink made by adding ginger essence, colouring and sweeteners to aerated water. Not as powerful in flavour as ginger beer.

Apple Buck ●●●●○
Basilian ●●●●○
The Big Easy ●●●●○
Bora Bora Brew (mocktail) ●●●○○
Brandy Buck ●●●●○
The Buck ●●●○○
Causeway ●●●●○
Cranapple Breeze ●●●●○

GINGER BEER

A fizzy drink flavoured with ginger - either non-alcoholic or only mildly so. Buy a quality brand or brew your own as follows:

Combine 2oz/56 grams of peeled and crushed root ginger, two lemons sliced into thick rings, one teaspoon of cream of tartar, 1lb/45o grams sugar and 1 gallon/ 4 litres water in a large stainless steel saucepan and bring to the boil. Stir and leave to cool to blood temperature. Stir in 1 oz/ 28 grams of yeast and leave to ferment for 24 hours. Skim off the yeast from the surface and fine strain the liquid into four sterilised 1 litre plastic bottles with screw caps. (Leave at least 2 inches/5cm of air at the top of each bottle and ensure all utensils are scrupulously clean.). Place bottles upright and release excess pressure after 12 hours. Check again after another 12 hours. Once the bottles feel firm and under pressure, place them in the refrigerator and consume their contents within three days.

Bomber ●●●●○

GRAND MARNIER

40% alc./vol.
(80° proof)

www.grand-marnier.com

Producer:
Marnier-Lapostolle
(Société des Produits), Paris, France.

Grand Marnier is one of the best known and most widely sold premium liqueurs in the world. With a cognac base, its unique flavour and aroma come from the maceration and distillation of natural, tropical orange peels.

Founded in 1827 by Jean Baptiste Lapostolle, Grand Marnier is still a family-run business today and continues to use traditional production methods and the original Grand Marnier recipe. Despite its traditional credentials and heritage, Grand Marnier is an essential cocktail ingredient in today's leading style bars. Grand Marnier is silky rich with a zesty, juicy flavour. It has a good underlying bite of bitter orange and hints of marmalade and cognac richness at the edges, making it the perfect cocktail partner.

Grand Marnier also produce two special cuvées or blends, 'Grand Marnier Cuvée du Centenaire', created in 1927 by Louis-Alexandre Marnier-Lapostolle to celebrate the 100th anniversary of the company's foundation; and 'Grand Marnier Cuvée du Cent Cinquantenaire', an exceptional Grand Marnier created in 1977 by the Chairman of the company, Jacques Marnier-Lapostolle, to celebrate the company's 150th anniversary.

Some cocktails in this guide which call for Grand Marnier may benefit from the extra complexity provided by these exceptional cuvées. I've marked these drinks with an '*' in the list below and after Grand Marnier in the recipe.

Agent Orange ●●●●○
The Alamagoozlum Cocktail* ●●●●●
Alfonso Martini ●●●●○
Alice From Dallas ●●●●○
Alice In Wonderland ●●●○○
Apple Of My Eire ●●●●○
Attitude Adjuster ●●●○○
B-52 Shot ●●●●○
B-52 Frozen ●●●●○
B. J. Shot ●●●○○
Bartender's Martini ●●●●○
Basil Grande ●●●●○
Basilian ●●●●○
Biarritz ●●●●○
Bingo ●●●○○
Black Magic
Blow Job ●●●●○
Blueberry Tea ●●●●○
Bombay ●●●●●
Bosom Caresser ●●●●○
Boulevard ●●●●○
Brandy Buck ●●●●○
Bull's Blood ●●●●○
Cactus Banger ●●●●○
Café Gates ●●●○○
Californian Martini ●●●●○
Caravan ●●●○○
Champagne Cup ●●●●○
Charente Collins ●●●●○
Chas ●●●●○
Claret Cobbler ●●●●○
Classic ●●●●●
Clockwork Orange ●●●●○
The Comet ●●●●○
Cosmopolitan Delight ●●●●●
Creamsicle ●●●●○

GRAPEFRUIT JUICE

This citrus fruit originated in Jamaica and may take its unusual name from the way the unripe fruit hangs in green clusters from the tree like bunches of grapes. Or then again, maybe some early botanist just got confused.

Grapefruit is a recognised antioxidant and pink grapefruit contains lycopene, which is thought to boost the body's immune system. Consuming large quantities of concentrated grapefruit juice can, however, produce reactions with certain prescription-only medicines.

As a rule of thumb – the darker the flesh, the sweeter the juice and the more beta-carotene and vitamins. But even the sweetest of grapefruits are wonderfully sharp and tart.

I must confess that I tend to use packaged 'freshly squeezed' grapefruit juice from the supermarket. However, this is a relatively easy fruit to juice yourself using a citrus press or an electric spinning juicer. Simply cut in half and juice away, taking care to avoid the pith, which can make the juice bitter. As with other citrus fruits, avoid storing in the refrigerator immediately prior to use as cold fruit yield less juice.

A.J. ●●●●○
Acapulco ●●●○○
Arizona Breeze ●●●●○
Baby Blue Martini ●●●●○
Bald Eagle Martini ●●●●●
Bitter Sweet Symphony ●●●●○
Blinker ●●●●○
Bloodhound ●●●●○
Buena Vida ●●●●●
Cherrute ●●●●○
Chihuahua Margarita ●●●●○
China Blue ●●●●○
China Blue Martini ●●●●○
Crimson Blush ●●●●○

GRAPES

Oddly, many of the grapes which are classically used for winemaking are not particularly good to eat. Only a few, like Gamay, Tokay, Zinfandel and Muscat, are used for both purposes.

The main commercially available table grapes are Concord, which gives a purple juice which is used for concentrates and jellies, Emperor, which is red and thick-skinned, and Thompson Seedless, which is green and sweet. Fresh grape juice has a delicate, subtle flavour which is very different from the syrupy stuff in cartons.

The best way to extract juice is to muddle the required number of grapes in the base of your shaker.

Recipes in this guide call for 'seedless red grapes' or 'seedless white grapes'. Obviously, if you've opted for a grape that has seeds you'll need to remove them yourself before you muddle the grapes. Crushing seeds releases bitter flavours which can spoil a drink.

Black Magic ●●●○○
Caipiruva ●●●●○
The Comet ●●●●○

GREEN BANANA LIQUEUR

Absinthe Without Leave ●●○○○
Bali Trader ●●●●○

GRENADINE

See 'Pomegranate (Grenadine) Syrup'

HALF AND HALF

This blend of 50% milk and 50% cream is relatively unknown in the UK. I've listed milk and cream as separate ingredients in both the American and the British versions of this guide.

HAZELNUT LIQUEUR

French hazelnut liqueurs are known as crème de noisette. Edmond Briottet is one of the better producers.

Apple Pie Shot ●●●●○
Bellissimo ●●●○○
The Bistro Sidecar ●●●●○
Black Nuts ●●○○○
Brazilian Monk ●●●●○
Butterfly's Kiss ●●●○○
Cherry & Hazelnut Daiquiri ●●●●○
Choc & Nut Martini ●●●○○
Creamy Bee ●●●●○
Cuppa Joe ●●●●○

HONEY

Many bartenders dilute honey with equal parts of warm water to make it easier to mix. I prefer to use good quality runny honey (preferably orange blossom) and dissolve it by stirring into the cocktail's base spirit prior to adding the other ingredients. This may be a tad time consuming but it avoids unnecessary dilution. Decant your honey into a squeezy plastic bottle with a fine nozzle for easy dispensing.

Aged Honey Daiquiri ●●●●○
Air Mail ●●●●○
Applily Married ●●●●○
Atholl Brose ●●●●○
Banana Smoothie (mocktail) ●●●●○
Basil & Honey Daiquiri ●●●●●
Bebbo ●●●●○
Bee Sting ●●●●○
Bee's Knees #1 ●●●●○
Bee's Knees #2 ●●●●●
Bee's Knees #3 ●●●●○
Blue Blazer ●●●○○
Canchanchara ●●●●○
Cappercaille ●●●●○
Cold Comfort ●●●●○
The Cold Winter Warmer Sour ●●●●○

HONEY LIQUEUR

There are many varieties of honey liqueur but the Polish brands claim the oldest heritage. Traditional Polish vodka-based honey liqueurs are thought to have originated in the 16th century. Besides the cocktails below, these liqueurs are worth enjoying neat and slightly warmed in a balloon glass – at London's Baltic they warm the bottle in a baby's bottle warmer.

Bohemian Iced Tea ●●●●○
Chinese Cosmopolitan ●●●●○
Creamy Bee ●●●●○

ICE CREAM (VANILLA)

Vanilla ice cream may not be exciting, but it is safe and almost universally liked. There are few people who can honestly say they hate the stuff, making it the obvious choice for a bar's freezer. Splash out on a decent brand. You'll taste the difference.

Barnamint ●●●○○
Black Irish ●●●○○
Brazilian Monk ●●●●○

INFUSIONS

Some recipes call for an infused spirit, such as vanilla-infused rum. You make this by putting three split vanilla pods in a bottle of rum and leaving it to stand for a fortnight. Warming and turning the bottle frequently can speed the infusion.

Other herbs, spices and even fruits can be infused in a similar manner in vodka, gin, rum, whiskey and tequila. Whatever spirit you decide to use, pick a brand that is at least 40% alcohol by volume.

Be aware that when the level of spirit in a bottle drops below the flavouring, the alcohol loses its preservative effect and the flavouring can start to rot. Also be careful not to load the spirit with too much flavour or leave it to infuse for too long. Sample the infusion every couple of days to ensure the taste is not becoming overpowering.

IRISH CREAM LIQUEUR

In November 1974 R&A Bailey perfected the technique of combining Irish whiskey, cocoa and fresh cream without souring the cream. Sales grew quickly and it is now the world's best selling liqueur. There are, however, many equally good alternatives.

A.B.C. ●●●●○
Absinthe Without Leave ●●●○○
After Six Shot ●●●○○
Apache ●●●●○
B5200 ●●●○○
B-52 Shot ●●●○○
B-53 Shot ●●●○○
B-54 Shot ●●●○○
B-55 Shot ●●●○○
B-52 Frozen ●●●●○
B. J. Shot ●●●○○
Baby Guinness ●●●●○
Bananas & Cream ●●●●○
Barnamint ●●●○○
Bazooka Joe ●●●○○
Beam-Me-Up Scotty ●●●○○
Beam-Me-Up Scotty Shot ●●●○○
Bit-O-Honey ●●●○○
Black Dream ●●●○○
Black Irish ●●●○○
Bumble Bee ●●●●○
Burnt Toasted Almond ●●●○○
Butterscotch Delight ●●●●○
Carrot Cake ●●●●○
Chill-Out Martini ●●●○○
Creamy Bee ●●●●○
Cream Cake ●●●●○

JÄGERMEISTER

Assisted Suicide ●●●○○
Crown Stag ●●●○○

JONGE JENEVER

Jenever (or genever) is a juniper-flavoured spirit from Holland and Belgium. The juniper means jenever is technically a gin and in fact it was the forerunner of the London dry gins popular today. There are three basic styles of jenever - 'oude' (literally, 'old'), 'jonge' ('young') and 'korenwijn' ('corn wine'). They differ according to the percentage of malt-wine (a kind of unaged whiskey) and botanicals contained.

Jonge jenever is so named because it is a modern, contemporary style. It was first developed in the 1950s in response to consumer demand for a lighter, more mixable jenever.

The Alamagoozlum Cocktail ●●●●●
Amsterdam Cocktail ●●●●○
Collins ●●●●○

KETEL ONE VODKA

40% alc./vol. (80°proof)

www.KetelOne.com

Producer: Nolet Distillery, Schiedam, The Netherlands.

Ketel One vodka is the creation of one of Holland's oldest distilling families, the Nolet family of Schiedam, who have been distilling since 1691 when Joannes Nolet started his distillation business.

The Dutch refer to their pot stills as 'ketels', thus this vodka is named after the Nolets' original coal-fired pot still number one, still used today in the production of Ketel One. After distillation,

this small batch distilled spirit is then slowly filtered through charcoal to ensure its purity.

Ten generations after Joannes, Carolus Nolet now runs the company with the help of his two sons, Carl and Bob. They introduced Ketel One to the US in 1991 where it has since enjoyed phenomenal growth. This looks as if it's being repeated in the UK where the brand was launched in 1999.

Ketel One's balanced and clean palate with its classic wheat character makes beautifully smooth Martinis while still showing the character of the grain from which it is made.

Absolutely Fabulous ●●●●○
After Eight ●●●○○
Agent Orange ●●●●○
Alabama Slammer #1●●●●○
Alexander The Great ●●●●○
Alien Secretion ●●●●○
Almond Martini #1●●●●○
Anis'tini ●●●●○
Anita's Attitude Adjuster ●●●○○
Apple & Elderflower Martini (Fresh Fruit) ●●●●○
Apple & Melon Martini ●●●●○
Apricot Cosmo ●●●●●
Asian Ginger Martini ●●●●○
Atomic Cocktail ●●●○○
Awol ●●●●○
B-53 Shot ●●●○○
Baby Woo Woo ●●●○○
Balalaika ●●●●○
Bali Trader ●●●●○
Ballet Russe ●●●●○
Banana Boomer ●●●●○
Barbara ●●●○○
Basil Grande ●●●●○
Basilico ●●●●○
Bay Breeze ●●●○○
Beach Iced Tea ●●●●○
Bellini-Tini ●●●●○
Beverly Hills Iced Tea ●●●●○
Big Apple Martini ●●●●○
Bingo ●●●○○
Bitter Sweet Symphony ●●●●○
Bitterest Pill ●●●●○
Black Cherry Martini ●●●●○
Black Forest Gateau Martini ●●●●●
Black Irish ●●●○○
Black 'N' Blue Caipirovska ●●●●○
Black Russian ●●●○○
Bling! Bling! ●●●●○
Bloodhound ●●●●○
Bloody Caesar ●●●●○
Bloody Mary (modern recipe) ●●●●●
Blue Champagne ●●●○○
Blue Kamikaze ●●●●○
Blue Lagoon ●●●○○
Blueberry Martini #1 ●●●●○
Blueberry Martini #2 (simple) ●●●●○
Blush Martini ●●●●○
Blushin' Russian ●●●●○
Boston Tea Party ●●●○○
Bullfrog ●●●●○
Burnt Toasted Almond ●●●○○
Caipirovska ●●●●○
California Root Beer ●●●●○
Californian Martini ●●●●○
Cape Codder ●●●○○
Casablanca ●●●○○
Cassini ●●●●○
Celery Martini ●●●●○
Cham 69 #1 ●●●●○

Cham 69 #2 ●●●○○
Cherrute ●●●●○
China Beach ●●●●○
Choc & Nut Martini ●●●○○
Chocolate Martini ●●●●○
Chocolate Mint Martini ●●●●○
Cobbled Raspberry Martini ●●●●●
Coconut Water ●●●●○
Collection Martini ●●●○○
Colorado Bulldog ●●○○○
Crown Stag ●●●○○
Cucumber Martini ●●●●●
Cucumber & Mint Martini ●●●●○
Cucumber Sake-Tini ●●●●○
Cuppa Joe ●●●●○

Brass Monkey ●●●○○
Cheeky Monkey ●●●●○
Chinese Whisper Martini ●●●●○
Citrus Caipirovska ●●●●○
Citrus Martini ●●●●○
Collection Martini ●●●○○
Colonial Rot ●●●○○
The Cold Winter Warmer Sour ●●●●○
Cosmopolitan #1 (simple version) ●●●●●
Cosmopolitan #2 (complex version) ●●●●●
Cosmopolitan #3 (Popular version) ●●●●●
Cranapple Breeze ●●●●○
Crimson Blush ●●●●○

KETEL ONE CITROEN VODKA

40% alc./vol.
(80°proof)

www.KetelOne.com

Producer: Nolet Distillery, Schiedam, The Netherlands.

Having already created what they and many top bartenders consider the perfect vodka for Martinis, the Nolet family wanted to create a flavoured vodka of equal excellence for making the ultimate Cosmopolitan. The family spent more than two years researching and evaluating different blending and infusion methods, before arriving at the costly but effective process of hand-crafting in small batches and infusing with natural citrus flavour until the perfect balance is reached.

Ketel One Citroen combines the smooth qualities of the original Ketel One Vodka with the refreshing natural essence of citrus fruit. To ensure continuity in the quality of Ketel One Citroen, a member of the Nolet family personally samples each batch produced prior to release.

There are few other citrus-flavoured vodkas with the rich, natural lemon peel oil flavours found in Ketel One Citroen. These combine with a clean grain character to make this vodka an ideal base for Cosmopolitans and other contemporary cocktails.

Allegrottini ●●●○○
Asian Mary ●●●●○
Basil Beauty ●●●●○
Blue Cosmo ●●●○○
Blue Fin ●●●○○
Bohemian Iced Tea ●●●●●

KETEL ONE ORANGE INFUSED VODKA

To make your own orange infused vodka:

1. Scrub two large oranges to clean and remove any wax coating.

2. Peel the zest from oranges using a knife or potato peeler. Be careful not to cut into white pith, or trim off white pith from peel after peeling.

3. Feed orange zest into an empty, clean bottle.

4. Fill bottle containing orange zest with Ketel One vodka using a funnel.

5. Replace cap securely and shake.

6. Leave to infuse for at least a week turning daily.

7. Your home infused orange flavoured Ketel One vodka is now ready to use.

Blood Orange ●●●○○
Blue Monday ●●●●○
Chill-Out Martini ●●●○○
Cordless Screwdriver ●●●○○
Creamsicle ●●●●○
Creamy Creamsicle ●●●●○
CVO Firevault ●●●●○

KETEL ONE VANILLA INFUSED VODKA

The pods of a tropical plant which belongs to the orchid family, vanilla has long been a prized flavouring. The vanilla orchid is cultivated in many different tropical regions. Bourbon vanilla is generally considered the finest kind, and Mexico and the Indian Ocean islands are popularly known as the best producers. Once the pods are harvested from the parent vine, they undergo months of curing to develop and refine their distinctive flavour.

To make your own vanilla infused vodka simply take two quality vanilla pods (roughly 6in/15cm long) and split them lengthwise with a sharp knife on a cutting board. Place them in a newly opened bottle of Ketel One vodka and leave it to infuse for a fortnight, turning occasionally.

Aphrodisiac ●●●●○
Apple Strudel Martini #2 ●●●●●
Banoffee Martini ●●●●○
Bon Bon Martini ●●●●○
Butterfly's Kiss ●●●●○
Cherry Alexander ●●●●○
Chocolate & Cranberry Martini ●●●●○
Crème Anglaise Martini ●●●●○
Crème Brûlée Martini ●●●●○

LEMONCELLO

See 'Luxardo Limoncello Liqueur'

LEMONS & LIMES

Originally from India or Malaysia, lemons are available throughout the year and in many different varieties, distinguishable by their shape, size and thickness of skin.

The smaller and more fragrant lime is closely related to the lemon. It is cultivated in tropical countries and is widely used in Caribbean and Brazilian cuisine.

Both these citrus fruits are bartender staples and their juice is used to balance sweetness and add depth to a bewildering range of cocktails. Lemon and lime juice will curdle cream and cream liqueurs but will happily mix with most other spirits and liqueurs. Limes generally pair well with rum while lemons are preferable in drinks based on whiskey or brandy.

Limes and lemons last longer if stored in the refrigerator. But you'll get more juice out of them if you let them warm up to room temperature and roll the fruit on a surface under the palm of your hand before you cut them. Save hard fruits for garnishing: soft fruits have more juice and flavour.

To juice, simply cut in half widthways and juice using a press, squeezer or spinning juicer, taking care not to grind the pith. Ideally you should juice your lemons and limes immediately prior to use as the juice will oxidise after a couple of hours.

I'd guess that, along with sugar syrup, these fruits are the most frequently used ingredients in this guide. Hence I've not even tried to index them.

LIME CORDIAL

Lauchlan Rose started importing lime juice from the West Indies to England in the 1860s, when ships were compelled to carry lime or lemon juice to prevent scurvy. In 1867 he devised a method for preserving juice without alcohol and created lime cordial, the world's first concentrated fruit drink. (What a spoilsport.) Thankfully all of the drinks in this guide that call for lime cordial are alcoholic.

Acapulco Daiquiri ●●●●○
Blue Heaven ●●○○○
Caribbean Breeze ●●●●○
Castro ●●●○○

LIMONCELLO LIQUEUR

See 'Luxardo Limoncello Liqueur'

LITCHI LIQUEUR

See 'Soho Lychee Liqueur'

LUXARDO AMARETTO DI SASCHIRA LIQUEUR

28% alc./vol. (56°proof)

Producer: Girolamo Luxardo SpA., Torreglia, Padova, Italy.

This delicate liqueur is an Italian classic, packed with the unique flavour of sweet almond, once sacred to the Greek goddess Cybele.

The Luxardo family have been distilling fine liqueurs in the Veneto region of Italy for six generations now. They make their amaretto with the pure paste of the finest almonds, from Avola in southern Sicily, and age it for eight months in larch vats to impart its distinctive, well-rounded taste. Their very contemporary amaretto is a vital tool in any mixologist's flavour armoury, with its palate of almond and marzipan.

A.B.C. ●●●○○
Alabama Slammer #2●●●●○
Almond Martini #2 ●●●●○
Almond Old Fashioned ●●●●●
Amaretto Sour ●●●○○
Artlantic ●●●○○
Atholl Brose ●●●●○
Autumn Punch ●●●●○
B-54 Shot ●●●○○
Bananas & Cream ●●●●○
Bella Donna Daiquiri ●●●●●
Bird Of Paradise ●●●●●
Blue Heaven ●●○○○
Blueberry Tea ●●●●○
Blush Martini ●●●○○
Blushin' Russian ●●●●○
Brake Tag ●●●○○
Brooklyn #2●●●●○
Bubblegum Shot ●●●○○
Buona Sera Shot ●●●○○
Burnt Toasted Almond ●●●○○
Canteen Martini ●●●○○
Caribbean Punch ●●●●○
Cham 69 #1 ●●●○○
Cham 69 #2 ●●●○○
Chas ●●●●○
Cicada Cocktail ●●●●○
Cranberry Cooler ●●●○○
Creamy Creamsicle ●●●●○
Cream Cake ●●●○○
Cruel Intention ●●●●○

LUXARDO LIMONCELLO LIQUEUR

27% alc./vol. (54° proof)

Producer: Girolamo Luxardo SpA., Torreglia, Padova, Italy.

Despite its vibrant yellow-green hue, this is an extremely traditional Italian liqueur – and, since the 90s, one of Italy's most popular. For generations, families have macerated lemon zest in spirit and sugar, encapsulating the mixologist's favourite combination of sour citrus, sweet and spirit: the formula at the heart of the Daiquiri, the Caipirinha and many more.

Luxardo limoncello delivers a rich sweet lemon flavour in a blast of sour citrus, lemon zest and candied citrus, which somehow remain pure and balanced. It is increasingly popular among bartenders seeking new ways of delivering that vital citrus tang.

Basilico ●●●○○
Bellissimo ●●●○○
Bon Bon Martini ●●●●○
Clementine ●●●○○

LUXARDO MARASCHINO ORIGINALE LIQUEUR

32% alc./vol. (64°proof)

www.luxardo.it

Producer: Girolamo Luxardo SpA., Torreglia, Padova, Italy.

Until well into the 20th century, the bitter Marasca cherry grew only on the Dalmatian coast. Now part of Croatia, Zara, Dalmatia, was Italian territory when Girolamo Luxardo's wife began producing a liqueur from the local cherries. So popular did her maraschino become that in 1821 Girolamo founded a distillery to mass-produce it. The business prospered until the

disruption of the Second World War, after which the family moved production to Italy. Today the Luxardos base their liqueur on cherries from their own 200 acre orchard and age it for two years in white Finnish ashwood vats. The silky palate features hints of dark chocolate, vanilla and marmalade alongside subtle cherry notes, with an elegant white chocolate and cherry finish, making it essential to a range of classic and modern cocktails.

Absinthe Italiano Cocktail ●●●○○
Aviation #1 ●●●●●
Aviation #2 (Classic Formula) ●●●●●
Beachcomber ●●●●○
Bensonhurst ●●●●●
Boomerang ●●●●○
Bourbon Crusta ●●●●●
Brandy Crusta ●●●●○
Brooklyn #1 ●●●●○
Casablanca #1 ●●●●○
Casino ●●●●○
Cherry & Hazelnut Daiquiri ●●●●○
Classic ●●●●●
Coronation ●●●○○
Coronation Martini ●●●○○
Cuban Cocktail No. 2 #1 ●●●●○

LUXARDO SAMBUCA DEI CESARI

38% alc./vol. (76°proof)

www.luxardo.it

Producer: Girolamo Luxardo SpA., Torreglia, Padova, Italy.

The elder bush, with its distinctive bunches of black berries, grows wild all over Europe. Along with anise, it is the vital ingredient in Luxardo Sambuca, which takes its name from the Latin term for the plant.

This clear liqueur is crafted from green Sicilian aniseed and elderberries grown in the Euganean hills. Uniquely, it is matured in Finnish ash wood vats.

The clean, rich aniseed palate is lighter and less syrupy than some other brands, with subtle hints of lemon zest. A star performer in a number of contemporary cocktails, it is also great served 'con mosca' – flamed in a glass with three floating coffee beans signifying health, wealth and happiness, to bestow good luck.

All White Frappé ●●●○○
Anis'tini ●●●●○
Bumble Bee ●●●○○
Crème De Café ●●●●○

LYCHEE LIQUEUR

See 'Soho Lychee Liqueur'

MADEIRA

Madeira is a fortified wine from the semi-tropical island of the same name in the Atlantic, 600km off the coast of Morocco. Until the opening of the Suez Canal, Madeira enjoyed a strategic position on the Atlantic shipping lanes and during the 17th and 18th centuries ships sailing from Britain carried the island's wine as ballast. The wine was slowly warmed during the voyage through the tropics, creating a mellow, baked flavour. This unusual, richly flavoured wine became popular. So the ships' effects were replicated on the island using a heating process called 'estufagem'.

There are four predominant styles of Madeira available: Sercial (dry), Verdelho (medium dry and traditionally referred to as 'Rainwater'), Bual (medium sweet) and Malmsey (sweet).

Baltimore Egg Nog ●●●○○
Bosom Caresser ●●●●○
Boston Flip ●●●●○
Casanova ●●●●○
China Blue ●●●○○

MANDARINE NAPOLÉON LIQUEUR

38% alc./vol. (76°proof)

www.mandarine-napoleon.com

Producer: Fourcroy S.A., Rue Steyls 119, B1020 Brussels, Belgium.

Emperor Napoléon Bonaparte's physician, Antoine-Francois de Fourcroy, created a special liqueur for the Emperor based on aged cognacs and exotic mandarine oranges. Mandarines, often known as tangerines, had been introduced into Europe from China in the 18th century and grew particularly well in Corsica, Bonaparte's birthplace.

Mandarine Napoléon was first commercially distilled in 1892, using the finest aged French cognacs and mandarine peels from the Mediterranean area blended with an infusion of herbs and spices. The distillate is aged for at least three years, until it acquires the rich mellow flavour which makes Mandarine Napoléon one of the great classic liqueurs of the world.

Mandarine Napoléon is brilliantly suited to cocktail mixing and distinctly different from other orange liqueurs on bartenders' shelves. Its luscious zesty tangerine flavour with a herbal backnote gives a sophisticated twist to a Cosmopolitan but is also superb on its own, long over ice with a splash of tonic.

Breakfast At Terrell's ●●●●○
Clementine ●●●○○

MAPLE SYRUP

The boiled-down sap of the North American sugar maple, authentic maple syrup has a complex sweetness appreciated all over the world. Please be wary of synthetic imitations, which are nowhere near as good as the real thing. Maple syrups are graded A or B – grade B, which is dark and very strongly flavoured, is sometimes known as 'cooking syrup'. The A grade syrups are all of equal quality and divided into categories according to their hue and level of flavour, most generally 'light amber', 'medium amber' and 'dark amber'. Confusingly, some Canadian and US states have their own names for these categories. I favour a medium amber or light syrup.

Maple syrup should be stored in the refrigerator and consumed within 28 days of opening. To use in a cocktail, simply pour into a thimble measure and follow the recipe.

Banoffee Martini ●●●●○
Bourbon Blush ●●●●○
Bull's Milk ●●●○○
Canadian Apple (Mocktail) ●●●●○
Che's Revolution ●●●●○

MARASCHINO LIQUEUR

'See Luxardo Maraschino Originale Liqueur'

MARASCHINO SYRUP

The sweet liquid from a jar of maraschino cherries.

MIDORI MELON LIQUEUR

20% alc./vol. (40°proof)

www.midori-world.com

Producer: Suntory Limited, Japan.

Midori is flavoured with extracts of honeydew melons and can rightly claim to be the original melon liqueur. Midori's vibrant green colour, light melon taste and great versatility has ensured its demand in bars worldwide. Launched in 1978 at New York's famed Studio 54 nightclub, Midori was shaken within sight of the cast of Saturday Night Fever. That same year, Midori won first prize in the U.S. Bartenders' Guild Annual Championship.

The name 'Midori' is Japanese for green and it is owned by Suntory, Japan's leading producer and distributor of alcoholic beverages. Midori is one of the most noted modern day cocktail ingredients due to its vibrant colour and flavour, being: fruity, luscious, lightly syrupy while retaining freshness, with honeyed melon and a hint of green apple. It is also great simply served long with sparkling apple juice or cranberry juice.

Alien Secretion ●●●○○
Apache ●●●○○
Apple & Melon Martini ●●●●○
Atomic Dog ●●●○○
Awol ●●●●○
Black Japan ●●○○○
Bubblegum Shot ●●●○○
Coco Cabana ●●●○○
Congo Blue ●●●●○
Cool Martini ●●●●○

MINT LEAVES

This perennial herb grows in most temperate parts of the world. The varieties which non-botanists call 'mint' belong to the genus mentha. Mentha species include apple mint, curly mint, pennyroyal, peppermint, pineapple mint, spearmint and water or bog mint.

Spearmint, or garden mint, is the most common kind and you may well find it growing in your garden. It has a fruity aroma and flavour and, like peppermint, has bright green leaves and purple flowers. Spearmint is generally used for cooking savouries, such as mint sauce.

Peppermint is the second most common kind. Its leaves produce a pungent oil which is used to flavour confectionery, desserts and liqueurs such as crème de menthe.

The main visible difference between peppermint and spearmint is in the leaves. Spearmint leaves have a crinkly surface and seem to grow straight out of the plant's main stem, while peppermint leaves have smoother surfaces and individual stems. Peppermint can also tend towards purple. Which type of mint you choose to use in drinks is largely a matter of personal taste: some recommend mentha nemorosa for Mojitos.

Growing your own mint, be it spearmint, peppermint or otherwise is easy – but be sure to keep it in a container or it will overrun your garden. Either buy a plant or place a sprig in a glass of water. When it roots, pot it in a large, shallow tub with drainage holes. Place bricks under the tub to prevent the roots from growing through the holes.

Aku Aku ●●●●○
Bajito ●●●●●
Beetle Jeuse ●●●●○
Bourbon Smash ●●●●○
Brandy Smash ●●●●○
Charente Collins ●●●●○
Che's Revolution ●●●●○
Colonial Rot ●●●○○
Cowboy Martini ●●●●○
Cranberry Delicious (Mocktail) ●●●○○
Cranberry & Mint Martini ●●●●○
Cucumber & Mint Martini ●●●●○

OPAL NERA BLACK SAMBUCA

40% alc./vol. (80°proof)

www.opalnera.com

Producer: Fratelli Francoli S.p.A., Ghemme, Corso Romagnano, Italy.

In 1989 Alessandro Francoli was on honeymoon in America, when he took time out to present his company's traditional Italian grappas and sambucas to a potential buyer. He noticed the interest the buyer showed in a coffee sambuca, and this dark liqueur set Alessandro thinking. He experimented with different flavours and created Opal Nera, a black coloured sambuca with a hint of lemon. Opal Nera's seductive and unmistakable colour comes from elderberries, a key ingredient in all sambucas: Francoli macerate their purple-black skins.

Opal Nera Black Sambuca is a favourite with many bartenders due to its colour and flavour, which includes aniseed, soft black liquorice, light elderberry spice and lemon zest.

Alessandro ●●●○○
Black Dream ●●●○○
Black Jack ●●●○○
Black Nuts ●●○○○
Black Widow ●●●○○

ORANGE BITTERS

Sadly, this key cocktail ingredient is hard to find in modern liquor stores. There are a number of brands that profess to be 'orange bitters' but many hardly taste of orange and are more like sweet liqueurs than bitters. Search the internet for suitable brands or make your own. See www.drinkboy.com/LiquorCabinet/Flavorings/OrangeBitters.htm

Absinthe Special Cocktail ●●●○○
Adonis ●●●●●
Alaska Martini ●●●●○
Almond Old Fashioned ●●●●○
Amsterdam Cocktail ●●●●○
Apricot Cosmo ●●●●○
The Argyll ●●●○○
Bamboo ●●●●●

Banana Bliss ●●●○○
Bijou ●●●●●
Blackthorn English ●●●●○
Boulevard ●●●●○
Bourbon Crusta ●●●●●
Bradford ●●●●○
Brass Rail ●●●●○
The Broadmoor ●●●●●
Californian Martini ●●●●○
Caprice ●●●●○
Casino ●●●●○
Causeway ●●●○○
Chancellor ●●●●●
Cheeky Monkey ●●●●○
Citrus Martini ●●●●○
Club Cocktail #1 ●●●●○
Colonel's Big Opu ●●●●○
Commodore #2 ●●●○○
Coronation Martini ●●●○○
Cosmopolitan #2 (complex version) ●●●●●
Cowboy Martini ●●●●●
Cuban Cocktail No. 2 #1 ●●●○○
Cuban Cocktail N0. 3 #2 ●●●●○

ORANGE JUICE

The orange is now so commonly available in our shops and markets that it's hard to believe it was once an exotic and expensive luxury. Although native to China, its name originates from 'naranga' in the old Indian language of Sanskrit.

There are many different types of orange but the best ones for bartending purposes are Washington Navels, which are in season from the end of October. These have a firm, rough skin perfect for cutting twists from and are juicy and slightly sour.

Simply cut in half and juice with a hand press. If using an electric spinning citrus juicer take care not to grind the pith.

Oranges are so widely available and easy to juice that as I write this I'm wondering why I so often buy packaged juice from the supermarket. My only defence is that I always buy freshly squeezed, refrigerated juice.

Abbey Martini ●●●○○
Agent Orange ●●●●○
Air Mail ●●●●●
Alabama Slammer #1 ●●●●○
Alabama Slammer #2 ●●●○○
Allegrottini ●●●○○
American Beauty #1 ●●●●●
American Beauty #2 ●●●●○
Amsterdam Cocktail ●●●●○
Apple Sunrise ●●●○○
Apricot Fizz ●●●●○
April Shower ●●●●○
Aunt Agatha ●●●●○
Aunt Emily ●●●●○
Bahama Mama ●●●●○
Banana Boomer ●●●●○
Beach Blonde ●●●●○
Bebbo ●●●●○
Bee's Knees #1 ●●●●○

Bee's Knees #2 ●●●●○
Bermuda Cocktail ●●●●○
Bermuda Rum Swizzle ●●●●○
Between Decks ●●●●○
The Big Easy ●●●●○
Bishop ●●●○○
The Bistro Sidecar ●●●●○
Blood & Sand #1 ●●●●●
Blood & Sand #2 (Difford's formula) ●●●●●
Blood Orange ●●●○○
Blue Star ●●●○○
Bolero Sour ●●●●●
Boston Tea Party ●●●○○
Brake Tag ●●●●○
Breakfast At Terrell's ●●●●○
Bronx ●●●●○
Buck's Fizz ●●●○○
Bull's Blood ●●●●○
Cactus Banger ●●●●○
Cactus Jack ●●●●○
Calvados Cocktail ●●●●○
Canaries ●●●○○
Carneval Batida ●●●●○
Casablanca ●●●○○
Castro ●●●○○
Cheeky Monkey ●●●●○
Chill-Out Martini ●●●○○
Chocolate Puff ●●●●○
Cinderella ●●●○○
Classic ●●●●●
Covadonga ●●●○○
Cranberry Cooler ●●●○○
Creamy Creamsicle ●●●●○
Cuban Master ●●●○○
Cumbersome ●●●●○
CVO Firevault ●●●●○

PARFAIT AMOUR LIQUEUR

A French, lilac coloured curaçao liqueur flavoured with rose petals, vanilla pods and almonds. The name means 'perfect love'.

Barnacle Bill ●●●○○
Blue Angel ●●●○○
Brazen Martini ●●●●○

PARTIDA TEQUILA

40% alc./vol. (80°proof)

www.partidatequila.com

Producer: Partida Distillery (NOM: 1454), Amatitán, Jalisco, Mexico

Partida is a super-premium 100% agave tequila made using agave grown on the 5,000 acres Partida family estate, just outside the village of Amatitán. The agave used to make Partida tequila are only harvested when at least ten years old to ensure

full development of the natural sugars in the plant so producing naturally sweet tequila.

Stainless steel ovens are used to bake the agave piñas (hearts) so avoiding the overbearing smoky flavour attributed to the use of old-fashioned soot-lined brick ovens. The cooked piñas are crushed to release the juice which is then fermented. The fermented juice is then double distilled using stainless steel pot stills.

Partida is aged in French-Canadian oak barrels previously used to age Jack Daniel's whiskey. The empty casks are hot-washed twice with distilled water so only a little of the 'toast' and Jack Daniel's character is left to subtly influence the tequila.

Partida is bottled without additives such as glycerine or caramel so often used to give mouthfeel and colour to lesser tequilas.

Acapulco ●●●○○
Adios ●●●○○
Alice From Dallas ●●●●○
Alice In Wonderland ●●●○○
All Fall Down ●●●○○
Almond Old Fashioned ●●●●○
Anita's Attitude Adjuster ●●●○○
Armillita Chico ●●●○○
Bald Eagle Shot ●●●○○
Bald Eagle Martini ●●●●○
Batanga ●●●●○
Beach Iced Tea ●●●○○
Bee Sting ●●●●○
Bird Of Paradise ●●●●●
Bloody Maria ●●●●○
Blue Margarita ●●●○○
Blue Velvet Margarita ●●●●○
Boston Tea Party ●●●○○
Buena Vida ●●●●○
Burning Bush Shot ●●○○○
C C Kazi ●●●●○
Cactus Banger ●●●●○
Cactus Jack ●●●●○
Chihuahua Magarita ●●●○○
Chimayo ●●●○○
Chocolarita ●●●●○
Cool Martini ●●●○○
Crouching Tiger ●●●○○

PASTIS

See 'Ricard Pastis'

PEACH SCHNAPPS LIQUEUR

The luscious peach originated in

China, where the tree has been cultivated since the 5th century BC. It reached Europe by way of Alexander the Great and the Greeks and its sweet, succulent flavour has made it a favourite liqueur ingredient since time immemorial.

During the 80s, peach schnapps appeared on the scene, and rapidly ousted the more syrupy, heavier peach liqueurs of old.

Achilles Heel ●●●●○
Aku Aku ●●●●○
Apple Spritz ●●●●○
Baby Woo Woo ●●●○○
Bellini #2 (Difford's formula) ●●●●○
Bellini-Tini ●●●●○
Bermuda Cocktail ●●●●○
Bikini Martini ●●●●○
Bohemian Iced Tea ●●●●○
Cream Cake ●●●○○

PEACHES

White peaches are preferable for use in cocktails. They have finer flesh and flavour, and produce more juice than yellow peaches, which generally mature later. When peeling peaches for muddling or pureeing, try plunging them into boiling water for thirty seconds first.

Bellini #1 (Original) ●●●●○
Bellini #2 (Difford's Formula) ●●●●○
Bellini-Tini ●●●●○

PEAR LIQUEUR

Apples 'N' Pears ●●●●●
Asian Pear Martini ●●●●○

PEAR JUICE

Western varieties of pear soften when ripe and tend to have quite a grainy texture; Asian types, such as the nashi pear, are crisp when ripe. Unless otherwise stated, pear in this guide means the Western varieties. Conference is widely available and works well in cocktails.

Pears will ripen after they are picked, but spoil quickly, so care is needed in storage.

The best way to extract the flavour of a pear is to use an electric juice extractor. Surprisingly, you'll find that beautifully ripe fruits yield little and much of that is in the form of slush. Instead, look for pears which are on their way to ripeness but still have a good crunch.

Remove the stalk but don't worry about peeling or removing the core. Cut the fruit into chunks small enough to push into the juicer. If you hate cleaning an electric juice extractor then use a blender or food processor.

Asian Pear Martini ●●●●○
Autumn Punch ●●●●●

PERNOD ANIS

40% alc./vol.
(80°proof)

www.pernod.net

Producer: Pernod Enterprise, France

Pernod's story starts in 1789 when Dr Pierre Ordinaire first prescribed his pain relieving and reviving 'absinthe elixir' in Switzerland. Ten years later, Major Dubied bought the formula and set up an absinthe factory in Couvet, Switzerland, with his son-in-law, Henri-Louis Pernod. In 1805, Henri-Louis Pernod established Pernod Fils in Pontarlier, France. The authentic absinthe, the original Pernod was created from a recipe that included 'artemisia absinthium': the plant of absinthe.

Pernod quickly gained fame as THE absinthe of Parisian café society. But a prohibitionist propaganda movement sprang up and a massive press campaign blamed absinthe abuse as the cause of socially unacceptable behaviour, insanity, tuberculosis and even murder. On 7th January 1915, absinthe was banned and Pernod Fils was forced to close. But by 1920, anise liquors were legalised again, albeit in a more sober form, and in its new guise Pernod remained as popular as ever. The Pernod we enjoy today is an historic blend of 14 herbs including star anise, fennel, mint and coriander.

Pernod is best served long with cranberry juice, apple juice or bitter lemon, diluted five to one.

Anis'tini ●●●●○
Appleissimo ●●●●○
Asylum Cocktail ●●●○○
Barnacle Bill ●●●○○
Blackthorn Irish ●●●●○
Bombay ●●●●●

PEYCHAUD'S AROMATIC BITTERS

Adelaide Swizzle ●●●●○
Algonquin ●●●●○
Auntie's Hot Xmas Punch ●●●●○
Behemoth ●●●●○
Bloomsbury Martini ●●●●○
Bourbonella ●●●●○
Brake Tag ●●●○○
Caramel Manhattan ●●●●●
Chocolate Sazerac ●●●●○
Concealed Weapon ●●●○○

PINEAPPLE JUICE

Pineapples are widely grown in the West Indies, Africa and Asia. There are many varieties which vary significantly in both size and flavour. When pineapples are ripe the skin changes colour from yellow-green to brown; over-ripe pineapples are yellow-brown.

Pineapples are tropical and tend to deteriorate at temperatures below 7°C (45°F) so are best left out of the refrigerator.

Pineapple is one of the most satisfying fruits to juice due to the quantity of liquid it yields. Chop the crown and bottom off, then slice the skin off, without worrying too much about the little brown dimples that remain. Finally slice the fruit along its length around the hard central core, and chop into pieces small enough to fit into your juice extractor. The base is the sweetest part of a pineapple, so if you are only juicing half be sure to divide the fruit lengthways.

For convenience I still often end up buying cartons of 'pressed pineapple juice' from the supermarket chill cabinet. As with all such juices, look for those labelled 'not from concentrate'. When buying supermarket own brand pineapple juice, read the label carefully to avoid stuff made from concentrate.

Abacaxi Ricaço ●●●●○
Abaci Batida ●●●●○
Acapulco ●●●●○

Aku Aku ●●●●○
Algonquin ●●●●○
Alien Secretion ●●●●○
Atlantic Breeze ●●●○○
Atomic Dog ●●●○○
Aunt Agatha ●●●○○
Awol ●●●●○
Baby Blue Martini ●●●●○
Bahama Mama ●●●●○
Bahamas Daiquiri ●●●●○
Bahia ●●●○○
Bali Trader ●●●●○
Banana Boomer ●●●●○
Banana Colada ●●●●○
Basil Beauty ●●●●○
Bay Breeze ●●●○○
Bermuda Rum Swizzle ●●●●○
Blade Runner ●●●●○
Blue Hawaiian ●●●○○
Blue Heaven ●●●○○
Blue Wave ●●●○○
Bossa Nova #2 ●●●●○
Brandy Fix ●●●●○
Brighton Punch ●●●●○
Buena Vida ●●●●○
Buzzard's Breath ●●●○○
Byzantine ●●●●○
Cactus Jack ●●●●○
Canaries ●●●○○
Cappercaille ●●●●○
Caramel Manhattan ●●●●●
Caribbean Breeze ●●●●○
Caribbean Cruise ●●●●○
Caribbean Piña Colada ●●●○○
Caribbean Punch ●●●●○
Caribe Daiquiri ●●●●○
Che's Revolution ●●●●●
Cinderella ●●●○○
Coco Cabana ●●●●○
Colonel T ●●●○○
Cool Orchard ●●●●○
Cox's Daiquiri ●●●●●
Cruel Intention ●●●●○
Cuban Master ●●●○○
Cuban Special ●●●○○
CVO Firevault ●●●●○

PISCO

A type of brandy and the national drink of both Chile and Peru, pisco probably takes its name from the port of Pisco in Peru.

The best pisco is made from the fermented juice of the Muscat grape, which grows in the Ica region of southwestern Peru and in Chile's Elqui Valley. There are many varieties of Muscat. The Quebranta grape is favoured in Peru where it is usually blended with one or two other varietals such as Italia, Moscatel, Albilla, Negra, Mollar and Torontel. In Chile Common Black, Mollar, Pink Muscat, Torontel, Pedro Jimenez and Muscat of Alexandria are all used.

Algeria ●●●●●
Charlie Lychee'tini ●●●●○
Cola De Mono ●●●●●

PLYMOUTH GIN

41.2% alc./vol.
(82.4°proof)

www.plymouthgin.com

Producer: V&S Plymouth Ltd, Black Friars Distillery, Plymouth, England

Since 1793, Plymouth Gin has been hand-crafted in England's oldest working distillery – Black Friars in Plymouth. It is still bottled at the unique strength of 41.2% alc./vol., and is based on a recipe that is over 200 years old. Plymouth Gin, which can only be produced in Plymouth, differs from London gins due to the use of only sweet botanicals combined with soft Dartmoor water. The result is a wonderfully aromatic and smooth gin.

Plymouth has been used by bartenders in cocktails since 1896, when it was first mixed in the original Dry Martini, and is favoured by many top bartenders due to its fresh juniper, lemony bite with deeper earthy notes.

Abbey Martini ●●●●○
Absinthe Special Cocktail ●●●○○
Ace ●●●●○
Adios Amigos Cocktail ●●●●○
Alaska Martini ●●●●○
Alaskan Martini ●●●●○
Alessandro ●●●○○
Alexander ●●●●○
Alexander's Big Brother ●●●○○
Alexander's Sister ●●●●○
Alfonso Martini ●●●●○
Angel Face ●●●●●
Anita's Attitude Adjuster ●●●●○
Apple & Elderflower Collins ●●●●○
Apricot Mango Martini ●●●●○
Apricot Martini ●●●●○
Arizona Breeze ●●●●○
Army & Navy ●●●●○
Arnaud Martini ●●●●○
Asylum Cocktail ●●●○○
Attitude Adjuster ●●●○○
The Atty Cocktail ●●●●○
Aunt Emily ●●●●○
Aviation #1 ●●●●●
Aviation #2 (Classic Formula) ●●●●●
Aviator ●●●●○
Baby Blue Martini ●●●○○
Barbara West ●●●○○
Barbary Coast Highball ●●●●○
Barbary Coast Martini ●●●●○
Barnum ●●●○○
Barranquilla Green Jade ●●●○○
Bartender's Martini ●●●●○
Basil & Lime Gimlet ●●●●●
Basil Bramble Sling ●●●●○
Beach Iced Tea ●●●●○
Bebbo ●●●●○
Bee's Knees Martini #2 ●●●●●
Bee's Knees #3 ●●●●○
Bermuda Cocktail ●●●●○
Bermuda Rose Cocktail ●●●●○

Between Decks ●●●○○
Beverly Hills Iced Tea ●●●●○
Bijou ●●●●●
Bikini Martini ●●●●○
Bitter Elder ●●●○○
Black Bison Martini ●●●●●
Black Jack Cocktail ●●●●○
Blackthorn Cocktail ●●●●○
Blackthorn English ●●●●○
Bloomsbury Martini ●●●●○
Blue Bird ●●●○○
Blue Lady ●●●○○
Blue Lagoon ●●●○○
Blue Moon ●●●●○
Blue Riband ●●●○○
Blue Star ●●●○○
Blue Wave ●●●○○
Boston ●●●○○
Boston Tea Party ●●●○○
Bradford ●●●●○
Bramble ●●●●○
Bramblette ●●●○○
Breakfast Martini ●●●●●
Bronx ●●●●○
The Buck ●●●●○
Byzantine ●●●●○
Caprice ●●●●○
Cardinale ●●●●○
Caruso Martini ●●●○○
Casino ●●●●○
Chelsea Sidecar ●●●●●
China Martini ●●●●○
Claridge ●●●●○
Clover Leaf Cocktail #1 ●●●●○
Clover Leaf Martini ●●●●●
Club Cocktail #2 ●●●●○
Colonel's Big Opu ●●●●○
Copper Illusion ●●●●○
Corpse Reviver #2 ●●●●○
Cosmopolitan #4 (1934 recipe) ●●●●○
Country Breeze ●●●○○
Cowboy Martini ●●●●○
Crimea ●●●○○
Crossbow ●●●○○
Cumbersome ●●●●○
Curdish Martini ●●●●○

PLYMOUTH SLOE GIN LIQUEUR

26% alc./vol. (52°proof)

www.plymouthgin.com

Producer: Coates & Co
Ltd, Plymouth.

The making of fruit
liqueurs is a long
tradition in the British
countryside and
Plymouth Gin stays true
to a unique 1883 recipe.
The sloe berries are
slowly and gently
steeped in high strength
Plymouth Gin, soft Dartmoor
water and a further secret
ingredient. It is an unhurried
process and the drink is bottled
only when the Head Distiller
decides the perfect flavour has
been reached. The result is an
entirely natural product with no

added flavouring or colourings.

This richly flavoured liqueur is
initially dry but opens with
smooth, sweet, lightly jammy,
juicy cherry and raspberry notes
alongside a complimentary
mixture of figs, cloves, set honey
and stewed fruits. The finish has
strong almond notes.

Alabama Slammer #2 ●●●●○
Blackthorn English ●●●●○
Charlie Chaplin ●●●●○

POMEGRANATE (GRENADINE) SYRUP

Originally grenadine was syrup
flavoured with pomegranate.
Sadly, most of today's commercially available grenadine syrups
are flavoured with red berries
and cherry juice. They may be
blood red but they don't taste of
pomegranate. Hunt out one of the
few genuine commercially made
pomegranate syrups or make
your own using one of the
following methods.

1. The simple method: Gradually
pour and stir two cups of
granulated sugar into a saucepan
containing one cup of Pom
Wonderful pomegrate juice and
gently simmer until the sugar is
dissolved. Consider adding half
a split vanilla pod for extra
flavour. Do not let the
pomegranate juice even come
close to boiling. Allow syrup to
cool and pour into an empty
bottle. Ideally, you should finely
strain your syrup into the bottle
to remove any undissolved
crystals which could otherwise
encourage crystallisation. If kept
in a refrigerator this mixture will
last for a week or so (please be
aware of the use by date of Pom
Wonderful).

2. Fresh & messy method:
Separate the seed cells from the
outer membranes and skin of
eight pomegranates. Simmer
these in a saucepan with
25ml/1oz of sugar syrup and 1/4
of a vanilla pod for each
pomegranate for at least an hour.
Allow to cool, strain through a
cheesecloth-layered sieve and
store in a refrigerator.

Ace ●●●●○
Alabama Slammer #1 ●●●●○
American Beauty #1 ●●●●●
American Beauty #2 ●●●●○
Apricot Martini ●●●○○
Armillita Chico ●●●●○
Asylum Cocktail ●●●○○

Aunt Emily ●●●●○
Avenue ●●●○○
Bacardi Cocktail ●●●●○
Bazooka ●●●○○
Bermuda Cocktail ●●●●○
Bermuda Rose Cocktail ●●●●○
Blinker ●●●●○
Bora Bora Brew (mocktail) ●●●○○
Bosom Caresser ●●●●○
Boston ●●●○○
Bourbonella ●●●●○
Caribbean Cruise ●●●●○
Caribbean Punch ●●●●○
Champagne Daisy ●●●○○
Cinderella ●●●○○
Clipper Cocktail ●●●●○
Clover Leaf Cocktail #1 ●●●●○
Clover Leaf Martini ●●●●●
Commodore #1 ●●●●○
Commodore #2 ●●●○○
Cosmopolitan #4 (1934 recipe) ●●●●○
Covadonga ●●●○○
Cranberry & Mint Martini ●●●●○
The Crow Cocktail ●●●○○
Cuban Cocktail No. 2 #1 ●●●●○

PORT (PORTO)

Port, or to give it its full name
'vinho do porto', is a Portuguese
wine from the area known as the
Upper Douro which starts 45
miles from the coast at the town
of Oporto and stretches east to
the Spanish border. Wine is
fortified with grape brandy, which
stops fermentation before it is
complete by raising the alcoholic
strength beyond that at which the
fermenting yeasts can survive.
This produces wines with
residual sugars, giving port its
inherently sweet style.

American Beauty #2 ●●●●○
Angel's Share #2 ●●●●●
Chancellor ●●●●●
Chatham Hotel Special ●●●●○
Chocolate Sidecar ●●●●○
Club Cocktail #1 ●●●●○
Basil Mary ●●●●○
Bishop ●●●●○
Bloody Joseph ●●●○○
Bloody Maria ●●●●○
Bloody Mary (modern recipe) ●●●●●

PUREES

Fruit purees are made from fresh
fruit which has been chopped up
and liquidised. When making
your own puree add roughly five
to ten percent sugar syrup to your
pureed fruit depending on the
fruit's ripeness. Commercially
available purees contain differing
amounts of added sugar and, if
using such a product, you may

have to adjust the balance of your
drink to allow for the extra
sweetness.

PUSSER'S NAVY RUM

47.75% alc./vol.
(95.5°proof)

www.pussers.com

Producer: Pusser's
Rum Limited,
Tortola, British
Virgin Islands.

The name 'Pusser'
is slang in the Royal
Navy for purser, the
officer with respon-
sibility for the issue of rum on
board ship. For more than 300
years the British Navy issued a
daily 'tot' of Pusser's rum, with a
double issue before battle. This
tradition, which started in
Jamaica in 1665, was finally
broken on 31st July 1970, a day
now known as 'Black Tot Day'.

In 1979 the Admiralty approved
the re-blending of Pusser's rum
to the original specifications by
Charles Tobias in the British
Virgin Islands. A significant
donation from the sale of each
bottle accrues to the benefit of
The Royal Navy Sailor's Fund, a
naval charity established to
compensate sailors for their lost
tot.

In our opinion, this is the best
Navy rum, delivering a rich
medley of flavours: molasses,
treacle, vanilla, cinnamon,
nutmeg, sticky toffee pudding,
espresso and creamy tiramisu
with subtle hints of oak.

Alexandra ●●●●○
All Fall Down ●●●●○
Aunt Agatha ●●●○○
Bahama Mama ●●●●○
Baltimore Egg Nog ●●●○○
Bee's Knees #1 ●●●●○
Boston Tea Party ●●●○○
Caribbean Breeze ●●●●○
Charles Daiquiri ●●●●○

PROSECCO SPARKLING WINE

Prosecco is a wine produced

around the towns of Conegliano and Valdobbiadene in the Italian province of Treviso. It can be still, semi-sparkling or sparkling, dry, off-dry or sweet. The style called for in this guide, and the preferred style for export, is dry and sparkling. 'Frizzante' means 'semi-sparkling' and 'spumante' means 'sparkling'.

The better wines from hillside vineyards are labelled Prosecco di Conegliano-Valdobbiadene. The best are 'Prosecco Superiore di Cartizze' from the great hill of Cartizze in the Valdobbiadene sub-region.

Bellini #1 (Original) ●●●●○
Bellini #2 (Difford's formula) ●●●●○

RASPBERRY (CRÈME DE FRAMBOISE) LIQUEUR

See 'Giffard Crème de Framboise Liqueur'

RASPBERRIES & BLACKBERRIES

Both these berries grow on brambly bushes and are related to the rose. Both can be cultivated in a wide range of colours, from white or yellow to orange, pink or purple, as well as the more common red and black.

The loganberry is a cross between a blackberry and a raspberry and is named after its Californian creator, James H Logan. Other later hybrids of the two fruits include the tayberry (named after the Scottish river) and the boysenberry (named after its creator).

The juice of both raspberries and blackberries is intense and a little goes a long way. Which is just as well because there's precious little juice in each berry and you'll find putting them through an electric juicer a complete waste of time. Instead, either blend them into a puree or (as I do) muddle the fruits in the base of your shaker or in the

glass. Recipes in this guide state how many fruits you should muddle for each drink.

Apple & Blackberry Pie ●●●●○
Berry Caipirinha ●●●●○
Black & White Daiquiri ●●●●○
Black & Blue Caipirovska ●●●●○
Blimey ●●●●○
Bling! Bling! ●●●●○
Blood Orange ●●●○○
Bourbon Smash ●●●●○
Brazilian Berry ●●●●○
Clover Leaf Martini ●●●●○
Cobbled Raspberry Martini ●●●●●

RICARD PASTIS

45% alc./vol. (90°proof)

Producer: Pernod (Group Pernod Ricard), Créteil, France.

A French classic, this liquorice based spirit is Europe's number one selling spirit brand and the third biggest brand worldwide. Created by Paul Ricard in Marseille in 1932, it is now produced in Bessan, Southern France. The unique flavour of this pastis derives from liquorice root, green anise, fennel and seven different aromatic herbs from Provence.

It is anethole, made from fennel and green anise, which produces Ricard's most distinctive effect: it turns milky on contact with water or ice.

Traditionally served over ice diluted with five parts of water, Ricard adds a rich aniseed flavour and distinctive cloudy appearance to a number of classic and modern cocktails. Besides the predominant aniseed, its dry palate features fennel, soft liquorice and a delicious minty lemon freshness.

Canarie ●●●○○

RUM

Rum is a spirit made from sugar cane or its by-products. The recipes in this guide call for a number of styles of rum, as explained below.

RUM - AGED (AÑEJO)

Like other distillates, rum is clear when it condenses after distillation. The fact that ageing in oak barrels improved the raw rum was discovered when ships carried rum on the long passage to Europe: it arrived darker in colour and with an enhanced flavour.

Today, rum is aged in barrels from France or the United States which have previously been used to age cognac, bourbon or whiskey. They may be charred or scraped clean to remove any previous charring before receiving the rum: the treatment of the barrels is reflected in the character they impart to the finished rum.

Aged Honey Daiquiri ●●●●●
Bahama Mama ●●●●○
Bolero Sour ●●●●●
Brass Rail ●●●●○
Castro ●●●○○
Cool Orchard ●●●●○

RUM - BERMUDAN DARK

A few recipes in this guide require the use of Bermudan rum, a distinctive dark blend.

Bella Donna Daiquiri ●●●●●
Bermuda Rum Swizzle ●●●○○
Bull's Milk ●●●○○

RUM - GOLDEN

An amber coloured rum aged in wood and often coloured with caramel.

Abacaxi Ricaço ●●●●○
Acapulco ●●●○○
Ace Of Clubs Daiquiri ●●●●●
Air Mail ●●●●○
Bajan Daiquiri ●●●●○
Bajan Mojito ●●●○○
Bajan Passion ●●●●○
Banana Colada ●●●●○
Bossa Nova #1 ●●●●○
Bossa Nova #2 ●●●○○
Butterscotch Martini ●●●●○
Chocolate Puff ●●●●○
Club Cocktail ●●●●○
Columbus Daiquiri ●●●○○
Commodore #1 ●●●●○
Crème De Café ●●●●○
Cuban Cocktail No. 3 #2 ●●●●○

RUM - JAMAICAN OVERPROOF

Originally gunpowder was used to determine the strength of a spirit. The tester would mix the spirit with gunpowder and attempt to light it. If the spirit did not ignite, it was underproof; if it burned steadily, it was proof; if it exploded, it was overproof.

Proof is measured differently in the UK and the US, but in the States 100°proof is double alcohol by volume (measured by the Gay-Lussac scale). Hence an overproof rum is over 100°proof or 50% alc./vol. in strength.

Afterburner ●●●○○
The Alamagoozlum Cocktail ●●●●●
Assisted Suicide ●●●●○
Awol ●●●●○
Beach Blonde ●●●●○
Bolshoi Punch ●●●●○
Caribbean Punch ●●●●○
Coco Naut ●●●○○
Cold Comfort ●●●●○

RUM - LIGHT/WHITE

Rum is termed 'light' or 'heavy', depending on the purity to which it was distilled. Essentially, the flavour of any spirit comes from 'congeners' – products of fermentation which are not ethyl alcohol. When alcohol is concentrated during distillation, the levels of congeners are reduced. The fewer congeners, the lighter the rum. The more congeners, the heavier.

The fermentation process also affects whether a rum is light or heavy. A longer, slower fermentation will result in a heavier rum.

The odour, texture and taste of light rums are more subtle and refined than those of heavy rums, which have a heavy, syrupy flavour to match their dark colour.

Light rums tend to originate from countries originally colonised by the Spanish, such as Cuba, the Dominican Republic, Puerto Rico and Venezuela.

Acapulco Daiquiri ●●●●○
Adelaide Swizzle ●●●●○
Adios Amigos Cocktail ●●●●○
Aku Aku ●●●●○
Alan's Apple Breeze ●●●○○
Anita's Attitude Adjuster ●●●○○
Apple Daiquiri ●●●●○

Apple Mojito ●●●●○
Apricot Lady Sour ●●●○○
Atlantic Breeze ●●●○○
Atomic Dog ●●●○○
Bahia ●●●○○
Bajito ●●●●●
Banana Cow ●●●○○
Banana Daiquiri ●●●○○
Basil & Honey Daiquiri ●●●●●
Beach Iced Tea ●●●○○
Beachcomber ●●●●○
Bee's Knees #1 ●●●●○
Between the Sheets #1 (Classic Formula) ●●●●○
Between The Sheets #2 ●●●●●
Black & White Daiquiri ●●●●●
Black Martini ●●●●○
Blade Runner ●●●●○
Blue Hawaiian ●●●○○
Blue Heaven ●●●○○
Blue Passion ●●●●○
Blue Wave ●●●○○
Blueberry Daiquiri ●●●●○
Bolero ●●●●○
Bomber ●●●●○
Brass Monkey ●●●○○
Bulldog ●●●○○
Bull's Blood ●●●○○
Butterscotch Daiquiri ●●●○○
Caipirissima ●●●●○
Canaries ●●●○○
Canchanchara ●●●○○
Canteen Martini ●●●○○
Caribbean Cruise ●●●●○
Caribbean Piña Colada ●●●○○
Caribe Daiquiri ●●●●○
Casablanca #1 ●●●●○
Charles Daiquiri ●●●●○
Cherry & Hazelnut Daiquiri ●●●●○
Che's Revolution ●●●●○
Chiclet Daiquiri ●●●○○
Cinnamon Daiquiri ●●●○○
Clipper Cocktail ●●●○○
Coconut Daiquiri ●●●●○
Cuba Libre ●●●●○
Cuba Pintada ●●●●○
Cuban Cocktail No. 2 #1 ●●●●○
Cuban Island ●●●●○
Cuban Master ●●●○○
Cuban Special ●●●○○
Cubanita ●●●●○
Custard Tart ●●●●○

RUM - NAVY

See 'Pusser's Navy Rum'

RUM - SPICED

Spiced rums are continuously distilled light rums flavoured with spices including ginger, cinnamon, clove and vanilla.

Black Beard ●●●○○
Bomber ●●●●○
Cable Car ●●●●○

RUM - VANILLA INFUSED

The pods of a tropical plant which belongs to the orchid family, vanilla has long been a prized flavouring. The vanilla orchid is cultivated in many different tropical regions. Bourbon vanilla is generally considered the finest kind, and Mexico and the Indian Ocean islands are popularly known as the best producers. Once the pods are harvested from the parent vine, they undergo months of curing to develop and refine their distinctive flavour.

To infuse your own rum, simply take two quality vanilla pods (roughly 6in/15cm long) and split them lengthwise with a sharp knife. Place them in the bottle of rum you want to flavour and leave it to infuse for a fortnight, turning occasionally.

Buona Sera Shot ●●●○○
Cherry Daiquiri ●●●●○
Coffee & Vanilla Daiquiri ●●●●○
Coquetail Au Vanilla ●●●●●
Cox's Daiquiri ●●●●●

SAKE

Sometimes described as a rice wine, sometimes as a rice beer, sake shares qualities of both. It is fermented from specially developed rice and water by brewmasters ('toji'). But, although sake is brewed like a beer, it is served like a wine and, like a wine, can either be dry or sweet, heavy or light. But it is slightly more alcoholic than wine - 14-18% alc./vol..

Sake (pronounced Sar-Keh – heavy on the K!) is native to Japan (and parts of China). The basic outline of production has changed little since the 11th century, but complex and fragrant sake has only been generally available since the 1970s.

Asian Ginger Martini ●●●●○
Bloody Maru ●●●○○
Charlie Lychee'tini ●●●●○
Cucumber Sake-Tini ●●●●○

SAMBUCA BLACK

See 'Opal Nera Black Sambuca'

SAMBUCA WHITE

See 'Luxardo Sambuca dei Cesari'

SCOTCH

See 'Whisky – Scotch'

SHERRY

A fortified wine produced around the region of Jerez, Spain. See below for styles of sherry used in this guide.

SHERRY – AMONTILLADO

An Amontillado sherry begins as a Fino, a pale, dry sherry produced under a layer of a kind of yeast known as 'flor'. Once the flor dies, increasing the oxidisation and changing the flavour of the wine, the sherry becomes an Amontillado. There are two distinct Amontillado styles. One is naturally dry, while the other is sweetened. Recipes in this guide which call for Amontillado sherry require the better quality, dry style.

Atomic Cocktail ●●●○○
Barbara West ●●●○○

SHERRY – FINO

Pronounced 'Fee-No' this pale, dry style of sherry is best drunk young. It is produced under a layer of a kind of yeast known as 'flor' which protects the wine from oxidation.

Adonis ●●●●●
Alaska Martini ●●●●○
Bamboo ●●●●●
Bartender's Martini ●●●●○
Charlie Lychee'tini ●●●●○
Club Cocktail #1 ●●●●○
Coronation ●●●○○
Coronation Martini ●●●●○

SHERRY - PEDRO XIMÉNEZ

A superbly rich dessert sherry made from sun-dried Pedro Ximénez (pronounced Hee-May-Neth) grapes.

Auntie's Hot Xmas Punch ●●●●○

SLOE GIN LIQUEUR

See 'Plymouth Sloe Gin Liqueur'

SOHO LYCHEE LIQUEUR

24% alc./vol. (48°proof)

Producer: Pernod (Group Pernod Ricard), Créteil, France.

Native to South China, the lychee's distinctive floral, fragrant flavour has a luscious delicacy which is distinctly Asian. Revered for over two thousand years as a symbol of love and romance, in part for its flavour and in part for its similarity to the heart, lychee is making waves in fusion food and cocktails around the world.

Pernod Ricard distil this clear liqueur in France, from Asian lychees. It has a distinct smoothness and a light, fresh taste of rich lychee and raspberry, alongside a touch of citrus and raspberry jam.

China Martini ●●●○○
Chinese Cosmopolitan ●●●●○
Chinese Whisper Martini ●●●●○
Crouching Tiger ●●●○○

SOUR APPLE SCHNAPPS LIQUEUR

In the following recipes, a standard apple schnapps liqueur will not work: a sour version is required.

Apple & Melon Martini ●●●○○
Apple Buck ●●●●○
Big Apple Martini ●●●○○
Curdish Martini ●●●●○

SOUR MIX

Sour mix is a term for a blend of lemon or lime juice mixed with sugar syrup. Commercial pre-mixed sour mix is available in a dried crystal or powdered form, often with the addition of pasteurised egg white. Margarita mix is a similar pre-mix, but with the addition of orange flavours. I strongly advocate the use of freshly squeezed juice and sugar syrup and in this guide they appear as separate ingredients.

SOUTHERN COMFORT

Alabama Slammer #1 ●●●●○
Alabama Slammer #2 ●●●●○
The Argyll ●●●○○
Avalanche Shot ●●○○○
Bazooka ●●○○○
Brake Tag ●●●●○
The Big Easy ●●●●○
Canteen Martini ●●●○○

ST. GERMAIN

24% alc./vol.
(48°proof)
www.stgermain.fr

Producer: The St. Germain Company, Saint Germain, Paris, France

St. Germain is a vintage liqueur made in late spring during the short season of the elderflower from which it takes its delicate, floral flavour. Hungarian and Romanian gypsies gather the small white blossom covering elder bushes growing wild in the French Alps. The gypsies ride their blossom laden bicycles to depots set up in the gardens of local homes where the flowers are weighed and the gypsies paid. The flowers are loaded into square baskets ready for collection and transportation to the distillery.

Speed is of the essence to capture the fresh taste of the blossoms as they quickly turn brown and lose their fragrance and a specialy developed, secret maceration process is used.

The quality of St. Germain's packaging reflects the expensive, artisan nature of its production, even recognising the important part the gypsies play with an illustration of a man and flower laden bicycle. The stunningly shapely eight-sided bottle was developed from an antique art-deco bottle and is finished with a heavy turned brass stopper. Each bottle is individually numbered and marked with the vintage year.

Apple & Elderflower Collins ●●●●○
Apple & Elderflower Martini (Fresh Fruit) ●●●●○
Bitter Elder ●●●●○
Charente Collins ●●●●○
Charlie Lychee'tini ●●●●○
Cyder Press ●●●●○

STRAWBERRY (CRÈME DE FRAISE) LIQUEUR

See 'Giffard Crème de Fraise de Bois'

SUGAR SYRUP

Many cocktails benefit from sweetening but granulated sugar does not dissolve easily in cold drinks. Hence pre-dissolved sugar syrup (also known as 'simple syrup') is used. Commercially made 'gomme sirop' (gum syrup) is sugar syrup with the addition of gum arabic, the crystallised sap of the acacia tree. Many bartenders don't like using gomme syrup but prefer to use simple or sugar syrup. Others prefer gomme as it adds mouth-feel and smoothness to some drinks.

Make your own sugar syrup by gradually pouring and stirring two cups of granulated sugar into a saucepan containing one cup of hot water and simmer until the sugar is dissolved. Do not let the water even come close to boiling and only simmer for as long as it takes to dissolve the sugar. Allow syrup to cool and pour into an empty bottle. Ideally, you should finely strain your syrup into the bottle to remove any undissolved crystals which could otherwise encourage crystallisation. If kept in a refrigerator this mixture will last for a couple of months.

A wide range of flavoured sugar syrups are commercially available. Orgeat (almond), passion fruit and vanilla are among the most popular. See also 'Pomegranate (Grenadine) Syrup'.

TEQUILA

See 'Partida Tequila'

TOMATO JUICE

Originally from Peru, the tomato was imported into Spain in the 16th century.

Buy a quality, chilled, freshly pressed juice or make your own. Avoid sweet packaged juices made from concentrate.

Basil Mary ●●●●○
Bloody Joseph ●●●○○
Bloody Maria ●●●●○
Bloody Maru ●●●○○
Bloody Mary (1930s recipe) ●●●○○
Bloody Mary (modern recipe) ●●●●●
Bloody Shame (mocktail) ●●●○○
Cubanita ●●●●○

TRIPLE SEC

An orange-flavoured liqueur often used in cocktails.

TUACA LIQUEUR

Apple Crumble Martini #2 ●●●●○
The Bistro Sidecar ●●●●○

VANILLA (SCHNAPPS) LIQUEUR

The term schnapps traditionally suggests a clear, strong spirit. However, in recent years the term has come to refer to sweet liqueurs of only 20-24% alc./vol., bearing no resemblance to the strong dry schnapps from which they take their name. I've added the term 'liqueur' in this guide to help make the type of vanilla schnapps called for more obvious.

Blush Martini ●●●○○
Cool Martini ●●●○○
Custard Tart ●●●●○

VERMOUTH EXTRA DRY

Vermouth as we know it today was invented during the 18th century in the ancient Kingdom of Savoy, which is now divided between north-west Italy and parts of southern and eastern France. At that time the region had an abundance of grapes and produced only very ordinary wines. As a result, enterprising types fortified wine, added herbs and spices, and created vermouth.

Adios Amigos Cocktail ●●●○○
Affinity ●●●○○
Alfonso Martini ●●●●○
Algonquin ●●●●○
Allegrottini ●●●●○
Almond Martini #2 ●●●●○
American Beauty #1 ●●●●●
American Beauty #2 ●●●●○
Apple Manhattan ●●●●○
Arnaud Martini ●●●●○
The Atty Cocktail ●●●●○
Aviator ●●●●○
Bamboo ●●●●●
Bartender's Martini ●●●●○
Bensonhurst ●●●●●
Black Bison Martini ●●●●●
Black Feather ●●●●○
Blackthorn English ●●●●○
Blackthorn Irish ●●●○○

Bloomsbury Martini ●●●●○
Blue Star ●●●○○
Bobby Burns ●●●●○
Boomerang ●●●●○
Boston Tea Party ●●●○○
Boulevard ●●●●○
Bourbonella ●●●●○
Bradford ●●●●○
Brainstorm ●●●●●
Bronx ●●●○○
Brooklyn #1 ●●●●○
Brooklyn #2 ●●●●○
Cajun Martini ●●●●○
Californian Martini ●●●●○
Caprice ●●●●○
Cardinale ●●●●○
Caruso Martini ●●●○○
Chancellor ●●●●●
China Martini ●●●○○
Chocolate & Cranberry Martini ●●●●○
Chocolate Martini ●●●●○
Chocolate Mint Martini ●●●●○
Claridge ●●●●○
Clipper Cocktail ●●●○○
Club Cocktail ●●●●○
Coronation ●●●○○
Coronation Martini ●●●○○
Cuban Island ●●●○○

VERMOUTH (SWEET)

Popular belief has it that Italian vermouth was originally sweet and produced from red wine, while French vermouth was typically dry and white. Hence, many old cocktail books refer to 'French' for dry vermouth and 'Italian' where sweet vermouth is called for. The truth is that the division between the styles of the two countries was never that defined and producers in both countries now make both sweet (rosso) and dry styles. Although red vermouth was initially based on red wine, now virtually all is made from white wine with caramel blended in to give an amber colour.

Abbey Martini ●●●○○
Adonis ●●●●●
Affinity ●●●○○
Alfonso Martini ●●●●○
Apple Blossom Cocktail ●●●●●
Apple Manhattan #2 ●●●●○
The Argyll ●●●○○
Aviator ●●●●○
Behemoth ●●●●○
Bijou ●●●●●
Blood & Sand #2 ●●●●●
Blood & Sand #2 (Difford's formula) ●●●●●
Bolero ●●●○○
Bombay ●●●●●
Boomerang ●●●●○
Bronx ●●●○○
Brooklyn #1 ●●●●○
Caramel Manhattan ●●●●●
Carrol Cocktail ●●●○○
Club Cocktail #1 ●●●●○
Club Cocktail #2 ●●●●○
Corpse Reviver ●●●●○
Covadonga ●●●○○

VIOLET LIQUEUR

A liqueur flavoured with the purple flowers from a small perennial plant. Usually from France, particularly Toulouse.

The Atty Cocktail ●●●●○
Aviation #2 (Classic Formula) ●●●●●
Blue Moon ●●●○○
Bramblette ●●●●○

VODKA - UNFLAVOURED GRAIN

See 'Ketel One Vodka'

VODKA — BISON GRASS FLAVOURED

See 'Zubrówka vodka'

VODKA — CITRUS FLAVOURED

See 'Ketel One Citroen'

VODKA — ORANGE FLAVOURED

See 'Ketel One Orange Infused Vodka'

VODKA - VANILLA FLAVOURED

See 'Ketel One Vanilla Infused Vodka'

WATER

The dilution of a cocktail is key to achieving the right balance. This varies according to how hard you shake, how cold your ice is and how much ice you use. Even if a recipe doesn't call for a splash of water, don't be scared to add some if you feel it needs it. Use spring or filtered water and keep a bottle in your refrigerator next to the bottle of sugar syrup.

WHISKEY - BOURBON

Bourbon can be made anywhere in the USA, but it is native to the South, and only Kentucky bourbon can advertise the state where it is made. Thus, there is no bourbon with Tennessee on the label.

Bourbons are produced in a specific way. A bourbon must contain at least 51% corn (but not more than 80%), be distilled to a strength of not more than 80% alc./vol., be stored in charred new white oak barrels at a strength no higher than 62.5% alc./vol. and aged for at least two years, and be reduced at the time of bottling to no lower than 40% alc./vol..

Straight bourbon whiskey must be aged for a minimum of two years in new, charred oak casks. Any whiskey which has been aged for less than four years must state its age on the label. Generally, two to four year old whiskies are best avoided. No colouring or flavouring may be added to straight whiskey.

Adam & Eve ●●●●○
American Pie Martini ●●●●○
Americana ●●●○○
Apple Manhattan #1 ●●●●○
Apple Manhattan #2 ●●●●○
Apricot Sour ●●●●○
Avenue ●●●○○
Barbary Coast Highball ●●●○○
Behemoth ●●●●○
Bensonhurst ●●●●●
Blinker ●●●●○
Boiler Maker ●●●●●
Boomerang ●●●●○
Borderline ●●●●○
Boston Flip ●●●●○
Boulevard ●●●●○
Bourbon Blush ●●●●●
Bourbon Cookie ●●●●○
Bourbon Crusta ●●●●○
Bourbon Milk Punch ●●●●○
Bourbon Smash ●●●○○
Bourbonella ●●●●○

Brainstorm ●●●●●
Brighton Punch ●●●●●
Brooklyn #1 ●●●●○
Brooklyn #2 ●●●●○
Caramel Manhattan ●●●●●
Casanova ●●●●○
Chas ●●●●○
Chocolate Sazerac ●●●●○
Colonel Collins ●●●●○
Colonel T ●●●●○
Commodore #2 ●●●○○
Cruel Intention ●●●●○
The Currier ●●●●○

WHISKEY - IRISH

Due to the domination of Irish Distillers, the producers' group now owned by Pernod-Ricard, as a rule Irish whiskey is triple-distilled and not peated and hence light and smooth. (The independent Cooley Distillery produces some notable exceptions to these rules.)

Blackthorn Irish ●●●●○
Causeway ●●●●○

WHISKEY - TENNESSEE

The main difference between bourbon and Tennessee whiskey lies in the Lincoln County Process, a form of charcoal filtration. In the 1820s someone (possibly Alfred Eaton) started filtering whiskey through maple charcoal. Tennessee whiskeys are now filtered through 10-12 feet of maple charcoal before they are bottled, removing impurities and giving a 'sooty' sweetness to the finished spirit.

A Tennessee whiskey must be made from at least 51% of one particular grain. This could be rye or wheat, but most often, as with bourbon, corn is the favoured base.

Bee Sting ●●●●○
Black Jack ●●●○○
Cherry Mash Sour ●●●○○
Cicada Cocktail ●●●○○

WHISKY — CANADIAN

John Molson, though better known for brewing, is credited with first introducing whisky to Canada in 1799. His lead was followed by Scottish emigrants who found their new home had plentiful and cheap grain. Whisky production started at Kingston, on Lake Ontario, and spread as farming developed. However, barley was not common, so they reduced the amount of barley and added corn, wheat and rye instead.

In 1875, government regulation specified that Canadian whisky must be made from cereal grains in Canada, using continuous distillation. The rules also state that Canadian whisky must be aged a minimum of 3 years and a maximum of 18 years in charred oak barrels.

Captain Collins ●●●○○

WHISKY - SCOTCH

For whisky to be called 'Scotch whisky' it must be a) made in Scotland and b) aged in oak casks for a minimum of three years. Malt whisky – based on malted barley - was the original Scottish whisky and is at the core of all decent Scotch. But, although it has recently become extremely popular, the majority of pot still malt whisky is sold in blends (which include non-malt whiskies), not as single malt whiskies (which do not). Blended Scotch whisky, or 'Scotch' for short is the world's most popular whisky and accounts for well over 85% of all Scottish whisky.

A standard blended whisky will probably contain 15-40% malt and have no age statement (though every whisky in it will have been aged at least three years). Some blends describe themselves as 'deluxe' - this is a reference to the percentage of malt whisky in the blend and the average age of the whisky. A deluxe brand will usually contain more than 45% pot-still malt and will show an age statement of 12 years or more.

Affinity ●●●○○
Aggravation ●●●●○
Apple Crumble Martini #1 ●●●○○
Apple Mac ●●●●○
Aquarius ●●●○○
Atholl Brose ●●●●○
Barbary Coast Martini ●●●●○
Bessie & Jessie ●●●○○
Blood & Sand #1 ●●●●●
Blood & Sand #2 (Difford's formula) ●●●●●
Bloody Joseph ●●●○○
Blue Blazer ●●○○○
Bobby Burns ●●●●○
Boston Tea Party ●●●○○
The Broadmoor ●●●●●
Brubaker Old-Fashioned ●●●●○
Cameron'tini ●●●●○
Cappercaille ●●●●○
Celtic Margarita ●●●●●

Chancellor ●●●●○
Chin Chin ●●●●○
Collar & Cuff ●●●●○
The Crow Cocktail ●●●○○

WINE - RED

The acidity in table wine can balance a cocktail in a similar way to citrus juice. Avoid heavily oaked wines.

American Beauty ●●●●○
Caravan ●●●○○
Cardinal Punch ●●●●○
Claret Cobbler ●●●●○
Cobbled Raspberry Martini ●●●●●
Cosmopolitan Delight ●●●●●

WINE - WHITE

The acidity in table wine can balance a cocktail in a similar way to citrus juice. The grassy notes in Sauvignon Blanc make this grape varietal particularly suitable for cocktail use.

Apache ●●●○○
Blueberry Martini #2 (simple) ●●●●○
Brazilian Berry ●●●●○
Canary Flip ●●●●●
Coronation ●●●○○

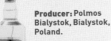

ZUBRÓWKA BISON VODKA

40% alc./vol. (80°proof)

Producer: Polmos Bialystok, Bialystok, Poland.

Pronounced 'Zhu-bruff-ka', this Polish vodka is flavoured with Hierochloe Odorata grass, a blade of which is immersed in each bottle, giving the vodka a translucent greenish colour and a subtle flavour. The area where this grass grows in the Bialowieza Forest is the habitat of wild Polish bison – so, although the bison don't eat this variety of grass, the vodka has the nickname 'Bison vodka'. The Hierochloe Odorata

grass is harvested by hand in early summer when its flavour is best, then dried, cut to size and bound in bunches for delivery to the Bialystok distillery. The vodka is forced through the grass to absorb its aromatic flavour rather as espresso coffee machines force water through coffee.

The palate is herby and grassy with flavours of citrus, vanilla, lavender, tobacco, cold jasmine tea and caffè latte, plus hints of dry chocolate/vanilla. This subtle and delicately flavoured vodka is extremely mixable.

Achilles Heel ●●●●○
Amber ●●●●○
Apple Breeze ●●●●○
Apple Pie Martini ●●●●○
Autumn Martini ●●●●○
Autumn Punch ●●●●●
Beetle Jeuse ●●●●○
Brazen Martini ●●●●○
Congo Blue ●●●●○
Coolman Martini ●●●●●
Cucumber Martini ●●●●●

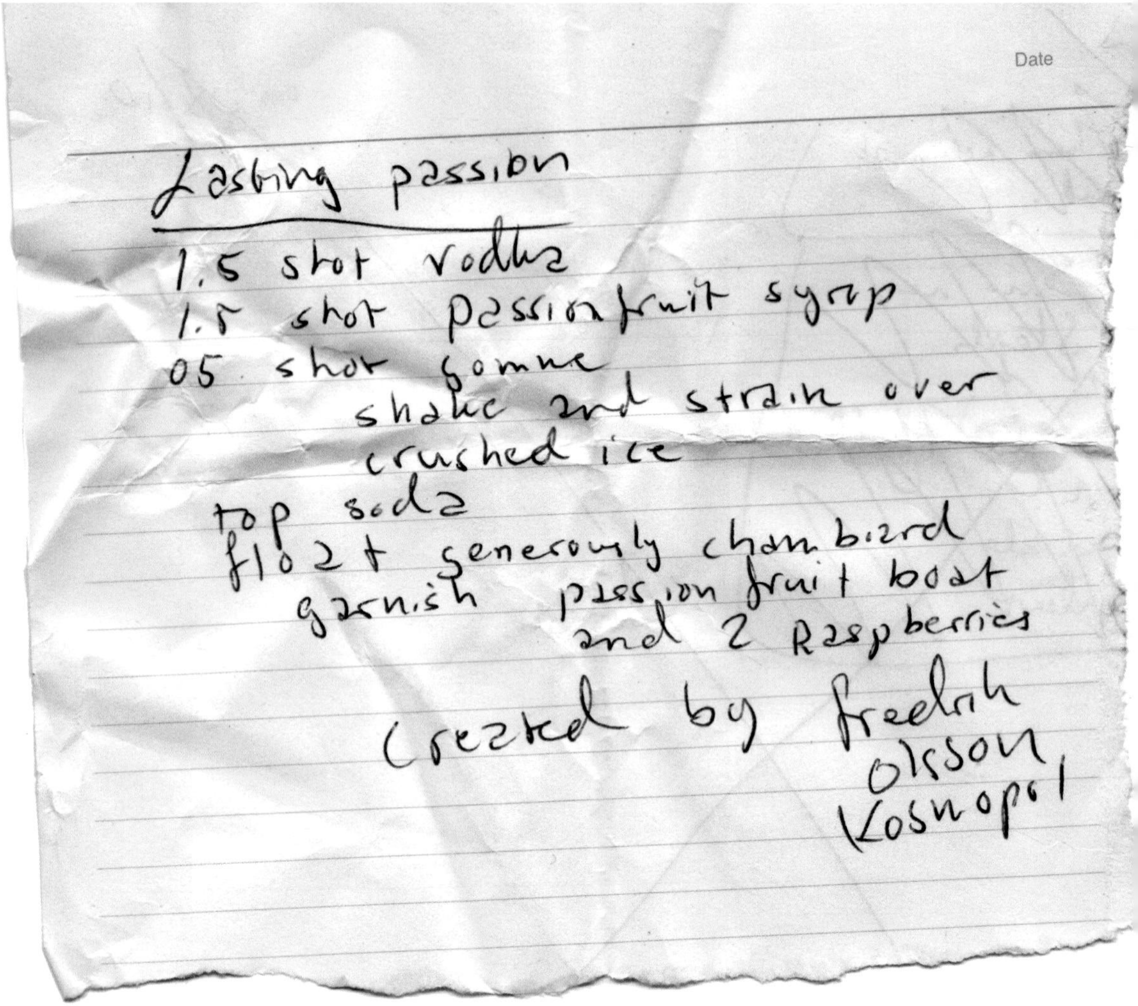

Date

Lasting passion

1.5 shot vodka
1.5 shot passionfruit syrup
05 shot gomme
        shake and strain over
        crushed ice

top soda
float generously chambord
garnish passion fruit boat
        and 2 Raspberries

Created by freelah
        olsson
        Kosmopol

READERS' RECIPES

I pick up new cocktail recipes on a daily basis, in bars and by email. I usually adapt recipes to fit our house style, both in the liquor brands specified and the way they're made. However, the recipes over the following pages are exactly as I received them. The best will find their way into the front pages of future guides and as always I'll credit creators, so please keep sending them in.

Once again I'd like to thank the many bartenders who have contributed to our guides.

Simon Difford
simon@diffordsguide.com

Hey Simon

This is Damon at Talulla's Bar in Chapel Hill, North Carolina. I was just writing to give you a new drink I came up with recently that I call Brazilian. I originally made it with shaved ice in a Highball, one shot of Gandaia cachaca, half shot of limoncello, a one count of sours and a float (which is actually a sinker) of Chambord. this is good as a cocktail, a highball or a shot. Thanks for the upkeep of good cocktails around the World.

Damon Shattuck
North Carolina, USA

• •

Hey Simon

Enjoyed reading Sauceguide to Cocktails UK Vol. 4. Its the only volume I've been able to find in the country (hey from Cape Town, South Africa). Anyway you might wanna try one of my more popular cocktails from the bar I manage.

VANILLA MELODY

Glass: I use an unusual version of an Old Fashion glass.
Steam honey, Galliano and cranberry with the spout of a coffee machine.
Stir. Layer cream and dust with cinnamon.

2 shots Galliano
3/4 shots runny honey
5 shots clear cranberry juice
2 shots heavy cream

Cheers

Justin Major
The Green Dolphin Jazz Restaurant, Cape Town, South Africa

• •

Hey Simon,

Our superstar 'drinksmith' at Bramble, David Cordoba, has long been coming up with tasty concoctions, many of which deserve to be served to one and all. I have attached some of these for you to trial, should you chose to, and perhaps even include them in future diffords-guides.

PERA CUBANA (CUBAN PEAR)

Glass: Highball
Method: Put all ingredients into a Boston glass add ice and shake vigorously. Single strain into a glass full of ice
Garnish: Two slice of pear with vanilla pod rim
50ml Havana Club Especial

20ml Apricot Brandy
100ml Pear pure
10ml Gomme syrup
1/4 Vanilla pod
Comments: This cocktail Won The International Havana Club Cocktail Grand Prix 2006 Competition Edinburgh Heat and came 3rd in the final.

BANGKOK BUFFALO

Glass: Martini
Garnish: One inch of Lemongrass cut diagonally in the rim
Method: Muddle honey, lemongrass, ginger and chilly. Add rest of ingredients, shake with ice and double strain.
35ml Buffalo Trace
12.5ml Benedictine D.O.M.
12.5ml Apricot brandy liqueur
35ml Freshly squeezed orange
2 spoon Runny honey
2 inch Lemongrass
2 inch Ginger
1/2 inch Red hot chilly
Comments: This cocktail won the best Buffalo trace cocktail in the Theme Awards'06 in Scotland Heat.

THE MAYAS DAIQUIRI

Glass: Coupette or Martini
Garnish: Two Pineapple leaf
Method: Muddle the avocado with the lime juice in Boston glass. Add rest of ingredients, shake vigorously and double strain into chilled glass.
50ml Havana Club especial
Half avocado
15ml Agave syrup
10ml lime juice
Comments: Made for the Havana Club Competition 2005 and featured on Bramble Bar cocktail menu.

ALMONDS ARE FOREVER

Glass: Martini
Garnish: Grated smoked almond
Method: Muddle the marzipan with vanilla syrup in a Boston glass, add rest of the ingredients and shake vigorously. Double strain into chilled glass.
35ml Stoli Vanilla Vodka
20ml Amaretto
5ml Vanilla syrup
1 inch Marzipan
Comments: This cocktail was created for Harvey Nichol's, Edinburgh cocktail menu.

GOOD MORNING... GOOD NIGHT

Glass: Cognac
Method: Muddle coffee beans in a Boston glass, add the rest of the ingredients, shake vigorously and double strain into a chilled glass.
50ml Cognac

12.5ml Caramel Carton Liqueur
12.5ml Benedictine
12.5ml Cinnamon syrup
20 Coffee beans
Comments: This cocktail was created for Harvey Nichol's, Edinburgh cocktail menu.

ROYAL PRIVILEGE

Glass: High Ball
Garnish: Three pineapple leaf
Method: Put the first five ingredients into Boston glass, add ice and shake vigorously. Single strain into ice-filled glass and top up with sparkling water.

50ml Tanqueray Gin Import
12.5ml Yellow Chartreuse
12.5ml Licor 43
70ml Pressed pineapple Juice
10ml Elderflower cordial
Top up with Perrier Sparkling Water
Comments: Finalist in the Bartender World Class Competition and now featured on Home-House Edinburgh cocktail menu.

Cheers

Jason Scott.
www.bramblebar.co.uk

• •

Simon

I am an avid subscriber and fan of your guides - keep up the great work. Just thought I would drop you a line with a drink created by myself, my friend Liam West with some significant help from Ago Perrone, the brilliant head bartender at Montgomery Place, Notting Hill.

We wanted to create a cocktail using the beautiful Compass Box Hedonism and came up with this. We called it Glased Over, in respect to the Compass Box founder John Glaser.

GLASED OVER

Glass: Martini
Garnish: Orange twist
Method: Shake all ingredients well with ice, double strain into Martini glass

60ml Compass Box Hedonism
15ml Bise-Dur (or other blackberry aperitif)
10ml Aperol
1 dash Angostura aromatic bitters
1 dash of orange bitters (Regan's)

Hope you like it.
Cheers
Mike O'Brien
London, England

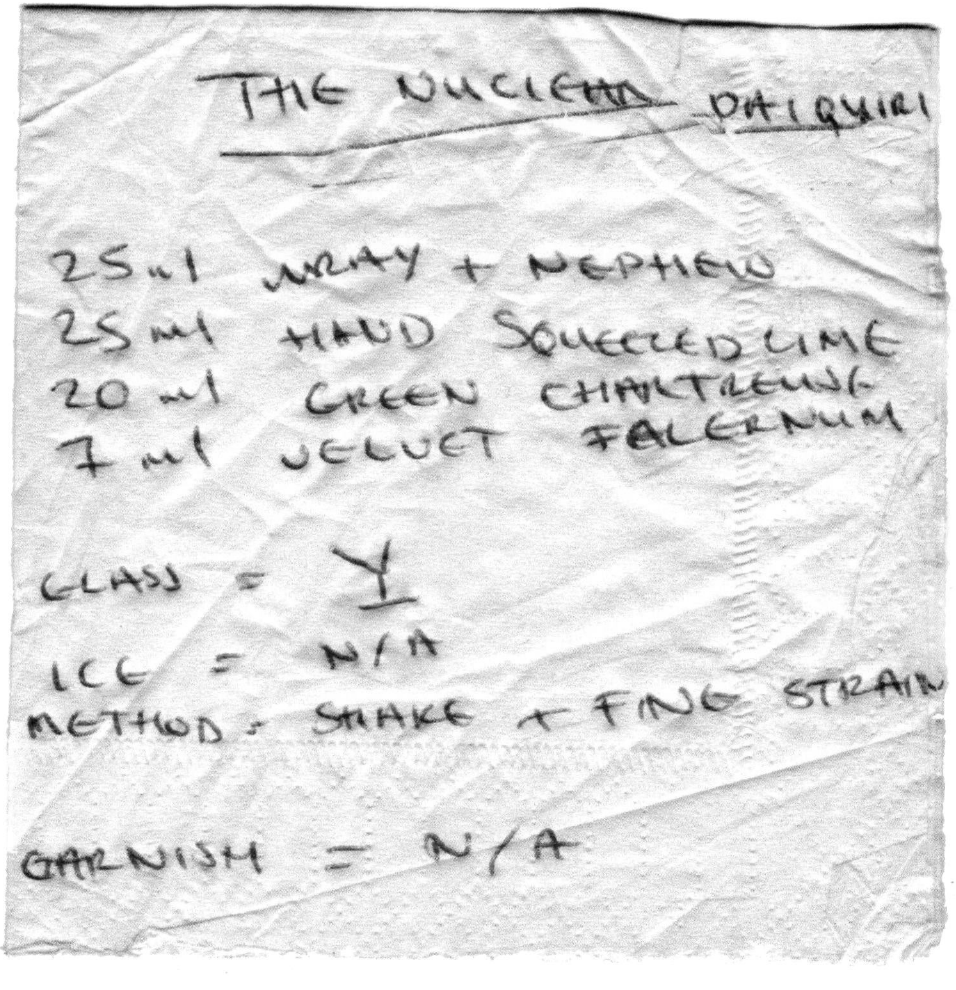

THE NUCLEAR DAIQUIRI

25ml WRAY + NEPHEW
25ml HAND SQUEEZED LIME
20ml GREEN CHARTREUSE
7ml VELVET FALERNUM

GLASS = Y

ICE = N/A

METHOD = SHAKE + FINE STRAIN

GARNISH = N/A

Spice of Life

Dry chillie

40 ml Morgan spice

15 ml Abricot du Roussillon

12,5 ml Caramel liqueur

Dash pineaple juice

garnish → slice of

chillie on the side of

Martini glass

gregory (century club)

Hi Simon,

It was great to finally meet you this past week. Here are three recipes, with a little background:

1)THE REVOLVER

2oz Bulliett Bourbon
3/4oz Tia Maria
2 Dashes Fee Brothers Orange Bitters
Burnt orange garnish

Pour all ingredients over ice, stir, strain into 5oz cocktail glass, flame orange peel over the top and drop it into drink.

This drink has been enormously popular at Bourbon and Branch, much more so than I could have hoped. It's basically a riff on a Manhattan, as you can see.

2)THE PEARL

1 1/4oz Plymouth Gin
3/4oz Aperol
1/2oz Lillet Blanc
2oz Enrico Prosecco
5 confectionary pearls
1 drop lemon oil

Pour Gin, Aperol and Lillet over ice, stir. Strain into a champagne flute, top with prosecco. Drop in pearls (these are used on cakes mostly, they're basically just hard shiny sugar balls), drop one drop lemon oil with eyedropper on top.

This drink won the Plymouth contest at Rye in October '06. They tell me it's been popular on their menue.

3) THE DEMOCRAT

2oz Bourbon
1/2oz Mathilde Peach
1/2oz Honey Water
1 1/2oz Lemon Juice

Combine all ingredients and shake over ice. Strain into a collins glass full of crushed ice. Garnish with a lemon (wheel, thumb, wedge, whatever really).

I wanted to make a drink as a kind of ode to the south and how it was a democratic stronghold for so long, etc. Harry Truman, our 33'rd President, only drank bourbon when he drank, and is considered by many to be our last great Democrat. All though he didn't like

anything in his bourbon except the occasional ice cube. This has also been more popular than I expected, I suspect it's the name.

Thanks for taking the time to check these out. Come back and visit soon.

Cheers,

Jon Santer
Bourbon & Branch, San Francisco, USA

• •

Hi Simon,

Here is a recipe that is a bartender favourite for birthdays/initiations/ leaving etc

BSUICIDAL
Layer like a B52
Kahlúa, Baileys, Cointreau (should be Grand Marnier I know) and then layer absinthe on top of that (Balkan 88%).

Not one for the connoisseurs but definitely a party piece, I do have more refined ones

Many thanks

Tim
Herts, England

• •

Hi,
Here is a simple cocktail I designed for a recent company competition sponsored by Bacardi-Brown Forman. I work for Pitcher & Piano and this competition is run every year with a cocktail knowledge test (both written and practical) followed by our own creations, between all the ambassadors (1 from each bar to make 23 this year). This drink and my knowledge WON me the competition and my creation is in the process of being placed in our drinks guide alongside some of the great classics. Not to mention it is universally loved by anyone who tries it!!

DIRTY GINNER
Glass: Rocks
Garnish: 'Dirty Ice' and Muddled Fruit
Muddle the orange & lime wedges with the syrup. Add the other ingredients and shake with one scoop of ice. Pour straight into the glass using the ice you shaked with, not strained over fresh ice, and the muddled fruit as a garnish.

2 Orange Wedges
2 Lime Wedges
10-15ml Simple Syrup
Grated Ginger (roughly a barspoon)
25ml Finlandia Cranberry Vodka
15ml Stolinchaya Vanilla Vodka
10ml Grand Marnier Orange Liquer
A fruity and refreshing drink, strong in flavour that concentrates upon the spirits used.

Alexander Evans
Harrogate, North Yorkshire, UK

• •

Hi,
My name is Damien McGuire and I'm duty manager/head mixologist at firefly bar in Leeds.

I recently created a new cocktail that I believe is worthy of your guide. Its name is Princess Karen (named after one of my staff) and it contains:

1 1/2 oz Cointreau
1/2 oz Chambord
4/5 fresh Raspberries
1/2 oz Raspberry puree
1/2 oz Lemon juice
1/2 oz Sugar (gomme) syrup
1 oz Cranberry juice
Muddle the raspberries first, add all the other ingredients, shake it up and strain into a martini glass. The garnish is a chunk of orange and a raspberry on cocktail stick balanced on the side of the glass.

Damien McGuire
Friefly, Leeds, England.

• •

Hey there Simon,
I'm just a bartender at a small diner that has all of your guides in Honolulu, Hawaii. Here is a smooth little cocktail with the new Stoil Blueberry Vodka

BLUEBERRY VESPER
1 1\2oz Stoli Blueberry
1 1\2oz Hendricks Gin
3\4 oz Maraschino Liqueur
Garnish with a lemon twist

You can use Tanqueray if you don't have Hendricks
Bottoms up!

Thomas Tsang
Big City Diner (Kaimuki)

ANNUAL GUIDES

diffordsguide to Cocktails #6

ISBN: 978-0-9546174-8-6
Cover price: UK £24.97, USA $34.97
A coffee table-style comprehensive hard-back A-Z guide to over 2,000 cocktail recipes, each accompanied by a colour illustrated photograph. A bigger, longer, completely indexed version of the cocktails at the back at this guide.

diffordsguide to London's Best Pubs & Bars

ISSN: 0-9546174-9-5
Cover price: UK £4.97
A pocket-friendly guide to the very best pubs and bars in London: more than 250 spaces reviewed and photographed.

WHERE TO BUY diffordsguide

WWW.DIFFORDSGUIDE.COM

For subscriptions, individual Issues and back copies

UK WIDE RETAILERS

Books etc
Tel: +44 (0)20 7379 7313,
www.bordersstores.co.uk

Borders Books & Music
Tel: +44 (0)20 7379 7313,
www.bordersstores.co.uk

Harvey Nichols
Department Stores
+44 (0)20 7235 5000,
www.harveynichols.com

Waterstone's
+44 (0)20 8742 3800,
www.amazon.co.uk

US WIDE RETAILERS

B-Dalton
Tel: 1 800 THE BOOK,
www.barnesandnoble.com

Barnes & Noble Superstores
Tel: 1 800 THE BOOK,
www.barnesandnoble.com

Books A Million
Tel: 1 800 201 3550,
www.booksamillion.com

Borders Books & Music
Tel: 1 888 81 BOOKS,
www.bordersstores.com

Tower Records
Tel: 1 800 ASK-TOWER
www.towerrecords.com

LONDON RETAILERS

The Conran Shop
81 Fulham Road, SW3 6RD
Tel: +44 (0)20 7589 7401, **www.**conran.com

The Conran Shop
55 Marylebone High Street,
W1U 5HS
Tel: +44 (0)20 7723 2223, **www.**conran.com

Daunt Books
83 Marylebone High Street,
W1U 4QW
Tel: +44 (0)20 7224 2295, **www.**dauntbooks.co.uk

Foyles
113-119 Charing Cross Road, WC2H 0EB
Tel: +44 (0)20 7437 5660, **www.**foyles.co.uk

Heal's Tottenham Court Road
196 Tottenham Court Road,
W1T 7LQ
Tel: +44 (0)20 7636 1666, **www.**heals.co.uk

Selfridges & Co.
400 Oxford Street, W1C 1JS
Tel:+44 (0)870 837 7377, **www.**selfridges.com

Stanfords Covent Garden
12-14 Long Acre, WC2E 9LP
Tel: +44 (0)20 7836 1321, **www.**stanfords.co.uk

Purves & Purves
222 Tottenham Court Road,
W1T 7QE
Tel: +44 (0)20 7580 8223, **www.**purves.co.uk

Vinopolis shop
1 Bank End, SE1 9BU
Tel: +44 (0)20 7940 8311, **www.**vinopolis.co.uk

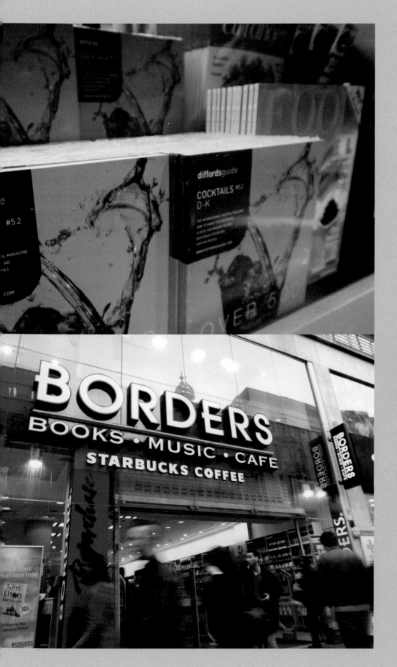

OTHER UK RETAILERS

Harris Interiors Gallery
33 Church Road, Lower
Parkstone, Poole, BH14 8UF
Tel: +44 (0)1202 744 081,
www.harris-interiors.co.uk

Villeneuves Wines
49 A Broughton Street,
Edinburgh, EH1 3RJ
Tel: +44 (0)131 558 8441,
www.villeneuvewines.com

Cornelius Wines
18-20 Easter Road, Edinburgh,
EH7 5RG
Tel: +44 (0)131 652 2405

Please look for our quarterly
guides on magazine racks as well
as the book shelves of book
retailers' cookery or travel
departments. We are proud to
produce publications which are
hard to pigeonhole.

ONLINE E-TAILERS

www.b-opie.com
www.amazon.com
www.amazon.co.uk
www.drinkon.com
www.shaker-uk.com
www.thedrinkshop.com
www.urbanbar.com

LAST ORDERS

JUST AS THE COSMO WAS LOOKING LIKE IT HAD RUN THE INEVITABLE COURSE FROM HIP DRINK TO NAFF BAR CALL, IT'S EMERGED THAT ITS ORIGINS MAY BE CLASSIC RATHER THAN CONTEMPORARY. WILL SUCH A REVELATION BREATHE NEW LIFE INTO THE COSMOPOLITAN AND LEAD ÜBER-COOL MANHATTANITES TO START REORDERING WHAT COULD NOW BE REGARDED AS A TWISTED CLASSIC?

NO, WE DON'T REALLY CARE EITHER SO WE WON'T BE ADDRESSING THAT QUESTION IN THE NEXT ISSUE. INSTEAD WE'LL BE LOOKING AT SOMETHING ELSE WE FEEL IS SET TO GO OUT OF FASHION - FLAVOURED VODKA. TRENDS COME AND GO AND BARTENDERS IN THE KNOW ARE INFUSING THEIR OWN – MUCH LIKE WE DID A DECADE OR SO AGO, BEFORE OUR SHELVES GROANED WITH BRANDED, ARTIFICIAL TASTING FLAVOURED VODKAS. WE'LL TASTE, EVALUATE AND, NATURALLY, SCORE A PLETHORA OF WHITE (AND NOT SO WHITE) SPIRITS TO SEE WHICH SHOULD BE SAVED AND WHICH ARE FOR THE HIGH JUMP. ON TOP OF OUR USUAL 500-PLUS COCKTAILS WE'RE PLANNING TO VISIT BARS IN LEEDS, WARSAW AND PARIS, AND WE'LL ALSO FIND SPACE FOR THE VERY LATEST FROM NEW YORK – PROMISE. SEE YOU IN THE SUMMER.